I0887654

Manifest in Words, Written on Paper

Producing and Circulating Poetry in Tang Dynasty China

Harvard-Yenching Institute Monograph Series 70

Manifest in Words, Written on Paper

Producing and Circulating Poetry in Tang Dynasty China

CHRISTOPHER M. B. NUGENT

Published by the Harvard University Asia Center
for the Harvard-Yenching Institute
Distributed by Harvard University Press
Cambridge (Massachusetts) and London 2010

© 2010 by the President and Fellows of Harvard College

Printed in the United States of America

The Harvard-Yenching Institute, founded in 1928 and headquartered at Harvard University, is a foundation dedicated to the advancement of higher education in the humanities and social sciences in East and Southeast Asia. The Institute supports advanced research at Harvard by faculty members of certain Asian universities and doctoral studies at Harvard and other universities by junior faculty at the same universities. It also supports East Asian studies at Harvard through contributions to the Harvard-Yenching Library and publication of the *Harvard Journal of Asiatic Studies* and books on premodern East Asian history and literature.

Library of Congress Cataloging-in-Publication Data

Nugent, Christopher M. B., 1969-
Manifest in words, written on paper : producing and circulating poetry in Tang Dynasty China / Christopher M.B. Nugent.
p. cm. -- (Harvard-Yenching Institute monograph series ; 70)
Summary: "This study aims to engage the textual realities of medieval literature by shedding light on the material lives of poems during the Tang, from their initial oral or written instantiation through their often lengthy and twisted paths of circulation"--Provided by publisher.
Includes bibliographical references and index.
ISBN 978-0-674-05603-9 (acid-free paper)
1. Chinese poetry--Tang dynasty, 618-907--History and criticism. I. Title.
PL2321.N84 2010
895.1'1309--dc22
2010029500

Index by the author

♾ Printed on acid-free paper

Last number below indicates year of this printing

18 17 16 15 14 13 12 11

To my family

Acknowledgments

Like the literary works it discusses, this book has benefited from the combined efforts of many different minds, hands, and voices (though its remaining flaws are entirely my own).

Stephen Owen has been an ideal mentor and a good friend. He is both inspiring in his dedication to his own scholarship and supremely generous in taking the time to help his students with theirs. His keen sense of what topics are interesting and important kept me on the straight and at least somewhat narrow through my many years working on this project.

Rare are the times in the last five years that I have run into Wilt Idema without hearing words to the effect of "So, how is the book coming?" Fortunately, that question, like its previous incarnation ("So, how is the dissertation coming?") has typically been followed by invaluable advice about everything from specific arguments to publication strategies. A book or article was often suggested (and usually lent) as well, and it was always the right one.

I have benefited greatly from numerous conversations with Xiaofei Tian about the issues I explore in this book. Her encyclopedic knowledge of sources has often pointed me to important texts, and her own innovative work on manuscript culture in medieval China has provided an excellent model for how to deal with these materials in interesting ways.

I have enjoyed the support and advice of many other scholars while working on this project. David Knechtges, Paul Kroll, and Martin Kern have offered carefully considered comments and corrections at various junctures and have improved my work considerably. Jack Chen has read a number of the chapters in this book and given valuable suggestions. I have been fortunate to have had the opportunity to share my work in presentations at a variety of talks and conferences and have especially benefited from perceptive comments by Paula Varsano, Robert Ashmore, Anna Shields, Lu Yang, Edward Shaughnessy, and Alexei Ditter. The Columbia Medieval Studies Workshop has proven a fruitful context in which to present work in progress and I thank Wendy Swartz for inviting me to participate.

Anonymous readers at *T'oung Pao*, *Asia Major*, and the Harvard University Asia Center Publications Program asked important questions and saved me from many errors. One reader for the Asia Center went above and beyond the call of duty in his or her careful and multiple readings of the manuscript. This book is a substantial improvement over that manuscript as a result.

A number of faculty and classmates at Harvard have been important to the development of many of the ideas in this book. I would like to thank in particular Peter Bol, Eileen Chow, Wiebke Denecke, Patrick Hanan, Natasha Heller, Li Wai-yee, Michael Puett, Zeb Raft, Paul Rouzer, and Wang Yugen.

Williams College has been a wonderfully supportive environment in which to teach and do research. I could not ask for better colleagues than those in the Chinese program. As chair, Neil Kubler consistently sacrificed his own time to ensure that junior faculty had the time and support to do their own research. I have learned much from him and from Cecilia Chang and Yu Li as teachers and colleagues.

Alexandra Garbarini and Micah Singer have provided good food and good company on more occasions than I can count. The last six years would not have been the same without them.

The love and support of my parents, Bill and Rita Nugent, and my brother David have allowed me to pursue my passions without fear.

Unlike Du Fu's son, my daughter Natasha has never recited any of her father's poems. For this we may all be thankful.

Finally, Sarah M. Allen has contributed more to this project than I could hope to enumerate. From late night conversations about issues and texts to meticulous editing and everything in between, she has lived with this book for as long as I have, and is possibly even more relieved than I am to see it done.

C. M. B. N.

Contents

Appendix

Reference Matter

Figures

Abbreviations

The following abbreviations are used in the text and notes. See *Works Cited,* pp. 313–332, for complete publication information.

JTS	Liu Xu, *Jiu Tang shu*
Ma	Ma Qichang, *Han Changli wenji jiaozhu*
Manuscrits	Bibliothèque nationale de France, *Manuscrits de Dunhuang et d'Asie Centrale Conservés à la Bibliothèque Nationale de France*
Qiu	Qiu Zhao'ao, *Dushi xiangzhu*
QTS	*Quan Tang shi*
QTW	*Quan Tang wen*
TZY	Wang Dingbao, *Tang zhiyan*
XTS	Song Qi and Ouyang Xiu, *Xin Tang shu*
Yingcang	*Yingcang Dunhuang wenxian*
YZJ	Yuan Zhen, *Yuan Zhen ji*
Zhu	Zhu Jincheng, *Bai Juyi ji jianjiao*

Manifest in Words, Written on Paper

Producing and Circulating Poetry in Tang Dynasty China

Introduction

What you are reading is only the dregs of the ancients. 君之所讀者古人之糟魄已夫

—Zhuangzi 莊子

Scholars of Tang dynasty 唐 (618–907) *shi* 詩 poetry are spoiled. Thanks to China's early invention of paper and its widespread use by the Tang period, devoted Song dynasty 宋 (960–1279) bibliophiles with a great fondness for Tang poetry, and an early and robust print culture, we enjoy access to received sources whose number and variety are surely the envy of scholars working on similar periods in other cultures. Yet the poetic culture of the Tang period itself was based not on printed editions carefully compiled and collated by scholars, published and spread through governmental and commercial concerns, but on handwritten manuscripts and oral performance and circulation. Today these manuscripts, with a few important exceptions, are lost, and the sounds of poems that were chanted and sung over a thousand years ago have faded away. We have almost no access to this poetry as it existed and was experienced in the period of its production and early circulation. This is no trivial matter; every Tang poem that we read today was by definition composed and circulated in the particular cultural and material contexts of the Tang period before its long and circuitous path to the present. If we do not understand how people of the Tang composed, experienced, and transmitted this poetry, then we are missing something very fundamental about the literature in its original contexts.

Scholarship on Tang poetry, whether in Asia or the West, has rarely occupied itself with answering questions of how people produced and circulated poetry during the Tang itself (as opposed to tracing different printed editions in later periods). Other than brief studies focused on the circulation of a single poet's works,[1] Fan Zhilin's 范之麟 two-part article in *Tangdai wenxue* 唐代文學 on the circulation of poetry in the Tang remains, to the best of my knowledge, the fullest treatment of the topic in any language.[2]

The specifically material aspects of poetry in the Tang have generally been ignored as well. Although scholars of medieval European literature have devoted considerable attention to the issues at stake when approaching handwritten manuscripts produced before the age of print, research on Tang poetry has rarely acknowledged these works and what relevance they might have for the study of the production and circulation of poetic literature in the particular manuscript culture of the Tang.[3] Indeed, unless they have done work with the manuscripts from Dunhuang 敦煌, many scholars of Tang poetry have never really examined Tang poems in something resembling their original forms. This state of affairs is understandable: much European literature considered to be medieval was produced more recently than the Tang and was written not on paper but on the far more durable (if expensive and difficult to manufacture) media of parch-

1. See, for example, Chen Shangjun, "Dushi zaoqi liuchuan kao," in his *Tangdai wenxue congkao*.

2. Fan Zhilin, "Tangdai shige de liuchuan (shang)" and "Tangdai shige de liuchuan (xia)."

3. There are some exceptions to this generalization. Stephen Owen notes the importance of textual history of Tang poetry and laments how little we know about it in *Great Age of Chinese Poetry*, 323–24*n*5. His most recent work treats questions of manuscript transmission and survival in substantially more detail. See Owen, *Late Tang*. Xu Jun is one of the few Chinese scholars to deal with the specific issues of manuscript transmission of Tang poetry. See Xu Jun, ed., *Dunhuang shiji canjuan jikao*, 8–52. It should also be noted that scholars working on earlier periods up through the Han have devoted considerable attention in recent years to issues of manuscript culture. See, for example, a number of the contributions to Kern, *Text and Ritual in Early China*; Kern's "Methodological Reflections"; Edward L. Shaughnessy's *Rewriting Early Texts*; and much of the work of William G. Boltz. Finally, Xiaofei Tian's recent work (*Tao Yuanming and Manuscript Culture*) on manuscript culture in the study of Tao Yuanming 陶淵明 (Tao Qian 陶潛) is an excellent example of how close attention to variants can enhance our understanding of poetic works from before the age of print.

ment or vellum,[4] and a good deal of it is still extant. The use of relatively cheap and easily obtainable paper in the Tang did ensure that literacy and textual production were significantly more widespread and common among the upper classes in Tang dynasty China than they were within the same group in medieval Europe. Yet the texts that Tang writers produced in such numbers were less able than parchment to withstand the forces of nature and time. A substantial number survived long enough to enter the print cultures of later periods and thus have been transmitted to the modern era through that route, but the original Tang manuscripts upon which these printed editions were ultimately based have mostly perished. With a paucity of actual manuscripts to study, it is not surprising that scholars have not made researching the peculiarities of physical manuscripts a priority.

In spite of its temporal distance, there is something about Tang poetry that remains intensely familiar. Not long after the dynasty itself came to an end, Tang period poetry achieved critical status as the apex of Chinese poetic achievement, a status that it has largely retained to the present day. The amount of *shi*-form poetry written after the Tang, indeed that written in the Song dynasty alone, dwarfs the output of Tang writers themselves. Yet poets of every succeeding period would look back to the Tang to find inspiration for their own works, works that they more often than not found wanting in comparison. Over a thousand years after the fall of the Tang and the death of its last poet, a wide range of people—from school children in East Asia to scholars in Europe and America—continue to study, recite, memorize, and imitate the poetic works of the Tang. Its dominant place in the Chinese poetic canon has helped it maintain a hold on a portion of both the literary and the cultural values of every succeeding era.

At the same time, this very familiarity can become a hindrance to a more thorough understanding of the original literary, cultural, and material contexts that produced poetry in the Tang. The seeming timelessness of a Wang Wei 王維 (701–61) poem about being "alone" in the mountains obscures the substantial differences between the literary culture in which Wang Wei originally produced the poem and that of succeeding

4. It has been estimated that a single copy of the *Book of Kells* produced around 800 CE required the slaughter of a herd of 150 calves. See Walther and Wolf, *Codices Illustres*, 18.

periods even a few centuries later, to say nothing of the new contexts in which such a poem would find itself today. We must be careful not to overlook the vast divide that separates us from this literature as it was produced and circulated in the Tang; what we think of as "Tang poetry" is a very different beast from "poetry during the Tang."

One aim of this study is to redirect our attention to the original contexts of poetry during the Tang and shed new light on questions of materiality and authorial control in particular. Scholars working on Tang literature still lag behind our Europeanist counterparts in developing methodologically and theoretically sound approaches to manuscript- and orally based material, and we have much to learn from the work that has already been done on medieval European manuscripts: both the successes and failures of these studies can be of great assistance to scholars of Tang poetry as we develop our own approaches. It is thus worth briefly discussing some of the important trends in how scholars over the last century have dealt with European texts from before the (Western) age of print. This discussion is by no means intended to be exhaustive and will focus primarily on aspects most applicable to the production and circulation of Tang poetry. My larger interest in this study is not with textual criticism *per se*, but as much textual criticism concerns itself with examining (and sometimes mitigating) the effects of different modes of production and circulation, understanding its different approaches and methods is important.

One major branch of Western textual criticism has concerned itself primarily with working backwards from extant texts to recreate an author's imagined autograph. As Paul Maas has stated, "We have no autograph manuscripts of the Greek and Roman classical writers and no copies which have been collated with the originals; the manuscripts we possess derive from the originals through an unknown number of intermediate copies....The business of textual criticism is to produce a text as close as possible to the original (*constitution textus*)."[5] Maas and many others took as their methodological basis the earlier work of the Prussian scholar Karl Lachmann (1793–1851), who developed a system by which extant texts would be grouped into families or "stemma" according to the

5. Maas, *Textual Criticism*, 1.

similarities found among their textual variants. Such texts were assumed to derive from a common ancestor, and the goal of the textual critic was "to methodically subtract manuscript 'descendents' that show scribal intrusions until one identifies the extant manuscript with the least scribal 'corruption,' that is, the manuscript closest to the author's original."[6] A strength of this method, as perceived by its practitioners, was that with it one could identify and eliminate errors and variation objectively, without having recourse to a vague sense of literary judgment. This process was called "recensio" and the method as a whole is thus often referred to as "recensionist" as well as "Lachmannian."

The recensionist approach, though influential in the study of classical texts for many decades, suffers from a number of flaws that eventually caused it to fall out of favor. It assumes that any one scribe would have been working from only a single copy text. The possibility otherwise would arise that he would "contaminate" a particular stemma by mixing families.[7] Bernard Cerquiglini opines that this sort of textual criticism is a "bourgeois, paternalist, and hygienist system of thought about the family; it cherishes filiation, tracks down adulterers, and is afraid of contamination."[8] Indeed, there is no reason to assume medieval scriptoria would be textual cleanrooms free from such contamination beyond the necessity of such a condition for the logic of the recensionist method to hold. Though the issue here is with written texts, there is ample reason to believe that medieval European scribes (and those of Tang China) would not only use more than one copy text, but might also copy down parts of a work from memory, using the copy texts to fill in gaps where their memory faltered. In either case textual alteration was always a real possibility regardless of its methodological inconvenience.

Lachmannian textual criticism further depends on the counterintuitive idea that scribes alter texts in the course of transmission in a very particular and consistent fashion. It assumes that in each instance of copying, all scribal alternations move away from the hypothetical autograph. New errors constantly creep in, but previous ones are perfectly preserved.[9] As

---

6. Bryan, *Collaborative Meaning*, 48. See also Thorpe, *Principles of Textual Criticism*, 108.
7. See Tansell, *Textual Criticism and Scholarly Editing*, 306.
8. Cerquiglini, *In Praise of the Variant*, 49.
9. Thorpe, *Principles of Textual Criticism*, 112.

Cerquiglini states, this form of textual criticism would collapse if it were forced to "think that a scribe, when confronted with an uncertain reading, for example, might be able to improve it or indeed even rediscover the 'original' reading."[10] Again, the only real justification for this assumption is that the internal logic of this particular method requires it. The recensionists thus not only desire to return to a pristine origin, but they also require an oddly pristine process of degeneration to accomplish this task.

Lachmannian-based approaches to textual criticism remained influential well into the 1960s, but as early as the first decades of the twentieth century, many scholars sought alternatives. Joseph Bédier was dissatisfied with what he saw as multiple levels of untenability in the Lachmannian approach, particularly as applied to medieval French manuscripts. Bédier instead focused on using his own knowledge of the literature in addition to "such criteria as coherence of sense, regularity of spelling, and form of grammar," to find a single "best text" from among extant witnesses, and reproduce it faithfully with little editing.[11] Unlike the recensionists, Bédier was not at all convinced that he could reliably identify certain usages as being errors or scribal changes rather than original authorial intent.[12] By choosing a single extant text as an exemplar, the Bédier method has the advantage of presenting a text that actually exists rather than a hypothetical text made up of a multitude of judgments by the textual critic. As David Hult points out, the Lachmannian approach takes the author as "unabashed hero" who has suffered from the villainous scribe defacing "original textual readings."[13] In this view, recensionists want to eliminate history and its contingencies whereas Bédier and his followers embrace a text's evolution and the fundamental materiality it displays.[14]

---

10. Cerquiglini, *In Praise of the Variant*, 49. See also Thorpe, *Principles of Textual Criticism*, 112: "A text is never self-correcting or self-rejuvenating, and the ordinary history of the transmission of a text, without the intervention of author or editor, is one of progressive degeneration." Although often critical of the Lachmannian approach, Thorpe seems to agree with its basic concept of unidirectional textual degeneration.

11. See Thorpe, *Principles of Textual Criticism*, 114; Tanselle, *Textual Criticism and Scholarly Editing*, 309–11; and Cerquiglini, *In Praise of the Variant*, 54–71.

12. Hult, "Reading it Right," 124.

13. Ibid., 119.

14. See Ibid., 122.

Much as the "best text" approach of Bédier might seem the complete antithesis of Lachmannian recensionism, they share a vulnerability to certain critiques. Recensionism pretends to eliminate judgment by a seemingly objective collation of errors, and Bédier, by presenting a text essentially "as is," purports to do the same. Yet both approaches ultimately fall back on personal judgment, whether in the identification of errors or in the choice of a "best text" and the slight editorial emendations which are made to it. Both Lachmann and Bédier sought to bring an air of the scientific to their endeavors, the former by embracing a carefully articulated method and the latter by attempting to avoid the errors and contradictions that would inevitably arise in creating a complex system of analysis. A. E. Housman succinctly punctured textual criticism's pretensions to true science by stating that such a practitioner "engaged upon his business is not at all like Newton investigating the motions of the planets: he is much more like a dog hunting for fleas."[15]

Beginning in the 1980s, an increasing number of studies of medieval European literature have taken up the ideas and terminology of more recent literary and cultural theory.[16] The new approaches exemplified by these works have soundly rejected the illusory certainty of the recensionist method. And while owing a substantial intellectual debt to Bédier, they have also moved well beyond the idea of a "best text." Modern medieval studies is a diverse field, and I limit my discussion of these new approaches (which have sometimes been called "the new medievalism"[17]) to a set of issues especially pertinent to the present study: the repudiation of the author as the final and preeminent determinant of meaning, the rejection of a critical text as a primary object of critical attention, an increased focus on the materiality of actual medieval manuscripts, and the idea that such new approaches to medieval texts actually represent a return to more typically medieval modes of experiencing texts. All of these ideas prove to be fruitful ways of engaging with Tang texts as well.

Recent studies of secular medieval literature have largely abandoned any notion of the author as Lachmannian heroic creator of the pristine

15. Housman, "Application of Thought," in his *Selected Prose*, 132.

16. For a general introduction and complaints that this new orientation was long overdue, see Finke and Shichtman, *Medieval Texts*, 1–11.

17. See Brownlee, *New Medievalism*, 1–2.

autographic manuscript. They thus reject one of the primary goals of earlier textual criticism: to come as close as possible to reclaiming this Eden of authorial intent. Scholars' justifications for rejecting this model are varied. For some, the theoretical issue of structural authority influences their approach. Elizabeth Bryan, in her study of a manuscript of Laȝamon's *Brut*, the first telling in English of the legend of King Arthur, finds in Jacques Derrida's work inspiration for a new way of considering textual authority. She writes of Derrida, "His ideas transfer rather easily to *any* situation involving a structure of authority that could be seen as oppressive, and that includes the textual structure of authority in which the 'author' has reigned supreme."[18] John Dagenais and others see author-centric approaches as inappropriate for the study of manuscript cultures, as such a perspective "carries with it both the implicit model of the printed book and all the baggage of the academic study of literary canons."[19] Printed texts, in Gerald Bruns's formulation, are closed. That is, they have reached a final form as "print closes off the act of writing and authorizes the results."[20] The author-ized results are the property of the author as creator. Manuscripts, instead, follow what Bryan characterizes as Roland Barthes's model of the "open, unendingly processual text."[21] Under such a model the author loses control at what may be an early point in the life of a work. Others can add, delete, and alter. In doing so they establish claims of their own on a work's meaning.

None of these medievalists go as far as to proclaim the author dead. They do, however, see him as operating in a larger context in which he is no longer the sole mover. Recent studies thus emphasize the idea of medieval writing as a collaborative endeavor in which the scribe plays a role equal in importance to the author. The debt to Bédier, with his acknowledgment that he "could not affirm the difference between an intelligent or gifted scribe and an author"[22] is obvious here. Yet even if Bédier had a "committed bias in favor of the scribes,"[23] the best scribe remained he who

18. Bryan, *Collaborative Meaning*, 52.
19. Dagenais, *Ethics of Reading*, xvii.
20. Bruns, "Originality of Texts," 113.
21. Bryan, *Collaborative Meaning*, 52.
22. Hult, "Reading it Right," 124.
23. Cerquiglini, *In Praise of the Variant*, 68.

created the "best text." In other words, the scribe was ultimately the transmitter and translator of the author, rather than a true collaborator creating meaning together with the author and others. Such scholars as Dagenais, on the other hand, do see the scribe as taking part in an aspect of medieval reading practice, in this case copying, that he considers to be arguably more important than authorial intent in situating the meaning of a given text. His statement that "the manuscript text is constituted by the individuals who created it: scribe, rubricator, corrector, illuminator,"[24] strikingly leaves out the author entirely. Authors do have a role to play in these new approaches to medieval texts, but it is as part of an ensemble cast.

Connected to the lowered position of the author in recent studies is a corresponding negative critique of excessive focus on the creation and use of critical texts. Variation implies a multiplicity of legitimate meanings—a key point of much recent literary theory but anathema to the very concept of a critical text. Focusing on the variation inherent in a manuscript culture, Bryan points out that "any two manuscripts will embed different sets of traces of signification and erasure, differently configured processes of meaning."[25] A critical text, on the other hand, is intended to eliminate variation so that it can present the one true meaning embodying the author's intent. It proclaims itself as the proper object of study, rather than the messy "fallen world of medieval manuscript textuality"[26] found in actual extant manuscripts. We thus return to the issue of authority. But again, this rejection is not complete; scholars critical of much traditional textual scholarship acknowledge a role for critical editions. William Paden sees a critical text as "an instrument of communication" that provides "transition between the medieval mode of existence of lyric song and a modern mode."[27] At the same time he agrees that the experience of reading a critical text necessarily distances one from the medieval world it purports to convey. These reservations are perhaps best seen less as a total rejection of critical texts than as an attempt to remind readers, and scholarly readers in particular, that critical texts are just that, works of criticism.

---

24. Dagenais, *Ethics of Reading*, 17.
25. Bryan, *Collaborative Meaning*, 52.
26. Dagenais, *Ethics of Reading*, 112.
27. Paden, "Manuscripts," 321.

They come with their own sets of judgments and cannot be accepted as transparent conveyors of the reality of medieval literature.

The focus on collaboration and a preference for actual manuscripts over critical editions has naturally led to a greater emphasis on the materiality of the textual record. There is precedent here too in the work of Bédier, for whom the medieval manuscript denotes a greater proximity to the original act of creation. Hult describes Bédier's views as holding that "the materiality of the manuscript texts becomes a part of the individual act of speech, our closest equivalent to the phonic resonances of voice within a literature whose spoken aspects are integral to it yet all but lost to us."[28] More recent scholars see the materiality of manuscripts as bringing us closer not to the author but to his collaborators. Transcendent meaning belongs to the realm of authorial intention; physical texts are the work of scribes and other participants in a manuscript culture. Bryan succinctly sums up the reasoning behind this turn to the material:

> Multiple meanings abound in manuscripts on several levels beginning with the very literal: Gaps and margins and erasures are literal. Multiple writing agents introduced multiple meanings: Actual humans apart from the author positioned organizational features like ornate initials or chapter divisions in page layout, and decided what script and quality of script to use, and entered corrections, and made annotations.[29]

This emphasis on different modes of meaning and contesting forces at work in a text is emblematic of the new medievalism, and the attention to margins, erasures, and multiple meanings betrays its debt to recent literary and cultural theory. Scholars such as Dagenais and Bryan are not trying to make medieval literature accessible to the casual reader. If anything, their focus on the material aspects of this literature can be intensely alienating: it forces us to be aware of the very real historical and cultural gaps separating the modern reader from the medieval text. These gaps may be discomforting, but only by acknowledging them can we understand this literature as people actually produced and circulated it.

Indeed, these scholars see themselves not as taking novel perspectives on medieval European literature but as returning to older ones. Post-

---

28. Hult, "Reading it Right," 123.
29. Bryan, *Collaborative Meaning*, 52.

structuralist theory may provide the immediate theoretical underpinnings, but these scholars argue that their new approaches are valuable because they ultimately come closer to the way writers and readers in medieval Europe themselves viewed their own literary products. This may seem too convenient, but the argument is a convincing one: there is much evidence that medieval authors themselves often considered their role as one of many in the production of literary texts. Amelia E. Van Vleck argues persuasively that twelfth-century troubadours not only accepted that their songs would be altered in the course of transmission, but that many actively promoted such a process at times.[30] Medieval texts are thus best thought of as collaborative because that is the way in which their creators conceived of them. We know that scribes felt at liberty to alter texts, sometimes substantially, because they in fact did so. Paden states, "Not only is the scribe capable of introducing innovative variant readings of a word, a phrase, or a line, but many editors believe that the isolated stanzas of certain songs that turn up in single manuscripts are also the work of the scribes of those manuscripts."[31] Variation and the multiple meanings it inscribes are thus not annoying inconveniences to be smoothed away by the critical text but are at the very heart of the medieval reading experience. As Dagenais points out, medieval readers did not have "the luxury of waiting around for an 'intelligible' text."[32] They read what they had. Likewise, the focus on the materiality of texts, from the handwriting and the layout to the marginalia and the scribal colophons, brings us back to texts as they were read, not as how the modern reader would find them easy to read. This is not to say that the methods of post-structural criticism and medieval reading practice are identical or even share similar goals. But the important role of difference and variation in each allows for a fruitful interaction in which one can help us understand the other.

My ultimate goal in this discussion of approaches to medieval texts in the West is to bring some of these ideas to the study of medieval Chinese manuscripts and the production and circulation of poetry in particular. The key question is whether or not the ideas of recent works on medieval Europe are applicable to the Chinese case, and I believe that they very

30. Van Vleck, *Memory and Re-Creation.*

31. Paden, "Manuscripts," 316.

32. Dagenais, *Ethics of Reading,* 112.

much are. This question has perhaps been made more complicated by an important and influential article on pre-modern Chinese attitudes towards textual change by Susan Cherniack. Cherniack's carefully researched study does a fine job of laying out a broad picture of Chinese textual criticism from the time of Confucius through the Qing, although her focus is on the Song period. She has read widely in the primary sources and has done the field a great service by bringing such disparate texts and secondary works together. However, her article also contains a number of problematic claims about the similarities and differences between Western and Chinese attitudes towards textual change.

The fundamental problem with Cherniack's argument is that she takes one particular school of Western textual criticism, the Lachmannian method, as the sole representative approach. She states, "Modern Western textual criticism has come to regard transmission as a wholly degenerative process through which texts become 'corrupted' and 'contaminated,'"[33] and that "The role assigned to the Western textual critic is to intervene in this historical process to purge the text of its accumulated filth and disease."[34] These comments would be accurate were they to refer primarily to the recensionist method. As a description of the ideas of Bédier or of the new approaches to medieval literature undertaken by scholars in the last twenty years, they are at best misleading and at worst wholly incorrect. Bédier certainly believed that texts changed in the course of transmission and that discovering the original author's intent was a worthwhile goal, but he quite explicitly objected to the idea that scribal changes were identifiable "filth" that had to be purged. These claims are even less accurate when applied to more recent studies that consider scribal contributions to be as important as authorial ones. Cherniack does note that the idea of a critical edition based on Lachmannian ideas has come under criticism by some "contemporary textual theorists,"[35] but fails to discuss any of the alternative approaches that they or earlier writers have both proposed and used for many years.[36]

---

33. Cherniack, "Book Culture," 6.

34. Ibid., 7.

35. Ibid., 8.

36. When Cherniack then goes on to contrast these supposed Western notions of inevitable textual degeneration with Chinese perspectives more open to the idea of textual

In fact, the similarities between East and West on this topic may well outweigh the differences. Modern Chinese scholars produce critical texts in much the same fashion as do their colleagues in the West. The recently published Shanghai guji edition of the Late Tang poet Wei Zhuang's 韋莊 (836–910) works takes as its base text for his epic poem "Qinfu yin" 秦婦吟 ("Lament of the Lady of Qin," of which I have much more to say below) not one of the Dunhuang manuscripts, that is, the only authentic Tang and Five Dynasties (907–60) versions of the work we have, but rather Liu Xiuye's 劉修業 critical 1947 edition, which is based on his composite editing of all the manuscripts available at the time.[37] Indeed, Cherniack herself makes even traditional Chinese editors sound like the precursors to Lachmann when she writes, "An explicit goal of traditional Chinese textual criticism has been to weed out unsanctioned changes in order to restore works to some former or original state 復其舊，復其原."[38]

But more important for my purposes here is the similarity between medieval European and medieval Chinese approaches to texts. Cherniack writes that "the traditional interpretation of Confucius's textual work as an act of transmission includes a concept of collaborative authorship that is excluded from the modern Western term."[39] Collaborative authorship, as we have seen, is not only the focus of recent Western critical approaches, it was the norm for medieval ideas on texts as well. Consider the comments of Derek Pearsal on the Ellesmere edition of Chaucer's writ-

---

changes, her argument relies on problematic chronological comparisons. To characterize Western approaches to texts, Cherniack focuses primarily on the twentieth century, with Lachmann himself being the only earlier figure noted. Turning to "Chinese attitudes towards textual change in transmission" ("Book Culture," p. 9), she begins with Zixia 子夏 in the fifth century BC, discusses Confucius as a foundational figure, and rarely moves past the Song. Comparing one particular school of twentieth-century Western criticism with general trends in Chinese textual approaches from Confucius to Zhu Xi 朱熹 (1130–1200) may be a worthy endeavor, but it fails to tell us much about the difference between "Western" and "Chinese" textual criticism overall.

37. Nie, *Wei Zhuang ji jianzhu*, 322–23. For a discussion of both modern and traditional Chinese textual criticism, see Guan, *Hanyu guji jiaokan xue*, and Cheng Qianfan and Xu Youfu, *Jiaochu guangyi*.

38. Cherniack, "Book Culture," 11. Later, in her discussion of Song critical approaches, she notes "the importance attached herein to 'author-based' authority in texts," 24.

39. Ibid., 17.

ings, which was put together just a few years after Chaucer's death. Pearsal writes, "...clearly the Ellesmere presents a text, not of what Chaucer wrote, but of what his editorial executors thought he should have written, or would have written if he had known as well as they did what he wished to write."[40] Cherniack is arguably correct that the common modern Western sense of the concept of "authorship" typically does not imply collaboration. Yet we must keep in mind that a notion of collaborative authorship has been the norm, not the exception, in recent scholarship on medieval Europe and in the period itself.

There is ample evidence that Tang compilers of literary collections similarly felt no compunction about editing the texts they put together, on the level both of individual poems and of larger-scale deletions of works that they felt did not fit their image of the poet in question. Lu Chun 陸淳 (d. 805?) produced a redacted version of the poet Wang Ji's 王績 (586–644) collection in which he "expunged those words of action and made complete [Wang Ji's] ambition to be unbound" 祛彼有爲之詞，全其懸解之志, so as to make the poet better conform to what Lu Chun saw as the ideal models of Tao Qian 陶潛 (365–427) or Ruan Ji 阮籍 (210–63).[41] Discussing the case of a Tang courtesan beloved by her patron for her ability to correct editions of Du Fu's 杜甫 (712–70) poems in such a way that made them more comprehensible to him, Xiaofei Tian writes, "To the degree that they were engaged in the production of manuscript copies by copying, editing, altering, and revising, we are no longer talking about the readers' reception of a stable text, but about the readers' dynamic participation in the very process of creating a text that is essentially protean."[42] The literary cultures of Tang China and medieval Europe were vastly different. Yet the technology of manuscript production and the realities of hand-copied texts resulted in a number of important similarities. Because of this, students of medieval Chinese poetry can greatly benefit by understanding and sometimes applying the practices of

40. Pearsall, "Editing Medieval Texts," 94.

41. Lu Chun, "Shan Donggaozi ji houxu" 删東皋子集後序 in Jin Ronghua, *Wang Ji shiwenji jiaozhu*, 388. I discuss this example in greater detail in Chapter 5. See also the discussion in Warner, *A Wild Deer*, 4–5.

42. Tian, *Tao Yuanming and Manuscript Culture*, 8. See also my further discussion in Chapter 4.

European medieval authors, scribes, and readers and the scholarly approaches of those who study them today.

The primary goal of this study is to shed light on the material lives that poems led during the Tang period, from their initial oral or written instantiation through often lengthy and twisted paths of circulation. Much of this work is thus descriptive. To the fullest extent possible, I articulate how authors in the Tang composed poems and how those poems spread to other people in both written and oral forms. Throughout, the focus is kept firmly on questions of materiality and process. We learn something different about poems when we examine them not as literary works transcending any particular physical instantiation but as objects that do have distinct physical attributes, whether as markings of ink on paper or sonic vibrations in the air. There is value in this information in and of itself. Reading a poem written on the wall of a monastery is a very different experience from hearing one sung in a tavern, and both are quite unlike reading a modern typeset critical edition. To fully understand literature from a given period and culture we need to have a good sense of how people in that era created, spread, and received it. These findings can also tell us a great deal about the roles that poems played in people's lives in the Tang, in such diverse contexts as intimate exchanges with good friends, attempts to curry favor with social superiors in order to gain employ, and even advertisements for brothels in the entertainment quarters.

From this base of detailed description, however, there are broader conclusions to be drawn. Like the literature of medieval Europe, poetry during the Tang dynasty underwent a continuous process of alteration as it passed through the hands, mouths, ears, and memories of those who composed and circulated it. Poetic texts, if we can use this term broadly to include not only written versions of poems but vocalized ones and even those stored in people's memories, were unstable in the Tang; they changed as they moved through time and space. The fact of instability, of the production of numerous non-identical versions of a given work, is not surprising. Chinese critics, just like European ones, have long understood that handwritten and orally declaimed texts are altered in the process of circulation (though in their critical practices they have often chosen to either ignore this fact or to understate its significance). Of greater interest are questions of *how* texts change and what attitudes people of the time had towards that process. A literary culture that accepts conscious revision of works in the course of transmission, as I argue the Tang did, is very different from one that recognizes the inevitability of change but fights it at every turn.

While textual instability may be the norm for poetry in the Tang, it is not the whole story. Just as certain cultural practices undermine the stability of texts, others encourage it. Different types of stability can grow out of practices that seem to work against each other. For example, the greatest form of instability is arguably extinction. Wide circulation can often ensure a poem's survival. At the same time, circulation in a manuscript and oral culture always involves textual movement in some direction. The poem will live on, but not as the same poem.

Textual instability also has important consequences for how we approach questions of a poem's authorship and a poet's control over his poem. By this I mean not control over different interpretations of a given work, but of its actual content and survival. Tang poetic texts were as much the product of numerous different hands as were the written works of medieval Europe.[43] Once a text left the hands or lips of its creator it began to slip out of his control in a much more unruly manner than we are accustomed to in our modern print culture. Different modes of circulation resulted in different types and degrees of change. Again we see contradictions. In a culture in which texts were copied individually by hand and spread rapidly through memorization and recitation, there was no circulation without change. The author who exerted absolute control over his works risked producing works that very few would see or hear. Not surprisingly, Tang poets were typically more concerned with circulation than with protecting their works from alteration.

The material reality of poetic production and circulation in the Tang was messy. This messiness is not without its consequences for critical approaches to Tang poetry. In some sense this study is concerned with the background to criticism. If a given poetic work is the object of criticism, my goal here is to illuminate what that object was in the early stages of its existence and how it may have changed over that period. These are issues that ought to be resolved before approaching the poem as an object of

43. There are, of course, important differences here in terms of the material details of the manuscripts. Tang manuscripts, as I will discuss further in Chapter 2, did not involve illuminators or other hands beyond those of the copyist.

criticism. The process of both post-Tang traditional criticism and modern scholarship on Tang poetry has tended to do the opposite: it has avoided the inconveniently untidy material history of its objects. Readers and critics have approached these poems as if the versions they are reading contain the exact words originally expressed by the poets themselves in response to particular knowable circumstances. Clearly readers have long known that there are variants in different poetic texts, as these are noted in any annotated edition, but there has always been a belief that the original and thus "correct" version could be ascertained by a sufficiently skilled reader.

Evidence of this approach is visible as far back as the Northern Song. In an anecdote from Ouyang Xiu's 歐陽修 (1007–1072) *Shihua* 詩話 ("Remarks on Poetry") we find an account of Chen Congyi 陳從易 obtaining a battered old edition of Du Fu's poems with the line "His body light: a single bird..." 身輕一鳥, missing a final character.[44] Chen's group of friends try in vain to fill in the missing word until they find an edition that has the character *guo* 過, "to pass by," which they are sure must have been Du Fu's original choice. The anecdote shows an awareness that there were many differing versions of Du Fu's poems, but also a belief that that when Du Fu's true words emerged, they would be instantly recognizable. The lynchpin of this approach is the connection between poet and poem; it is a criticism based on biographical knowledge. This connection finds its roots in the "Daxu" 大序 to the *Shi* 詩 ("The Poems," often referred to as the *Shijing* 詩經 "Classic of Poetry") which portrays poetry as the expression of a distinct individual in particular circumstances. As Steven Van Zoeren has pointed out, "...the reading of poetry was thus often conceived in terms of a process of coming to know the poet as a person."[45] In a world in which poems passed through many hands in the course of circulation, and where every instance of transmission carried the potential for departure from an original, such a mode of interpretation is dubious at

44. Translation from Owen, *Readings in Chinese Literary Thought*, 370. See Ouyang Xiu, *Ouyang Xiu quanji* 歐陽修全集, 1036.

45. Van Zoeren, *Poetry and Personality*, 15. In a similar vein, Owen (*Traditional Chinese Poetry and Poetics*, 57) explains that "the traditional Chinese reader had faith that poems were authentic presentations of historical experience. Poets wrote and readers read, under those assumptions."

best. One of the larger aims of this study is to demonstrate that the assumption that the totality of a poem can always be unquestionably tied to a single authorial hand and directly linked to the specific experiences of that author is simply untenable.

This study begins by engaging directly with the material reality of poetry as it was produced and circulated during the Tang by looking closely at a set of surviving manuscripts from the period. My particular focus is eight Dunhuang manuscript copies of Wei Zhuang's lengthy narrative poem "Qinfu yin," which tells of the sack of Chang'an 長安 during the Huang Chao 黄巢 rebellion in the late ninth century. Rather than address the poem as a literary work as others have done, I approach the manuscripts as distinctly physical objects whose numerous differences may well be as important as their similarities to our understanding of the actual material contexts in which Tang poetry was produced and circulated. I then use the categories of variants established by this examination to discuss a small number of other poetic texts from Dunhuang. Looking closely at the types and implications of variations among the different manuscript versions of a given poem allows us to gain a better understanding of the technology and process of the written text as it existed in the Tang.

As the first chapter examines concrete examples of Tang poetic manuscripts, the rest of the study tells the different possible stories behind these objects. Using a range of received sources, from prefaces to individual poems and collections to anecdotal literature, I reconstruct the material contexts of poetic production and circulation that led to the creation of these tangible traces of the vast world of poetry in the Tang.

The Tang was perhaps the most literate civilization on the earth in its time, yet memory continued to play an important role in both the educational system and the ways that the literate populace interacted with texts. Memory is the original form of "textual" storage. In the second chapter I look at both the content and the methods of memorial practices in the medieval period in general with a focus on the Tang. Memory is properly viewed as a technology of textual storage. The well-trained memories of literate men and women in the Tang were important sources of stability in a way that our comparatively less meticulously trained and thus weaker textual memories today are not. By spending countless hours reciting and copying texts until they were internalized, people in the Tang had substantial stores of knowledge at their immediate disposal. These memories were not passive storehouses where texts languished unused; as sources of inspiration for new literary works, they provided the basis for a common language of literary expression.

Chapter 2 also deals with the substantial differences between medieval Chinese memorial practices and those developed in similar periods in Europe. These differences, not surprisingly, result in different strengths and weaknesses. Considering medieval Chinese methods carefully allows us to move past the myth of perfect memory so often connected to traditional Chinese learning. Tang memories were arduously trained and significantly more capable than our memories in the modern West, but they were still far from infallible. Even the classics tested on the exams were memorized incompletely, while many other works were just "largely" set to memory. The ability to fully and accurately recall a wide variety of texts verbatim was clearly the exception rather than the rule. With a good deal of poetic reproduction and circulation having been based on recitation from memory, imperfect memories inevitably introduced change in the course of transmission.

Much of the second chapter deals with memory in general, but in the final section I focus on its role in the circulation of poetry in particular. The needs and strengths of memory shaped the forms of literature themselves, and the more memorable structures enjoyed more opportunities for circulation. Though the goals of the literary figures instrumental in the development of popular forms of poetry were not specifically concerned with creating patterns that were easy to memorize, the fact that poems utilizing these patterns could be quickly set to memory unquestionably aided their dissemination and popularity.

The connection between memory and orality was a very close one in the Tang. Given the prevalent role of oral expression, with both reading and writing typically accompanied by vocalization, it is clear that people memorized poems (and probably many other texts) as sounds, not as the graphic representation of those sounds.[46] The third chapter investigates the different functions and meanings of orality in Tang poetic culture, ar-

46. When writing down poems, people obviously converted these sounds into characters, but the basis of their memorization appears to have been aural, rather than visual.

guing that orality was not a result of an immature literary culture (as is sometimes claimed about orality in medieval Europe), but represented conscious aesthetic choices made by Tang poets and their audience. Looking at accounts of oral composition, I demonstrate that this method of composing poetry was connected to a particular set of associations with moral authenticity that poets would often exploit to give a presumption of emotional and moral depth to their works. This chapter also addresses the issue of oral circulation. Memory and oral circulation worked together, with memory storing poetic works and speech using that storage as a base from which to spread poems to a wider audience. As perhaps the most basic aspect of the stability of poetic works is simple preservation, oral circulation was an important force in maintaining that stability. Poems that people memorized and repeated, whether from father to son or from singing girl to audience, tended to survive and enjoy additional opportunities to spread. The ability of oral circulation to disseminate poems rapidly to a wide audience was especially important in certain commercial contexts in the Tang. Oral poetry was not a true commodity in the Tang, but it had an important role to play in some marketplaces.

Oral circulation helped poems spread but could serve as a destabilizing force as well. Imperfect memories stored and reproduced poems imperfectly, no matter how amenable their forms were to memorization. In some performance contexts, poems would be intentionally altered, both to fit musical requirements and to please different audiences. Performance was an important mode of poetic circulation, but it inevitably changed the works it spread.

Turning to the written aspects of poetry in the fourth chapter, I address the tension in accounts of written composition between spontaneity and a more prolonged process of working on a poem. My examination of written circulation, a slower process than its oral counterpart but one that was crucial to the long-term preservation of Tang poetry, focuses on copying practices and their implications. While the first chapter shows the end result of textual change, this chapter looks closely at how that change occurred, citing numerous accounts of readers, copyists, and others altering poems in the course of transmission.

Writing *was* a source of stability for poetic works. Oral manifestations of poems in the Tang were by nature transitory—brief vibrations in the air—while written texts have persevered over vast stretches of time and space. We can never hear a Tang recitation of a poem (which is a very different thing from a recitation of a Tang poem); we can read (provided we make a trip to London or Paris) the exact same texts of "Qinfu yin" that were produced in Dunhuang monasteries over a thousand years ago. A single manuscript could thus circulate and provide many people with the same version of a given poem. Written texts can surely be altered, whether through erasures, damage, or complete destruction, but they tend to be less fallible than human memory.

Yet written circulation typically did not involve the circulation of a single copy; it rather consisted of multiple reproductions of texts based on different sources. This textual reproduction served stability in that it was a force for preservation; the only reason we have almost *any* versions of poems from the Tang is because written copies survived to be printed in the Song. However, as I will show in a number of contexts, textual reproduction in the manuscript culture of the Tang was never exact duplication. The interval between original and reproduction truly did witness a new production. Even when a copyist, whether he was a professional scribe or simply a reader who wanted his own copy of a poem, may have intended to stay fully true to the original, changes inevitably crept in. Many examples we will see are far more drastic; copyists undertook significant revisions to "improve" the poems they copied or make them better conform to their expectations. Though there is little evidence of a commercial market for poems to be enjoyed as literature, they were bought and sold in connection with certain practices surrounding the exam system and the related pursuit of patronage. In these commercial contexts poems would not only be changed, but intentionally circulated under false names. Like memory and orality, the written culture of Tang poetry both preserved and altered poetic texts.

The fifth and final chapter examines one of the key means of preserving and circulating written poetry during the Tang: literary collections consisting of the works of a single author. Literary collections were not new in the Tang, but in the course of the dynasty they reached a level of popularity that was previously unknown. Individual literary collections, especially by the Mid- and Late Tang, were read widely and constituted one of the primary means of access to the works of poets from earlier in the dynasty. Perhaps more importantly, these collections, along with the Tang anthologies for which they were often the source texts, ultimately formed the basis for Song printed editions, the primary avenue through which Tang poetry survived into later periods. The first part of this chapter examines the full process of compiling a literary collection in the Tang, from collecting the poems to editing and copying them into a formal collection, as revealed in prefaces to those collections. It is thus a fitting conclusion to the discussion that began in the first chapter, which describes the material reality of Tang poetry. In this final chapter we get a glimpse of what it was like for compilers and readers in the Tang to confront that reality. Collections clearly stabilized the link between authors and their works, but by the time they became parts of collections, the works were often different from what the authors had originally produced. When people compiled written and oral texts into individual literary collections, they also changed them, both revising individual works and, just as importantly, deciding which works to include and omit. Compilers were not objective conservators so much as opinionated editors. I conclude this chapter by briefly discussing some distinctions between the attitudes of Tang collectors and compilers towards their work and the attitudes of those who would undertake similar endeavors in the Song. Those Song attitudes were very different, but we can see their beginnings in new approaches to collections in the Mid- and Late Tang.

Before concluding this introduction it is worth briefly discussing the limits of this study, those both self-imposed as well as those due to the nature and number of available sources. My focus here is on the Tang itself. I will not discuss how poetic texts circulated during the Song or in later periods. While such phenomena are certainly worth examining (and there is a substantial amount of scholarship on such topics), the issues involved move well beyond those concerned with manuscript culture alone. Thus it is important to be clear that when I speak of variation and change in poetic works, I am specifically talking about change during the Tang itself. If we have a single manuscript copy of a poem from Dunhuang and another copy from a printed edition in the Ming, there is little if anything that we can learn about variation in Tang manuscript circulation specifically by comparing them. Likewise, though a genre such as tomb texts (*muzhiming* 墓誌銘) that involved the burial of an original version of the work would appear to present an ideal test cases for textual variation, unless we have other found copies of the same text extant from the Tang itself, as opposed to received through later print traditions, no comparison can tell us about textual change in the Tang manuscript culture *per se*.

A related limitation is that of genre. I will address other sorts of writing at times, in the second chapter's examination of memory for example, but my focus here is strongly on poetry. There are a number of reasons for this. Poetry is clearly the genre with which the Tang has been most closely associated in both traditional and modern histories of Chinese literature. It suffused the life of the educated elite in the Tang in a way that no other form of literature did. As a result there are far more accounts of composing and circulating poetry than of other genres in the Tang. Most importantly, poetry regularly involved a wider range of circulation practices. Works in other genres were no doubt transmitted orally at times, but there is no evidence this happened with anything near the extent that it did with poetry. The same holds true for such modes of written circulation as writing on walls and other such surfaces.

The implications of this study are themselves by no means limited to the study of poetry. As this is ultimately a series of arguments about how people in the Tang created and circulated texts, and as texts are ultimately the basis for most of what we know about the Tang, my hope is that this work will influence the way historians and scholars of religion approach Tang materials, whether received or recently discovered, as well. Textual reproduction was, after all, undertaken on a massive scale by both the state and religious organizations, and reproducing texts from memory was an important requirement for becoming either an ordained monk or a member of the official bureaucracy. A concluding section addresses some of the broader implications of my findings for other disciplines.

Other limits are imposed by the available sources. Many of the issues with which this study is concerned were not of great interest to Tang writers themselves. The material aspects of how they produced and circulated poetry were the basic fabric of their everyday lives and not a frequent topic of their writings. Consequently, the evidence is diffuse and often incidental to the larger works that contain it. It is to be found in such diverse sources as official histories, poems, Tang prefaces to Tang collections and poems, and anecdote collections from both the Tang and Song. For some sources, such as prefaces to Tang poetry collections, I only use materials written in the Tang by those who compiled the collection themselves or knew those who had. With anecdote collections and histories, I have cast a wider net while still focusing primarily on sources that were compiled no later than the Song, with very few exceptions. There is no question that using such a diverse set of sources means that we are dealing with writings that have very different origins and agendas. Nevertheless, none of these sources should be out of bounds. A late Tang anecdote about a poetic performance by Li Bai 李白 (701–62) a century earlier may not offer a guarantee of exact historical accuracy, but it still has important things to tell us about what the culture accepted and valued. Likewise, though anecdote collections compiled in the Song are farther removed from the events they describe, Song compilers had access to far more surviving Tang sources than we have today. Finally, because so many of these anecdotes are concerned with matters other than the basic ways in which poetry was produced and circulated, be it the culture of the exam system or allure of a certain courtesan, they are perhaps less likely to exaggerate and distort the more quotidian aspects of the contexts they describe, that is, the very aspects with which this study is concerned.

Another issue that must be addressed is the prominent role played here (and in any examination of composing and circulating poetry in the Tang, especially when literary collections are discussed) by the writings of Bai Juyi 白居易 (772–846). There are far more surviving writings from Bai Juyi and, to a lesser extent, Yuan Zhen 元稹 (779–831), that deal with the process of producing, circulating, and storing poems than from any other Tang writer. Throughout this study I have been careful to limit the degree to which arguments depend primarily on examples from Bai Juyi. It is worth noting in this context that essentially all the secondary materials in Chinese and Japanese that deal with these topics are far more heavily dependent on examples from Bai Juyi than am I. At the same time, an argument can be made that Bai Juyi is indeed a valid example. As noted above, much of what we are examining here was part of the everyday lives of Tang poets, and it was not until the later parts of the dynasty that poets began focusing more on the mundane details of their lives (with the influential exception of Du Fu). Bai Juyi was the great poet of the everyday and it is thus not surprising that we have so much writing by him about the process of writing, circulating, and preserving those writings. It is likely that most elements of these practices were not at all unique to him; he just bothered to write about them more than most others did. We can likewise assume that other poets ate bamboo shoots and possessed interesting rocks, even if they did not write about them with the same frequency and relish.

Bai Juyi's ample writings on these topics notwithstanding, the number and types of primary sources limit what we can do: arguments about the historical development of practices throughout the Tang period are often difficult if not impossible to make. The amount and detail of writing about the issues with which we are concerned herein are far greater for the second half of the dynasty than for the first. As a result, the data points for the early Tang are usually insufficient to make a valid comparison with later periods.[47] In some cases we have legitimate grounds for informed speculation, but it is important to acknowledge that it is often just that. For example, as discussed in Chapter 3, fewer poems specifically described as orally composed survive from the latter half of the dynasty. While one might argue that the specific claim of oral composition held less rhetorical value in this period than in the first part of the dynasty, one cannot extrapolate from this to assume that the actual *practice* of oral composition likewise diminished. Even for later periods, evidence for trends in certain practices is suggestive but far from conclusive. On the issue of commercial markets for poetry, the very limited sources allow for no more than assertions that there were, indeed, connections between commerce and poetry in some contexts during the Tang. We have evidence that writings including poetry were bought and sold. Yet we know very little about who bought them, who sold them, what poems were popular in this context, and how much they cost. There is simply not enough evidence to do the sort of detailed sociological examination of the market for Tang poetry or for different levels of taste that would be possible for the commercial printing industry in later periods. At the same time, even sketching the outlines of such a market in the Tang can tell us important things about the contexts in which poetry circulated.

This study deals more with the material and cultural history of poetry during the Tang than with Tang poetry as literature. Critical discussions

---

47. We obviously have a great number of *poems* that survive from earlier parts of the dynasty, and scholars thus can and have made legitimate studies of historical changes to poetic styles in the Tang. What we lack are writings about the process of composition and circulation.

of poems, prefaces, historical anecdotes, and other primary sources in a specifically literary mode are infrequent, though not totally absent. The issues addressed, however, have a significant impact on how we can engage with Tang poetry from a literary critical perspective. Thus in a brief concluding section I discuss some of the repercussions of this study and some further directions in which these and related issues might be explored. Only by improving our understanding of the full material context in which Tang poetry was first produced and circulated can we hope to gain better critical insights into this important stage of the development of literature in China.

ONE
Textual Variation in Poetic Manuscripts from Dunhuang

"Now, medieval writing does not produce variants; it *is* variance."

—Bernard Cerquiglini

Chronological, technical, and cultural differences make it impossible for us to truly experience a Tang poem as its original audience would have. There are, however, ways we can approach texts that allow us to reconstruct certain aspects of those earlier readers' experiences. With its numerous manuscript versions surviving in the Dunhuang caves from during or just after the Tang, Wei Zhuang's "Qinfu yin" provides a unique opportunity to engage a Tang poem in something like its original states of existence, with all the disorder and irregularity they entail.[1] When we consider these manuscripts not merely as flawed embodiments of an imagined original, but as examples of the kinds of texts Tang copyists and readers would actually create and encounter, we gain important insights into the literary world in which Tang poetry was first composed and circulated.

EPIGRAPH: Cerquiglini, *In Praise of the Variant*, 77–78.

1. In addition to the "Qinfu yin" manuscripts, I will briefly discuss a small set of shorter poems by the High Tang poet Gao Shi.

The story of the finds at the oasis city of Dunhuang, fascinating in its own right, has been told in many places and need not be repeated in great detail here.[2] Briefly, somewhere near the turn of the twentieth century and no later than 1900, either a Daoist monk named Wang Yuanlu 王圓籙 (1849–1931) or his assistant noticed a crack in the wall of one of the temple caves in the Mogao 莫高 complex at Dunhuang.[3] Behind the wall he discovered a massive cache of stacked manuscripts. The bulk of these eventually found their way into the hands of the British archaeologist Mark Aurel Stein (1862–1943) and the French scholar Paul Pelliot (1878–1945) in 1907 and 1908 respectively, and later to the collections of the British Museum and the Bibliothèque nationale de France.[4] Examination of the manuscripts eventually revealed a date range of 406 to 995 CE,[5] along with evidence that the caves were sealed in the year 1035 or 1036.[6]

The total number of Dunhuang manuscripts, including numerous fragments, is now thought to be near 50,000. Whereas most of the manuscripts consist of copies of known Buddhist scriptures, there are also significant numbers of works such as popular narratives and vernacular

---

2. The fullest discussion of the discovery and early history of the Dunhuang finds in English is Su Ying-hui's "On the Tunhuang Studies," 64–88. For a general introduction to the Dunhuang manuscripts see Ji Xianlin, *Dunhuangxue da cidian*. For a description of the physical and formal characteristics of the manuscripts, see Fujieda, "Dunhuang Manuscripts." Although Fujieda discusses in some detail the characteristics of the paper, handwriting, and writing instruments of the manuscripts, his focus is primarily on Buddhist texts. However, his observation that the "informal" scrolls (i.e., other than the canonical Buddhist, Daoist, and Confucian texts) from the ninth and tenth centuries were often written with a wooden pen introduced by the Tibetans is worth noting. Such a writing implement appears to have been used for sections of some of the "Qinfu yin" and Gao Shi manuscripts that I will discuss below. For a general study of the Dunhuang documents that were written in Chinese, see Ikeda, *Tonkô kanbun bunken* 敦煌漢文文獻.

3. This possibility is noted in Wilkinson, *Chinese History*, 826.

4. Other groups of manuscripts were acquired by assistants of Ôtani Kôzui, Sergei Oldenburg, and Petr Kuz'mich Kozlov and taken to Japan and Russia. A number were also eventually obtained by the Beijing Capital Library and various collectors. See Wilkinson, *Chinese History*, 828.

5. See Twitchett, "Chinese Social History," 35.

6. This was the time of the Tangut or Xixia invasion of the area. Victor Mair notes that there are no documents in the Xixia language among the manuscripts despite their subsequent occupation of the area. See Mair, *T'ang Transformation Texts*, 5.

poetry and prose that have changed the way the development of these genres is now viewed. In addition to the wealth of vernacular and folk literature, there are many examples of what would be considered the "high" literary culture of the Tang by such poets as Wang Wei, Li Bai, Bai Juyi, and Gao Shi 高適 (716–65), among others. The importance of the Dunhuang finds to scholars of Tang poetry became apparent soon after their discovery, with one of the highlights being Lionel Giles's identification of the full text of Wei Zhuang's lengthy narrative poem "Qinfu yin." However, serious work on the full corpus of Tang poetry from Dunhuang did not begin in earnest until many years later when the texts, those gathered by Paul Pelliot and held in the Bibliothèque National de France in particular, became available in photo-reproduced form to scholars in China, Taiwan, and Japan.[7]

These finds have opened a new avenue of inquiry in the study of Tang poetry, though one that scholars have approached with caution. Such caution is only appropriate given the limitations of these sources. The Dunhuang manuscripts are the fullest set of poetic texts from the Tang period itself or soon after, unmediated by the selection and editing process of Song print culture. At the same time, we must not overstate the extent to which these texts can be taken as fully representative of Tang literary culture, especially that of the capital region. Some scholars have perhaps been overly sanguine in this respect. Victor Mair points out that with the exception of the Tibetan occupation from 781–848, there was "constant communication between Dunhuang and the rest of China throughout most of the period from the Han to the Tang."[8] Xu Jun states that the general situation of poetic manuscripts in Dunhuang accurately reflects "the true shape of the circulation of poetic works in the typical manuscript age of the Tang, Five Dynasties, and early Song."[9] These claims should not be dismissed, yet we must keep in mind that Dunhuang had ceased to be a part of the Tang realm with the Tibetan invasion and did not again fall under Chinese

7. Such studies as Gao Song's *Dunhuang Tangren shiji canjuan kaoshi* and Huang Yongwu's *Dunhuang de Tangshi and Dunhuang de tangshi xubian* are representative.

8. Mair, *T'ang Transformation Texts*, 2.

9. Xu Jun, *Dunhuang shiji*, 11.

imperial rule until many centuries later. Communication did allow a large inflow of Tang cultural products and influences, but it did not turn Dunhuang into a Chang'an on the frontier.[10]

Some scholars have also assumed that, as manuscripts from the period of the Tang or shortly thereafter, the Dunhuang texts are closer to the "original" versions of whatever poem is being discussed than versions surviving in print editions. Huang Yongwu, while accepting that there are sometimes "errors" in the Dunhuang versions,[11] nevertheless often uses the texts to correct what he sees as mistakes in the received versions of poems that have come down to us through later print cultures. For instance, when asserting that the Dunhuang version of a poem by Li Bai contains the poet's "original writing" (*yuanwen* 原文),[12] he neglects to take into account the fact that we cannot know the number of reproductions, possibly both oral and written, that had taken place prior to the version preserved in the manuscript in question. It is certainly possible that the version of a poem preserved by the Song printers is closer to Li Bai's original composition. There is no way to know without a clearly delineated line of transmission from the author to the later text in question. Unfortunately, there are no occasions in which such a knowable line of transmission exists. In short, the Dunhuang manuscripts cannot provide us with the original versions of Tang poems as they left their authors' brushes. They can, however, provide important insights into how a manuscript culture strongly influenced by and closely connected historically to the Tang reproduced some of the poetic products of that culture. They are not the ideal representatives of Tang manuscript culture, but they are the only ones we have.

10. Xu Jun (*Dunhuang shiji*, 30) notes that most poetry collections found at Dunhuang are by poets from the central regions of China proper, whereas many individual poems are from poets from Dunhuang itself.

11. Huang, *Dunhuang de Tangshi*, 9.

12. Ibid., 3.

The "Qinfu yin" Manuscripts

"Qinfu yin" itself may seem an odd choice for the basis of larger claims about Tang poetic circulation.[13] As the longest surviving poem from the Tang it is, by this fact alone, exceptional. It is a very late Tang poem, dated by Chen Yinke to 886, and thus not necessarily representative of how poetry was circulated, for example, in the capital region prior to the An Lushan Rebellion.[14] While these objections are valid, they are legitimately outweighed by the primary advantage of "Qinfu yin" as an object for this type of textual study, namely the exceptionally large number of copies of it available in manuscript form. Few if any other poems in the Dunhuang manuscripts exist in more than a handful of manuscript copies from the period. As such, they provide only very limited evidence for the extent of variation between multiple copies. Because of its numerous versions, "Qinfu yin" offers a wealth of opportunities to observe the variations in a text through many different versions. Moreover, the ample length of the poem makes it especially useful for this type of examination as it effectively cancels out the statistical impact of each individual variant. In a typical five-character, eight-line regulated poem, any single variant character represents a variation rate of 2.5 percent of the entire poem. In a work the length of "Qinfu yin," at some 238 lines of seven characters each

---

13. As noted in the Introduction, I will not be addressing "Qinfu yin" as a literary work in this chapter. For such perspectives on the poem see, for example, Robin Yates, *Washing Silk*, and Levy, *Chinese Narrative Poetry*. "Qinfu yin" was one of the first poetic works found among the Dunhuang manuscripts to enjoy concerted scholarly attention. Lionel Giles, in his 1926 *T'oung Pao* article, "The Lament of the Lady of Ch'in" (305–80) describes discovering three manuscript copies of the poem in the Stein collection of manuscripts in 1919, just over a decade after Stein took them from Dunhuang. These are the manuscripts that later came to be numbered s692, s5476, and s5477. The great Chinese scholar Wang Guowei had previously discussed the content and dating of the poem in his 1923 article "Wei Zhuang de Qinfu yin." For an account of the other early scholarship on the poem see Xu Jun, *Dunhuang shiji*, 230–31. See also Giles, "Lament"; Wang Guowei, *op cit*; and Chen Yinke, "Du 'Qinfu yin.'" For a summary of various readings of the poem, including recent Marxist criticisms of Wei Zhuang as a reactionary, see Gao Guofan, *Dunhuang suwenhua xue*, 514–22. Finally, most of the important (and less important) pre-1990 Chinese scholarship on the poem, including many of the articles cited above, can be found in Yan Tingliang and Zhao Yiwu, eds., *"Qinfu yin" yanjiu huilu*.

14. Chen Yinke, "Du 'Qinfu yin,'" 953. This date continues to be disputed, with Nie Anfu in the Zhonghua critical edition noting that some date it to 884.

(1,666 characters in all), depending on the version in question,[15] much of the statistical "noise" of a single mistake is smoothed out and we can develop a more accurate picture of the real types and degrees of variation.

Beyond such practical concerns, "Qinfu yin" is also a particularly interesting case of the ability of an author in the Late Tang to maintain control over his literary works after they had begun to circulate beyond his family or very close circle of friends. This extremely popular poem brought Wei Zhuang a measure of fame and quite literally made his name. In his work *Beimeng suoyan* 北夢瑣言 ("Chit-chat of the Northern Dreamer"), the tenth-century author Sun Guangxian 孫光憲 (d. 968) relates that the poem became so popular that Wei Zhuang became known as the "'Lament of the Lady of Qin' Graduate" 秦婦吟秀才.[16] The multiple copies of the poem found in the caves at Dunhuang prove that the poem circulated beyond the formal boundaries of the Tang state during Wei Zhuang's own lifetime. Yet later in life Wei Zhuang himself came to regret the poem's success. Sun Guangxian claims that the couplet, "The Inner Treasury was burned to ashes of brocade and embroidery/On the Street of Heaven everywhere one stepped were the bones of officials" 內庫燒爲錦繡灰，天街踏盡公卿骨 offended surviving officials and that Wei Zhuang thus began treating his own poem as taboo.[17] When he later composed his "Family Regulations" (*Jiajie* 家戒), reports Sun, "he did not permit the hanging of screens with 'The Lament of the Lady of Qin'" 不許垂秦婦吟障子.[18] Moreover, the work was not included when his brother Wei Ai 韋藹 compiled the *Washing Flowers Collection* 浣花集 of Wei Zhuang's poems. More recent scholars have speculated that it was, in fact, portions of the poem that could be interpreted to show Wei Zhuang's later patron Wang Jian 王建 in a bad light that caused the former to disown his famous work.[19]

---

15. As described below, some versions have extra characters, and others omit certain characters.

16. Sun Guangxian 孫光憲, *Beimeng suoyan* 北夢瑣言, 6.47.

17. Ibid. These are lines 145 and 146 of the poem.

18. Ibid. Note that this may be a reference to the text of the poem or to paintings on the topic of "Qinfu yin."

19. See discussion in Robin Yates, *Washing Silk*, xii, 254–55, and Chen Yinke, "Du 'Qinfu yin.'" The following articles in Yan and Zhao focus on this issue though others ad-

The popularity of "Qinfu yin" also raises questions about whether or not it should really be viewed as an exception. It is the longest surviving poem from the Tang, but there is no reason to believe that there were not many other poems of similar length that were quite popular in the Tang. Lengthy narrative poems of this sort did not catch the fancy of compilers of literary anthologies and collections in the Song and were rarely reproduced by the burgeoning print culture. "Qinfu yin" itself is, of course, a perfect example of a poem highly popular and well known in its time that disappeared from the received corpus of Tang poetry, yet exists in far more copies from Dunhuang than any other poetic work whether long or short. The differences between this work and an eight-line poem from the High Tang are obvious, but do not preclude us from concluding that "Qinfu yin" might well be representative of a larger body of Tang works that simply did not meet the tastes of later collectors.

Wei Zhuang both succeeded and failed in his attempts to control "Qinfu yin." The initial loss of control involved a failure to foresee unintended consequences. When he originally composed the poem, probably around 886, it would have been impossible for him to predict that five years or so later he would be serving Wang Jian, who himself had served under Yang Fuguang 楊復光 in a region through which the poem's eponymous lady was shown to pass through with some difficulty due to the depredations of local officials.[20] Of the concrete measures Wei Zhuang took to distance himself from the poem, we know of only the two noted above: forbidding family members to hang scrolls of the text and keeping it out of his primary collection.[21] The poem indeed appears to have disappeared at some point in the Song (save for the two lines quoted by Sun Guangxian), probably due more to decreased popularity in that

dress it as well: Huang Guangsheng, "Wei Zhuang zijin 'Qinfu yin' yuanyin zai xi," 218–26; Ma Maoyuan and Liu Chutang 劉初棠, "Wei Zhuang huiyan 'Qinfu yin' zhi you ji qita," 275–87; and Zhang Tianjian 張天健, "'Qinfu yin' hui yin kao," 288–95.

20. Robin Yates, *Washing Silk*, 254.

21. The *Washing Flowers Collection* was compiled by Wei Ai in Wei Zhuang's lifetime and with his assistance. It is thus reasonable to assume that the poem was excluded at his request.

period than to specific efforts by Wei Zhuang.[22] Thus even if he could not control interpretations of his work, his desire that its textual manifestations disappear was apparently fulfilled.[23] Or so it would have seemed for just over one thousand years after his death. In fact, dry desert air and some diligent copyists accomplished what Song print culture could not and preserved multiple copies of Wei Zhuang's disowned poem.

In what follows I use a number of approaches influenced by recent work on European medieval literature to discuss a set of manuscript copies of Wei Zhuang's "Qinfu yin." My interest here is not in creating a new critical text (or criticizing previous ones), determining Wei Zhuang's original intent, or discussing the literary merit of the poem. Rather, my goal is to take the initial steps towards articulating how Tang and Five Dynasties readers would have interacted with texts of the poem. I thus focus heavily on the materiality of these manuscripts, on what makes each one an individual text different from other versions of the poem. Tang poetry consisted not of disembodied works but of oral declamations and hand-written texts. In our age of print and electronic textual reproduction on a massive scale, it is easy to forget the importance of the physical for a manuscript culture. Tang readers did not go to a bookstore and buy a book of poems. The poems they read were likely either copied out by a friend or the reader himself. The "Qinfu yin" manuscripts thus provide us with a narrow but revealing window onto Tang poetic literature as it was copied, circulated, and read during the Tang and just after. Acknowledging that it is not a perfect representative of what we ordinarily think of as Tang poetry, after examining this poem in detail, I briefly look at a set of shorter works from earlier in the dynasty that were found in Dunhuang as well.

---

22. Were Sun's claim that it was these very lines that so distressed the poet correct, their status as sole survivors would be keenly ironic, though other explanations for Wei's actions are more convincing.

23. The key issue here may be that there is no record of the poem ever being printed. Had it been, its textual history might have been very different. Dore Levy has suggested that the later history of narrative poetry in China would have been quite different as well. See Levy, *Chinese Narrative Poetry*, 120.

If we are serious about dealing with poems as material objects, we must begin with a concrete description of the different texts we are to discuss, as they vary significantly in terms of their physical and visual attributes as written texts.[24] In this section I thus outline the basic physical characteristics and facts of production to the fullest extent possible for each of these eight manuscript copies of "Qinfu yin." I then look at visual presentation, from layout to punctuation, and discuss the general content of the manuscripts aside from the words of the poem proper, ranging from colophons to correction marks and various forms of marginalia. When we look at the texts from this perspective, it becomes clear that variations among them go beyond the differing words of the poem to the very experience of reading and engaging with them as material objects.

Dates and Copyists[25]

There is no definitive scholarly consensus as to when Wei Zhuang composed "Qinfu yin." Thanks to colophons on the manuscripts, however, we can date five of the eight Dunhuang versions of the poem with some precision. In many cases, these colophons also provide limited information about the copyists responsible for the texts.

P3381: According to a colophon, this manuscript was copied in 905 (天復五年乙丑歲十二月五日) by scholar (*xueshi* 學仕) Zhang Gui 長龜

24. Although such an approach is unusual when dealing with Chinese literature (with the exception of recent work on excavated bamboo texts), it is common in scholarship on medieval European manuscripts. See, for example, Bryan's exhaustive descriptions of manuscripts of Laȝamon's *Brut* in *Collaborative Meaning*, 63–95. For a fine example of this type of approach towards medieval Chinese religious texts, see Stephen F. Teiser's *Scripture on the Ten Kings*.

25. For my analysis of the "Qinfu yin" manuscripts I have used high-quality photographs that have recently been published in both book form and on the website of the International Dunhuang project. The sources are as follows: P2700: *Manuscrits*, 17.297–300; P3381: *Manuscrits*, 24.40–42; P3910: *Manuscrits*, 29.203–7; P3953: *Manuscrits*, 30.278; P3780: *Manuscrits*, 28.35–37; S692: *Yingcang*, 2.116–17; S5834: *Yingcang*, 9.172 (note that this is a small fragment that appears to have come from P2700. I thus treat it as part of the latter text in my analysis); S5476: *Yingcang*, 7.172–77; S5477: *Yingcang*, 7.177–82. For manuscripts from the Stein collections, I also made extensive use of the images found at the International Dunhuang Project website. See <http://idp.bl.uk/>.

of the Jinguangming Monastery 金光明寺 in Dunhuang Commandery.[26] The text shows minimal damage and appears to contain the entire 238 lines of the poem.[27] If it was indeed copied in 905, this would make it the only one of the surviving manuscripts copied during the Tang[28] and within the lifetime of Wei Zhuang himself.

P3780: This manuscript includes conflicting colophons, making it difficult to determine definitively the copyist and the date of copying. Immediately following the text of the poem itself and the title is one column of text written with a brush in a very rapid hand. It names one Yang Dingqian 楊定遷 as the copyist and gives the date of copying as the second year of the Xiande period, seventeenth day of the second month of the *dingsi* year 顯德二年丁巳歲二月十七日, that is, 955 (which contains an error, as it was the fourth year of the Xiande period that was a *dingsi* year). However, following this column and another in the same hand that repeats part of the date are two columns written with a Tibetan wood pen, like the text of the poem itself. These identify the copyist as Scholarly Gentleman (*xueshi lang* 學士郎) Ma Fude 馬富德 and give the same date of copying. To complicate matters, after a few random characters written with a brush, another column in pen again names Ma Fude as copyist, but describes him as junior scholar (*xueshi tonger* 學士童兒). A new date is also given with the year being the fourth of the Xiande period. This is quite clearly written as *dingji* 丁己, though this must be an error for *dingsi* as there can be no *dingji* year: both *ding* and *ji* are heavenly stems and thus do not combine in the sexagenary cycle (and, as just noted, the fourth year of the Xiande period was indeed a *dingsi* year). The day in this column is listed as being the nineteenth and the month remains the

26. Giles ("Lament," 307–308*n*2) notes that Dunhuang manuscript S2711 (which does not contain any portion of "Qinfu yin"), dating from the early tenth century, contains a list of sutra copyists (*xiejingren* 寫經人) from the Jinguangming Monastery. The list, however, notes neither Zhang Gui nor the An Yousheng 安友盛 stated as being the copyist for S692 from the same monastery. Giles takes this as indicating that neither were considered skilled enough scribes to work on scriptural projects.

27. This manuscript is thus used by Xu Jun as his base text.

28. The lack of Tang sovereignty over Dunhuang since the late eighth century perhaps makes this fact less important.

same. Xu Jun notes that the correct date should be the fourth year of the Xiande period and thus dates the manuscript to 957. These two copyists continue their back and forth on the opposite side of the scroll with Yang Dingqian insisting that he "copied it with his own hand and that is that" 學仕郎楊定遷自手書記之耳也. Xu Jun sides with Ma Fude; as the columns in pen that identify him as the copyist match the calligraphic hand of the poetic text, I do as well. This manuscript contains the entire poem, but has suffered extensive damage to the first third of the text, making much of it difficult to decipher.

P3910: In booklet rather than scroll form, this manuscript is the only one of the "Qinfu yin" texts to be included in a set of other, unrelated texts.[29] The text has suffered minimal damage but only contains the first two thirds of the poem. A colophon giving the date and identifying the copyist implies that either the copyist was working from a truncated version of the poem or simply cut his copying effort short. The two-line colophon appears to identify Mi Zhaoyuan 彌趙員 of the Jingtu Monastery 淨土寺 as the copyist. Based on a date given in the colophon, Xu Jun dates the text to 979. He further speculates that it should be attributed to the same copyist as that of S5477, identified as Servant Yin 陰奴兒.[30] There is no information in colophons to either of these texts that would definitely prove this authorship, and I thus assume Xu Jun is basing his conclusion on the similarities in handwriting and textual variants. I also believe that the copyist for P3910 did indeed copy at least part of S5477, though the latter may well have been copied by more than one hand.

P3953: This manuscript is best termed a fragment as it contains less than a third of the full text of the poem found in other manuscripts. The beginning and end of the poem are missing and it is impossible to either date it or identify the copyist.

S692: A colophon dates this manuscript to 919 (貞明伍己卯歲四月十一日) and attributes it to Scholarly Gentleman An Yousheng 安有盛, who, like the copyist of P3381, was associated with the Jinguanming Mon-

29. These are the *Chajiu lun* 茶酒論, the *Xinhe qianwen huangdi ganci* 新合千文皇帝感辭, and the *Xinhe xiaojing huangdi ganci* 新合孝經皇帝感辭.

30. Xu Jun, *Dunhuang shiji*, 232.

astery. The opening portion of the text is missing and appears to have been torn off, with the remaining text beginning with line 40 and running to the end of the poem.

P2700 and S5834: Two portions of the main text, P2700, appear to have been torn from the scroll. Part of one of these sections is found in a fragment in the Stein collection labeled S5834. A partial colophon found in the latter dates the text to 920 (貞明陸年歲在庚辰拾貳月) but does not identify the copyist.

S5476: A self-contained booklet, this text is missing sections at the beginning and end and thus cannot be dated or attached to a specific copyist.

S5477: This manuscript is also a self-contained booklet missing sections at the beginning. It starts at line 19 and then continues to the end of the poem. Just after line 135, in very light ink, the name Servant Yin 陰奴兒 appears. Xu Jun attributes P3910 to the hand of this scribe as well, though does not explain the discrepancy in names (as the short colophon to P3910 names Mi Zhaoyan as the copyist). This manuscript appears to have been copied in more than one hand, though the question is complicated by the fact that some parts are written with a brush and others with a Tibetan wooden pen.[31] These different writing utensils might produce substantially different calligraphic styles even if used by the same person. Based on the similarities in handwriting between P3910 and at least parts of S5477 and on similar patterns of variants (see more detailed discussion of this topic below), I agree with Xu Jun that the same scribe had some involvement with copying both of these texts.

We thus find substantial variation within this set of manuscripts when looking simply at their copying dates and scribes. For dated texts there is a range from the last years of the Tang (905) to the early years of the Song (979). There are also a number of different scribes connected with the texts in question, with only one pair of texts at least partially copied by the same person. Yet there are also commonalities. At least one pair of texts

31. Fujieda ("The Dunhuang Manuscripts, part II," 21) claims that even after Tibetan rule ended, "[t]he brush was used only by the privileged people." The fact that both types of utensils appear to have been used in some of these manuscripts calls this into question.

(s692 and P3381) was copied in the same monastery and another pair, s5477 and P3910, probably shared a scriptorium as well. All the texts for which we have colophons that state where the copy was made were copied in Dunhuang and not brought in from elsewhere, and it is highly likely that this holds true for the other manuscripts as well.

Formal Variation

There are two basic formats found in these manuscripts, and they offer the reader very different modes of interacting with the texts. Our typical image of reading in the Tang involves scrolls, and half of the "Qinfu yin" manuscripts follow this format, with P3381, P3780, P2700, and s692 all in scrolls of differing sizes. To take two examples, the sheets of paper attached to make the scroll for s692 are about 27 cm in height; those for P2700 are approximately 22 cm in height. Other than a few random names and dates, none of these scrolls have writing on the reverse side. Three of the manuscripts—P3910, s5476, and s5477—are not scrolls but rather bound booklets. S5476, for example, consists of eighteen page-sides approximately 14.5 cm high by 10.2 cm wide. These pages are thus substantially smaller in terms of height than the papers used in the scrolls. The poem is written on both sides of pages bound in the butterfly style in which pages are folded in half and then attached by either glue or string.[32] Multiple string holes are visible near the tops of the pages with a single set near the bottom. S5477, which was also bound in this style, though probably with glue rather than string, has approximately the same dimensions. With a sample of only eight manuscripts it is difficult to draw conclusions about which format was more popular. My sense is that the greater number of scroll-form manuscripts probably reflects the norm in more central areas of the Tang state. It is true that booklets using butterfly binding techniques are not attested to in central China until the Song, yet the numbers of manuscripts in this form for a wide variety of genres found at Dunhuang, from religious tracts to secular poems, are substantial, and it seems unlikely that a technique so common in Dunhuang would not be used in numerous

32. For a detailed description of this style of binding see Pan, *Zhongguo kexue*, 334–37, and http://idp.bl.uk/education/bookbinding/bookbinding.a4d#2.

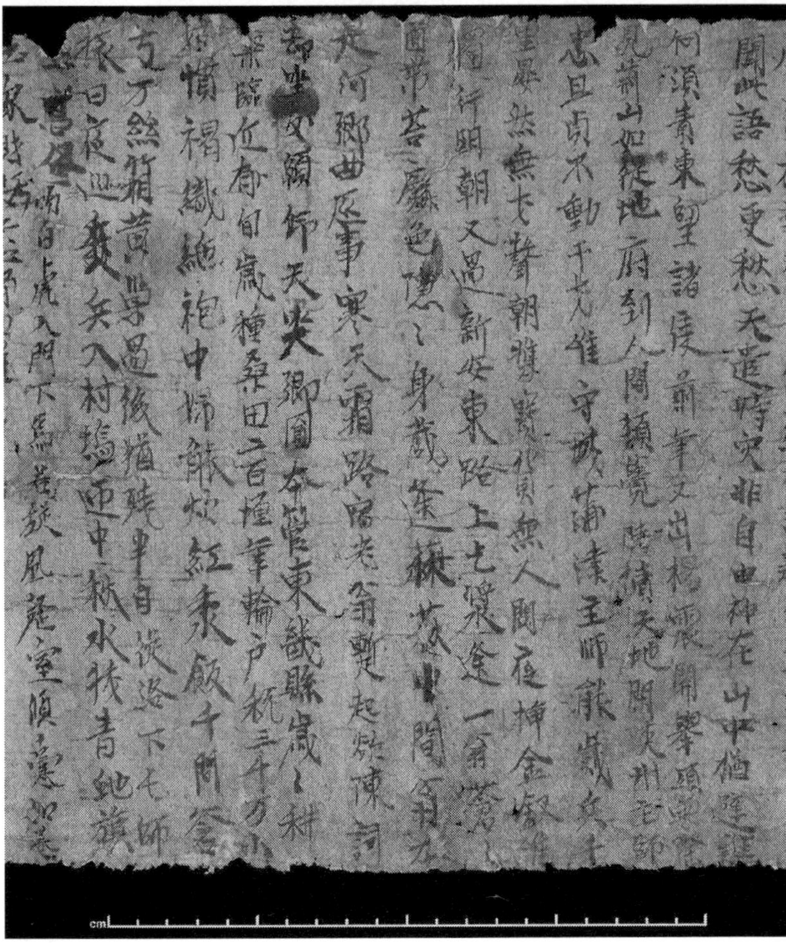

Fig. 1 Manuscript s692

other locales as well. This suggests that though scrolls were more popular and widespread, booklets probably also existed elsewhere in Tang and Five Dynasties China.

One would expect hand-copied texts to display a degree of variation in the size and layout of the characters, and this is indeed the case with the "Qinfu yin" manuscripts, though there is some consistency as well. For the manuscripts in scroll format, the column length ranges from the 18 or 19 characters per column found in P2700 to the 29 to 30 characters found in the columns of P3780. The other three scrolls are closer to P2700 in

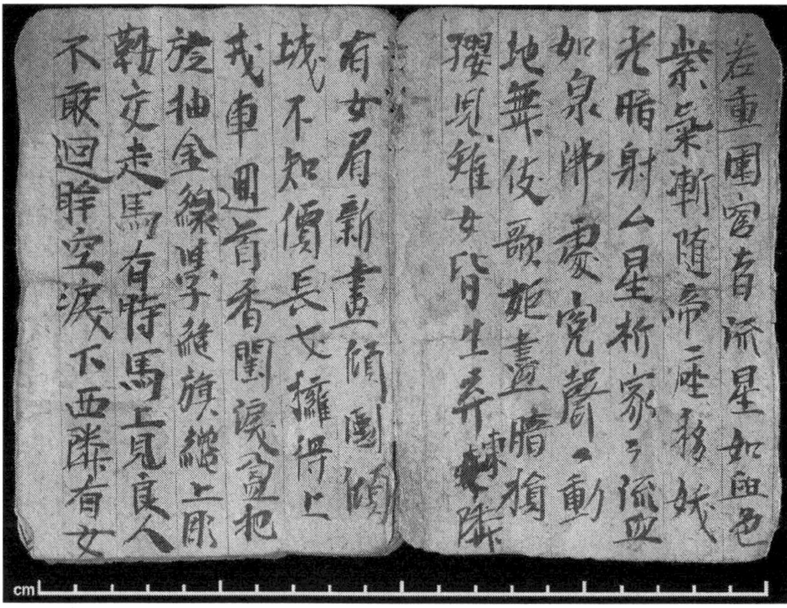

Fig. 2 Manuscript S5476

average line length with lines of over 23 characters being unusual. The characters in both P2700 and S692 are typically about 1.5 cm in height. This height appears to be standard for most other "Qinfu yin" scrolls except for P3780 in which the characters are about a third smaller and in P3953 in which they are about a third larger. As the photo-reproductions of the Pelliot manuscripts do not give any indication of measurements and scale, some of these measurements can only be conjectural.[33] The height of the characters found in the booklets S5476 and S5477 also tend to be between 1 cm and 2 cm high. S5477, however, displays a much greater degree of variance in the size of its characters. This may be because of the two or more different copyists involved, the poor writing skills of those copyists, and their alternating use of a brush and a Tibetan wooden pen at different points in the manuscript.

---

33. I was able to determine character sizes for P2700 because of the fragment of the text that made it into the Stein collection as S5834. The photo-reproductions of all Stein manuscripts helpfully include scale measurements. My conclusions for other Pelliot manuscripts are based on comparing the relative sizes of the curatorial stamp and the characters, as the photos in *Manuscrits* do not contain any measurements or scales.

In spite of the general consistency in the size of the characters within this set of manuscripts, there is substantial calligraphic variation. I will leave aesthetic judgments to the art historians, but it is clear to even the untrained eye that none of these texts were copied with the care and precision often found in Buddhist sutras and even certain other poetic texts from Dunhuang. That being said, some hands still can be considered more steady and consistent than others. The copyist for P3780 writes in the clearest hand: every stroke is easy to identify and the characters have a consistent style and form. The copyist for P3910 (and at least part of S5477) has the sloppiest writing: the sizes of his characters are inconsistent and the same character is written with differently angled strokes at different occurrences. It also appears that he had not mastered the use of a brush, as the strokes do not show the practiced application of pressure at different points in the lines that one would expect from an experienced calligrapher. Finally, he tended to dip his brush in ink only when it had almost run dry and the characters were barely visible. These were immediately followed by much darker characters in which the fresh ink soaked deeply into the paper and spread out. Other manuscripts fall between these two poles, with P3381, S5476, and P3953 being more consistently written and P2700 and S692 being less so. It is worth noting that the scribes for the latter two manuscripts have much more controlled hands than the scribes for P3910 and S5477, who simply appear to have written out the texts more quickly, frequently merging strokes. All of P3780 and one portion of S5477 are written with a wooden pen; the other six manuscripts are written with a brush. Other than P2700 and P3953, all the manuscripts contain lightly drawn lines to demarcate columns. S692 is the only manuscript to contain any sort of punctuation. For the first 72 lines of the poem there is a mark off to the side after every seventh character (i.e., at line breaks in the poem) similar to the *dunhao* 頓號 used in modern Chinese punctuation (、).

The primary content of these manuscripts is obviously the words of the poem itself. But as we are examining manuscripts as physical objects, it is important to look closely at elements other than words. These elements include information about the title of the work, the copyists, the dates of copying, and even mistakes in the copying process that give a fuller sense of the contexts in which late medieval Chinese readers would have

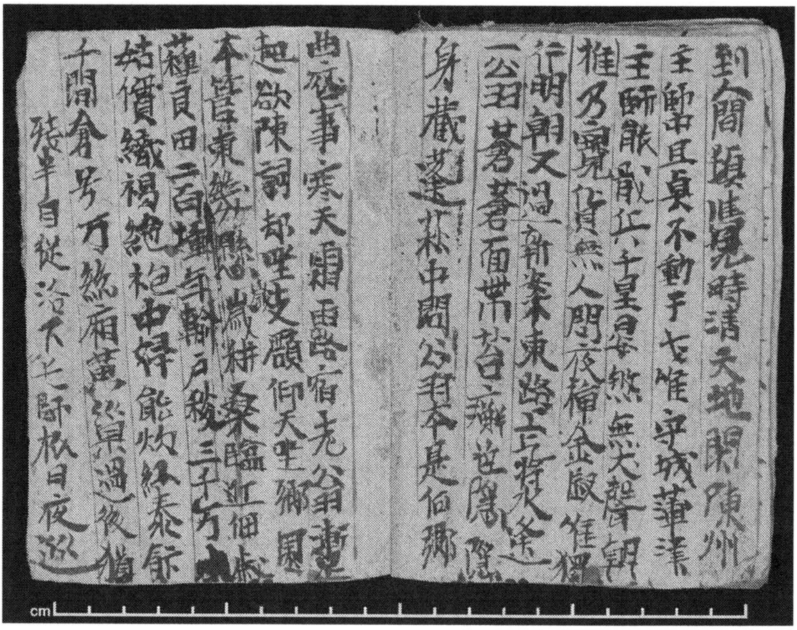

Fig. 3 Manuscript S5477

encountered the poem itself. Perhaps the most mundane content is simply the title of the work and attribution to a specific author, but even here there is some variation. Of the texts that include the beginning of the poem (those that have not suffered substantial physical damage at the beginning of the manuscript), all four include the title of the poem as "Qinfu yin," with the scribe for P3910 writing it twice in succession, the second time in darker ink. P3381 and P3780 further note after the title that the poem is in "one scroll" (*yijuan* 一卷). All of these texts may well have originally listed the author as well, though in some cases physical damage to the beginnings and endings of the texts makes it impossible to say. P3910 follows the title of the poem with the phrase "Composed by Rectifier of Omissions Wei Zhuang" 補闕韋莊撰. P2700 more specifically cites the text as being "Composed by Right Rectifier [of Omissions] Wei Zhuang" 右補□韋莊撰. Finally, P3780 includes this same full position title (including the character 闕, missing in P2700 where the text is torn), though the portion of text that would contain the name "Wei Zhuang" itself has been damaged.[34] Of the four manuscripts that include the end of the poem, P3381, P3780, S692, and S5477 all conclude with the phrase "'Qinfu yin' one scroll" 秦婦吟一卷 and do not list the author or his position again.[35]

Identifying the title and author of a literary work is a textual convention familiar to us from the print tradition. Corrections of copying mistakes included in a text itself, however, put us firmly in the world of manuscripts and are a consistent reminder that with the "Qinfu yin" texts we see the constant possibility and reality of human error. These are, as Housman has put it, "the frailties and aberrations of the human mind, and of its insubordinate servants, the human fingers."[36] There are two general categories of corrections in these texts: those for errors recognized immediately and corrected before continuing with copying, and those noted and corrected at some later point. The first category is easily identified by the placement of the corrected characters. If they directly follow the mistaken character in line of text, we can be confident that the copyist himself probably made them in the course of his labors. That is, before he filled the following space with the next character in the text, he recognized an error in what he had just written and corrected it. In most cases these corrections take the form of a character that the scribe has crossed out and immediately re-written. Sometimes it was clear that the crossed-out character and the correction are essentially the same; the scribe had either made some small error in writing the character or was simply dissatisfied with his calligraphy. In other cases the crossed-out character is a different character altogether, having resulted from reversing characters from his copy text, writing a character with a similar sound, or another of the common types of variation that I discuss in more detail below. The mistaken or dissatisfying character is typically crossed or smudged out

34. Wei Zhuang was appointed to this position in 900, though it is unclear whether his actual appointment was as Rectifier of Omissions for the "Right" or "Left." See Nie, *Wei Zhuang ji*, 521.

35. Note that P3910 does not contain the last portion of the poem found in other texts not due to physical damage, but because the copyist simply concluded early, as indicated by the inclusion of a date at this point. See further discussion below.

36. Quoted in Tanselle, *Textual Criticism and Scholarly Editing*, 337, from Housman's address to the Classical Association in 1921.

with brush or pen strokes and followed by the correct character, though at times a mark to the side of the mistaken character indicating deletion may be used instead. For example, in P3780 the character 避 ("to escape," "to avoid") has a deletion mark next to it and is immediately followed by the phonologically and orthographically similar character 璧. In this context the latter is part of the compound 銜璧, a reference from the *Zuozhuan* 左傳 that refers to holding a jade tablet in one's mouth to show submission.[37] The character marked for deletion would clearly have been an error. Whether the offending character is crossed out or otherwise indicated as an error, these immediate corrections of errors are common and appear in every one of the "Qinfu yin" manuscripts.

Other corrections appear not in the lines of text proper, but either in the space between columns or in the margin above the text and indicate corrections made at some point after the original copying. These corrections take a number of different forms. Some are similar to the crossed-out characters just discussed, but have the correct character written to the side of the column. In other instances characters that were mistakenly omitted in the original copying are written in smaller script next to where they should have originally appeared. One interesting marginal correction is a caret-like mark (ˇ) written next to a character to indicate that it and the preceding character should be transposed. For example, in five of the six manuscripts that contain line 91, the line reads 一從陷賊經三載 ("It has been three years since I fell into the rebels' clutches"). In manuscript S692, the characters 經 and 三 are transposed and a caret mark has been written next to the former. These marks appear with some frequency in four of the eight manuscripts and are especially abundant in S692. Because these corrections, whether in the form of editorial marks or characters filled in between columns, are not written in the text proper, we can assume that they correct errors that were discovered only after the scribe had copied either the whole text or at least these portions of it. This indicates that all of these texts were probably proofread after their scribes had copied them, either by the scribe himself or someone else.

37. Entry from the Sixth Year of Duke Yi 僖公六年. Ruan, *Shisanjing*, 7.214.

These formal differences in the "Qinfu yin" texts should not be ignored, as they contribute to very different reading experiences. The effect of differences between the scroll and booklet formats is a clear example. A scroll puts more restrictions on the reader: he will typically start at the very beginning. Although the beginning may be a very good place to start, it is not the most dramatic point in the poem and is unlikely to be the portion most savored upon rereading. The reader can skip ahead, but this would probably require skimming text. The scroll thus forces a certain level of engagement with the text it contains and dictates the order of the reading experience. If the reader is to open them up, scrolls also require more space or a take-up reel, in which case the text would have to be re-rolled when finished. Thus this format puts restrictions not only on the activity of reading itself, but also on the context in which reading is likely to occur.

Booklets, on the other hand, offer the reader greater freedom. To begin with, they are more compact, both in terms of the size of the page and bulkiness of the shape. The page height of the various "Qinfu yin" scrolls is about the same as the height of a volume of a large modern dictionary such as the *Hanyu da cidian*, while the two booklets in question are, intriguingly, similar in both height and width to mass-market or "pocket-sized" paperback books currently sold in the United States. Booklets also allow the reader to more easily mark and skip to a specific point in the poem without skimming through earlier sections. Finally, booklets are not only portable, but they can also be opened and read without a surface on which to spread them out.[38] I note above that the number of surviving "Qinfu yin" manuscripts is too small to lead to definitive conclusions about the relative popularity of various formats. The fact that Dunhuang was an outpost that was clearly visited by many travelers, however, might explain the substantial number of booklet-format texts found there. Booklets allowed the poem to travel and perhaps circulate more widely than scrolls alone would have.[39]

38. For a discussion of changes in furniture used by European monks to copy manuscripts being dictated by different book formats, see Saenger, *Space Between Words*, 252–53.

39. For a discussion of a Buddhist text from Dunhuang in booklet form, see Teiser, *Scripture on the Ten Kings*, 93–101.

The significant differences in both the size and style of the written characters in these texts would have resulted in very different reading experiences as well. Reading a carefully copied manuscript like P3780 would unquestionably have been easier than reading a more briskly copied text such as P2700 or S692. Modern printed editions use different sizes and styles of print as well, but it is worth noting that they tend towards a much higher degree of uniformity than do the handwritten "Qinfu yin" texts. To give a general analogy, if the writing of P3780 is like the careful script of a primary school teacher's writing on a backboard, P2700 is closer to the script a college student might use in quickly taking notes in class, and S5477 might be akin to the writing of a high school student scribbling a message to pass on to a friend. Though all of these are legible, they make for a diverse set of reading experiences.

Finally, the formal aspects of these texts give us an indication of the reasons why they were copied. One of the conclusions the first scholars to discuss these manuscripts drew about them is that the quality of the calligraphy and the diversity of character forms indicate that at least some of these texts were probably mere calligraphy exercises for novice monks. Examination of the formal and visual aspects of these texts, however, implies otherwise. It seems clear that these texts were copied not for the sake of copying itself, but to be read. They were, after all, bound. It is unlikely that one would go to the trouble of binding together, either in a booklet or scroll, a set of handwriting exercises. The scrolls in question, moreover, with the exception of some scribbling about the copying dates, are blank on the reverse side from the poetic text. Paper in Tang China may have been cheaper and easier to produce than parchment was in medieval Europe, but it was still precious enough that it was often reused if a blank side were available. In fact, many of the Dunhuang texts most important for our understanding of household registration practices and taxation come from registration rolls on the backside of other texts. One can imagine that mere copying exercises would not be accorded the honor of virgin paper, or if they were, both sides would eventually be put to use.

The written words themselves also indicate that these texts were copied not for the sake of copying itself but to be read. In some of the manuscripts there are various bits of marginalia that would be useful to readers but probably not worth replicating in a copying exercise. For example, in

P2700 and P3780, the final character in line 134, 殍 (*phiaw´*), is followed by the characters 眇音 indicating how it should be pronounced.[40] There are similar notes found in both P3910 and S5477. The presence of colophons for many of these texts further implies a level of formality greater than what would likely be accorded practice sheets. As we have seen, many of these texts are precisely dated, with the copyist and his monastery noted as well. Most tellingly, one such colophon, found in S692, indicates that the copyist would typically expect payment for his work. He writes the following brief bit of doggerel: "Today I have finished copying, and should have five measures of rice / Yet the price is high and I can't get it, what a disaster!" 今日寫書了，合有五升米·高代(貸)不可得，環(還)是自身災.[41] This short verse is similar to certain scribal comments found in medieval European manuscripts in its use of the vernacular where the original poem itself is in a more literary mode. Xu Jun points out that very similar verses are found in colophons to a number of Dunhuang manuscripts of a diverse range of genres.[42] We know very little of the economics of the book market in Dunhuang, but it does appear that scribes like the copyist of S692 were not merely working on their brushwork. They were copying out texts that others would read and they were (or at least would have wanted to have been) paid accordingly for their labors.

Before even addressing the poem itself, we have through these texts drawn closer to the experience of late medieval Chinese literature as it was enjoyed by its actual practitioners. Critical texts and print-set editions, useful though they are for many purposes, elide the real circumstances of literary production that existed a thousand or so years ago. The "Qinfu yin" manuscripts reveal a world of diverse reading experiences and texts that were far from standardized. The writing in some of these texts is sloppy and the copyists less than skilled, but they may well represent the conditions under which much Tang dynasty poetry was produced, reproduced, and enjoyed before and even well into the age of print.

---

40. All transcriptions of Tang period pronunciations are from Edwin G. Pulleyblank's reconstructions of Late Middle Chinese found in his *Lexicon of Reconstructed Pronunciation*. I will use the reconstructed Tang pronunciations only when it is important for the argument being made, not for every character cited.

41. This reading is suggested by Xu Jun (*Dunhuang shiji*, 252).

42. Ibid., 36–37.

Textual Variation: General

The variation in the material and formal aspects of these manuscripts is an important part of the textual world of the Tang and Five Dynasties. Yet no one would consider the actual poem "Qinfu yin" to have changed in a meaningful way in the course of transmission simply because different versions appeared on different sizes of paper in different handwriting. Indeed, formal variation is only one aspect of the differences between these texts. I now turn to the focal point of this chapter: the variation found among the words of the poetic texts themselves. After a brief introduction to methodology I discuss overall rates of variation between the manuscripts and then address in detail the specific types of variation that I have found in these different texts. My analysis shows that there is a wide range in both the rates of variation between sets of texts and in the types of variation that appear most frequently. Finally, I draw some tentative conclusions as to what this data can and cannot tell us about how the poem "Qinfu yin" might have circulated in the Late Tang and Five Dynasties periods.

Because my goal here is to give a sense of what the actual textual environment might have been like, my approach is to compare pairs of texts. With eight texts in all, there are a total of twenty-eight possible pairs. The most basic comparison gives us the overall rate of variation. To calculate this figure I note each instance of textual variation and divide the total number of character positions containing instances of variation by the total number of eligible character positions for the given pair. A character position is considered eligible only if both of the manuscripts in a given pair contain physically intact text at that point. If one or both are damaged then the position is not counted, as that would not necessarily indicate variation in the text as originally copied, but possibly damage that occurred years or centuries later.[43] I have repeated this process for each of the twenty-eight pairs and have further broken down the results into a number of categories of variation.

43. Note that if one text includes a character that another omits not because of textual damage but simply as an omission, this does count as an eligible character position and an instance of variation.

There are many advantages to this approach. Looking at pairs of manuscripts and treating them all equally avoids setting off any single text as better than any other or implying it is a more accurate match to an imagined original. My interest is in differences between actual texts rather than between the texts and an abstract ideal of the poem. Another important aspect of this method is that it tells us exactly how much any given text differs from any other given text. This, I believe, provides a more useful picture of how readers in this period would have actually encountered literary works. To a reader, the difference between pairs of texts, say my copy of "Qinfu yin" and my friend's copy, would surely be more important than the differences across a group of texts. Finally, the data derived from twenty-eight comparisons allows us to tell if certain types of variation are more common in some pairs than in others and thus to make educated guesses about some of the circumstances of copying and transmission for specific manuscripts.

If there is one dominant trend in the variations between these manuscripts it is, well, variety. We find a range from nearly identical to substantially different. The pair that shows the highest rate of variation is P3780 and S5477, with variation between the two texts in 280 of 1342 character positions, or 20.9 percent. This means that, on average, these two texts differ from one another in at least one character position in every seven-character line of the poem. The actual patterns of variation, of course, are not this consistent. Some lines have no variants and others contain many. Overall, these two texts differ in some fashion for over a fifth of the poem. At the opposite end of the spectrum is the pair of P3381 and S692. Out of 1366 eligible character positions, these two manuscripts display variation in only 77, for a rate of 5.6 percent. Between these two extremes we find a fairly even distribution of rates with an average of 12.8 percent variation and median of 12.85 percent variation.

When we look more closely at these numbers, certain patterns emerge that give hints about the relationships between some of the manuscripts. We cannot know which of these texts most closely resembles Wei Zhuang's original intention for his poem, but we can see that one of these versions differs from its peers more than any other. Of the top ten pairs in terms of variation rate, six of them include S5477. It differs from most other texts at a rate ranging from 15.5 percent (P3381) to the 20.9 percent variation with P3780 noted previously. In fact, the only text with which it displays substantially less variation is P3910, which was clearly copied at least in part by the same scribe. Even more surprising is that these two texts, despite sharing a copyist, still differ at a rate of 12.6 percent, just below the average rate but more than double the rate of some other pairs by different copyists.[44] Though these two texts were copied at least in part by the same person at the same place and probably in close chronological proximity, on average they display variation in almost every line of the poem.[45]

In other cases, similarity in some of the key circumstances of copying indeed results in far more similar textual products. From colophons we know that P3381 and S692 were copied approximately fourteen years apart and by different copyists. Surprisingly, these copyists produced texts with a rate of variation less than half that of P3910 and S5477. The colophons also tell us that both P3381 and S692 were copied at Dunhuang's Jinguangming Monastery and this may be the key to their similarity. It raises the possibility, though it can be no more than speculative, that these copyists were working from base texts that were closely related or identical, or that S692 was actually copied from P3381. Of course this would likely have been true of the two texts produced in part by Servant Yin as well.

Types of Variation

The substantial differences between multiple pairs of "Qinfu yin" manuscripts give us only a general picture of textual variation. To understand how texts change over time and in what fashion, we must determine not merely the presence of variation but the specific types. Below I identify eleven different categories of variants in the twenty-eight pairs of "Qinfu yin" texts, give examples, and note the percentage of overall variants that each category itself represents.[46] Many of these categories will be familiar

44. Interestingly, P3910 is present in each of the other four pairs that round out the ten with the highest variation rates.

45. In fact, the variation between these texts is even more extreme than this variation rate would imply. As I will discuss in more detail below, P3910 is missing the last third or so of the poem. This omission is not due to damage, but is simply because the scribe cut the poem short.

46. My description here will be brief and primarily serve as a reference point for the discussion that follows. I have included fuller descriptions of each category with more examples and reference to specific lines where they appear in manuscripts in the

to students of Chinese textual criticism and textual change in Chinese print culture. Indeed, a number have been described in Susan Cherniack's article discussed above.[47] Yet these categories have not, to the best of my knowledge, been applied fully to variation in manuscripts or quantified in a set body of texts as I do here.

Before examining the variants, however, we must be clear about the limitations of this and any other categorical scheme when dealing with texts as removed from us culturally, chronologically, and linguistically as the "Qinfu yin" manuscripts. Some of these categories, such as missing characters or reversed characters, are straightforward. Others depend very much on the judgments made by the examiner. Such categories as characters that are phonologically related but graphically dissimilar require subjective judgments as to what constitutes similarity and difference. And while many characters have retained the same basic orthographic form over time or can be found in other texts, with phonology we enter into very uncertain territory: reconstructing pronunciations is always an inexact science. Accuracy here is further compromised by the fact that we are examining texts written and recited not in Tang dynasty Chang'an or Luoyang, but in a distant frontier region where numerous different languages and dialects were both spoken and written. Our guesses at how these characters would have been pronounced and heard by the copyists of these "Qinfu yin" texts are thus tentative at best. Even if one can reconstruct rhyming categories with some accuracy, it is doubtful that they would fully represent the range of sounds that might be mutually confused, especially when pronounced with a dialectical or even "foreign" accent. In short, the categories employed here should be taken for what they are: provisional judgments that are open for revision. There is no doubt that another reader examining these same texts would arrive at somewhat different numbers than those given below. I am, however, confident that any informed reader would find the same general trend of variants I propose here.

Appendix. That discussion also notes different rates for the types of variants in different manuscript pairs.

47. Cherniack, "Book Culture," 102–25.

1. Variant Forms

Variants a contemporary reader would not see as representing different words or meanings. Examples: 门 and 門; 娉 and 騁 or 䮁; 壹 and 一. These represent 21.8 percent of overall variation.

2. Graphically and Phonologically Similar

Variants for which the form and sound of the character are both significantly similar. Examples: 城 (*ʂɦiajŋ*) and 成 (*ʂɦiajŋ*); 警 (*kiajŋ´*) and 驚 (*kiajŋ*). These represent 17.4 percent of overall variation.

3. Graphically Similar, Phonologically Distinct

Variants that have similar forms but substantially different pronunciations. Examples: 里 (*li*) and 重 (*trɦywŋ`*); 盡 (*tsɦin`*) and 畫 (*xɦwa:jk*). These represent 13.1 percent of overall variation.

4. Phonologically Similar, Graphically Distinct

Variants that have similar pronunciations but substantially different graphic forms. Examples: 塵 (*trɦin*) and 陳 (*trɦin*); 氣 (*kʰi`*) and 起 (*kʰi´*). These represent 10.1 percent of overall variation.

5. Semantic Similarity

Variants that have similar meanings or categories of meanings, but substantial graphic and phonological difference. Examples: 賊 (*tsɦəǎk*), ("bandit" or "rebel") and 寇 (*kʰəw`*) ("bandit" or often "raiders"); 烟 (*ʔjian*), ("smoke" or "mist") and 塵 (*trɦin*) ("dust"); 子 (*tsẓ´*) ("son") and 女 (*nriǝ̆´*) ("daughter"). These represent 4.5 percent of overall variation.

6. Reversed Characters

Variation where in a pair of texts, two adjacent characters appear in inverted positions. Example: 向走 and 走向. These represent 9.3 percent of overall variation.

7. Extra Characters

Variation in which one text includes characters not found in another (in violation of the set seven-character line length). Example: 仰天掩面哭

一聲 instead of 仰天哭 (at end of a line where there should only be three characters). These represent 8.6 percent of overall variation.

8. Missing Characters

Variation in which one text is missing characters found in another (in violation of the set seven-character line length). Example: 溝壑漸平人漸少 and 溝壑漸少. These represent 11.3 percent of overall variation.

9. Commentarial Characters

Variation in which commentarial characters have become part of the text proper. Example: In manuscripts P3780 and P2700, the characters 眇音 (*mjiaw´ ʔim*) are written horizontally in small script after the character 殍 (*pĥiaw´*), apparently as an explanation of the latter's correct pronunciation. In P3910, however, the character 殍 itself is omitted while the characters 眇音 appear as vertically written, regularly sized parts of the text proper. This is the only instance of this type of variation in the manuscripts.

10. Split Characters

Variation in which the scribe has written the radical and phonetic components of a single character as two separate characters. Examples: 携 and 推乃; 公羽 and 翁. These represent less than 1 percent of overall variation.

11. Variant Drift

Variants with little or no discernable connections sometimes explainable by a chain of variation through a succession of manuscripts. Examples: 事 (*ʂĥɨ̣`*) and 對 (*tuaj`*); 烟 and 陳. These represent 2.9 percent of overall variation (though this total is very tentative).

UNDERSTANDING VARIATION

If we are only interested in approaching "Qinfu yin" as a disembodied literary work free from any material context, the usefulness of these statistics may seem obscure. But "Qinfu yin" was never free from specific material contexts to those who encountered it in the Tang and Five Dynasties. Every "Qinfu yin," whether recited or read, was unique in ways that literary works would not always be in the age of print. And thanks to the

Dunhuang finds, in this particular case modern scholars can get a sense of what the earlier experience of this poem might have been like, if we set aside the various critical editions that have appeared in the last seventy years and return to the manuscripts themselves. The variants I detail above may not bring us any closer to understanding the poem as it originally existed in Wei Zhuang's own mind or on his lips or paper. But they do go a long way towards helping us understand how the poem was experienced by readers and copyists (two categories that heavily overlap in late medieval China) close to its period of greatest popularity. In this final section I discuss what conclusions we can and cannot draw from both the extent and the different types of variation found in these texts.

One of the most important implications of these variants is that it can be difficult if not impossible to distinguish between scribal error and scribal choice in many (but certainly not all) instances of variation. In the Appendix I identify a number of such cases; it is worth examining one particularly complex example here in detail. Variants in Category 3, which are graphically similar but have very different pronunciations, would appear to be clear examples of scribal errors: the copyist meant to write a certain character but accidentally wrote one very similar. Yet when we look closely at some instances of this type of variation, the assumption of error becomes less reliable.

In line 85 we find a confluence of different variants that make it exceedingly difficult to determine which variants represent a "correct" reading of the line. In the fifth character position of this line, the manuscripts P3910 and S5477 both have the character 金 (*kim*), meaning metal, while the four other texts with this line use the orthographically similar character 全 (*tsɦyan*), meaning "complete" or "to keep whole, keep safe, preserve." The context for these variants varies by manuscript because of the presence of variants elsewhere in the line. In P3381, S692, and S5476 the line reads: 妾身幸得全刀鋸 ("I was fortunate to be able to keep myself safe from their weapons of torture").[48] In the version contained in P3910 and S5477 the third character position has the character 行 (*xɦjia:jŋ*),

48. Literally, "knives and saws." The compound is a reference to tools of punishment and torture. Robin Yates translates this line as "But, as luck would have it, I managed to keep myself/safe from sword slashes." See Yates, *Washing Silk*, 113.

meaning "to walk, to go" or "conduct, action," rather than 幸 (*xɦjiaːjŋ*), meaning "fortunate."[49] My tentative reading of the line in this form is "If I were to have gone, I would have met with their metal weapons of torture" 妾身行得金刀鋸.[50] Had the character 金 appeared in the fourth character position of P3381, S692, or S5476, it would have been simple to write it off as an error, as it would make little sense for the line to read, "I was fortunate to have met with their metal weapons of torture." When 行 rather than 幸 is used in the third character position, however, the presence of 金 is more plausible. At the same time, a reasonable argument could be made that 全 still makes more sense than 金 even in P3910 and S5477. The line would then read, "I myself went out and was able to keep safe from their weapons of torture" 妾身行得全刀鋸. A few lines later in the poem we learn that the woman in whose voice this line is written did indeed leave and go with the rebel forces, giving additional support for this reading.

Complicating matters further, the full line in P2700 reads: 妾身行德全刃鋸 ("I conducted myself virtuously and kept safe from their weapons of torture"). In this context, 行 works better than 幸 but 全 is also clearly superior to 金. Again we find that it is difficult to choose one variant or set of variants over another. Moreover, any given variant can have an effect that goes beyond the character position in which it appears, changing our reading of other characters and lines as well. We have moved beyond a simple notion of scribal errors in such cases and must acknowledge that copyists may be consciously reshaping the poem in the course of transmission.

Another particularly interesting type of variation that hints at a longer process of change through the course of transmission is that of my final category above, what I call "variant drift." On the face of it, these are variants that simply do not fit into any of the other categories. They may be nothing more than a choice by a given copyist, as the variants often seem to make sense, albeit different sense, in context. In many instances of this type of variation, it may also be the case that the characters did indeed sound more alike to the Tang ear (or Dunhuang ear) than we now realize through our reconstructed pronunciation. However, another explanation

49. This type of variant falls into category 4. See further discussion below.
50. This is an unnatural reading, as the translation is intended to reflect.

for some of these confusing variants is variant drift. This is a phenomenon, well attested to in manuscript cultures, of a single word changing in different directions through multiple reproductions. In other words, some transmission lines might vary according to sound value while others will change along orthographic lines.[51] The comparison pair P3780 and P3910 offers two interesting examples of this phenomenon. In the sixth character position of line 4 (a position rich in variants), P3780 has the character 烟 and P3910 has 陳. These characters bear no relation to each other phonologically, orthographically, or semantically. If we had only these two manuscripts it would be difficult to find any connection between the two. However, we do have one additional text that is intact at this character position: P3381. The latter's use of 塵 in this position provides a link between 烟 and 陳. It is connected to the first through meaning ("dust" vs. "smoke" or "mist") and to the second through pronunciation (*trhiin* in both cases). The third character position of line 34 is a similar example with two seemingly unrelated characters: in P3780, 綠 (*lywk*), meaning "green" and in P3910, 薗.(*yan*), meaning "garden." The four other manuscripts with this portion of text provide a possible missing link with the character 緣 (*jyan`*), here meaning "to climb," which shows an orthographic link to 綠 and a phonological link to 薗.

These cases are fairly straightforward and understandable because we have additional texts with different variants beyond the pair in question. One could, however, easily see how variant drift, when continued across many generations of textual reproduction and transmission, could produce variants whose paths and origins are much less obvious. In tracing these connections I am not implying a direct link between any of these texts. I would not claim, for example, that the scribes for P3381 and P3910 worked from the same source text and erred or altered it in different directions. Rather, the idea of variant drift provides a useful and in some cases convincing description of a process that probably took part at vari-

51. This type of variation has been found in some of the earliest manuscripts from China. See Edward Shaughnessy's discussion of the variants 柬, 東, and 簡 in bamboo strips from Mawangdui and other sites in *Rewriting Early Chinese Texts*, 18–19.

ous stages in the transmission process of these texts, the length and number of textual generations of which we cannot know.

By examining these manuscripts in a manner that pays close attention to the types of variants they contain and other textual clues, we can also draw conclusions both firm and tentative about how "Qinfu yin" might have circulated in its day. The two general categories of transmission for texts in a manuscript culture are memorial/oral and written.[52] In the former, works are memorized and transmitted orally until they are eventually written down (*if* they are written down). Pure written transmission would entail a series of scribes working with physically present source texts from which they would copy new manuscripts.[53] It should be noted that there are many plausible situations that would be a combination of these two categories, such as one scribe reading aloud from a written text while another copies down his spoken words. Not long after their discovery, scholars tagged the "Qinfu yin" texts from Dunhuang as evidence of memorial transmission. Both Giles and Robin Yates have speculated that, to quote Yates, "many of the errors in these manuscripts...were the result of these novices' memorizing the text without learning the correct form of the graphs."[54] Close examination of the patterns of variants in these texts, however, reveals that though memorial transmission at some point in the process of transmission could explain some of these variants, the concrete evidence from the manuscripts primarily indicates scribes working from written sources when they made these copies.

Before addressing the specific question of memorial versus written transmission, I would note that most of the variation between these texts is comprehensible. That is, we can usually find reasonable connections between variants, whether they exist through sound, shape, or meaning. Even with category II, some of the seemingly unrelated variants can be attributed to variant drift. If we had a fuller set of manuscripts, I have no doubt that more connections like this would become clear. One obvious

---

52. We will look at both these modes of transmission in far more detail in Chapters 3 and 4.

53. Memory could play a role in written transmission as well, as people copying a familiar text may well have used their recollection of the text rather than an exemplar at hand as their base.

54. Robin Yates, *Washing Silk*, 254.

trend found in these texts is that the more qualities these variants have in common, for example sharing similar sounds *and* shapes *and* meanings, the more likely they are to occur. As we have seen, the most common variant category overall is variant forms of the same character. These variants have the same meaning and sound, and often very similar graphic forms (though there are exceptions to this, such as the variant form 壹 and 一). The next most common category is characters that share both the same sound and very similar graphic forms. It should not be at all surprising that a scribe, whether working from his memory or another text, might write the character 何 when he meant to write 河, or 城 when he intended to copy 成. These examples provide specific evidence of neither written nor memorial transmission, but they do remind us that even if scribes sometimes changed texts intentionally, they often simply made mistakes as well.

Looking at the types of variants found in these manuscripts, we do find hints of memorial transmission; conclusive proof, however, remains elusive. Homophones that are graphically dissimilar, the fourth category discussed above, are often cited as evidence of memorial transmission in Chinese texts beginning with the *Shi* and seem to be what Yates has in mind when he speaks of copyists "memorizing the text without learning the correct form of the graphs."[55] Indeed, we could easily imagine how such variants would be common in texts written out based on memorized sounds. However, there is no reason to believe that these changes would not also occur in texts copied directly from another written text. In a culture in which most reading was done aloud, including the reading involved in transcribing a text, writing rarely occurred without an oral component. The typical process of copying from a written text, even in modern reading cultures in which vocalized reading has largely disappeared, still introduces a word's sound into the process. The copyist looks at the written base text and "vocalizes" the part he is about to copy, if only

55. Note that Yates is using the term "text" in a broader sense than I do. He seems to be referring to the poem in the abstract, while I use "text" to refer to specific written instantiations of the poem. With my terminology it would thus not make sense for someone to memorize the text but not the graphs. The graphs (and the paper on which they are written) *are* the text.

in his head, and then turns to a separate blank sheet to write it out anew. There is ample evidence from both Europe and China that vocalization while copying results in the same sorts of variants as would copying purely from memory or from hearing another read or recite aloud. Graphically distinct homophonic variants thus may be the result of memorial transmission, but there are other explanations for them as well.

Another category of variation that might appear to provide more convincing evidence for memorial transmission is that of graphically and phonetically distinct synonyms. It is less likely that someone working directly from a text, whether speaking aloud, working silently, or having someone else dictate, would confuse 塵 and 烟. Had people memorized all or parts of the poem, however, it would not be surprising for them to remember the basic sense of a line, especially in a narrative poem with a distinct plot like "Qinfu yin," while occasionally switching words for near synonyms. This type of variation is quite common in the received versions of Tang poems that have come down to us through later print culture and in this case we imagine the print culture is simply reproducing the variation found in the manuscript culture upon which it was ultimately based.

At the same time, there are valid explanations for this type of variation other than memorial transmission. People copying texts in both medieval Europe and Tang China, whether professional copyists or simply avid readers, would change words in an attempt to "improve" the work they were copying. These changes were especially likely with such noncanonical works as contemporary poetry.[56] When copyists think of themselves as potential collaborators or critics rather than simply agents of mechanical reproduction, we cannot write off changes in the course of transmission as mere errors. We can explain some variants this way, but clearly not all of them, as we have seen in the above discussion of a number of ambiguous cases. Thus variants of this sort neither indicate copying "errors" *per se* nor serve as definitive proof of any particular mode of circulation.

Perhaps more significantly, "Qinfu yin" lacks the one pattern of variation that does point directly to memorial transmission. In his work on the role of memorization in the transmission of the Middle English romances,

---

56. See further discussion in Chapters 4 and 5.

Murray McGillivray writes that memorization at some stage can be definitively proven only by "memorial transfer," defined as, "the movement of material from one part of a text to another part which is physically remote, but which is liable to confusion with it because of similarities of situation, content, or language."[57] As a lengthy poem with a number of similarly worded sections, "Qinfu yin" would seem to be prime ground for just such a phenomenon, yet it does not appear in any of the extant manuscripts.

The evidence for written transmission of "Qinfu yin" is much stronger and can be broken down into two types: (1) evidence of copying from written texts at some point in the transmission process, and (2) evidence that the scribes copying these particular texts were working from physically present written models. Any given manuscript will likely contain changes introduced when it was copied as well as changes that were introduced at any given point earlier in the transmission process, and it is most often impossible to distinguish between the two.[58] The presence of marginalia and the accidental integration of commentarial characters into the text proper are two examples of evidence for written transmission of these texts that I have noted above. As we have seen, some of these texts contain marginalia indicating how a particular character is pronounced, while in another text it appears that these same marginalia have been mistakenly integrated into the text proper rather than appearing as smaller horizontally written characters. The presence of marginalia of this sort strongly suggests that these texts had been circulating in written form, as such annotations would be out of place in the transcription of a text that had theretofore only circulated orally. The same holds for commentarial characters accidentally making their way into the text proper. The splitting of a single character into two characters made up of its two graphic elements is an additional example of variation that could only occur through written transmission at some point. In both these cases, there is no way to de-

57. McGillivray, *Memorization in the Transmission*, 5.

58. Thus even the numerous "errors" noted by Giles and Yates do not prove that our novice Dunhuang monks were poor copyists. By the time the extant Dunhuang versions of "Qinfu yin" were copied, the poem had surely been transmitted countless times by others. Though it is extremely unlikely, the possibility exists that these monks may well have made perfect reproductions of variant-filled texts.

termine when the variation first happened. Servant Yin may have had sloppy handwriting, but it is very possible that he reproduced rather than introduced this particular variant.

Line skips, also called "eye skips," in which it appears a copyist has jumped from one point in a text to a later point, thereby missing the characters in between, are strong evidence of written transmission and are also sometimes evidence of variants that occurred with the copying of the text in question. Line 132 of manuscript P3910 is a good example. As noted above, while the other seven manuscripts have the line reading 溝壑漸平人漸少 ("Ditches and gullies gradually filled [with bodies] while the people grew few"), P3910 reads 溝壑漸少 ("Ditches and gullies grew few"). By consulting multiple texts we can clearly see that the copyist must have skipped from one 漸 to the other in the same line. Similarly, line 198 of manuscript P3780 contains the extra characters 户叁阡, which appear in no other text. However, as they do appear two lines later we can be confident that a copyist's eyes skipped ahead somewhere in the transmission process.[59]

These eye skips could have occurred at any point in the transmission process, with later copyists simply faithfully reproducing the texts they had. There is one example, however, that seems to have occurred during the copying of the text we have today. In the beginning of line 66 in S5477 our old friend Servant Yin has prematurely written the characters 出朱𠃜. These same three characters (with the full version of 門) are found at the end of the next line, line 67. I would suggest that this indicates that Yin skipped ahead but realized his error in mid-character. These two and a half characters also appear to be written in lighter ink than the surrounding characters. We might speculate that this copyist may have been taking a break after completing line 65. When he returned to his copying, he mistakenly began farther down in the text than he should have. Realizing

59. For another example, see lines 212–13 in which the phrase 一身苦 is found both at the end of 212 and the beginning of 213 as an intentional repetition (i.e., it conforms to the seven-character line length). Two of the manuscripts, however, simply skip over the second repetition and thus merge the two lines.

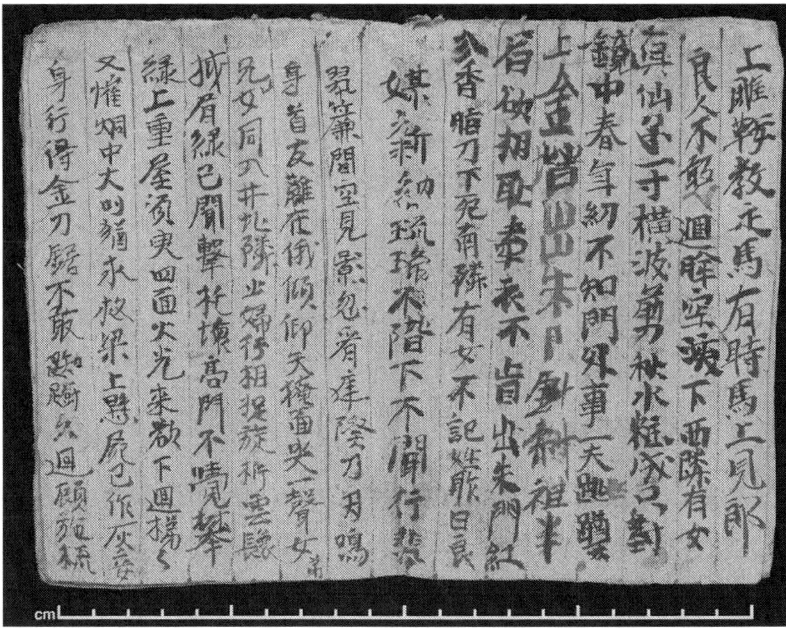

Fig. 4 Manuscript S5477

his mistake, he also re-inked his brush before beginning again.[60] This is indeed more evidence that Yin was not the most fastidious copyist. Yet it also shows that he was almost definitely working from a written model and not from his memory.[61]

The overall rates of variation between different pairs of texts make it clear that there were many different versions of "Qinfu yin" in the half century or so after it first appeared. This raises the question of whether or not these different "versions" should, in fact, be considered to be the same poem. In the course of his discussion of different versions of works created by the same author (for example, original manuscript, corrected galley proofs, first edition, etc.), James Thorpe concludes that "The basic proposition which I submit about works created by authorial revision is

---

60. In personal correspondence about this variant, Sarah M. Allen has raised the possibility that the text was covered up with a light pigment as a form of "white-out" that has since partially faded. Without closer examination of the manuscript, it is impossible to tell for sure.

61. It should also be noted that the presence of corrections in so many of these texts also implies that they were read over and compared to another written text.

that each version is either, potentially or actually, another work of art."[62] The situation we find with the "Qinfu yin" manuscripts is quite different from Thorpe's focus on authorial revision in that we have no way of knowing whether any of the variation in the "Qinfu yin" texts is due to different versions all created by or approved of by Wei Zhuang himself. Thorpe's focus on the author as the only legitimate creator is out of place when we are dealing with texts produced and transmitted in the very different circumstances of Tang and Five Dynasties China where numerous actors beyond the author himself had opportunities to introduce variations. If we afford copyists respect on a level approaching that of authors, we would then be talking about not one "Qinfu yin" but many.

But by what measure could we declare that these texts meaningfully represent distinct works of art? Falling back on numbers to make the determination, one inevitably encounters the Sorites paradox. What precise amount of variation results in a new literary work? In the final analysis I am not sure such a determination would tell us more than do the bare numbers that underlie it. What is clear is that someone reading the poem found in manuscripts S5477 or P3910 would have a very different experience from someone reading that written out by the copyist of P3780. They will encounter numerous lines that differ not only in the form of the words but in their meaning as well. Given the tendency in traditional Chinese literary criticism to focus very closely on single words and compounds as examples of literary achievement, these differences might well add up to different judgments on the merit of the poem. And this does not even take into account the fact that P3910 omits about a third of the poem found in other texts without noting as much, which would surely lead to even greater discrepancies in reader and critical responses to these different texts.

The scholarship on medieval European literature discussed earlier highlights the importance of differences between texts and the value of taking into full account the material aspects of literary works from the period. These ideas provide much of the justification for the approach I have taken here. But what of the larger claim that many of these scholars make that scribes and other copyists should be considered as equals to the

---

62. Thorpe, *Principles of Textual Criticism*, 37.

author and that works produced in such contexts are truly collaborations? Can we draw similar conclusions based on the evidence the "Qinfu yin" manuscripts provide? Perhaps not. These texts give us clear evidence for the fact of textual variation and change produced by hands other than the author's. They do not, however, tell us much about the intentions behind those changes. Some of these variants may well have been the result of conscious efforts by copyists to improve the work they were copying. Or they may simply have been mistakes. The manuscripts themselves can point us towards the possibility of each conclusion but do not definitively prove either. Moreover, as we do not know when in the process of transmission these variants were introduced, we also do not know who was responsible for them. If a single scribe intentionally altered a text so much that twenty percent of it differed from its source, we might indeed consider him to be an active collaborator in the creation of a new work. If, however, this same variation is the result of fifty different scribes each introducing a single variant, we would be less inclined to afford them the same stature.

Shorter Works from Earlier in the Dynasty: Gao Shi

What I think we can claim is that the changes that occur in the process of circulation, whether at the hands of a single opinionated scribe or a hundred careless ones, undermine the direct connection between an author and the works we attribute to him. Even if we were to make the highly dubious assumption that one of these manuscripts contains the exact version of "Qinfu yin" as Wei Zhuang himself produced it, then we would have to acknowledge the other seven manuscripts do not. They all vary in ways sometimes trivial, but sometimes important as well.

There are other examples of poems from Dunhuang in multiple copies (though rarely more than two), and the contexts in which we find them imply an even more substantial undermining or at least obscuring of the connection between author and poem. As I explain in at the beginning of this chapter, because of its length and the great number of copies of it that were found in Dunhuang, "Qinfu yin" is a very useful object of study for establishing the wide range of possible variants and getting a good sense of how often they occur. At the same time, focusing on this work does raise the question of whether or not these findings are relevant to shorter poems and those composed in earlier periods of the dynasty. Fortunately, there are opportunities, albeit limited ones, to examine some concrete evidence concerning these poems and how they might have circulated.

The High Tang poet Gao Shi has far more works that appear in the Dunhuang manuscripts than does any other poet. These include a partial copy of a collection of his poems containing forty-nine pieces in all.[63] He is also one of the only High Tang poets to have poems appear in multiple copies from Dunhuang.[64] Unlike "Qinfu yin," however, none of Gao Shi's poems exist in more than two copies from Dunhuang and it would thus be impossible to get the same extent of data that one can extract from examining copies of Wei Zhuang's work.[65] Yet by looking at multiple examples of Gao Shi's poems with two versions each, we can get at least a general sense of whether or not the patterns present in the "Qinfu yin" texts are applicable to other styles of poetry from earlier periods. For purposes of comparison I have chosen six of Gao Shi's poems for which there are two copies each surviving in Dunhuang. They range in length from 28 characters to 112 and are as follows: "Jiuri chou Yan shaofu" 九日詶顏少府 ("Answering District Defender Yan on the Ninth Day"),[66] "Fengqiu zuo" 封丘作 ("Composed in Fengqiu"),[67] "Zi Ji bei gui" 自薊北歸 ("Returning North from Ji"),[68] "Yanbie Guo jiaoshu" 宴别郭校書 ("A Fare-

63. See P3862 in *Manuscrits*, 29.17–21. See also Xu Jun's (*Dunhuang shiji*, 392–411) discussion and annotations. For additional annotations of Gao Shi's Dunhuang poems, comparisons to their printed versions, and a more thorough discussion of their importance, see Huang Yongwu's section on Gao Shi in *Dunhuang de Tangshi xubian*.

64. Li Bai is another, though he has far fewer poems in the Dunhuang manuscripts.

65. Huang Yongwu (*Dunhuang de Tangshi xubian*, 131–44) notes that Gao Shi's "Yangexing" 燕歌行 survives in six Dunhuang manuscripts. However, most of these are fragments, some of only a few characters.

66. Found in P3862, *Manuscrits*, 29.20. See also Xu Jun, *Dunhuang shiji*, 405 and Liu Kaiyang, *Gao Shi shiji*, 76. The second version of this poem from Dunhuang has a different title: "Jiuyue jiuri denggao" 九月九日登高 ("Climbing to a High Place on the Ninth Day of the Ninth Month"), and is found in P3619, *Manuscrits*, 26.109.

67. Found in P3862, *Manuscrits*, 29.17. See also Xu Jun, *Dunhuang shiji*, 394 and Liu Kaiyang, *Gao Shi shiji*, 230. The second version, which is untitled and does not name the author, is found in P2976, *Manuscrits*, 20.298.

68. Found in P2976, *Manuscrits*, 20.299. See also Xu Jun, *Dunhuang shiji*, 92 and Liu Kaiyang, *Gao Shi shiji*, 46. The second version is found in P2552/2567, *Manuscrits*, 15.324 and has the same title.

well Feast for Secretary Guo"),[69] "Saishang ting chuidi" 塞上聽吹笛 ("Listening to Someone Playing the Flute on the Frontier"),[70] and "Bie Dong Lingwang" 別董令望 ("Seeing Off Dong Lingwang").[71] These twelve individual poems appear in five different Dunhuang scrolls.

In material terms, the range of these manuscripts is not as broad as that found with the "Qinfu yin" texts. All of the manuscripts are in scroll form with similar sizes of paper. The handwriting is also better on average than that found in the "Qinfu yin" texts, with most versions written in a very clear and controlled hand equal to or better than the best copies of the latter. There is, however, some variation. P2555 and P2976 appear to have been written much more quickly and with a brush, while P3862 and P2552/2567[72] are very clear and probably written with a wooden pen. P2555 is written in multiple hands and the scribe for P3691, though a single person, begins writing his characters about a third smaller half-way through the scroll. There is substantial variation in likely dates of copying as well. Based on the particular taboo characters avoided, we can definitively date two of the scrolls to the Tang period (and in the case of P2567/2552 give a likely date of 793 with a broader range of 753–805). One

---

69. Found in P2976, *Manuscrits*, 20.229. See also Xu Jun, *Dunhuang shiji*, 93 and Liu Kaiyang, *Gao Shi shiji*, 335–56. The second version is entitled "Yan Guo jiaoshu yin zhi you bie" 宴郭校書因之有別 ("Having a Feast for Secretary Guo to See Him Off"), and is found in P2552/P2567, *Manuscrits*, 15.324.

70. Found in P2552/P2567, *Manuscrits*, 15.322. See also Xu Jun, *Dunhuang shiji*, 84. The poem "Matching Wang the Seventh's 'Listening to Someone Playing the Flute at Yumen Gate'" 和王七玉門關聽吹笛 (Liu Kaiyang, *Gao Shi shiji*, 347) is clearly related to this poem and shares a number of lines with slight differences. It is different enough that I do not think we can call it the same poem. Marie Chan (*Kao Shih*, 97) claims to translate the version of the poem found in *Quan Tang shi*, 214.2243, which is identical to that found in *Gao Shi shiji*. However, it is clear that she is using a version probably based on the Dunhuang texts and definitely not on the version found in the *QTS* and the *Gao Shi shiji*. The second version of this poem from Dunhuang is found in P2555, *Manuscrits*, 15.334, and does not indicate a title or author.

71. Found in P2567, *Manuscrits*, 15.325. See also Xu Jun, *Dunhuang shiji*, 95 and Liu Kaiyang, *Gao Shi shiji*, 193. The second version, with no indication of title or author, is found in P2555, *Manuscrits*, 15.334.

72. For an explanation of why this scroll has two different Pelliot numbers, see Xu Jun, *Dunhuang shiji*, 41.

scroll was clearly copied after the Tang and two others are most likely post-Tang as well but difficult to date.[73]

In terms of format, the differences in these texts are more significant. In only one of the poem pairs, "Returning North from Ji," do both versions of the poem have the same title. In three of the six pairs, one version has no title whatsoever. The same lack of consistency holds for the identification of the author, with Gao Shi noted as such in both poems in only one pair.[74] Moreover, the five manuscripts that do not identify the author are all collections of poems by different authors with no indication of where works by one author end and those of another begin. Thus, for almost half of these poems a reader would not know to whom the work is attributed and for a quarter of them both the author and title would be unknown. Finally, while none of the poems contain any punctuation, most do indicate by means of blank space where one poem begins and another ends.[75]

Looking at variation in the content of the poem, we find much that is familiar from our examination of "Qinfu yin." The overall rates of variation for these pairs range from a low of 5 percent to a high of 14 percent with an average of 9 percent. That these are all lower than the corresponding rates for "Qinfu yin" is to be expected; the latter is a work of 1666 characters while the longest of these Gao Shi poems is less than a tenth of that length. Regardless of the mode of circulation, it is not surprising that shorter poems would be passed on with a higher rate of fidelity. Of the eleven categories of variants established above, we find variants in these texts in all but three: reversed characters, commentarial characters entering the text, and split characters. As with "Qinfu yin," variants that are close to each other in multiple factors such as sound and graphic form are

73. For discussion of P2567/2552 see Xu Jun, *Dunhuang shiji*, 41–43. The other scroll clearly copied in the Tang is the collection of Gao Shi's poems, P3862.

74. Even in this pair, the situation is ambiguous. None of the poems in P3862, a scroll of forty-nine poems all by Gao Shi, identifies the author. However, as the beginning and the end of the scroll are missing and all of the poems are by Gao Shi, it seems reasonable to assume that he was originally identified as the author at one of these points.

75. The scribe for P2976 apparently forgot to leave such a space in some instances. In its place he (or possibly a later reader) sometimes inserts a small mark (a reverse of ┌). I will discuss the general lack of "extra-linguistic markers" in Chapter 3.

the most frequent. In other words, both the types and the frequency of variants in these shorter poems from earlier in the dynasty bear a strong similarity to those found in the much longer and later "Qinfu yin." Wei Zhuang's poem may be an outlier in terms of its length, but the patterns of variants it developed in the course of transmission is likely representative of what we would find in a much broader range of widely circulated poems.

There is, however, one particularly interesting anomaly in these patterns. Variants that share semantic similarity, which made up only 4.5 percent of the overall variants in "Qinfu yin," account for about 15 percent of the total in these shorter poems. This would reinforce the possibility that these types of variants might indicate oral/memorial transmission at some point in the process of circulation. In spite what some scholars have assumed about "Qinfu yin," it stands to reason that a poem of 28 characters is more likely to be set to memory than one of well over a thousand. In a poem committed to memory, it is not surprising that one would replace 行子 with 客子, both of which indicate someone traveling away from home, as we see in "Answering District Defender Yan on the Ninth Day" and "Climbing to a High Place on the Ninth Day of the Ninth Month." We also cannot dismiss the possibility that someone in the chain of transmission simply replaced one of these with the other.

The variations in "Qinfu yin" and the Gao Shi poems ultimately point to the many ways in which a poetic work could become disconnected from its author in the Tang. Given its popularity, it is likely that "Qinfu yin" would be recognized by most members of the literate audience of the time as being the work of Wei Zhuang. Indeed, his close association with the poem proved politically problematic for him. Moreover, all the copies of "Qinfu yin" for which we have intact texts specifically identify Wei Zhuang as the author. At the same time, even if Wei Zhuang was connected with a work entitled "Qinfu yin," the high rates of variation in the available texts show that the actual versions of the work that circulated, in Dunhuang at least, often differed substantially from what he originally composed. In the case of Gao Shi's poems, there is less variation overall (though some poems still contain variants in every line on average). We can at least speculate that these poems are slightly closer to what Gao Shi might have intended, though that must always remain a conjecture. Yet for a number of these poems, the reader would be given no indication that they were the work of Gao Shi in the first place, as neither he nor anyone else is named as author.

We cannot know how representative the Dunhuang scrolls in which Gao Shi's poems appear are of general Tang practice. Our sample is simply too small. It does, however, seem likely that people might have written down poems in this fashion—as a set of verses they had heard or read but about which they knew very little. Indeed, as we shall see in Chapter 4, some poetry manuals from earlier in the dynasty suggested to poets that they keep a "notebook" in which to write down poems and lines to look to for inspiration when stymied in their own compositions. Poets who followed this advice might have noted the author and full title of these works and excerpts, but it would not be surprising if they sometimes did not, especially if poems came from sources that themselves lacked such information. These were not the types of "anthologies" that included prefaces explaining their aesthetic ideals and that showed up in later literary histories, but they were likely a far more common way of encountering poems for the average literate person in the Tang.

The "Qinfu yin" and Gao Shi poetic manuscripts are important as a window into the world of Tang literary culture. However cloudy that window may be, it provides insights not found in either texts received through hundreds of years of printing or in modern critical editions. In most cases the latter is all we have. However, when exceptional finds such as the Dunhuang manuscripts present themselves, we must take advantage of them. Manuscripts can show us not only the end product, but parts of the process that produced it. Glimpsing at this process, we are reminded that the world in which this literature was produced was very different from the world in which we read it today. All of these manuscripts were copied in the same place and at roughly the same time by people who probably spoke the same dialect and had similar levels of education, yet the resulting texts are often substantially different. There can be little doubt that if we had Tang and Five Dynasties copies of these works from other regions of China, we would see even more variation.

In this chapter I have examined traces of the material reality of Tang poetic literature. These traces tell us that for Tang readers, textual variation was an important part of the experience of interacting with poetic texts. The Dunhuang manuscripts also provide evidence for a wide range of transmission practices, from memorization and oral recitation to copying from a written model. Yet as useful as these traces may be for giving us a glimpse of Tang literary practices, they are ultimately end products of a process for which no explicit descriptions are provided. In subsequent chapters I tell the story behind these traces. The manuscripts themselves cannot describe the process of their creation, but many other sources do tell us something about how poetic works were created and circulated. The manuscripts may not reveal the intentions of the copyists who altered them as they copied, but such actors were not silent about their aims, and they made their intentions known in other contexts. The notion of copyists and readers as authorial collaborators has a meaningful role in how we think about poetry from Tang dynasty China. It is only by considering the concrete examples of textual production found in the Dunhuang manuscripts, together with the contemporaneous descriptions of practices I examine in subsequent chapters, that we can understand how oral, memorial, and written modes of production and circulation could have produced these enduring and valuable traces.

TWO

The Roles of Textual Memory and Memorization in Medieval Literary Culture

The Dunhuang manuscripts are concrete examples of how people in the Tang transmitted and stored texts through the technology of writing—in the simplest terms, the manipulation of material objects to preserve language. Human memory, trained and honed through a variety of methods, was also a vital means of preserving language in the Tang. In its more developed forms, memory is no less a technology than is writing.[1] For nonliterate cultures, it is the only way to store linguistic data. Though the development of writing changes the role of memory in a society, it does not eclipse it. As Mary Carruthers writes:

> Because oral cultures must obviously depend on memory, and hence value memory highly, such valorization has come to be seen as a hallmark of orality, as opposed to literacy. This has led to a further assumption that literacy and memory are *per se* incompatible, and that a "rise of literacy" will therefore bring with it a consequent devalorizing and disuse of memory. It is this assumption that my study calls particularly into doubt. For the cultivation and training of memory

---

1. Daniel M. Veidlinger usefully defines "technology" in such contexts as "the application of human knowledge to fashion a system that solves a particular problem." See Veidlinger, *Spreading the Dharma.*

was a basic aspect of the literate society of Rome, and continued to be necessary to literature and culture straight through the Middle Ages.[2]

The Tang period was witness to a highly literate culture in which the material technology of writing (and near the end of the period, printing) was arguably more advanced than it would be anywhere else in the world for centuries, yet as in Europe, memory continued to play a crucial role in the circulation of literature in both oral and written forms. Its part in oral transmission is obvious; however, written texts as well were often copied not only from direct recitation or an original written copy, but from memory. Given its influence on how poetry was transmitted and reproduced during the Tang, it is crucial that we gain a meaningful understanding of how textual memory functioned and what its cultural roles were in the period.[3]

Scholars have long been aware that, whether in Europe or China, educated persons' memories were far better trained in centuries past than they are today. Memorization, especially in the West, is now often seen as a sometimes necessary burden at best, and a stifling damper on creative thinking at worst. Writers and thinkers in medieval China (and before and after) instead considered it a basic mode of interacting with important texts. It was a key aspect of developing one's own moral outlook and literary style, both of which were always seen as best grounded on internalizing successful models of the past. A strong memory (*qiangji* 強記) was regarded as an impressive trait in an individual, as frequent biographical claims from the Tang and earlier that a person was so gifted attest.

Focusing on these very real differences, however, risks seeing memory in times past as more different from today than it really was. We must be fully aware of the superior memorial skills of the literate elite in the medieval period, while avoiding the trap of exaggeration. Educated people in this era memorized many texts, but far fewer than they read and studied without doing so. Moreover, for the texts they did set to memory, the ultimate goal was not necessarily the ability to reproduce a text exactly, but rather to internalize its fundamental ideas and general literary style. To put it simply, the trained memories of educated people in the Tang and

---

2. Carruthers, *Book of Memory*, 10.

3. The focus of this chapter is "textual memory," by which I mean memory of oral and written texts, as distinct from memory of past events, places, emotions, and so forth.

earlier were strong enough to make large-scale oral circulation of poetic works possible, but also sufficiently fallible to ensure that texts would continually change when circulated through modes that depended on memorization.

This conclusion departs from the assumptions that underlie many scholarly discussions of learning and education in the medieval period in general and the Tang period in particular, which typically avoid detailed discussions of textual memory and memorization. Terms such as "memorization corpus" are often used vaguely and uncritically in ways that imply there was a vast set of works, often assumed to include all the classics, their commentaries, the *Wenxuan*, and sundry other texts and commentaries, that every educated man in the Tang had set to memory and could access and reproduce accurately at will. When we look at the available sources for concrete evidence to support such assumptions, not only is it difficult to find, but there is much that calls these assumptions into question.

My interest here is in examples of memorization that hew closely to our accepted definitions of that word in English, that is, to be able to reproduce a text from memory, either verbally or in writing, without having recourse to the text itself. One can be very familiar with a given work, even to the extent of alluding to it in complex ways and playing off of specific aspects of its style, without having set it entirely to memory. In literary composition, it would typically not matter if a writer has perfectly memorized the entire work to which he alludes in a new composition. For the purposes of the present study, which concerns itself with the concrete ways that poetry was reproduced and circulated during the Tang, the distinction between knowing well and truly memorizing is a very important one.

Tang accounts of memorization use a number of different terms to indicate someone had set a piece to memory. The most common claim is that a person could "recite" (*song* 誦) the text in question. *Song* could refer to reading aloud in some contexts, but its primary meaning was to recite from memory. *Fengsong* 諷誦, *ansong* 暗誦, *jisong* 記誦, *songyi* 誦憶 and *songde* 誦得 were used in similar ways. All these terms describe a form of textual reproduction as proof of memorization; the reciter demonstrates that he has memorized a text by producing an oral "copy" of that text. Other terms point to the psychological or mental aspects of remembering. *Jilan* 記覽 (or sometimes *lanji* 覽記) specifically describes setting a text to memory through reading. These latter terms emphasize the process of memorization, rather than displayed proof of the result. Finally, such terms as *jiyi* 記憶 and *anji* 暗記[4] refer to memory in a more general sense—not only recalling the words of written sources, but remembering landscapes, faces, or oral sources as well. Writers sometimes use *anji* to specifically indicate setting something to memory without the use of vocalization, thus distinguishing the practice from those that involved reciting aloud to help fix a text in the mind. Just as important are the terms that do not, in and of themselves, indicate memorization. Such words as *du* 讀 ("to read"), *xue* 學 ("learning"), and a variety of terms indicating intensive study such as *tongxi* 通習 ("to penetrate thoroughly," "to have thorough knowledge of")[5] describe activities than can involve memorization, but they cannot be taken to clearly indicate it without additional textual evidence.

In what follows I examine memory from a number of different angles. The scope of investigation will be more extensive here than in other chapters, with greater attention paid to accounts from earlier periods (Eastern Han through Six Dynasties).[6] I also consider memory's roles in literary culture in general, rather than focusing only on poetry. The first section discusses general cultural attitudes towards memory by looking at accounts of exceptional memory, that is, of people performing memorial feats well beyond that of the average literate person. These accounts indicate that memory was indeed a skill valued in and of itself. In some con-

---

4. This is sometimes written 闇記.

5. To give one example, Charles Hartman (*Han Yü*, 164) translates the term *tongxi* 通習 (from Han Yu's "Shishuo" 師說 ["Discourse on Teachers"] [Ma, 1.44]) as "memorize," when a more appropriate rendering would be something like "penetrate thoroughly," as the term sometimes takes as its object things that cannot properly be "memorized" (as we use the term in English), such as *jingyi* 經義, the "meaning of the classics" (Beishi 北史, 40.1465).

6. There appears to be little significant change in memorial methods in this period. People in the Tang used the same basic memorial methods as did their counterparts in the Six Dynasties (316-589). Anecdotes dealing with memorization are not common in any period, and by broadening my chronological scope I am able to give a fuller picture of the practices as they existed in the Tang. Memory was arguably even more important prior to the medieval period, but to deal adequately with earlier periods would take us much further afield. For an excellent discussion of memorial practices in the Han and earlier, see Brashier, "Text and Ritual," 249–84.

texts it could be employed primarily as an entertaining parlor trick, yet in others it was a part of performances that implied moral and intellectual achievement. Anecdotes of exceptional memory also provide a contrast with more quotidian memorial abilities and thus serve to clarify the limits of those skills. I turn next to ordinary memory—memory as trained and utilized by the typical member of the literate class. The main issues here are the types of works people memorized and the methods they used to do so. In terms of the latter, I contrast the memorization techniques used in medieval China with those employed in medieval Europe. Though educated people in both cultures set large amounts of text to memory, the differences in their methods for doing so are substantial. As noted, in spite of their ample strengths, medieval Chinese memorial techniques had their limitations as well. I thus consider these limits and what they say about the effects of memorial transmission on textual fidelity. Finally, I close by looking at contemporary poetry and the role of memory in its circulation. Contemporary poetry was not set to memory with the systematic effort used in memorizing classical texts, yet its basic structures are ones that made it especially easy to memorize, even after limited exposure to a given poem. Of contemporary literary genres in the Tang, it was clearly the one most dependent on memorial transmission for many aspects of its circulation.

Extraordinary Memory

One important function of memorization was to serve as a form of textual storage. On the level of the individual, memorization meant constant access to texts that would not otherwise be on hand. In a broader sense, it preserved texts that might otherwise be lost. Fragile written works often suffered lamentable fates, and the limited numbers of available texts in the medieval Chinese manuscript culture made the loss of those texts all the more tragic when it occurred.[7] From the Qin burning of the books to the Huang Chao rebellion that destroyed many literary collections in the later years of the Tang, memorized versions of literary works were often all that survived times of war and chaos. Cai Yan 蔡琰 (b. ca. 178) was the daughter of the prominent literary and political figure Cai Yong 蔡邕 (133–92). She famously endured abduction and twelve years of life with

7. See Chapter 5 for further discussion of textual loss.

the Xiongnu (including a forced marriage to one of their leaders which produced two children) before being ransomed by Cao Cao 曹操 (155–220) in 206. The following account of her partial reconstruction of her father's extensive library shows both the extent of loss when such collections of writing were destroyed and the role of memory in keeping that loss from being total.[8]

Cao thereupon asked, "I have heard that your family previously had many ancient writings, are you able to recall them?" Wenji[9] said, "In the past, the writings left by my late father were over four thousand *juan*, but they have been scattered and lost in the mud and ashes. There are none that survive. Those that I can recite from memory number only just over four hundred." Cao said, "I will send ten clerks today to go to you and copy them down." Wenji said, "I have heard that in the separation of men and women, propriety forbids personally handing things to each other. I beg to be given paper and brush, and will use standard or cursive script, according to your command." Thereupon she wrote out a fair copy and sent it to him. The writing contained neither omissions nor errors.
操因問曰：聞夫人家先多墳籍，猶能憶識之不？文姬曰：昔亡父賜書四千許卷，流離塗炭，罔有存者．今所誦憶，裁四百餘篇耳．操曰：今當使十吏就夫人寫之．文姬曰：妾聞男女之別，禮不親授．乞給紙筆，眞草唯命．於是繕書送之，文無遺誤．[10]

Even in a period in which people memorized numerous classical texts, the ability to recite from memory four hundred works would be impressive. Keeping in mind that Cai Yan had been married off at age fifteen and thus presumably had not had access to her father's library for some thirteen rather tumultuous years, her achievement would be all the more unusual. There are a number of seemingly minor yet telling details in this account. It is clear, for example, that Cao Cao had some expectation that Cai Yan would have set many of the works from her father's library to memory and that she would still be able to recall them, implying that memorization was a common way of dealing with texts in the period. He also tells her that he will be sending scribes to record what she remembers, indicating that the predominant mode of reproducing memorized texts was oral recitation. He did not expect Cai Yan to write down the texts

8. For an examination of Cai Yan's life and her writings, see Frankel, "Cai Yan," 133–56.
9. Cai Yan's courtesy name.
10. *Hou Han shu*, 84.2801.

from memory herself and she must cite extenuating moral circumstances in asking to be allowed to do so.[11]

Memory here also serves as a method of cultural conservation whose import transcends the specific texts in question (which the anecdote never names). Cai Yan was not simply remembering old texts; she was bringing back part of what her father had passed on to her and bridging a gap between her past as the daughter of a nobleman and literatus and the new life commencing with her return to her native Han culture. The years as a captive of the Xiongnu represent personal loss and suffering, but also a broader loss of Han virtue to foreign barbarity. By reconstructing a small portion of her father's literary holdings, she not only proves that she has held on to her true identity, but also ensures that part of the literary past connected to that identity would now be preserved. The act simultaneously recognizes a sense of loss that cannot be ignored, yet shows that that loss is not total. Cai Yan's life was the source of many stories, some less in accord with historical fact than others. Whether or not the incident in question truly occurred, it gives us a glimpse of some of the less concrete but no less important roles that memory could play in society.

In spite of the great proliferation of texts in the Tang compared to earlier periods, works could still be lost, whether from turmoil or simple neglect. Those with extraordinary memories were sometimes called on to fill textual gaps in this period as well. The Mid-Tang figure Jiang Yi 蔣乂 became known as a youth for his rapid memorization and recitation of Yu Xin's "Rhapsody Lamenting Jiangnan" (哀江南賦) and his ability to "memorize without tiring" 記覽不倦.[12] The loss of a set of important texts provided him the opportunity to further show his quality:

The Emperor [Dezong] once climbed Rising Beyond the Mist Pavilion and saw that the left wall was crumbling and peeling. The written characters were incomplete, with only three or five characters in each line. He ordered that the text be

11. It is unclear how her reciting while scribes wrote down what she said would constitute "personally handing things to each other" 親授. It was perhaps the required physical proximity to which she objected. There is also the curious note that "the writing contained neither omissions nor errors." As Cao Cao presumably lacked additional copies of these texts, thus necessitating retrieving them from Cai Yan's memory, there would be no way to gauge the accuracy of her recollections. Questions of accuracy become more explicit in other examples that we will encounter below.

12. *JTS*, 149.4026.

copied so that the Grand Councilor could be questioned about it. The Grand Councilor was quickly summoned but could not come up with a response. He then ordered that Yi be summoned. [Yi] responded, "These are encomium verses for portraits of officials[13] from the Shengli[14] reign period. I have set them all to memory." He then recited them before the Emperor to fill in what was lost and did not miss a single character. The Emperor sighed, saying, "Even Yu Shinan's silently copying the *Biographies of Exemplary Women* from memory has nothing on this."

上嘗登淩煙閣，見左壁頹剝，文字殘缺，每行僅有三五字，命錄之以問宰臣．宰臣遽受宣，無以對，即令召乂至，對曰：此聖曆中侍臣圖贊，臣皆記憶．即於御前口誦， 以補其缺，不失一字．上歎曰，虞世南暗寫列女傳，無以加也．[15]

Rising Beyond the Mist Pavilion was a memorial pavilion housing the portraits of various exemplary officials and loyal generals of the Tang. Through the course of the dynasty the ranks of those honored were enlarged and changed as various figures fell in and out of the court's favor. Victor Cunrui Xiong writes, "These paintings represented the political iconography of the Tang court, for they were intended to eulogize loyalty to the court and to inspire political adhesion."[16] Jiang Yi's accomplishment is thus elevated beyond simple skill at memorizing. By accurately reconstructing the poetic verses of praise that accompanied the portraits, he aided in restoring important symbols of imperial military power and political unity. Moreover, the fact that Jiang Yi had memorized the verses implies, following basic Confucian theories of literature and education, that he had inculcated the values that they praise, thus making him a worthy and loyal official himself.

This anecdote further demonstrates the fluidity with which texts would pass between written and oral forms in the Tang. Jiang Yi presumably memorized the original verses from written texts (probably the wall itself). When those texts were lost, Jiang Yi reproduced them through his oral recitations, which scribes copied down (and then recopied onto the walls of the pavilion). His recitation itself is considered

---

13. These were praise poems written either on or above the portraits of the officials in the Rising Beyond the Mist Pavilion.

14. December 20, 697 to May 26, 700.

15. *JTS*, 149.4027.

16. Victor Cunrui Xiong, *Sui-Tang Chang'an*, 64.

sufficient evidence that he memorized the verses correctly. As with the story of Cai Yan, though the account claims that he did not miss a single character, there would have been no way to know. The conceit of the anecdote, at least, is that no written texts were available to restore the verses, thus the value of Jiang Yi's performance.[17]

This provides an interesting distinction between Jiang Yi's accomplishment and those of the Early Tang writer Yu Shinan 虞世南 (558–638), noted by the Emperor at the end of the passage.[18] Emperor Taizong once ordered Yu Shinan to copy the *Biographies of Exemplary Women* onto a screen. As there was no text available to him at the time, he "wrote it silently from memory" 暗疏之.[19] Yu Shinan's feat was thus a response to a test: he was ordered to write a copy of the text without having access to it not because the text was really lost, but as a challenge.[20] Moreover, the writing he produced could then be compared with a written text of the original to justify the conclusion that he, in the same words applied later to Jiang Yi, "did not miss a single character" 不失一字. But in both cases we see texts transmitted and reproduced with memory as the intermediate state of storage between an "original" (which itself was probably a copy) and its reproduction.

The moral role of memory implicit in the accounts of Cai Yan and Jiang Yi points to interesting comparisons between medieval European and Chinese notions on the subject. Carruthers notes that medieval Europeans considered a well-developed memory not merely a tool of learning, but proof of a certain moral virtuousness in and of itself.[21] This notion works primarily on two levels. The first is the internalization of examples of past moral models through memorization:

---

17. It is, however, likely that other copies of the verses would have been preserved by the court.

18. For a discussion of Yu Shinan's poetry and thought, see Stephen Owen, *Poetry of the Early T'ang*, 42–52.

19. *JTS*, 72.2566. For another version of the Yu Shinan story see Liu Su 劉餗, *Sui Tang jiahua* 隋唐嘉話 ("Beautiful Talk of the Sui and Tang"), from *Suitang jiahua, Chaoye qianzai* 隋唐嘉話、朝野僉載, 15. Note that the phrases cited above, while having the same meaning as the *Jiu Tang shu*'s wording, differ slightly, being 暗書之 and 一字無失 respectively.

20. I will discuss further examples of testing memory below.

21. Mary Carruthers, *Book of Memory*, 71.

And this memorized chorus of voices, this ever-present florilegium built up plank by plank continuously through one's lifetime, formed not only one's opinions but one's moral character as well. Character indeed results from one's experience, but that includes the experiences of others, often epitomized in ethical commonplaces, and made one's own by constant recollection.[22]

The ideas here fit well with traditional Chinese moral notions, which perhaps put even more stress on looking to the past for ethical models. From the *Shi* hailing King Wen's 文王 example[23] to Mencius speaking of the ancient sage king Yao and claiming that "if you wear Yao's clothes, recite Yao's words, and do what Yao did, this is itself being Yao" 子服堯之服、誦堯之言、行堯之行，是堯而已矣,[24] internalizing past moral exemplars was a foundational part of ethical theory.[25] Its force continued through Tang times and beyond and often served as the ethical justification for stressing memorization on the exams.

Carruthers also argues that a strong memory as a skill in and of itself was associated with morality in medieval Europe. She points out that "the memory feats of saints are frequently stressed in hagiography, even of saints who were not scholars...not to show off their intellectual prowess, but to stress their moral perfection."[26] This is different from the idea that memorizing a text such as the *Analects* makes one more moral because of the particular attributes of that text and its author. In the former case it is the ability to memorize that is important, in the latter it is the act of having internalized the language and ideas in a text through memorization.

It may seem that this notion would be at odds with Chinese moral ideas. There are, however, analogies in the Chinese case to the idea that a strong memory itself has moral value independent of the texts memorized. As noted in the opening of this chapter, claims that their subjects possessed a strong memory are common in biographies from the Han through the Tang. Han Yu 韓愈 (768–824) in particular focuses on

22. Carruthers, *Book of Memory*, 179.

23. See, for example, "This rite is modeled on King Wen's rules, which daily pacify the four directions" 儀式刑文王之典，日靖四方. Ruan, *Shisanjing*, 19.716.

24. Ruan, *Shisanjing*, 12.209.

25. See also Brashier's ("Text and Ritual," 257–58) discussion of this topic. He notes that Wang Chong, whose excellent memory was noted below, is one of many thinkers to comment on this idea.

26. Carruthers, *Book of Memory*, 71.

memorization abilities in a number of his writings. His "Three Encomiums on Three Worthies of the Later Han" 後漢三賢贊三首 praises the ability of Wang Chong 王充 (27–97), author of the *Lunheng* 論衡, to memorize rapidly and paraphrases the *Hou Han shu* 後漢書 entry describing it.[27] In "Seeing Off Zhuge Jue Who Is Heading to Suizhou to Study" 送諸葛覺往隨州讀書, he commends Zhuge Jue 諸葛覺 in similar fashion, writing, "As a man his strength is in memorization / when something passes before his eyes he does not read it a second time" 爲人強記覽，過眼不再讀.[28] Han Yu goes into more specific detail in his "Postface to the Biography of Zhang Zhongchen" 張中丞傳後敘, written about the military hero Zhang Xun 張巡 (709–57).[29] The postface cites a story that Zhang Ji 張籍 (776–ca. 829) heard from Yu Song 于嵩, an acquaintance of Zhang Xun's, describing the latter's almost perfect memory:

He once saw Song reading the *Han shu* and asked him, "Why do you keep reading this?"
Song replied, "I've not yet mastered it."
Xun said, "My way with books is that I read something no more than three times and I never forget it for my whole life."
He then recited the book that Song was reading and did not get a single character wrong in the entire scroll. Song was surprised and thought that Xun just happened to be familiar with this scroll. He then randomly pulled out other rolls to test him and it was like this for all of them. Song took still more books from his shelves and tested Xun with questions. Zhang Xun smoothly recited each without hesitation. Song accompanied Zhang Xun for a long time and never saw him reading much.
嘗見嵩讀漢書，謂嵩曰：何爲久讀此？嵩曰：未熟也．巡曰：吾於書讀不過三遍，終身不忘也．因誦嵩所讀書，盡卷不錯一字．嵩驚，以

---

27. Ma, 1.58–59. The original passage from the *Hou Han shu* reads, "His family was poor and lacked books. He would often visit the markets and shops of Luoyang and read the books they sold. After seeing them once he was instantly able to recite them from memory" 家貧無書，常游洛陽市肆，閱所賣書，一見輒能誦憶. See *Hou Han shu*, 49.1629. A similar story is told of Sun Yue 孫悅 in the *Hou Han shu* (62.2058). It includes the identical phrase "His family was poor and lacked books" and notes that he would "read something once and usually be able to recite it from memory" 一覽多能誦記.

28. Qian Zhonglian, *Han Changli shiji*, 12.1273.

29. Zhang was famed for his valiant if ultimately failed attempt to hold the key city of Suiyang 睢陽 when surrounded by An Lushan's armies.

為巡偶熟此卷，因亂抽他帙以試，無不盡然．嵩又取架上諸書試以問巡，巡應口誦無疑．嵩從巡久，亦不見巡常讀書也．[30]

Though Han Yu never explicitly states that Zhang Xun's extraordinary memory is connected to his moral character, such a connection is implicit in Han Yu's claim that he wrote the piece to emphasize both the practical and moral legitimacy of Zhang Xun's doomed defense of Suiyang.[31] It is also worth noting that the anecdote makes it clear that Zhang's ability is indeed extraordinary. Yu Song is surprised to discover the extent of Zhang's memorization, implying that it is far beyond what one would be expected to have accomplished.

Han Yu's account brings together two themes that are common in anecdotes about extraordinary memories: speed and proof of accuracy. Zhang Xun claims that he reads works "no more than three times" and never forgets them. Yu Song finds the claim dubious and repeatedly tests him with different volumes from his library. There are similar claims of near instantaneous memories in numerous biographies from the Han on, often expressed with such phrases as "after reading something once he was usually able to recite it from memory" 一覽多能誦記,[32] "Whatever his eyes saw, he could instantly recite. Whatever his ears happened to hear, his heart would not forget" 目所一見，輒誦於口，耳所暫聞，不忘於心,[33] or "When he read something once, he wouldn't forget it for the rest of his life" 一閱籍，終身不忘.[34] An account of the poet Wang Can 王粲 shows him not only memorizing a stele on the side of the road and reciting it perfectly after a single reading, but also recreating the positions of all the pieces on a chess board after it had broken.[35]

30. Ma, 2.77.

31. In this context of Han Yu's association of memory with morality, it is noteworthy that his own son had little talent for memorization. Han Chang's 韓昶 "Autobiographical Funerary Inscription" ("Zi wei muzhiming" 自爲墓誌銘) notes that in his youth he "could not memorize. When he reached adulthood he was unable to recite three or five hundred characters" 不能闇記書．至年長．不能通誦得三五百字. *QTW*, 741.7666. See also Hartman's discussion (*Han Yü*, 362, n. 67).

32. *Hou Han shu*, 62.2058. For another example see *Liang shu* 梁書, 50.726.

33. *Hou Han shu*, 80.2653.

34. *XTS*, 168.5127.

35. *Wei shu*, 21.599.

Of particular interest in terms of poetry is an anecdote from the Northern Qi period about Xing Shao 邢邵. The account begins by noting his strong memory and his daily recitation of over ten thousand words, going on to claim that when he was "tired from drinking and playing around, he looked broadly through the classics and histories. He read through them quickly, remembering them after a single glance and not forgetting a thing" 飲讌倦，方廣尋經史，五行俱下，一覽便記，無所遺忘.[36] This sense of casualness continues through a description of an incident when he was traveling and drinking with a group of friends:

They composed poems together, many dozens in all and left them with the host's servant. The next morning the servant had left and they looked for the poems but couldn't find them. Shao recited them all for them. Some of the people didn't recognize their poems, but when the servant returned and they got the originals, he hadn't erred by a single word. They took him as the equal of Wang Can. 相與賦詩、凡數十首，皆在主人奴處．旦日奴行，諸人求詩不得，邵皆爲誦之，諸人有不認詩者，奴還得本，不誤一字．諸人方之王粲．[37]

Like Wang Can, Xing Shao applies his facile memory not only to memorizing classical texts (a task that seems to have provided him few challenges) but to new works that he encounters as well. The proof of accuracy here is accidental, and only comes about when the original texts reappear. We also see that although Xing Shao's companions, as literate men, must have had experience memorizing texts as well, his ability to recall all the poems perfectly goes well beyond what they could do or would expect one of their peers to be capable of. The degree of skill shown by Xing Shao is said not to be the result of intensive training, but of some unusual talent.

As we have seen in Han Yu's writings, the ability to memorize continued to be highly valued in the Tang as well. Fittingly for this period, there is an increased emphasis on public performance and gaining fame for one's abilities. In an anecdote from the *Da Tang xinyu* 大唐新語 ("New Words from the Great Tang"), memory serves as an entertaining parlor trick:

Once at an official banquet a guest wrote a draft preface of five hundred words. Feng Gu looked at it and said, "This is all old writings." He then picked up a

---

36. *Bei Qi shu*, 36.475.
37. *Bei Qi shu*, 36.475.

brush and wrote it out backwards. The drafter was silent and disconcerted and the assembled guests all applauded. Feng Gu slowly smiled and said, "I just then read it and set it to memory, it's not really an older work." Because of this he became well known.

嘗日公讌，有客草序五百言·奉古覽之曰：皆舊文·援筆倒疏之·草序者默然自失，列座撫掌·奉古徐笑曰：適覽記之，非舊習也·由是知名·[38]

This seemingly insignificant prank actually reveals much about memorization in the Tang. It shows that most people would not be expected to be able to read through a text quickly once and be able to reproduce it verbatim immediately. Memory required repetition and effort. At the same time, people were expected to have parts of many texts set to memory. Feng Gu proves his claim that the preface is "all old writings" by showing that it is something he had memorized. This claim of memorization is further bolstered by his ability to write out the text backwards—as I discuss below, an ability much prized in medieval Europe but not often mentioned in Chinese texts. Finally, Feng Gu's ability to memorize so quickly is enough to bring him a measure of fame. Such rapid memorization was apparently both esteemed and rare.

Performance for an imperial audience represented the height of achievement in many fields of endeavor in the Tang, and memorization was no exception. Lü Cai's 呂才 biography claims that when Taizong heard he could recite the *Yijing* 易經 ("Classic of Changes") and *Shi* at a young age, he summoned the boy and presented him with a gift of silk for his talent.[39] The *Minghuang zalu* 明皇雜錄 ("Miscellaneous Records of the Brilliant Emperor") records the following account of the monk Yixing 一行 that highlights the performative aspects of rapid memorization:

The monk Yixing was surnamed Zhang. He was from Julu and his original name was Sui. Tang Xuanzong summoned him for an audience and said, "What can you do?" He answered, "I am only good at memorization." Xuanzong ordered an official in charge of the palace women to get the palace women's writings and show them to Yixing. When he finished reading them all, he repeated them, reciting from memory with great familiarity as if they were pieces he had long practiced reading....[Xuanzong] hailed him as a sage.

38. Liu Su 劉肅, *Da Tang xinyu*, 8.120.

39. *JTS*, 79.2727.

僧一行姓張氏，鉅鹿人，本名遂．唐玄宗既召見，謂曰：卿何能？對曰：唯善記覽．玄宗因詔掖庭，取宮人籍以示之，周覽既畢，覆其本，記念精熟，如素所習讀．．．呼為聖人．[40]

The testing here is explicit: Xuanzong gives Yixing writings that he could not possibly have seen before, and he must reproduce them after what was presumably a quite limited timeframe. The most revealing aspect of this account is the way it elevates memory as having value completely apart from its content. The cultural roles of the texts that Yixing sets quickly to memory, poems by the imperial consorts, could not be farther from the classics or Buddhist texts memorized by exam candidates and monks. Internalizing their language and ideals would have been unlikely to make Yixing a more morally upright individual. Moreover, whereas Zhang Xun's remarkable memory was just one of his many admirable traits, Yixing himself modestly claims that memorization is his only ability. In spite of this, Xuanzong declares him a sage on the basis of his memory alone.

An anecdote from the *Tang yulin* 唐語林 ("Forest of Words from the Tang"), is arguably the fullest account of how memory might be tested in a context that was official, but outside of the structure of the formal exam system.

At the beginning of the Kaiyuan reign period, Chang Jingzhong of Luzhou passed the *mingjing* exam at age fifteen and after several years fully penetrated all of the five classics. He presented a memorial recommending himself that said, "I can recite from memory one thousand words after reading them once." The emperor summoned him to the Secretariat for testing. Zhang, the Duke of Yan,[41] asked him, "If the scholar can recite a thousand words from memory after reading them once, can you recite ten thousand after reading them ten times?" He responded, "I've never tested myself." The Duke of Yan then took out a book; it was not one that anyone had ever seen before. He said to [Jingzhong], "Please recite it after ten times." Jingzhong knelt down respectively and read. For each time through he made a mark on the ground to record it. When he had read through seven times, he got up and said, "I can already recite this." The Duke of Yan said, "You may complete the ten readings." Jingzhong said, "If it's ten readings, then it would be reciting after ten readings. Now after seven readings I've already achieved it. What need is there to complete ten?" The Duke of Yan took up the

40. Zheng Chuhui 鄭處誨, *Minghuang zalu* 明皇雜錄, 42.

41. That is, Zhang Yue 張説 (667–731).

volume and read it without a break. Jingzhong recited it to the end without missing a single character. Everyone who saw it gasped.

開元初，潞州常敬忠十五明經擢第，數年遍通五經．上書自舉，云：一遍誦千言．敕赴中書考試，張燕公問曰：學士能一遍誦千言，十遍誦萬言乎？對曰：未曾自試．燕公遂出書，非人間所見也，謂之曰：可十遍誦之．敬忠危坐而讀，每遍畫地爲記．讀七遍，起曰：此已誦得．燕公曰：可滿十遍．敬忠曰：若十遍，即是十遍誦得；今七遍已得，何要滿十？燕公執本觀覽不暇，而敬忠誦畢不差一字，見者莫不嗟嘆．[42]

Here again we are firmly in the realm of performance. While Chang Jingzhong had indeed mastered the classics sufficiently to have gained official recognition through the exam system, his justification for presenting himself to the emperor is not his scholarly achievements, but rather his ability to memorize new texts almost instantaneously; the emphasis is on memory as an independent skill. Indeed, we are never told the content of the book that Zhang Yue uses to test Chang, only that "it was not one that anyone had ever seen before." From the beginning, the set-up is both a test and a performance. Chang is presented with a challenge and responds with theatrical flourish, marking the ground after each read through the material. Finally, he not only meets the challenge but surpasses it, completing the memorization with even fewer repetitions than allowed, and reciting the text without a single error.

These three accounts, of Xing Shao, Yixing, and Chang Jingzhong, bring us close to the European notion of memory as a separate area of endeavor, a skill that exists independent of knowledge of any particular text. Even if these examples are exceptional, they show that the culture of these periods valued the ability to set texts to memory. In more extreme cases, this ability could be used as a form of showing off for entertainment purposes, but the same could be said for poetry composition and calligraphy in certain contexts, also skills that were regarded as possessing fundamental value. Memorial abilities, regardless of the content of what one memorized, pointed to something more than a parlor trick. Yet these accounts further demonstrate that that ability to set substantial amounts of text to memory after only a limited number of readings was indeed exceptional.

---

42. Wang Dang 王讜, *Tang yulin*, 3.311–12.

Ordinary memorial practices did not confer upon their practitioners these particular abilities. It is to these practices that we now turn.

Ordinary Memory

CONTENT: WHAT DID PEOPLE MEMORIZE?

Memorization was an important aspect of education for the entire imperial period. From the Han dynasty on there is abundant evidence that male children began training their memories at a very early age. Most historical accounts start their descriptions of early education at the point at which boys began memorizing the classics or such works as the *Analects* or the *Laozi* 老子. Particularly precocious children are said to have memorized a classic or two, typically including the *Shi*, by around the age of seven *sui* 歲 (about six years of age in Western reckoning), though children who could recite even a single classic from memory by seven *sui* were clearly exceptional. We can probably assume a gap of at least a year or two between when a child would begin learning to read and write and when he would start setting his first classical text to memory. This period would be filled partly by learning the various primers I discuss below. Anne Kinney suggests that male children in the Han would have begun practicing reading and writing by eight *sui*,[43] and Charles Hartman gives a similar figure for the Tang.[44] The few biographies of Tang figures that mention the age at which they began studying, rather than when they had mastered certain texts, also give dates in this range. For example, the great Early Tang scholar Kong Yingda 孔穎達 (574–648) who is said to have "begun his studies at eight *sui*, reciting over a thousand words a day" 八歲就學，日誦千餘言,[45] is probably typical in terms of age, if not accomplishments.[46]

43. Kinney, *Representations of Childhood*, 15.

44. Hartman, *Han Yü*, 235.

45. *JTS*, 73.2601.

46. The physician Sun Simiao 孫思邈 (ca. 581–682), one of the few other Tang figures for whom an age is given for beginning his studies, is said to have begun at seven *sui* and is also credited with reciting a thousand characters a day. See *JTS* 191.5094. The latter claim is a formulaic statement in a number of biographies from the Six Dynasties and Tang periods.

Though an ability to memorize the classics at a young age is often the first mention of study in most biographies that include such details, male children in the Tang began their education not with the classics themselves but with various primers that would introduce them both to writing and to many of the historical figures, events, and themes that they would later encounter in more difficult texts. The most prominent among these is *Qianzi wen* 千字文 ("Thousand Character Text") by the early sixth-century author Zhou Xingsi 周興嗣, which enjoyed widespread popularity in the Tang. An anecdote in the *Tang zhiyan* 唐摭言 ("Collected Statements of the Tang") notes that after fleeing the Huang Chao rebellion and facing a series of other misfortunes, the calligrapher and *Yijing* specialist Gu Meng 顧蒙 fled to Guangzhou where he "suffered an itinerant life, going so far as teaching writing the *Qianzi wen* to the ignorant and vulgar in exchange for meager wages" 困於旅食，以至書千字文授於聾俗，以換斗筲之資.[47] The text is mentioned in a more positive light in the "Memorial Presenting the *Meng qiu*" 薦蒙求表 by Li Han 李翰, which notes that "in recent times Zhou Xingsi composed the *Qianzi wen* and it has indeed spread throughout the realm" 近代周興嗣撰千字文・亦頒行天下.[48] The *Meng qiu* 蒙求 ("The Child Seeks") is itself a primer intended for young students in the early stage of their studies prior to tackling classical texts.[49] Presented to the throne in 747, it includes a preface by Li Hua 李華 (d. 769) explaining that the work "enumerated the beautiful and the foul of the words and deeds of men of old and joined them with rhyme in order to instruct children" 列古人言行美惡・參之聲律・以授幼童.[50] One other text, *Kaimeng yaoxun* 開蒙要訓 ("Important Instructions for Beginners"), is a Six Dynasties work recovered at Dunhuang that served similar purposes.[51]

---

47. *TZY*, 10.118.

48. *QTW*, *Tangwen shiyi* 唐文拾遺, 19.10574.

49. The title comes from the opening of the discussion of the hexagram *meng* 蒙 from the *Yijing*, which reads, "It is not I who seeks the young fool, the young fool seeks me" 匪我求童蒙，童蒙求. Translation from Wilhelm, *I Ching*, 20–21.

50. "Mengqiu xu" 蒙求序, *QTW*, *Tangwen shiyi*, 19.10574.

51. See Hsiung Ping-chen, "Erh-t'ung wen-hsüeh," 32. For a more detailed analysis and a typeset version of the text, see Zheng Acai and Zhu Fengyu, *Dunhuang mengshu yanjiu*, 51–68. For one Dunhuang manuscript of the text, see P2578 in *Manuscrits*, 16.83–85.

Texts such as these show the close connection between reading and memorizing in childhood education. One function of the primers was clearly to lead young students to recognize as many new characters as they could in a limited period of time and with as little text as possible. The *Qianzi wen*, for example, never repeats a character, thus introducing students to one thousand distinct words. Even the longest, the *Meng qiu* at 2384 characters, is substantially shorter than any classical text other than the *Xiaojing* 孝經 ("Classic of Filial Piety") (1799 characters), which itself is essentially a primer. The structures of these works, however, demonstrate that they were not meant merely to be read, but to be set to memory. All three are written in rhyming parallel couplets of four-character lines and are divided up according to specific themes. The *Qianzi wen*, for example, begins with descriptions of the physical world, then moves on to sections on such themes as politics, morality, and history. These structural features, both in terms of content and linguistic patterning, are mnemonic devices intended to make the texts "easy to recite" 易於諷誦, as Li Hua's "Preface to the *Meng qiu*" explicitly states.[52] It is important to keep in mind in this context that these children learning the written Chinese of the time were not simply learning to read a language they already knew how to speak; rather, they were essentially learning a new language. The vernacular and literary languages had grown apart by this point;[53] the grammar and meanings of words of a great part of the written literary language would have been at least somewhat alien to young children just beginning their education. Memorization allowed them not only to recognize new characters, but to begin building a store of the types of diction and allusions that would form the basis for their own writing when they reached the stage of composing original pieces themselves.

Important though primers were for the beginning stages of a young boy's education, they were ultimately preparation for the more important task of learning selected classics and other texts of both professional and social importance. An educated man would be expected to display familiarity with all of the classics, but not to fully memorize each one. Different

52. *QTW*, *Tangwen shiyi*, 19.10574.

53. For phonological changes see Pulleyblank, *Middle Chinese*, 1–4. For a good overview of the distinctions between classical, literary, and vernacular Chinese, see Hartman, "Literary Chinese," 92–97.

texts played different roles in the educational process, differences which are reflected in the extent to which they were commonly set to memory. From the Han on, biographies that claim precocious memorization skills on the part of their subjects typically name the *Shi* as the first classic set to memory.[54] This is not surprising, as rhyme, repetitive structures, and the short length of many of the poems would have made this work easier to memorize than other classical texts that, though shorter overall in some cases, were written in prose and contained more complex diction. It is likely that the *Xiaojing* was memorized even earlier by most students, but accounts note it by name less often.[55] Given its brevity, memorizing it at an early age was perhaps not considered worthy of mention. Other classics precocious children would sometimes memorize included the *Analects* and the *Yijing*, though these appear less frequently.[56]

Memorization of classical texts was not the sole preserve of the very young, but rather an educational endeavor that continued throughout a boy's education. Successful performance on the civil service exams was a key goal of male elites for much of the Tang (in spite of the fact that they were not yet as important a road to social and political success as they would become in the Song and later periods), and their requirements can tell us quite a bit about the aims and content of textual memorization. The two exams that had the most influence on elite education in the Tang were the *mingjing* 明經 ("illuminating the classics") and *jinshi* 進士 ("presented scholar"), both of which required some degree of memorization. The *mingjing* was the focus of the state educational system[57] and involved more memorization (a feature for which it was increasingly criticized throughout the period) than the *jinshi*. It thus serves as a good

54. Examples prior to the Tang are numerous. For a few examples, see *Hou Han shu*, 16.599; 20.850, 28.962, 14.1330; and *Liang shu*, 50.724. Biographical mentions of childhood memorization of the classics are less frequent in the Tang, perhaps as memorization became more common due to the increasing importance of the exams, but examples do exist. See *JTS*, 51.2167, 79.2727; and *XTS*, 109.4106. See also discussion in Brashier, "Text and Ritual," 260–61.

55. Some instances when it is mentioned include *Nan Qi shu* 南齊書, 23.435; *Liang shu*, 8.165; and *TZY*, 10.221.

56. For the *Analects* see *Nan Qi shu*, 54.928; *Liang shu*, 8.165 and 50.724; *JTS*, 51.2167; and *QTW*, 563.5706.

57. See Herbert, "Curriculum and Content," 152. See also McMullen, *State and Scholars*, 22–26.

indication of the state's memorization requirements in their strictest form. Candidates were not expected to have set all of the classics to memory; they focused instead on a smaller subset of texts. The basic requirement was mastery of the *Xiaojing* and the *Analects*, with the rest of the classics broken into categories of long, medium, or short.[58] P. A. Herbert points out that though students could choose to pursue degrees in anywhere from two to five texts beyond the basic requirement, "the number of classics studied does not seem to have been considered important, so naturally candidates preferred easy options."[59]

This structure meant that the number and length of the texts candidates for the *mingjing* set to memory could vary widely. The easiest option was the degree in two classics, which included the *Xiaojing* and the *Analects* (as the base requirement) to which a candidate would add either a long and short classic, or two medium classics. The *Xiaojing* and the *Analects* together total just under fourteen thousand characters. If a candidate added to this two medium classics such as the *Shi* (about thirty-nine thousand characters) and the *Zhouli* 周禮 ("Rites of Zhou") (about forty-six thousand characters), the total number of characters tested would be just under a hundred thousand. A *mingjing* degree in five classics, which would include both the *Liji* 禮記 ("Record of Rites") and the *Chunqiu Zuozhuan* 春秋左傳 ("Zuo Commentary on the Spring and Autumn Annals"), would involve a figure almost three times that. Following Herbert, we must assume that the smaller number was a more common goal for the average exam candidate. Indeed, as Li Bincheng 李斌城 et al. have pointed out, few people focused on the longer classics.[60]

Exam success was not, however, the only goal of education in the Tang, and the fact that most students preferred not to be tested on such difficult and lengthy works as the *Zuozhuan* should not be taken to imply that they did not study and often set at least substantial parts of them to memory. The *Jiu Tangshu* ("Old Tang History") biography of Fu Bi 父泌 notes that "He enjoyed study as a youth, penetrating the Five Classics. He was especially fond of the *Shi*, *Yi* and *Zuo's Spring and Autumn Annals*,

58. This discussion is heavily based on the charts provided by Herbert, "Curriculum and Content," 159–62.

59. Herbert, "Curriculum and Content," 154.

60. See Li Bincheng 李斌城, et al., *Sui Tang Wudai shehui*, 346.

and was able to recite the commentaries [to these texts]" 少好學，通五經，尤嗜詩、易、左氏春秋，能諷其章句.[61] Facility with these texts would have served Fu Bi well on the exam, yet this passage claims something aside from ambition as his motivation for learning: he simply enjoyed them. Such was his fondness for these classics that he set even the commentaries to memory. Moreover, texts that people set to memory for their own pleasure and enjoyment went well beyond the classics. The biography of Liu Gongquan 柳公權 states that "he had an especially acute understanding of the *Zuozhuan*, the *Guoyu*, the *Documents*, the *Mao Shi*, and the *Zhuangzi*. Whenever explaining a point of significance, he was sure to recite many pages" 尤精左氏傳、國語、尚 書、毛詩、莊子・每説一義，必誦數紙.[62] Such texts as the *Guoyu* ("Sayings of the States") and the *Zhuangzi* were not part of the official memorization corpus for the exam. They were, however, works that educated people would be expected to know well.

Examples like this show that the requirements for the exams reveal only a small portion of what the educated elite actually memorized in practice. Exams were an official arena for testing knowledge; they codified an expectation that was a part of wider elite life in which memorization was not exceptional, but rather the typical mode of interacting with certain types of texts. Having works at one's immediate mental disposal was necessary (but not sufficient) evidence that one had mastered such writings, and was an important aspect of argumentation, whether in writing or in oral debate (much as quoting the *Shi* played a key part in interstate diplomacy in the pre-Qin period). For Liu Gongquan, memorization was part of the process of gaining a deeper understanding of a text. When he recited lengthy portions of the texts he studied, it was not simply to show that he could memorize, but to provide evidence to bolster arguments that he was making in the course of conversation or debate.

Another goal of memorization was internalization. Works set to memory as a student became a part of one's compositional repertoire. They taught the modes of expression that were acceptable in a range of genres from formal memorials to poetry written to entertain friends. This was particularly important for learning a language that, though most of-

---

61. *JTS*, 159.4190.
62. *JTS*, 165.4312.

ten recited aloud, was not typically spoken in a conversational mode the way vernaculars were. Young students did not learn literary Chinese through conversation with adults, as they would the spoken language, yet their learning was by no means passive. They developed the ability to compose by actively reading, listening to, and imitating model works by others. By memorizing such works, students made them their own. Ideally they would ultimately create their own style, but it would always be a style that grew out of the works they had set to memory from the time they began their studies.

These models included not only the classical texts but later poetic works as well. In this context the most important set of model works for students hoping for literary accomplishment or success on compositional portions of the exams was clearly the *Wenxuan* 文選 ("Selections of Refined Literature"), compiled by Crown Prince Xiao Tong 蕭統 (501–31) of the Liang 梁 (502–57). Many scholars have referred to the *Wenxuan* as part of the "memorization corpus"[63] for the exams in the Tang and have gone as far as to say that "for centuries from Tang times onward, every civil examination candidate had memorized the *Wenxuan*...."[64] The influence of the *Wenxuan* on literary works from the Tang on in a number of genres is beyond dispute, and there is no question that children memorized works it contained. Numerous biographical accounts demonstrate the importance afforded to memorizing works from poetic genres in particular. Su Jie 素節 was said to "be able to recite over five hundred words of old poems and rhapsodies a day" 能日誦古詩賦五百餘言.[65] I note earlier that Jiang Yi was known for his memorization skills at an early age; his biography states that at the age of seven *sui*, he "recited Yu Xin's 'Rhapsody Lamenting Jiangnan.' After several times he could recite it

---

63. Hartman, *Han Yü*, 238.

64. Kern and Hegel, "A History of Chinese Literature?" 168–69. See also Kōjirō, "Tu Fu's Poetics and Poetry," 9, for the specific claim that Du Fu had memorized the *Wenxuan*. David Knechtges more conservatively (and, in my opinion, accurately) notes, "In the Tang, the *Wen xuan* became an important text that was studied by degree candidates. Young boys were expected to master its contents and imitate its style in order to perform well in the literary examinations." Xiao Tong 蕭統, compiler, and Knechtges, trans., *Wen xuan, vol. 1*, 54.

65. *JTS*, 86.2826.

from memory" 七歲時，誦庾信哀江南賦，數遍而成誦在口.[66] The specific claim that all exam candidates or even just Du Fu memorized the entire *Wenxuan* anthology, however, deserves closer examination.

Most mentions of memorization refer to setting an entire text to memory. We can assume that when a biography notes that its subject "could recite the *Mao Shi*" 能誦毛詩 (that is, the *Shi*), it does not mean that he could recite parts of them or only a few entire poems. Accounts do, however, sometimes make distinctions between the thorough memorization indicated by the ability to recite a text aloud, and a less complete level of memorization in which a person was able to "generally" or "largely" (*lüe* 略) recall a text. One account claims that when the poet Lu Zhaolin 盧照鄰 (634–ca. 684) served as a document clerk for one of the imperial princes who had a library filling twelve cartloads of writings 王有書十二車, "Zhaolin was always spreading out the scrolls and reading them and was by and large able to remember them" 照鄰總披覽・略能記憶.[67] This is a testament not to the kind of complete memorization the exam would test, but to simply having a good memory for what one read.

From the Six Dynasties period on, writers typically use descriptions of this sort in reference to texts other than the classics, and to learning the *Han shu* 漢書 ("Han History") with particular frequency. Xing Shao's biography claims that:

> He was bright and had a good memory, reciting over ten thousand words a day...Once because of a long period of rain, he read the *Han shu*. After five days he was largely able to remember the whole thing.
> 聰明強記，日誦萬餘言・・・嘗因霖雨，乃讀漢書，五日，略能遍記之・[68]

The biography of the Liang figure Lu Yungong 陸雲公 (511–47) similarly notes that "Yun could recite (誦) the *Analects* and the *Mao Shi*. At nine *sui* he read the *Han shu* and was largely able to remember it" 雲公五歲誦論語、毛詩，九歲讀漢書，略能記憶.[69] While such comments for Tang figures appear less often, the biography of Hao Chujun 郝處俊 notes that "when he was older he liked studying. He was fond of the *Han*

---

66. *JTS*, 149.4026.
67. *Taiping guangji* 太平廣記, 198.1484.
68. *Bei Qi shu* 北齊書, 36.475.
69. *Liang shu*, 51.724.

shu and could largely recite it from memory" 及長，好學，嗜漢書，崖略暗誦.[70] These frequent mentions of Ban Gu's famous historical work make it clear that it was a popular and important object of study for both its factual content and its stylistic excellence, but it was neither a classic nor a text that would ever show up on the section of the exams that specifically required memorization. Educated men read it and many apparently set large sections of it to memory, but they did not memorize it with the rigor reserved for the true "memorization canon."[71]

What then of the *Wenxuan*? Evidence that people memorized the entire anthology the way they did the *Shi* or the *Analects* is scarce. Biographies frequently note their subjects reciting these classics from memory in their youth (and committing large portions of such non-classical texts as the *Han shu* to memory later in life), yet one finds few similar comments about the *Wenxuan*. There are possible exceptions: Du Fu encourages his son to "thoroughly master the order of the *Wenxuan*" 熟精文選理[72] and notes that he recites it together with him.[73] In his epitaph for his son-in-law's father Li Ping 李邴, Han Yu claims that "at age fourteen or fifteen, he had been able to memorize the *Analects*, the *Documents*, the *Mao Poems*, the *Zuozhuan*, and the *Wenxuan*, in all over a million words" 年十四五，能闇記論語尚書毛詩左氏文選，凡百餘萬言.[74] One might argue that setting the *Wenxuan* to memory was so common that it did not merit mention. But the same should then hold true for the *Analects* or the *Shi*, two of the basic texts for elite education, and they are noted with some frequency.

My sense is that it is substantially overstating the situation to imply that the Tang literary elite memorized the *Wenxuan* the way they memorized certain classical texts for the exams. There is no doubt that the liter-

70. *XTS*, 115.4215.

71. In this context, recall Yu Song's surprise that Zhang Xun had apparently set this entire text to memory.

72. Du Fu, "Zongwu shengri" 宗武生日, Qiu, 17.1477.

73. Du Fu, "Shuige zhaoji fengjian Yun'an Yan Mingfu" 水閣朝霽奉簡雲安嚴明府, Qiu, 14.1248. The line in question reads 續兒誦文選 and seems to indicate that Du Fu is filling in when his son gets stuck in his recitations. It is worth noting that we cannot tell for sure if Du Fu is doing this from memory or is looking at a text as his son recites.

74. Han Yu, "Zhong dafu Shanfu zuosima Li gong muzhiming" 中大夫陝府左司馬李公墓誌名, in Ma, 7.542.

ary models found in the *Wenxuan* were crucially important for the composition section of the *jinshi* exam and that candidates were expected to demonstrate great familiarity with the texts it contained when composing their own exam compositions. As David McMullen notes:

> The *Wenxuan* was never, like the Confucian canons, an "established" text, no statutory provision existed for teaching it officially, and, essential though mastery of it was for composition skills, its status was guaranteed by the great prestige of the *belle lettres* it incorporated rather than by official provision.[75]

He later points out that its prestige suffered in the period after the An Lushan Rebellion when many scholars attacked the importance given to compositional skills on the exams.[76] But the key issue is not so much whether people could accurately recite the *Wenxuan* from beginning to end, but rather how people related to such texts. The issue of internalization is again a critical one here. It is clear that the "order" or "order of things," the *li* 理,[77] embodied in the literary models of the *Wenxuan* were a part of literary training, as Du Fu's admonition to his son demonstrates. Internalization of this "order" initially proceeded not from detached criticism, but from reciting the text until it was deeply familiar. Exam candidates and indeed literate men in general would have been expected to comprehend and use allusions from the *Wenxuan* and be able to imitate its style. Memorizing the full text would have made such endeavors easier, but it was not necessary.

Method: How Did They Memorize?

Medieval Europeans employed a wide array of carefully honed techniques to set texts to memory. Scholars such as Mary Carruthers and Francis Yates have shown that a "trained memory" in that period was "educated and disciplined according to a well-developed pedagogy that was part of the elementary language arts—grammar, logic, and rhetoric."[78] Practitio-

75. McMullen, *State and Scholars*, 224.

76. Ibid., 225.

77. For the reasons for translating *li* as "order" in this context see Owen, *Late Tang*, 158.

78. Carruthers, *Book of Memory*, 7. See also Francis Yates, *Art of Memory*; Coleman, *Ancient and Medieval Memories*; and Carruthers and Ziolkowski, eds., *Medieval Craft of Memory*.

ners of these memorial techniques were able to keep huge amounts of text in their heads for ready recall whenever needed—a skill that was particularly important in an era in which texts were not always easy to obtain. Chinese in the period roughly from the end of the Han through the Tang faced fewer limitations imposed by material culture. In the Tang especially, widespread use of paper meant that texts were much easier to acquire, reproduce, and circulate. At the same time, scholarly norms and the exam system required the literate elite in China to set to memory substantial amounts of text.

With memorization playing such an important role in education, we might expect that the Chinese would have developed their own carefully articulated theories and treatises on memorization by the Tang period. Surprisingly, they did not. There are no received texts that point to the sort of sustained discourse on systematic practices to train and improve one's memory that were common in medieval Europe. When we examine accounts of either extraordinary or ordinary memories for the type of detailed descriptions of method that European writings provide, we are left with little to go on in terms of theoretical treatments. Consider the account of Chang Jingzhong discussed above. Zhang Yue never tests Chang on his original claim of being able to recite one thousand words after reading them once, but instead offers to test a logical extension of that claim based on a correspondence between repetition and length, rather than, say, time and length. The assumption is that only through repeated readings would it be possible for Chang to remember this new material. In essence, Zhang expects him to engage in a condensed version of the type of method used by children and adolescents memorizing the classics that we will see below. And Chang indeed does use repetition. Though he does not need the full number allotted, he also does not claim to have achieved his goal after a single time through. The only conclusion we are left to draw is that perhaps Chang was simply gifted with a better memory than most, and that he, Xing Shao, and Yixing were indeed lucky enough to have exceptional talents in a culture that valued such things greatly.

This lack of a theoretical discourse does not, however, imply lack of method. We know that people did memorize substantial amounts of text and that they therefore must have followed certain established practices of doing so. The challenge then is to examine these practices not through prescriptive historical treatises on them (which we lack), but by looking at descriptions of the practices themselves.

For Tang children, true memory training probably began with such primers as the *Qianzi wen* and the *Meng qiu*, noted above. Unlike texts they would encounter later in their education, these primers were specifically written to aid memorization. As Li Hua points out in his preface to the *Meng qiu*, the incidents it narrates were set to rhyme in order to make the text "easy to recite." The method here is thus part of the structure of the text. Material is ordered on the phonetic level through this use of rhyme. Metrically similar lines of four characters further reinforce the rhyme by putting the phonetic repetition in the same place. Rhyme appears to be an almost universal way of making language more memorable. As the cognitive psychologist David C. Rubin points out, "The repetition of sound is an aid to memory. When a sound repeats, the first occurrence of the sound limits the choices for the second occurrence and provides a strong cue for it."[79] Rhyme provides a phonetic context in which to place data and make it easier to bring back to one's active consciousness. This quality of rhyme, which seems intuitively clear, is also backed by modern research showing its effectiveness in aiding memory.[80] While many of the texts they would memorize later, such as the *Analects* and even the *Xiaojing*, are not in rhyme, training in memorization with the easier primers accustomed children to setting chunks of language to memory.

The content of primers also helped students to more easily memorize classical texts by, indeed, "priming" their minds through introducing many of the historical figures, themes, and events they would encounter in later works. The *Qianzi wen* includes lines about historical personages ranging from Yao 堯 and Shun 舜 to Mencius 孟子 and even the famous beauty Xi Shi 西施; tells of the rise and fall of the Xia 夏, Shang 商, and Zhou 周 dynasties; and sets down rules of proper behavior and decorum in both the royal court and the home. The *Meng qiu* has similar aims, with each of its 596 lines introducing an important figure from the past, whether historical or legendary. In his preface, Li Hua claims of children who study the *Meng qiu* that, "of what is important in the classics, the histories, and [the writings] of the Hundred Schools, they will get four or

79. Rubin, *Memory in Oral Traditions*, 75.
80. Ibid., 75–76.

five out of ten" 經史百家之要，十得其四五矣.[81] The motivation behind such works was no doubt primarily to introduce young readers to historical and moral ideals for the sake of those ideas themselves, that is, to start them down the road to becoming moral and knowledgeable adults. At the same time, the primers ensured that when students encountered important figures, themes, and events in the classics and histories, they would already have at least a passing familiarity with them, a base which would make later learning more meaningful. Modern research shows that meaningfulness matters for retention. The psychologist and memory expert Alan Baddeley has noted that "a crucial factor in deciding whether something will be learned and remembered is the meaningfulness to the learner."[82] Just as rhyme provides a phonetic context, familiar terms and names benefit from a "semantic context" that facilitates memory.

There is some question as to whether or not Tang children beginning their education truly understood what they were setting to memory. Charles Hartman writes of the Tang educational process:

> In traditional China this process began when a child of six or seven copied out and memorized selected passages of text, even though those passages made little or no sense to him when read aloud. This process continued until the age of eleven or twelve, at which time a teacher began to explain the meanings of individual graphs and specific phrases.[83]

Certain texts and parts of texts that children memorized in the Tang may well have been abstruse to them without instruction, and especially when encountered only aurally. The *Qianzi wen* is an uneven mix in this regard.

---

81. *QTW*, *Tangwen shiyi*, 19.10574.

82. Baddeley, *Essentials of Human Memory*, 72.

83. Hartman, *Han Yü*, 235. If Hartman is correct, this would be an interesting example of Tang memorization practices taking advantage of a surprising feature of memory: though texts that are meaningful to the memorizer are easier to set to memory, they are also more likely to be altered in the process of recollection due to interference from newly learned and related materials, as Baddeley has noted. See Baddeley, *Human Memory*, 246–47. George Dreyfus (*Sound of Two Hands Clapping*, 95) has discussed this phenomenon in relation to memorization practices in Tibetan Buddhism in which monks are taught a technique of "disassociating texts from meaning before committing them to memory." Because the monks then memorize sonic patterns rather than meaningful linguistic constructions, the verbatim text remains more deeply inscribed in their memories. Of course the fact that written Chinese does not use a phonetic alphabet complicates this issue.

A line like "Women respect the chaste and pure / men model themselves on the talented and good" 女慕貞絜，男效才良, was probably close enough to the spoken vernacular and sufficiently free of allusions that it would have been readily understandable to a seven-year-old child. Yet "turning over the throne and yielding the realm / there were the rulers of Yu, Tao, and Tang" 推位讓國，有虞陶唐, with its political language and references to early sage kings, would surely have required more explanation. The lines in the *Meng qiu* are even more seemingly cryptic, with each line consisting of a two-character name followed by a two-character phrase to characterize that person. Without explanation, a child would be unlikely to understand that a line such as "Yang Xu suspends a fish" 羊續懸魚 refers to being an incorruptible official and thus failing to win high office.[84]

Assuming that primers were the types of texts that students would begin learning at age six or seven, the evidence suggests that they learned the meaning of what they memorized from the very beginning. Such scholars as Gu Meng were paid to offer instruction in the *Qianzi wen* and we can assume he would discuss the meaning of the passages he taught rather than limiting his instruction to teaching his students how to write and pronounce the characters. In Li Hua's preface to the *Meng qiu* he emphasizes the historical figures and facts that children would learn from it and notes that Li Han includes his own explanatory notes of the terse lines of the rhyming text.[85] Hartman is surely correct that students practiced reciting texts before they fully understood them, just as children today memorize prayers or recite the "Pledge of Allegiance" before they grasp their full meaning and history and before they understand such individual words as "hallowed" or "indivisible." This is quite different, however, from spending five or six years learning seemingly meaningless sound patterns and symbols. The content of these works mattered; it was important for students to understand what the words they were learning meant before moving on to work on the classical texts. It is thus doubtful that their teachers would have neglected to teach them the "meanings of individual graphs" until years later. The use of primers in the Tang and earlier strongly implies that "meaningful" instruction in texts began quite early

84. For the background to this line see Watson, *Meng Ch'iu*, 58–59.

85. *QTW*, *Tangwen shiyi*, 19.10574.

in the educational process and well before students would tackle the classics themselves.

Whether for learning a children's primer or the *Analects*, the preferred method of memorization itself from antiquity through the Tang (and beyond) was rote repetition. Students learned texts by spending untold hours repeating them, primarily through oral recitation but also by copying them out in writing. This method of memorization simultaneously served as a means of textual reproduction and storage. Each session of practice produced a new copy of the text that would exist for only fleeting moments in the case of oral recitation, or much longer if it involved creating a new written text. From not long after paper became the predominant medium for written works, there are examples of students copying out texts as part of the process of setting them to memory. The following account from the biography of Ge Hong 葛洪 (283–343), author of the *Baopuzi* 抱朴子, is typical:

> In his youth [Ge] Hong was fond of study. As his family was poor, he would chop kindling himself to trade for paper and brushes. At night he would always copy out writings and study by reciting.
> 洪少好學，家貧，躬自伐薪以貿紙筆，夜輒寫書誦習。[86]

Here we see the close connection between reproducing texts orally and through writing; both activities serve to fix texts in the memory through repetition. The more times someone reproduces a text, the more likely he is to remember it. Given the mention of Ge Hong's poverty, it is likely that he was copying texts that he did not himself possess. A similar account of the Wei figure Li Biao 李彪 makes such a connection explicit. After mentioning Li's poverty, his biography notes that his friend Gao Yue's 高悅 family had many books and that "when Biao was at [Gao] Yue's home he would copy things out and recite them, not stopping to sleep or eat" 彪遂於悅家手抄口誦，不暇寢食.[87]

Both these accounts point to different levels of possessing a text. Copying provided Ge Hong and Li Biao with physical copies of the books they sought; it gave them new material possession of the texts they reproduced. Material possession, however, did not indicate possession on the level of

---

86. *Jin shu* 晉書, 72.1911.
87. *Wei shu* 魏書, 62.1381.

internalization, that is, making the texts their own by setting them to memory. In each case the biographies thus specify that they combined copying with recitation. Because of their financial straits, we can assume that they would copy a given text only once (thus avoiding the cost of extra paper). To commit the text to memory and truly possess it not just as a physical object, but as a store of internalized knowledge, required the hard work of repeated recitation.

Sources mention recitation far more often than copying in the context of memorizing texts, and it is clear that the practice would be conducted repeatedly and over long stretches of time. We saw above how Kong Yingda and Sun Simiao were said to recite a thousand words a day in their studies starting from a very young age. There are similar accounts of other Tang figures: Kong Shaoan 孔紹安 "shut his door and read, reciting many millions of words of collected ancient writings" 閉門讀書，誦古文集數十萬言.[88] Lu Yuqing 陸餘慶 similarly "shut his door and recited works for three years" 閉户誦書三年.[89] The term *song* can mean both to recite while reading a written text and to recite from memory. Though the latter meaning was more common in the Tang, the connection between the two is telling: the goal of reciting while reading a text, especially in any educational context, was often to set that text to memory. When proof of memorization was offered, it was typically through oral recitation (with some sections of the exams that I discuss below being exceptions).[90]

Memorization as a key goal of study was common to students and scholars in both medieval Europe and Six Dynasties and Tang China, yet the methods could not be more different. Medieval Europeans relied heavily on mental manipulation of texts and visual associations. The memorizer would break texts up into manageable pieces and arrange them in a structure of his own fashioning so that they could be retrieved at will and in any order. Carruthers notes that:

---

88. *JTS*, 190.4983.

89. *XTS*, 116.4239.

90. Though as of the exam reform of 737, the *mingjing* exams included an oral portion on the "general meaning of the classics" which would surely have involved some recitation to bolster the candidates' arguments. See Herbert, "Curriculum and Content," 156.

One accomplishment which seems always to have been greatly admired by both ancient and medieval writers was the ability to recite a text backwards as well as forwards, or to skip around in it in a systematic way, without becoming lost or confused. The ability to do this marked the difference between merely being able to imitate something (to reproduce it exactly) and really knowing it, being able to recall it in various ways.[91]

Discussions of this type of memory feat are extremely rare in the case of medieval China. There are scattered descriptions of people reciting or copying texts out backwards,[92] but these do not figure in most accounts of even the most prodigious memories. Indeed, the memorial practices that formed the foundation of learning in the Tang and before would have been shown little respect by their European counterparts. As Carruthers explains, "Rote repetition, since it is not 'found out' by any heuristic scheme, is not considered recollection or true memory (*memoria*)."[93]

Another important difference between these two traditions is the role of the visual in memorial practices. European techniques depended heavily on the creation of mental images to attach to lines and portions of text for rapid recall later.[94] As Carruthers demonstrates, the illuminations found in so many medieval European manuscripts were not merely for decoration, but rather played important roles in providing "mnemonically valuable images" for their readers.[95] In the Chinese case, there is little evidence that texts of the classics or other parts of the "high" literary tradition were intentionally arranged or illustrated in ways that would have provided clues for visual memory. Texts often lacked punctuation, and the physical layout for poetry would have been no different from that for prose. Written texts were, to some extent, more like transposed recitations than carefully laid out arrangements of visual mnemonic clues. In-

---

91. Carruthers, *Book of Memory*, 18.

92. For an account of Lu Zhuangdao 盧莊道 reciting texts backwards (*daosong* 倒誦) on command, see *Taiping guangji*, 174.1286. See also the discussion of Feng Gu writing backwards noted earlier in this chapter.

93. Carruthers, *Book of Memory*, 20.

94. Ibid., 59.

95. Ibid., 243. For her full discussion of the mnemonic roles of book decoration see 242–57. For a good example of the use of visual images in medieval European memorial techniques, see Thomas Bradwardine (ca. 1300–1349) (Carruthers, trans.), "On Acquiring a Trained Memory," in Carruthers and Ziolkowski, *Medieval Craft of Memory*, 205–14.

deed, though most memorization in the Tang and Six Dynasties was textually based, a physical text was not necessarily a requisite for memorization, as the following anecdote concerning Gu Huan 顧歡 of the Southern Qi 南齊 dynasty shows:

> There was a school in their village, but as [Gu] Huan was poor he had no means to pursue his studies. He would lean on the back of the school's wall and listen, not forgetting a thing. By eight *sui*, he could recite the *Xiaojing*, the *Shi*, and the *Analects*.
>
> 鄉中有學舍，歡貧無以受業，於舍壁後倚聽，無遺忘者．八歲，誦孝經、詩、論．[96]

The point of this passage is Gu Huan's excellent memory, yet it also reaffirms the importance of repeated recitations. As he leaned against the school wall, Gu Huan would presumably hear not only the teacher's explanations of the text at hand, but also his and the students' continuous oral recitations of that text. Even without a written copy, Gu Huan could practice along with the unseen students using a very similar method. Unlike medieval Europeans, scholars of the Tang and Six Dynasties *did* value reciting classical texts exactly (and in the original order) and indeed considered this to be proof of "really knowing it."

Indeed, when Matteo Ricci introduced to some of his acquaintances in Ming dynasty China the European method of the "memory palace" or loci method,[97] they were impressed but showed no great interest in adopting the method themselves.[98] Rote repetition may not lend itself to discussion in treatises, but it clearly worked. We know this to be the case from the ample evidence that medieval Chinese scholars set to memory many hundreds of pages of difficult texts before they had reached adulthood. They also kept these texts in their memories to the extent that reciting portions of them became almost second nature.

---

96. *Nan Qi shu*, 54.928.

97. The many variations of the loci method, typically based on placing items to be recalled in specific geographic or architectural locations, either real or imaginary, are discussed in detail throughout both Francis Yates and Carruthers, *Book of Memory*. The psychologist Kenneth L. Higbee provides a straightforward description of loci methods and how they remain in use in modern times in *Your Memory*, 144–156.

98. Jonathon Spence, *Memory Palace of Matteo Ricci*, 4.

Modern research on memory has further demonstrated the effectiveness of Chinese techniques. As we have seen, these practices essentially involve spending an extended amount of time, often decades of one's life, reproducing texts repeatedly, primarily through recitation but also through copying. Psychological experiments have clearly shown that the amount someone can remember and the accuracy of that memory is to some extent determined by the amount of time they spend studying the items to be recalled. This is called the "total time hypothesis."[99] Memory is further enhanced by structuring trials, or occasions on which the subject would be called upon to demonstrate that he has memorized a text by repeating it aloud or reproducing it in written form, such that they occur repeatedly over a prolonged period of time, what is referred to as the "distribution of practice effect."[100] Though we do not know a great deal about the specifics of instructional educational practices in medieval China, it does seem that teachers would frequently call upon students to recite substantial portions of the texts they were studying. Were students to make mistakes, the teachers would then correct them and eventually test the students in a similar manner at sometime in the future.[101] Given that students often engaged in this type of study from as early as age seven to adulthood, it is little surprise that they were able to memorize substantial amounts of text.

Limitations and Accuracy

The bulk of our discussion thus far has focused on the strengths of memorial practices in medieval China. There is no question that educated men of this period were skilled memorizers who spent a good deal of their education reciting and copying classical texts until they knew them intimately. At the same time, as I caution in the introduction to this chapter,

---

99. Baddeley, *Essentials of Human Memory*, 72.

100. For further discussion see Bahrick, "Long-Term Maintenance of Knowledge," 355. See also Baddeley, *Essentials of Human Memory*, 73; Landauer and Bjork, "Optimal Rehearsal Patterns and Name Learning," 625–32; and Goody, *Interface Between the Written and the Oral*, 177.

101. McMullen (*State and Scholars*, 18) notes that instruction in the classics and commentaries in the state academy directorate, which focused on preparing students for the civil service exams, involved "regular internal examinations to monitor progress."

it is important that we not exaggerate these memorial abilities. The question of limitations is a complex one that benefits from examination from a number of different angles. I first return to comparisons between medieval European and medieval Chinese techniques. We should not assume that these vastly different approaches for setting texts to memory produced similar results, and I therefore look at some possible differences. A larger question with which this study is concerned is the stability of texts through the process of transmission. I thus also address the question of how accurate textual memories in this period really were and to what extent we should assume they transmitted texts faithfully. While we cannot know for certain how accurately educated people in the Tang memorized texts, the type of memorization tested on the exams, for example, can give us a general sense of expectations. Related to this is the role of memorized texts in composition, both on the exam and elsewhere. Though memorization was an important part of learning to write literary Chinese for younger students, exact recollection of past texts was not strictly necessary when adults composed.

The primary area in which we might conclude that Chinese methods are lacking in comparison to those of their medieval European counterparts is at the level of encoding. Related to this is the ability to rapidly memorize new texts without spending substantial time on repetition. Turning again to modern research on memory, we find evidence that while rote repetition is effective, it is less so than more elaborate encoding techniques. Rote repetition is sometimes referred to as "maintenance rehearsal" in contrast to "elaborative rehearsal, in which information is meaningfully related to other information, presented either previously or currently."[102] The latter has been proven to be more effective, as "the greater the elaboration—or extensiveness—of one's encodings, the better the subsequent memory."[103] The European memorial methods that Carruthers and Yates describe, whether based on variations of the loci method or on visual associations with particular portions of a text (and both would often be used in conjunction), appear to involve substantially more elaborate encoding than Chinese methods did. As Carruthers de-

102. Brown and Craik, "Encoding and Retrieval of Information," 96.

103. Ibid. See also Craik and Tulving, "Depth of Processing and the Retention of Words in Episodic Memory," 268–94.

scribes it, "Recollection occurs consciously through association: one finds or hunts out the stored memory-impressions by using other things associated with it either through a logical connection or through 'habit' (*consuetudo*), the sort of associations taught by the various *artes memorativa*."[104] Chunks of texts are placed within a complex semantic and visual web of associations that have often been pre-established by the learning as part of a larger mnemonic structure. This allows sections of text to be retrieved through a variety of avenues, as Carruthers notes. While it is possible that medieval Chinese might have created similar webs of associates for the texts they had memorized through repeated recitations, there is no extant evidence for it. The lack of any treatises on such practices further implies that they were at least not commonly used.

There are interesting hints of dissatisfaction with the practice of rote memorization within the Chinese tradition itself. Even Confucius, who famously extolled the value of learning the *Shi*, implied that rote memorization alone had its limits:

> The Master said, "Imagine a person who can recite the several hundred odes by heart but, when delegated a government task, is unable to carry it out, or when sent abroad as an envoy, is unable to engage in repartee. No matter how many odes he might have memorized, what good are they to him?
> 子曰：誦詩三百，授之以政，不達；使於四方，不能專對；雖多，亦奚以爲。[105]

The question here is specifically of use. The *Shi* were not to be memorized for the sake of memorization alone. They were memorized, in part, as an aid to interstate diplomacy, forming a set of common references shared by the various states, and could thus be used as a rhetorical element in speeches and debates. This called for an ability to locate the proper portion of the appropriate poem quickly and without recourse to a written text. It is just this sort of retrieval that is the strong point of more complex mnemonic systems. Carruthers notes that such a system "provides one with a 'random-access' memory system, by means of which one can immediately and securely find a particular bit of information...."[106] More-

104. Carruthers, *Book of Memory*, 20.
105. Ruan, *Shisanjing*, 13.116. Translation from Slingerland, *Analects*, 141.
106. Carruthers, *Book of Memory*, 7.

over, as Confucius is concerned not simply with the speed of retrieval, but with the appropriateness of a given passage to the context at hand, a system that encodes in part through the use of semantic associations might be particularly useful. There can be no doubt that talented students who had memorized the *Shi* could also quickly come up with passages fitting to specific contexts, but their method of setting the text to memory does not appear to have been designed to facilitate such a skill.

An additional consequence of the less complex if more grueling techniques used by Chinese students and scholars is that they did not lend themselves to quickly learning new material. Because such techniques as the loci method essentially create a substantial apparatus in which to insert new material continuously, they are particularly useful for organizing information that one encounters for the first time.[107] For obvious reasons, such a system would not be necessary in a context in which one was expected to spend most of the years of childhood and adolescence learning a previously delineated set of classical texts. It would, however, be very useful in memorizing new works that one had only heard or read once or twice.

Anxiety about the accuracy of memory can be taken as a feature of the modern period in which we are unaccustomed to relying on memory as a way to meaningfully interact with texts. As Carruthers points out, "medieval scholars simply did not share our distrust of memory's 'accuracy.'"[108] Rather, they saw memory as no less reliable (and sometimes more reliable) than the various manuscripts that circulated with so many variants. The question of accuracy is even more difficult to examine in the Chinese case, as the discourse on memory is so relatively sparse. We have seen how accounts of exceptional memory often claim that the subject reproduced memorized texts without a single error (even when there were no original texts against which to check). Accounts of more quotidian memory, such as common biographical notes that someone had a strong memory or could recite a classic or two at an early age, rarely touch on the question of exact accuracy.

---

107. For this reason, such techniques are widely used by entertainers and others who are presented as having "photographic memories." For a well-known and studied example, see Luria, *Mind of a Mnemonist*.

108. Carruthers, *Book of Memory*, 160.

I would argue that the available evidence implies that perfectly accurate textual memories were probably the exception rather than the rule. The only explicit and official testing of memorization in the Tang in a non-religious context occurred as part of the *mingjing* and *jinshi* exams, both of which for most of the dynasty included sections requiring candidates to reproduce only very small portions of classical texts with perfect accuracy. Beginning in 681, the exams tested pure memorization primarily by means of the *tiejing* 帖經 method, in which strips of paper would be used to cover up three consecutive characters in a number of lines of a given classical text. The candidate would have to fill in the missing characters to prove that he had accurately set the text to memory.[109] Such a test ostensibly determined whether or not a candidate had fully memorized a given classic, but as it did so by means of a random sampling, there would always be substantial room for doubt. A candidate who had not fully set the required texts to memory could simply be fortunate enough to encounter sections that he had, and the provision of the text surrounding the covered characters certainly made the task far easier. As candidates were only required to provide three characters out of a larger portion of text, a candidate who recognized the passage and knew its general intent might well be able to guess the correct characters. More likely, cheating rather than luck often played a part; it would be all too easy for word of what passages the examiners had chosen to leak out prior to the exam, rendering its effectiveness as a true test of memorization even less valuable.[110]

There are examples of more rigorous requirements for exact memorial reproduction of texts, but they are typically found in religious contexts. For example, to become ordained, the state required monks to pass a recitation exam consisting of a set number of pages of sutras. Erik Zücher points out that "the general picture is one of an erratic policy, without stable guidelines and subject to great fluctuation. The amount of memorization varied from a very reasonable 150 pages (about one-half of the *Lo-*

109. Herbert, "Curriculum and Content," 156.

110. Herbert ("Curriculum and Content," 156) notes of the *tiejing* portions that "They were open to abuse by candidates and examiners alike and their objectiveness and effectiveness were seriously questioned. Nevertheless, they remained a part of the *mingjing* and *jinshi* examinations throughout the dynasty."

tus sutra) to the extreme demand of 1,000 pages."[111] Recall that candidates for the *mingjing* exam were responsible for between one hundred and three hundred thousand characters. As Zürcher estimates that a sutra page would consist of about five hundred characters, at various points in the dynasty ordination candidates would have been required to recite from memory between seventy-five thousand and five hundred thousand characters. Not only could this amount to far more text than was required for even the most difficult combination of classics for the *mingjing* degree (a combination which, moreover, few if any candidates were willing to be tested on), the texts had to be recited completely from beginning to end, a task more difficult by many orders of magnitude.[112] As the *jinshi* exam, which became a far more prominent and popular path to officialdom as the Tang progressed, required even less explicit memorization than did the *mingjing*, it is clear that contexts requiring perfectly accurate textual reproduction of any substantial length were rarely encountered by adults who did not intend to become ordained.

In fact, while there are many examples of adults memorizing texts in medieval China, the kind of systematic memorization tested by at intervals by recitation with pedagogical corrections appears to be primarily a feature of childhood and adolescence. Again we see a contrast with the situation in medieval Europe in which memorial techniques were used and practiced as much by adults as by younger students. European techniques developed systems that could be applied to any new texts one encountered. Chinese practices required instead a great outlay of time for learning any lengthy text. It is thus not surprising that the bulk of memorization took place before the demands of adulthood meant that substantial blocks of time would not be available.[113]

---

111. Zürcher, "Buddhism and Education in T'ang Times," 33.

112. It is not clear how many errors in such recitations would be allowed. We find similar requirements in Tibetan Buddhist monastic practices. Dreyfus (*Sound of Two Hands Clapping*, 90) writes, "The liturgy of these [Tibetan] monasteries includes hundreds of folios whose memorization requires several years of extremely demanding effort. The knowledge of new monks is tested: on a number of occasions they must recite the entire liturgy of the monastery in front of their peers."

113. The question of why such different techniques were used in medieval Europe and China is an interesting one but would take us well beyond the boundaries of this study. Everything from the greater accessibility of texts in China, especially by the late medieval

This distinction between different stages in one's education and linguistic abilities also provides a useful approach to the issue of the roles memorized texts played in literary composition in medieval China. I argue above that memorization was an important aspect of how younger students learned to function in literary Chinese. Setting both primers and portions of classical texts to memory gave them the basic vocabulary of words, phrases, and allusions that they could draw on when composing their own pieces. There is no question that early compositions would be highly imitative, with numerous phrases taken directly from the student's memorized store of source texts.[114] Again, literary Chinese was a language learned not through conversation with other people, but through continuous encounters with texts, whether written or intoned aloud. Memorizing those texts made them a part of one's own linguistic foundation.

---

period, to the state's interest in promoting a particular type of learning and the different contexts in which people would be called upon to rely on their textual memories clearly played a part. The mental rearrangement of texts, which Carruthers (*Book of Memory*, 164) notes "violates most of our notions concerning 'accuracy,' 'objective scholarship,' and 'the integrity of the text,'" might also have seemed problematic to medieval Chinese scholars. For such texts as the *Shi* and the *Chunqiu*, the order in which passages appeared was considered to convey subtle judgments made by Confucius himself. It is certainly conceivable that mental manipulation of this order would have been seen as violating these texts in a fundamental way.

114. Hartman (*Han Yü*, 235–36) discusses in detail the process of learning to compose. While I agree with the general notion that juvenile compositions would have been highly imitative, I do not accept many of Hartman's larger claims here. The notion that "every graph constitutes an allusion to the memorization corpus" (236) appears to imagine the Tang brain as containing perfectly articulated hypertext in which every word instantly brings up all its previous instances of use. This seems to me an overly idealized portrait of how people related to texts in this period. Were all educated people to have mastered a true "memorization corpus" to this extent, the tests of memorization on the exams would have been essentially meaningless. Also problematic is the comment that "Since the meanings of the graphs are learned from a designated corpus of texts, there is little room for the variations in meaning that arise when an author confronts words as they relate in a living language to the real world" (236). The fact that literary Chinese was learned from texts rather than the real world does not seem to imply that there would be "little room for the variations in meaning." If anything, we might imagine the opposite to be true. Spoken languages typically function within a constant feedback loop. If someone does not understand my intended meaning, I am more likely to pick up on this and correct him than, for instance, a written text would be. The notion that there would be little room for variation in the meaning of texts such as the *Shi* as it was received in the Tang is simply untenable.

It is clear that the literary past, from the classics to the works contained in the *Wenxuan* anthology, continued to play an important part in compositional practices when adults set brush to paper as well. Descriptions of composition from the medieval period invariably note the importance of basing one's own writing on the models provided by certain earlier texts. Lu Ji's 陸機 (261–303) *Wenfu* 文賦 ("Poetic Exposition on Literature") speaks in typical terms when it says the writer "nourishes feeling and intent in the ancient canons" 頤情志於典墳 or "roams in the groves and treasure houses of literary works" 游文章之林府.[115] Liu Xie's 劉勰 (ca. 465–522) *Wenxin diaolong* 文心雕龍 ("The Literary Mind and the Carving of Dragons") from the late fifth or early sixth century likewise describes the classics as "the profound source of all writings, and the spiritual realm in which talent and imagination make their abode" 實群言之奥區，而才思之神臯.[116] This emphasis on the literary past in composition continues throughout the Tang (and indeed through the entire imperial period). As McMullen points out, the early Tang court "set value on an effortless command of the inherited tradition and on dexterity in composing."[117] Such Tang writers as Han Yu use phrases similar to those in the *Wenfu* and *Wenxin diaolong* in descriptions of composition. In his famous "Letter in Reply to Li Yi" 答李翊書 Han Yu claims that his writing "travels to the source of the *Shi* and the *Shu*" 游之乎詩書之源.[118] In all these cases the composer is assumed to have a deep familiarity with the literary tradition and to base his writings on it to some extent.

A key distinction must be made between the type of relationship with past literary models described in these passages and memorization *per se*. I would contend that what we see here are descriptions of internalization based on a profound understanding of the texts in question. This is ultimately not a question of exact words, but of ideas and ways of thinking, of cultural forms.[119] In fact, we find numerous criticisms of excessive reliance on the exact words found in past texts, even those of the classics, and

115. Zhang Shaokang, ed., *Wenfu jiyi* 文賦集釋, 20. Translation from Owen, *Readings in Chinese Literary Thought*, 87, 92.

116. Liu Xie 劉勰, *Wenxin diaolong zhu* 文心雕龍諸, 615. Translation from Vincent Yu-chung Shih, *Literary Mind*, 397.

117. McMullen, *State and Scholars*, 211.

118. Ma, 3.170.

119. Bol, *This Culture of Ours*, 76.

praise for original wording. In the *Wenxin diaolong* Liu Xie says of the great poets of the *Chuci* 楚辭 ("Lyrics of Chu") Song Yu 宋玉 and Qu Yuan 屈原 that although they "followed the example of the *Shi* poets...they did not use their old diction" 號依詩人・・・莫取舊辭.[120] This criticism becomes more pointed in the Tang, with Bai Juyi complaining that students "recite the texts of the *Shi* and the *Shu*, but do not understand the meaning of the *Shi* and the *Shu*" 誦詩書之文而不知詩書之旨.[121] Bai saw students slavishly preparing for the exam without bothering to ponder the real meaning and implications of what they were so diligently setting to memory. Han Yu, while he acknowledged the importance of the literary past, also differentiated between the exact words and phrases of those texts and the basic tenets that they embodied. In his "Letter in Reply to Liu Zhengfu" 答劉正夫書 he advises the recipient to engage with the ancients by "taking their ideas as a model, not taking their diction as a model" 師其意，不師其辭.[122] Similarly, in his "Letter in Reply to Li Yi," the same piece in which he claims his writings "travel to the source of the *Shi* and the *Shu*," he notes his efforts to expunge "clichés" 陳言 from his compositions.[123] Finally recall that Du Fu specifically advised his son to master the "order" of the *Wenxuan*, rather than emphasizing the ability to reproduce the texts verbatim.

The distinction here between memorization and mastery of cultural forms or internalization is an important one if we are to get a sense of the role of precise memorization in medieval society. If internalization was the preeminent goal for Tang writers, a goal that did not depend on scholars' long-term ability to recall the exact words of texts, then this is further indication (in addition to the limited memorization requirements of the exams) that educated people in the Tang were *not* expected to hold perfect copies of texts in their heads. Indeed, there were numerous works written specifically to take the place of memorized texts. The essay enti-

---

120. Liu Xie, *Wenxin diaolong zhu*, 615.

121. Bai Juyi, "Celin liushi, jiaoxuezhe zhi shi" 策林六十、教學者之失 ("Forest of Policy Essay, Number 60: Omissions in Education"), Zhu, 65.3535.

122. Ma, 3.206. This translation follows Hartman's (*Han Yü*, 254).

123. Ma, 3.170. Liu Zongyuan's 柳宗元 ideas on composition follow similar lines. See discussion in Bol, *This Culture of Ours*, 140–43.

tled "Discussion of Literary Ideas" 論文意 from the *Bunkyō hifuron* 文鏡秘府論 anthology (eighth century)[124] states:

All poets themselves copy out the fine sections of poetic language from ancient times and today. These are called 'personal notebooks' and are used to keep melancholy at bay. If the inspiration to compose does not come, then you should look at your personal notebook to bring it forth.
凡作詩之人，皆自抄古今詩語精妙之處，名爲隨身卷子，以防苦思。作文興不來，即須看隨身卷子，以發興也。[125]

The advice in this passage acknowledges the role of the literary past (and present) as inspiration for one's own writings, but it does not assume that the poet would have continuous mental access to those works. Here, I think we are seeing the effect of cheap and available paper. In a written culture based on parchment and vellum, like that of medieval Europe, it would have been substantially more expensive to keep "personal notebooks" for writing down lines of poems that struck one's fancy. The increasing technological maturity of written culture in the Tang may not have replaced a trained memory, but it was beginning to change the role that memory played.

A more complex example of this is found not in poetry manuals like the "Discussion of Literary Ideas," but in the genre of *leishu* 類書.[126] McMullen refers to such works when he notes that in the medieval period "mastery [of the inherited tradition] had been facilitated by short reference works and by larger reference collections."[127] The *leishu* genre comprises a wide range of different works, from smaller sets of poetic quotes associated with certain topics, to massive collections with copious writings on topics ranging from government to natural history. They con-

124. A collection of Six Dynasties and Tang writings on poetry and poetics preserved in Japan. See Kūkai 空海 (Zhou Weide, ed.), *Wenjing mifulun* 文鏡秘府論. For a translation and discussion of the *Bunkyō hifuron*, see Bodman, "Poetics and Prosody."

125. *Wenjing mifulun*, 132.

126. While *leishu* is often translated as "encyclopedia," a more accurate rendering would be something like "writings divided by category." *Leishu* are a massive topic and I will only touch on them in the most cursory fashion here. Some useful introductions include Liu Yeqiu, *Leishu jianshuo*; Hu Daojing, *Zhongguo gudai de leishu*; and DeWoskin, "Lei-shu." McMullen lists some important Tang and pre-Tang examples in *State and Scholars*, 357*n*8.

127. McMullen, *State and Scholars*, 211.

sisted not of original writings, but of selections from previously circulated works, ranging from the classics to recent poetry. Like the personal notebooks described in the *Bunkyō hifuron*, these collections served, in some sense, as replacements for extensive memorization. If a poet wanted to see the ways past writers had dealt with a poetic topic or image, he could consult an appropriate *leishu* and find a wealth of examples.

The similarities between medieval European memorial techniques on the one hand and *leishu* on the other are intriguing.[128] Recall that these memorial techniques often focused on tying information together in complex but systematic ways. They embedded pieces of texts in webs of connecting ideas and images. *Leishu* do something very similar in written form, as they synthesize a larger body of knowledge into smaller chunks organized by a variety of schemata including rhymes, generic divisions, and topics.[129] In fact, it is not at all unlikely that exam candidates and other educated people would have set substantial portions of *leishu* to memory as part of their literary education. Because of their organizational schema, these works would have represented a more efficient means of preparing for compositional portions of the *jinshi* exam than would attempting to memorize the entire *Wenxuan*. A candidate who had prepared for the exam with an appropriate *leishu* would have come in with a comprehensively ordered set of quotations from past works on any topic that he was likely to encounter on the exam. He might not have remembered every poetic exposition in the *Wenxuan*, but he would have been likely to know the accepted ways of writing about topics covered in those works. We do not, unfortunately, have specific descriptions of people memorizing portions of *leishu* in biographic writings from the Tang, and this is not entirely surprising. Such books did not themselves have the status of many of the works they excerpted, no matter how useful they might have been.

Human memories always have been and always will be prone to error, and the memories of educated people in medieval China were no exception. The human brain is not a hardwired computer whose circuits never

128. Some of my thinking on this topic has been influenced by personal communications with Robert Ashmore.

129. DeWoskin, "Lei-shu," 526. For more detailed descriptions of these organizational schemata see Hu Daojing, *Zhongguo gudai de leishu*, 8–14.

change, but ultimately a malleable organ shaped by the forces of evolution for purposes other than memorizing written texts. The strong memories of the literate audience in the Tang facilitated oral and written reproduction of texts without an original at hand on a large scale. They did not, however, make it infallible. The ability to memorize accurately all the poems produced in a night of revelry *was* exceptional. More importantly, it is abundantly clear that there were very few contexts in which perfect recollection of texts was necessary or expected. Composition was based on earlier models, but in most cases it was the ideas and general style of those models, rather than their exact words, that were important. Skilled composition required understanding the *li* of past models, the inherent order that they exhibited. Precise memorization may have played an important part in internalizing texts in the earlier stages of education, but its role was diminished as writers matured and found their own voices.

These limitations of memorial skills in medieval China are presented not as faults, but as a piece in the puzzle of how texts changed in the course of transmission. Imperfect memories reproduced literary works imperfectly. The constant flow of texts from oral to written form and back again, from person to person, and from one day to the next, inevitably produced the kind of variance and textual destabilization that we have seen in concrete form in the manuscripts examined in the first chapter and that we will continue to discuss throughout this study.

Memory and Poetic Circulation

To conclude this chapter I would like to turn briefly to the role of memorization in the circulation of contemporary poetry in the Tang, one of the larger concerns of this study. The connection between memorization and contemporary poetry presents an interesting set of issues, particularly for the topic of circulation.[130] This chapter has argued that textual memory in medieval China was valued and strong, but lacked the types of well articu-

130. In terms of poetic production, the points made about the role of memorization in composition above apply. As noted, internalization and memory in a broad sense are important aspects of composition of poetry and other genres. Memory is, of course, key to understanding allusions. But again, general memory here is very different from precise memorization. Allusions do not require perfect textual memory for either use by the author or understanding by the reader.

lated methods developed in medieval Europe and was far from infallible. In the Tang in particular, there is little evidence that contemporary non-poetic texts, ranging from personal letters to memorials, were regularly set to memory and circulated orally. As I argue above, medieval Chinese memorial techniques would not have been particularly efficient at setting new texts to memory. Texts that were regularly set to memory were done so through constant repetition, a practice that had additional goals beyond memorization *per se*. Finally, there was no exam-based incentive for candidates to specifically memorize contemporary works, whether of poetry or prose, as they would not even have been expected to show familiarity with these works on the compositional sections, let alone to memorize them for the *tiejing* portion.[131]

At the same time, the widespread oral circulation of poetry examined in Chapter 3 shows that contemporary poetry was indeed set to memory and recited with great frequency, not only by adults, but by children as well. There is evidence that the poems of Du Mu 杜牧 (803–52), Yuan Zhen, and Bai Juyi were taught to young children in schools late in the Tang, and we know that Du Fu taught his son Zongwu 宗武 to recite his poems.[132] In a memorial criticizing the exam system, Yang Wan 楊綰 (d. 777) laments that "when the young are capable of studying, they all recite contemporary poetry" 幼能就學，皆誦當代之詩.[133] The *Tang zhiyan* includes an interesting account of one Duan Wei 段維, who though not a child, was illiterate until the age of forty. When he sought instruction in the classics from teachers in the Zhongtiao Mountains 中條山, they first tested his memory with contemporary poems:

> The people there would not teach him the classics because he was an adult yet had not learned to read and write. Someone said, "Give him over a hundred regulated poems and have him chant them from memory." The next day [Duan] Wei

131. There was, of course, great incentive to become skilled at the composition of contemporary poems for the *jinshi* exam. This meant that candidates no doubt set substantial numbers of poems to memory as part of their practice of learning how to compose poems themselves, a practice to which Yang Wan, cited below, and many others objected.

132. For Du Mu see *QTS*, 614.7083. This is noted as well in Ji Yougong 計有功, *Tangshi jishi* 唐詩紀事, 66.994. For Yuan Zhen and Bai Juyi see Yuan Zhen, "Baishi changqingji xu" 白氏長慶集序, Zhu, "fulu" 2.3973. I will discuss the case of Du Fu teaching his son in Chapter 3.

133. Yang Wan, "Tiaozou gongju shu" 條奏貢舉疏, *QTW*, 331.3357.

was able to remember them all well. All the scholars thought this extraordinary...They thereupon taught him the *Xiaojing*.
眾以年長猶未發蒙，不與授經．或曰：以律詩白餘篇俾其諷誦．翌日維能強記，諸生異之．．．因授之孝經．[134]

The scholars here regard contemporary poems as the easiest type of text to remember. Before they will even begin instructing Duan Wei on the shortest of the classical texts, they expect him to prove himself by memorizing a set of regulated poems. This is still sufficiently difficult that the scholars are surprised that he remembers them all well, yet it is clear that they considered this a lesser task than those he would face later in his education. There is no doubt that contemporary poems were set to memory in great number in the medieval period, and the answer as to why is found not in the details of memorial techniques but rather in the structure of the poems themselves.

Put simply, certain popular forms of poetry, especially in the Tang, were almost perfectly structured to support memorization. Research on the psychology of memory provides an interesting perspective on why verse is generally much easier to remember than other literary forms. We know that in the Tang and pre-Tang periods, poems, whether from the *Shi* or by one's father, were some of the first works that children would set to memory.[135] Similarly, we have seen that early primers, with their use of rhyme and parallelism, were intentionally designed so that they could be easily memorized. The most complex structures of one of the most popular forms of poetry in the Tang, regulated verse (*lüshi* 律詩, also referred to as "recent style poetry" *jintishi* 近體詩),[136] however, go much farther in terms of having characteristics that aid memory. In what follows I first give a general description of the forms of regulated verse and then discuss how modern psychological research on memory can shed light on the effects of these features on memorability.[137]

---

134. *TZY*, 10.112.

135. For a discussion of the role of the *Shi* in memorial culture in the Han, see Brashier, "Text and Ritual," 259–62.

136. Note that I will typically use the term "regulated poetry" or "regulated verse" to refer generally to both Tang recent style poetry and pre-Tang proto-regulated verse that shares most of the characteristics of Tang regulated verse.

137. It should be noted that many of the points in this discussion would apply to some extent to the genre of "parallel prose" as well. See Hightower, "Some Characteristics of Parallel Prose."

Regulated verse grew out of the aesthetic and phonological concerns of writers in the poetry salons of the Six Dynasties.[138] The famous "Eight Defects" (*babing* 八病) described by the poet Shen Yue 沈約 (441–513)[139] and the "Twenty-eight Defects" (*ershibabing* 二十八病) found in the *Bunkyō hifuron* were gradually adjusted to form a set of basic parameters that poets would, more or less, adhere to when writing in this form. Regulated poems are written in lines of either all five or all seven characters. They are typically made up of either two couplets or four, and thus consist of either four or eight lines, though there is a longer form known as the *pailü* 排律 that was less common. The key features of regulated verse for our purposes are as follows:

Caesural divisions. Each line is divided by a caesura that falls after the second syllable in a five-syllable line and after the fourth in a seven-syllable line.[140]

Rhyme. The rhyme falls on the last syllable of even-numbered lines, though in some cases both lines of the first couplet will also rhyme on the last syllable.

Tonal alternations. For the purposes of tonal alternation, medieval Chinese was broken into two tonal categories, level (*ping* 平) and deflected (*ze* 仄). Certain positions in each line, typically the second, fourth, and fifth in a five-character line and the second, fourth, sixth, and seventh of a seven-character line, have specific tonal requirements. Within a line, syllables in even-numbered positions should alternate between level and de-

---

138. I will go into more detail about the historical and literary context in which regulated verse developed in Chapter 3. My interest here is specifically in the relationship between certain structural aspects of regulated verse and memory. A full discussion of its evolution and detailed structures is beyond the scope of this study. An excellent summary of the rules for rhyme and tonal alternations is found in Downer and Graham, "Tone Patterns in Chinese Poetry." For a much more detailed examination of tonal patterns see Wang Li, *Hanyu Shilüxue*. For tonal patterns, parallelism and other structural issues, see Owen, *Poetry of the Early T'ang*, 234–55 and 425–31; Yu-kung Kao, "The Aesthetics of Regulated Verse," 332–85; Shuen-fu Lin, "The Nature of the Quatrain," 296–331; Hsieh, *Evolution of Jueju Verse*; and Mair and Mei, "Sanskrit Origins of Recent Style Prosody." For a summary of earlier scholarship on tonal prosody prior to the Tang, see Meow Hui Goh, "Wang Rong's Poetics," 5–21.

139. See Mather, *The Poet Shen Yüeh*.

140. This and a number of other characteristics apply to "ancient style" (*gutishi* 古體詩) as well. For the sake of simplicity, I will focus here just on regulated verse.

flected tones. If the second syllable is in the level tone, the fourth should be in a deflected tone, and so forth. Tonal alternation is also required between corresponding even-numbered line positions in a couplet. Thus if the second syllable of the first line is in the level tone, the second syllable of the second line should be in the deflected tone. Finally, syllables that carry the rhyme are typically in the level tone.

Parallelism. The middle two couplets of an eight-line regulated poem[141] (and sometimes the first couplet as well) typically feature syntactical parallelism between corresponding positions in each line. In addition, there will be conceptual and often antithetical parallelism between positions as well. For example, were there something high (such as the sky 天 or a mountain 山) in a given position in the first line of a couplet, that position in the second line might have something low (such as earth or river). Some other frequent pairings include near and far, and sight and sound.

Even the very simplified version of these features just described can seem dauntingly complex on first glance. Yet as G. B. Downer and A. C. Graham have shown, the most complicated aspect, tonal alternation, allows only four different sequences of tones.[142] Moreover, once the poet has made his tonal choice for the second syllable of the first line and the last of the second, the rest of the pattern is essentially determined.[143]

As I will argue in the next chapter, the poets who developed the poetic structures that became regulated verse in the Tang were motivated by aesthetic concerns. Put simply, they felt that poems following these parameters sounded good. At the same time, some of the great popularity that regulated verse enjoyed in the Tang and afterwards can be attributed to the fact that the structures of regulated verse made such poems, once one internalized the basic rules, easy to compose and easy to remember.[144]

---

141. Parallelism is not required in the shorter form of *jueju*.

142. Downer and Graham, 148. Bodman argues that, useful though Downer and Graham's analysis is, it suffers from certain limitations and leaves out some possibilities for variation. See Bodman, "Poetics and Prosody," 108–110.

143. It is also important to keep in mind that these rules were often violated in ways both large and small in poems that we would consider essentially regulated.

144. Ease of composition and memorability are closely linked, as both involve a limiting of possible choices for a given position. In this discussion I will focus on memorability and turn to ease of composition in the next chapter.

Each one of the properties of regulated verse outlined above involves qualities that modern psychological research has shown to aid memorization. Psychologists measure predictability through the "cloze technique," in which subjects are given writings with every fifth word removed.[145] Texts for which subjects have an easier time guessing the missing words accurately tend to be easier to remember.[146] Thanks to a strict set of compositional standards, regulated poetry is arguably the most predictable and thus memorable of all genres of Chinese literature.

This memorability begins with the most basic structure of the line. The accepted wisdom is that people can retain about seven separate items in their short-term memory at a time.[147] This number can be significantly increased by the use of chunking, or grouping items in a series into larger meaningful units.[148] Not only is each line of a regulated poem within the "magic seven" parameter, the use of caesural divisions clearly functions as a form of chunking, with each segment of the line frequently standing as a grammatically self-contained unit.[149] Chunking is most effective in terms of short-term memory,[150] but as each line in a poem gives indications as to what will appear in the next line, this can make a difference in the comprehension and retention of the poem as a whole. Caesural breaks also divide each line into rhythmic units, which Rubin notes "create slots or gaps that need to be filled; they do not allow for the omission of a part of a rhythmic unit."[151] The pause after the second or fourth syllable of a line of

145. Baddeley, *Essentials of Human Memory*, 87.

146. Ibid., 88.

147. The origin of this figure comes from George Miller's paper "The Magic Number Seven." The term "short-term memory" has fallen out of fashion in many circles of cognitive psychology, sometimes being replaced by or subsumed into the concept of "working memory." These debates are complex and as they do not directly bear on my argument here, I will not address them. See Baddeley, "Short-Term and Working Memory," 77–78.

148. Brown and Craik, "Encoding and Retrieval of Information," 97.

149. In lines of seven syllables the four syllables before the first caesural break are often made up of two distinct units, such as adjective-noun/adjective-noun as well.

150. It is worth noting that short-term memory typically refers to the ability to remember items for less than a minute. While this would obviously not be useful in actual oral transmission (as we can assume a break of more than a minute before a poem would likely be circulated orally), stronger encoding at the stage of short-term memory often means a more likely transition to long-term memory. See Brown and Craik, "Encoding and Retrieval of Information," 93–94.

151. Rubin, *Memory in Oral Traditions*, 86.

regulated verse indeed serves this purpose, allowing the reader or listener to anticipate what will come next.

The phonological qualities of regulated verse are another factor that substantially increases its memorability. We have already discussed rhyme, often referred to as providing a "sensory-context" cue,[152] in the context of children's primers. It serves the same function in regulated poems. The latter, however, add an additional set of sensory-context cues through the use of tonal alternations. Phonological constraints thus come into play not only in the last position in a couplet, but in at least two or three of the other character positions in each line as well. So long as one knows the tone of the second syllable of the first line, one can predict the tonal designations for almost every restricted position to follow.

Such sensory-context cues as rhyme, tonal alternation, and rhythm, though effective at aiding memory themselves, become even more potent aids to retrieval when combined with semantic-context cues at the point when the memory was originally encoded.[153] We see the most obvious use of semantic-context cues, which are based on the meanings of the words in question rather than the sounds, in parallel couplets. Expectations for the second line of a parallel couplet are primed by the content of the first. A given image in the first line of a couplet automatically creates an expectation of what will come in the corresponding positions in the second. This moment of expectation followed quickly by discovery is indeed one of the pleasures of regulated verse (provided it is done well). Though the parameters of parallelism can be quite broad beyond the basic syntactic constraints (which themselves are not always closely followed), thus leaving a substantial range for creativity in such couplets, when the semantic-context cues of parallelism are combined with the sensory-context cues of either tonal alternation and/or rhyme, the probable depth of encoding and thus memorability is quite substantial.

Perhaps the most important factor in the memorability of regulated poetry in the Tang is the people who were attempting to set it to memory. Expertise in a subject can be a decisive factor in how quickly and accurately one can memorize material dealing with it. Baddeley notes experi-

152. Ibid., 78.

153. Brown and Craik, "Encoding and Retrieval of Information," 99–100. Rubin (*Memory in Oral Traditions*, 86) notes this as well.

ments in recalling patterns of chess pieces, bridge hands, and electronic circuits that showed, perhaps unsurprisingly, that subjects skilled in these areas remembered the patterns accurately after much shorter times of observation than did those with little expertise. "In each case," he explains, "the expert is able to organize the material into a meaningful and lawful pattern."[154] Unlike the case with most art forms and literary genres in modern times, the audience for Tang poetry was made up almost entirely of people who composed poetry themselves and typically did so with great frequency. These were people for whom the rules of regulated poetry would have been second nature by the time they were adults, allowing them to almost subconsciously absorb the patterns in any given work and be likely to remember those patterns at a later time.

The structure of regulated poetry was initially dictated largely by the aesthetic concerns of a small number of poets in the courts of the Southern Dynasties. There is no indication that a desire to make the poems easy to remember itself determined these concerns. At the same time, the fact that this particular style of poetry succeeded not only in its original setting, but eventually dominated poetic production for centuries after, owes a great deal to the ease with which regulated poems were set to memory. From poetry competitions in the imperial entourage to gossipy verses in the entertainment quarters, the ideal combination of a literate populace with well-trained memories and a form that lent itself perfectly to memorization with minimal effort ensured that this poetry would circulate quickly and widely.

Memory mattered in medieval Chinese society. As we have seen from accounts of those with unusually strong mnemonic abilities, these abilities were valued in and of themselves, not merely because they demonstrated knowledge of specific culturally important texts. Memorization also played an important role in education. It was the basic way that students interacted

154. Baddeley, *Essentials of Human Memory*, 99. Interestingly, this does not mean that chess masters, for example, tend to have better memories overall than the average person. When such subjects were shown a chess board with the pieces set up randomly rather than in a fashion that would occur in the course of an actual game, their ability to recall the order of the pieces was no better than a novice. See Brown and Craik, "Encoding and Retrieval of Information," 98.

with a substantial set of texts from the time they began their education to the time they became adults and, in many cases, were examined on their ability to reproduce portions of texts from memory. Moreover, their foundation in the written language of the day was built up through learning past exemplars. Even if these past texts were not memorized with precise accuracy, they provided a set of common phrases, themes, images, and styles that literate men would all be expected to both recognize and use. Finally, in spite of the fact it was not accorded the respect of the classics or even the *Wenxuan*, it is clear that contemporary poetry was frequently set to memory as well. This was made possible not by any particularly well-developed memorial techniques, but rather by the fact that its basic structures and phonological qualities made it especially easy to set to memory.

At the same time, I hope that some common misconceptions about memory in this period have been shown to be just that. The fact that educated men in medieval China had memorial abilities far surpassing those of most moderns must not lead us to unnecessarily idealize those abilities. There was a memorization corpus of sorts, but it was much more limited than has often been supposed. The notion that it included all the classics and the entire *Wenxuan* at a bare minimum is simply not supported by the available sources. The widespread use of *leishu* and promptbooks shows that students and scholars by the Tang period at the very latest had clearly begun the process of relying on technologies other than human memory for storing important information. If memorial techniques in medieval China were not as well developed as those of medieval Europe, it is perhaps because they did not have to be.

Like the technology of manuscript production, memories were imperfect replicators of texts. The process of remembering, from the initial moments of encoding to retrievals that might be attempted years later, offered innumerable opportunities for textual alteration. From our perspective as modern scholars, this may seem troubling in terms of its inevitable introduction of textual instability. From the perspective of medieval Chinese writers, readers, singers, and listeners, this would have simply been the reality of the literary context in which they lived.

THREE

The Roles of Orality in Tang Poetic Culture

The *Book of Documents* (書經 or 尚書) long ago promised that "song makes language last" 歌永言. If there is a certain irony in a work so titled serving as a starting point for a discussion of the oral aspects of Tang poetry, it is one that runs through any discussion of the seemingly oxymoronic topic of "oral literature."[1] Song does indeed make language more durable. Patterning—whether in the form of rhyme schemes, tonal alternations, or parallelism—aids memory, composition, and transmission. At the same time, the oral aspects of Tang poetry were the first to be lost; documents, not sounds, are all that survive. Each instance of a poem's oral manifestation was necessarily ephemeral, hemmed in by the limitations of human lungs and vocal cords. Sounds were often recorded in writing, but writing is always different from sound, especially in a non-alphabetic written script like Chinese, where for the majority of words, phonetic rather than orthographic aspects have changed the most over the centuries since the Tang.[2]

---

1. Walter Ong objects to the use of the term and finds solace in his belief that it is "losing ground." See Ong, *Orality and Literacy*, 10–15. Ruth Finnegan, on the other hand, holds that "the term is so widely accepted and the instances clearly covered by the term so numerous, that it is an excess of pedantry to worry about the etymology of the word 'literature'" See Finnegan, *Oral Poetry*, 16.

2. Note that saying written Chinese is and was non-alphabetic, is very different from saying that characters did not have set phonetic values, which, as logographs, they clearly did from the very beginning of their development. See Boltz, "Language and Writing," 112.

Ephemerality, however, does not imply irrelevance. In spite of being part of what was the world's most literate culture at the time, poetry in the Tang was an intensely oral phenomenon. This is different from saying that it was "oral poetry" as literary scholars of the last fifty years have commonly used the term. In his important work *The Singer of Tales*, Albert Lord builds on the research of his teacher, Milman Parry, to construct a theory of oral poetry "composed in a manner evolved over many generations by singers of tales who did not know how to write."[3] Parry and Lord focused their research on very particular types of narrative poetry (some of which, such as the works of Homer, had long been available only in textual form), yet the close association they present between orality and illiteracy has permeated scholarly discourse on the topic of oral poetry.[4] The vast majority of work on this topic almost completely ignores examples from China and tends to make divisions between the oral and written that typically do not fit the historical reality of late-medieval China. Although I focus my discussion on examples from the Tang and Six Dynasties period, many of my broader points apply equally well to later periods in Chinese history, when poetry continued to be a very oral phenomenon, despite the great value placed upon writing and written texts among the educated elite. Orality in the medieval and post-medieval periods in China was an aesthetic choice, not a tendency resulting from lingering habits of any recent pre-literate past.

Recent scholarship has called into question this emphasis on a "pure" orality and argued that the realms of the oral and the written overlap so thoroughly that differentiation becomes problematic at best. In her important work on oral poetry, Ruth Finnegan takes issue with Lord's restrictive definitions and claims that "there *is* no clear-cut line between 'oral' and 'written' literature...."[5] Rosalind Thomas comes to a similar

---

3. Lord, *Singer of Tales*, 4. Lord here is specifically defining the narrative poetry he refers to as "oral epic song." However, in his more general definition in the entry on oral poetry in *The New Princeton Encyclopedia of Poetry and Poetics*, he again emphasizes the importance of illiteracy, referring to it as "poetry composed and transmitted mainly but not exclusively by people who cannot read or write." See Preminger and Brogan, *New Princeton Encyclopedia*, 863.

4. Egan gives a good overview of oral theory as it applies to poetry and related genres such as ballads in his article "Were *Yüeh-fu* Ever Folk Songs?"

5. Finnegan, *Oral Poetry*, 2.

conclusion based on her studies of the role of orality in ancient Greece, pointing out that it is "difficult, if not impossible, to make hard and fast distinctions between what is 'oral' and what is 'written' except in the most literal sense."[6] It goes without saying that Tang poetry came into being in a cultural context that was thousands of years removed from what Walter Ong has called "primary orality," by which he means "a culture totally untouched by any knowledge of writing or print."[7] Tang poets were a highly literate bunch and bore as little resemblance on the one hand to Lord's illiterate bards as they do on the other to a modern Western poet sitting before his computer screen. We must thus move beyond Lord's restrictive definition of oral poetry and consider orality in a broader sense when applied to the Tang.

We have seen that a number of the characteristics of Tang poetry, and regulated poetry in particular, lend themselves to rapid memorization. These same characteristics are ones that literary scholars in the West have often associated with orality. Finnegan identifies tone repetition (or rhyme) and parallelism as "important structural device[s] in oral poetry,"[8] noting that some scholars go as far as to consider such formal repetitions as parallelism to be "the yardstick by which oral can definitively be distinguished from written literature."[9] Rhyme and parallelism (in addition to such similar repetitive phonetic qualities as tonal alternation) are some of the defining characteristics of regulated verse, as discussed in Chapter 2. These qualities would indeed be aids to oral composition, especially composition performed on the spot and essentially simultaneous with presentation of the poetic work to an audience. In terms of sounds, rhyme and tonal patterning reduce the number of possible candidates for a given position affected by these regulations in a poem. Parallelism creates conceptual limits just as rhyme and tonal patterning create phonetic limits; but in addition, it also provides the composing poet with pre-determined sets of categories to put in parallel positions, such as mountains and water, heaven and earth, up and down, and so forth. As Owen has noted, "...where a premium was placed on speed of composition, these rules and

6. Thomas, *Literacy and Orality in Ancient Greece*, 73.
7. Ong, *Orality and Literacy*, 11.
8. Finnegan, *Oral Poetry*, 96, 98.
9. Finnegan, *Oral Poetry*, 128.

conventions facilitated extempore versifying without awkwardness."[10] If mnemonic ease is a question of knowing what to expect when reading or recalling a poem, compositional ease is a question of reducing the possible moves expected of the composing poet.

Yet given that the Tang was not a culture of primary orality, but one in which poets and their audience were highly literate, the necessities of oral composition and transmission themselves cannot fully account for the origins and presence of these "oral characteristics." This situation is not unique to Tang dynasty China; European cultures from ancient Greece to Tudor England existed in a state that some scholars have referred to as "mixed orality" where a vibrant oral culture co-existed with widespread use of writing, typically in manuscript form.[11] Ong sees oral characteristics that continue to exist in literate cultures and are used by literate authors as a kind of "oral residue" consisting of "habits of thought and expression tracing back to preliterate situations or practice, or deriving from the dominance of the oral as a medium in a given culture, or indicating a reluctance or inability to dissociate the written medium from the spoken."[12] For Ong, such writers function in a "marginal position" between fully pre-literate and print cultures,[13] the oral elements in their works surviving because the manuscript cultures in which they composed "retained very lively connections with the old pre-literate oral-aural world."[14]

Such a model is clearly problematic for the Tang case. Essentially all regulated poetry contains characteristics associated with oral poetry, and we know that it was not all actually composed orally. The model proposed by Ong and other scholars would force us to conclude that these oral elements are holdovers from a pre-literate time in which Chinese poetic cul-

---

10. Owen, *Poetry of the Early T'ang*, 8.

11. See Gellrich, *Discourse and Dominion*, 3.

12. Ong, "Oral Residue in Tudor Prose Style," 146.

13. Ibid.," 150.

14. Ibid., 153. Note also that Ong's belief that cultures of primary orality are fundamentally different from those with any form of writing leads him to see manuscript cultures as marginal in that they are neither pre-literate nor print based. This assumes a natural evolution from full orality to manuscript and then to print. Yet while writers in a manuscript culture may well have realized that there was a time before there was writing, one doubts that they saw themselves as waiting around for the invention of print. The notion that they are truly "marginal" in a way that sets them off definitively from print culture is problematic. See further discussion of this issue in Chapter 4.

ture could not survive without such devices as rhyme, tonal patterning, and structural parallelism for both composition and transmission.[15] This conclusion does not fit with the historical realities of the development of pre-print Chinese literary culture in general or the evolution of regulated poetry in the Tang in particular. "Oral characteristics" cannot, in and of themselves, prove that any given poem was actually composed (and/or transmitted) orally. Other compositional circumstances and aesthetic goals can and have resulted in poetry that has such characteristics but was initially composed in writing.[16]

The notion of a "residual orality" assumes that literary culture progresses in a linear fashion away from orality and towards an increased emphasis on writing. This may be true in larger sociological terms, but it does not account for the possibility that poets and their audience might consciously prefer oral elements for reasons beyond force of habit inherited from an earlier age. Regulated poetry is a telling example in this case. Its defining characteristics—those very elements that would appear to be holdovers from previous oral practices—were in fact developed not in the misty reaches of the pre-literate past but in the hyper-literate settings of the poetry salons of the Six Dynasties and Early Tang. In their important article, "The Sanskrit Origins of Recent Style Prosody," Victor Mair and Mei Tsu-lin persuasively argue that the tonal properties of regulated verse were developed in Six Dynasties poetry salons "in order to reproduce, in Chinese, the same euphonic effect achieved by meter in Sanskrit."[17] Shen Yue's "Eight Defects" and the "Twenty-eight Defects" found in the *Bunkyō hifuron*, which we have seen articulated the rules that formed the foundation of what would become regulated verse in the Tang, were thus

---

15. Gellrich takes a similar perspective throughout *Discourse and Dominion*.

16. Finnegan has noted that "one cannot necessarily discriminate between 'oral' and 'written' on the basis of a 'formulaic' style alone." See Finnegan, *Oral Poetry*, 70. Thomas makes a similar claim. See Thomas, *Literacy and Orality in Ancient Greece*, 74.

17. Mair and Mei, "Sanskrit Origins of Recent Style Prosody," 380. The question of the true origins of regulated verse and its direct antecedents has been long debated and continues to be a topic of some contention. While Mair and Mei are far from the first to suggest a connection with Sanskrit sutra chanting (that would be Chen Yinke in a 1934 article in *Qinghua xuebao*), their arguments are detailed and, in my opinion, strong. For an overview of this issue and a review of some of the major criticisms of Mair and Mei's position, see Wu Xiangzhou, *Tangshi chuangzuo yu geshi chuanchang guanxi yanjiu*, 128–43.

not an unconscious oral residue in the minds of Six Dynasties poets but rather the result of a very conscious attempt to create a certain original (to the Chinese) sonic effect in this new style of poetry.

This interest in the "new" sounds of Sanskrit poetry found fertile ground in the particular social contexts in which poets in the Six Dynasties and Early Tang periods composed, namely poetry salons and the courts of the ruling families of the Qi 齊 and Liang 梁 dynasties where courtiers would compose poems in response to imperial commands (*yingzhao* 應詔) or as a part of a linked verse (*lianju* 聯句) composed with their peers.[18] Tellingly, these contexts bore a certain resemblance to those in which oral poetry was the norm: they emphasized rapid composition and performance before an audience. As Mair and Mei point out, the poetry salon gatherings in which Shen Yue and others worked out the details of the new rules of prosody were very competitive environments, "where budding literati could show off their skills in front of their elders."[19] Such a context, in which numerous poets were expected to quickly come up with short poems that could be easily judged, meshed perfectly with a set of increasingly formal rules to govern composition and assessment. Rules make competition possible, and competition inevitably tests such regulations in turn, leading to change and refinement.[20] This particular competitive aspect of poetry continued into the Early Tang, where courtiers would be called upon to compose extemporaneously to topics assigned by the emperor, princes, or their peers. As Owen points out, the "unwritten rules" of court poetry from this period "permitted the ordinary courtier to write a poem that could stand without too much embarrassment beside the work of the greatest court poets."[21]

---

18. For a fuller set of terms used for social verse in these contexts, see Hsieh, *Evolution of Jueju Verse*, 167. For more specific descriptions of poetry salons in this period, see Morino Shigeo, *Rikuchuō shi no kenkyū*, 251–53, 263–64.

19. Mair and Mei, "Sanskrit Origins of Recent Style Prosody," 398.

20. Mair and Mei also note that these regulations and the corresponding ease of assessment made recent style poetry an acceptable part of the *jinshi* examinations. For a brief discussion of Xie Lingyun's 謝靈運 (385–433) contribution to poetry as competition, see Rouzer, *Articulated Ladies*, 138–40. McMullen (State and Scholars, 225–27) briefly discusses poetry competitions in the Early Tang court. Thomas addresses the role of competition in the context of orality in ancient Greece. See Thomas, *Literacy and Orality in Ancient Greece*, 107.

21. Owen, *Poetry of the Early T'ang*, 8.

These features of regulated poetry do not indicate that the poems were necessarily orally composed. Indeed, the limited anecdotes we have describing poetry salons in the Six Dynasties and Early Tang almost all describe poets composing their poems in writing, not orally. What these features tell us is that orality in general was an important aspect of poetry (and indeed most writing) at the time. Sounds mattered in Tang poetry. As Mair and Mei have conclusively shown, it was attempts to imitate the specifically euphonic qualities of Sanskrit verse that led to the development of many of the key tonal rules for regulated poetry. The meaning of the original Sanskrit verse was not a significant source of inspiration for these innovating poets. In fact, it is unlikely that most of these men would have even understood the Sanskrit verses whose sounds they found so appealing.[22] And while most accounts of poetry salons describe courtiers writing out their poems, there is evidence that they would recite them aloud soon after doing so.[23] The scholar Ren Bantang 任半塘, in his meticulous study of poetry set to music in the Tang, *Tang shengshi* 唐聲詩, has demonstrated beyond any doubt that a great deal of Tang poetry was both accompanied by instrumentation and sung, in addition to being recited and chanted aloud without musical accompaniment.[24]

Poetry was never far from the oral realm in the Tang even when it was in written form. This is particularly clear when looking at the types of terms used to describe reading, as opposed to reciting from memory.

---

22. Mair and Mei ("Sanskrit Origins of Recent Style Prosody," 391) note that "what Buddhist biographies really mean when they say that Chinese Buddhist monks and laymen 'had made a profound study of the Sanskrit language,' is that they were instructed in *Siddham*—the principles of Sanskrit script, spelling, and pronunciation that every Indian child had to learn as he began his education."

23. Owen (*Poetry of the Early T'ang*, 257) notes that "We do not know if poems were chanted aloud as they were completed or simply handed in for judgment, but in many of the series we can see poems that seem to respond to each other."

24. This particular contention is developed by Wu Xiangzhou (*Tangshi chuangzuo yu geshi chuanchang guanxi yanjiu*) in some detail as well, with his work building on that of Ren. Ren's work on oral and musical performance has proven invaluable to scholars working on the question of performance in Tang poetry. For a general overview of his scholarship, see Wang Xiaodun and Li Changji, "Ren Zhongming xiansheng he ta suo jianli de sanquxue, Tangdai wenyixue." As Ren's work is both comprehensive and well-known, I will repeat little of it here, citing it only when his insights on performance are pertinent to my specific arguments. For a study of poetic performance in the Tang see Ashmore, "Hearing Things."

When context makes it clear that there was a written text present, poetry was still read not silently but aloud. Reading, whether indicated by the verbs *lan* 覽 or *du* 讀, is time and again described as including vocalization. Luo Yin's 羅隱 (833–909) "Answering Qiu Guangting" 酬丘光庭 includes the line "I recite while walking and sit to read, my mouth never tiring" 行吟坐讀口不倦.[25] In his "Weeping for a Mountain Friend" 哭山友, Du Xunhe 杜荀鶴 (846–904) promises a friend that "I read out the lines of your poems in a loud voice, / fancying that the highest heavens should hear them too" 把君詩句高聲讀，想得天高也合聞.[26]

Descriptions of reading so frequently note vocalization that there is little doubt that it was the typical mode of reading texts in the Tang. When we look at Tang manuscripts themselves, whether poetic or otherwise, we find further strong indications from their formal aspects that they were typically read aloud. Recent scholarship on reading practices in the West has drawn intriguing connections between transcriptions systems, levels of literacy, and modes of reading. Katherine O'Brian O'Keeffe notes the substantial differences in the modes of transcription for Old English and Latin works during the Anglo-Saxon period in England. Whereas texts written in Latin "are regularly transmitted in a format familiar to modern readers—verses are set out one to a line of writing, capitals begin each line, and often some sort of pointing marks the end of each verse[27]—writings in Old English manuscripts lack such "extra-linguistic markers."[28] O'Keeffe concludes that these differences are due to the fact that for the scribes and readers of these texts, Old English was very much an orally and aurally alive language. Readers could thus use "knowledge of the conventions of the verse to 'predict' what is on the page" in a way they could not when reading Latin texts.[29] The latter, divorced from an oral context, required extra-linguistic markers to tell readers how texts should be parsed.

Tang poetic manuscripts are more akin to the Old English texts in this example. As we know from the Dunhuang manuscripts examined in the first chapter and from the early print tradition, texts in this period,

25. *QTS*, 665.7619.
26. *QTS*, 692.7960.
27. O'Keeffe, *Visible Song*, 23.
28. Ibid., 136.
29. Ibid., 40.

whether poetic or otherwise, provided few visual cues to assist readers in decoding the written word. At the same time, the particular relationship between texts, orality, and literacy in the Tang calls into question the universality of O'Keeffe's model and its connotations for literacy. For O'Keeffe, the formal structure (or lack thereof) of the Old English texts she examines reflects a "persisting residual orality" in that particular literary culture.[30] Putting the case more starkly, she writes, "The higher the degree of conventional spatialization in the manuscript, the less oral and more literate the community."[31] Following this logic, the lack of conventional spatialization and other extra-linguistic markers in Tang manuscripts should indicate a community only recently emerging from primary orality and with a low degree of literacy even among the readers of the texts in question. The assumption would be that Tang readers depended on orality to decipher written texts. The absence of such markers as spatialization and punctuation would indicate not only that readers in the Tang typically did vocalize when reading, but also that they had to do so to understand what they read.

I would contend instead that the high degree of orality present even in the specifically *written* aspects of Tang literary culture is a matter not of a low level of literacy among Tang poets and their readers, but rather of the aesthetic norms the culture embraced. Tang readers read texts aloud because they wanted to, not because that was the only way they could understand them. In his influential study on the development of silent reading and word separation in the West, Paul Saenger appears to draw conclusions similar to O'Keeffe's when he writes, "In the West, the ability to read silently and rapidly is a result of the historical evolution of word separation that, beginning in the seventh century, changed the format of the written page, which had to be read orally and slowly in order to be comprehended."[32] At the same time, Saenger notes recent research demonstrating that "the Chinese graphic tradition provides optimal conditions for rapid lexical access and allows Chinese children to develop silent

30. Ibid., 5.
31. Ibid., 25.
32. Saenger, *Space Between Words*, 6.

reading at an earlier age than in Burma or the West."[33] The particular textual-visual aspects of Chinese thus do not appear to have presented the same barriers to silent reading that Western languages did before the widespread use of such conventions as word separation and punctuation. We know that Tang China was a highly literate culture for whom cultural and social achievement revolved around mastery of the texts and the written word. It was as far removed from the *necessity* of orality as perhaps any culture with which it was contemporaneous. Further, due to the graphic particularities of the written language and the metrical properties of poetry in particular, it had little need of word separation or punctuation to facilitate silent reading.[34] Rather, part of the aesthetic pleasure of poetry lay in its patterning of sound, patterning that became codified in regulated verse and similar genres.

Problematic notions of a "pure" oral culture or "residual orality" can only obscure the important reality of how orality actually functioned in the Tang. It was a set of presentational modes that, as we shall see below, included both a father teaching his poems to his son and a singing girl entertaining her clientele, and that presented poems ranging from a drunkenly exclaimed verse to an impassioned lament for a fallen dynasty. None of these modes existed free of written methods of composition and circulation. We can assume, and the evidence from the Dunhuang texts of "Qinfu Yin" and other works clearly implies, that most poems in the Tang that survived for any length of time were, on various occasions and in certain contexts, encountered and transmitted in both oral and written forms. These poetic experiences were not mutually exclusive, but they were different, and by understanding the unique aspects of orality we can come closer to understanding how people in the Tang composed and experienced their era's poetry themselves.

---

33. Ibid., 2. It is true that this research focused on vernacular Chinese written in the modern style with full punctuation, not on Tang poetic manuscripts. The main conclusion, however, appears to be that it is the specifically graphic nature of Chinese that allows for ease of silent reading, and that would obviously have been true for the Tang as well.

34. As any reader of literary Chinese can attest, some form of punctuation does indeed make many prose genres of literary Chinese easier to quickly read and comprehend. Because of such features as rhyme and meter, this would be far less true of most poetic genres.

In what follows I explore the senses in which Tang poetry could be called "oral" and the different roles that orality played in the poetic cultures of the Tang.[35] If orality was integral to Tang poetry, how was it manifested? Ruth Finnegan provides a useful set of guidelines, while admitting that ideal definitions are hard to come by. She writes, "The three ways in which a poem can most readily be called oral are in terms of (1) its composition, (2) its mode of transmission, and (3) (related to [2]) its performance. Some oral poetry is oral in all these respects, some in only one or two."[36] I take Finnegan's lead and examine each of these categories of orality, though focusing more heavily on the first two. After defining some important terms, I present evidence from numerous contemporary accounts of the contexts in and the methods by which Tang poets and their audience intoned their works.[37] We will see that orality had a part in the composition, circulation, and performance of poetry throughout the dynasty. As such it was fundamental to the existence and survival of many poems.

Beyond this, however, the *idea* of orality influenced the interpretation of poems as well. Orality often functioned as trope through which spontaneous oral composition claimed emotional authenticity and moral authority in poetic expression. In terms of circulation, orality was tied to developing quasi-commercial contexts of literary production and circulation. Claims of oral circulation were simultaneously claims of popularity and value. Yet poems that spread orally, no matter how rapid and extensive their circulation, lived a tenuous existence. They escaped the control of their creators and often simply faded away if they did not eventually find their way into textual form. If they did continue to spread, many of the contexts of oral circulation, especially performative ones, could substan-

35. I will not, however, be addressing larger questions of the role of orality in Tang society as a whole. For example, the oral aspects of prose literature or the role of oral networks for news and gossip, while interesting and important topics, are beyond the scope of this discussion.

36. Finnegan, *Oral Poetry*, 17.

37. Graham Sanders has reasonably argued of anecdotes concerning poetry that "they cannot be used as a reliable basis for reconstructing how poetry *really* was performed and received in ancient China; the only historical fact that we can be sure of is that these narratives were written down at some point." See Sanders, *Words Well Put*, 6. My argument does not, however, depend on the various anecdotes I cite being specific historical fact, but simply plausible in their details to their intended audience and thus reflective of certain aspects of common practice at the time.

tially alter a poem's content, further destabilizing both the "text" of the poem and its connection with its author.

Composition

On the face of it, oral composition seems an uncomplicated concept. Ren Bantang defines it straightforwardly as "at the time of composing a poem, [the poet] has no writing materials at hand. He gets [the poem] in his heart and speaks it out his mouth."[38] Finnegan offers a similarly basic definition of a poem composed "without reliance on writing."[39] Yet beneath these simple notions we find a great variety of compositional circumstances. Some poets compose spontaneously in a social setting while others, like the Eskimo and Gilbertese poets Finnegan describes, might spend hours and even days working out a poem in isolation before finally declaiming the whole work in front of others. Some chant their poems to an audience themselves, while others recite them quietly to a performer who then presents them to a larger audience.[40] All of these circumstances involve methods of composition that are clearly oral, yet they sometimes differ from each other more than they differ from certain written modes of poetic composition.

For my purposes here, the broadness of Ren and Finnegan's definitions is a virtue. I follow their lead and define oral composition quite simply as composing a poem without recourse to writing as a primary part of the act of composition itself. In this scheme, the fate of the poem after composition does not have any bearing on the question of whether or not we will consider it orally composed. If an anecdote describes a poet working a poem out in his head and then declaiming it orally to a scribe who immediately writes it down, he has composed orally. At the same time, the mere presence of an oral component in the compositional process does not in itself denote an instance of oral composition. A poet who tries out each line of a poem orally just before he writes it down is not composing orally in a way that is meaningful to our discussion here, nor is one who vocalizes while he writes (as this could arguably include all poets and poems in the

---

38. Ren, *Tang shengshi*, 17.
39. Finnegan, *Oral Poetry*, 17.
40. Finnegan, *Oral Poetry*, 80–83.

Tang). Such a definition of oral composition, broad though it is, will inevitably exclude some oral practices related to poetic composition, but it will also bring some cohesion to our discussion that a definition that included any and all oral aspects would not.

The poet who composed orally in the Tang had at his disposal a long tradition of literary precedents and ideas that presented poetry as a distinctly oral act.[41] Considering the *Shi* as the beginning of Chinese poetry, a strong argument can be made that the dominant mode of expression in the earliest and most influential stage of Chinese poetry about which we have any knowledge was oral. The earliest strata of the *Shi* survived in oral form for centuries prior to being written down. Many of the Zhou ritual hymns are believed to have been composed as early as 1200 or 1000 BCE, but the corpus was probably not recorded in writing until ca. 600 BCE. C. H. Wang has argued that large sections of the *Shi* show evidence of the sorts of oral-formulaic composition described by Parry and Lord in their seminal work on oral literature and composition.[42] He further claims that even the shorter poems can be classified as oral compositions, though his evidence here is suspect with regards to true formulaic structures.[43]

The early critical apparatus that grew up around the *Shi* and came to be the defining notion of poetic production for much of imperial history focused on the poems as specifically oral manifestations as well. The "Daxu" 大序 ("Great Preface [to the *Poems*])," now believed to have been put together in its final form in the first century CE by Wei Hong 衛宏 (fl. ca. 25 CE), states that "The affections are stirred within and take on form in words. If words alone are inadequate, we speak them out in sighs. If sighing is inadequate, we sing them" 情動於中而形於言，言之不足故嗟歎之，嗟歎之不足，故詠歌之.[44]

41. For a more detailed discussion of orality in early China than I can offer here, see Goh, "Wang Rong's Poetics," 59–74.

42. Lord, *Singer of Tales*.

43. C. H. Wang, *The Bell and the Drum*. Note that Wang's specific claims have been widely criticized. See for example Egan, "Were *Yüeh-fu* Ever Folk Songs?" 46. See also Knechtges's citation of William R. Baxter's phonological arguments in "Questions About the Languages of *Sheng Min*," 15–16.

44. Translation from Owen, *Readings in Chinese Literary Thought*, 41. For additional discussion see 37–56. For a more detailed examination of the dating and composition of the "Great Preface" see Van Zoeren, *Poetry and Personality*, 80–115.

Poetic production here is involuntary, a natural response to the world and to specific situations therein. Moreover the focus is not on writing characters, but on producing sounds, a decidedly oral response unmediated by textuality.

Later writers would create models of literary composition that went well beyond and even contradicted many of the ideas contained in the "Daxu," yet these notions continued to exert a strong influence on how poetic composition and reception were envisioned and would be returned to again and again for justification of certain modes of expression. In his preface to the *Benshi shi* 本事詩 ("Original Instances of Poems"), Meng Qi 孟棨 (fl. 841–86) opens by defining a poem with a line from the "Daxu" cited above: "The affections are stirred within and take on form in words." He then goes on to further emphasize the oral aspects of poetry:

> Beautiful works that give voice to feelings and elegant words that admonish are written in the various books. Though they fill up cabinets and overflow shelves, those among them in which one was inspired to chant [a poem] when encountering an event especially focus one's emotions.
>
> 抒懷佳作，諷刺雅言著於群書雖盈廚溢閣：其間觸事興詠，尤所鐘情。[45]

Meng Qi acknowledges a more complex relationship between orality and poetry than the older text he quotes: where the "Daxu" took it for granted that poetic expression would be oral, the tremendous growth of literacy in the Tang meant that Meng Qi could no longer do so, and had to separate out orally performed or composed poetry as a specific category of literary response. But ultimately he also privileges oral composition, granting particular power to instances when the poet was "inspired to chant" by proximate events.

Tang writers themselves were unlikely to find the process of oral composition sufficiently novel to record in great detail. Indeed, for most of Chinese literary history prior to the Tang, especially before the widespread use of paper as a relatively inexpensive writing material, oral composition of some sort was likely more the rule than the exception in most contexts. The *Wei shu* 魏書, in a typical example, describes Cao Pi 曹丕

---

45. Meng Qi 孟棨, *Benshi shi* 本事詩, in Wang Meng'ou, *Tangren xiaoshuo yanjiu sanji*, 29.

(187–226), emperor of the Wei, as skilled at oral composition in a range of literary forms:

> He was fond of literary writing. He would compose poems, rhapsodies, epitaphs, and hymns to his heart's content. There were great literary works that he would dictate orally on horseback, without a single character to be changed when they were complete.
> 好爲文章，詩賦銘頌，任興而作．有大文筆，馬上口授，及其成也不改一字．[46]

An element of hyperbole is to be expected in accounts of rulers, but it is the composer who is exceptional here, not the mode of composition itself. Rulers would, of course, also be surrounded by scribes and others at the ready to record their important utterances and would not need to go to the trouble of recording their words themselves.[47] What is striking is that the oral dictation is said to serve as a final draft: Cao Pi is so skilled at on-the-spot oral composition that he does not need to revise what he has dictated.

References to oral composition of poetry itself, though frequent enough to corroborate that oral composition was a common practice in the Tang, tend to be cursory. Casual oral composition of poems in social settings would not have been worthy of special notice beyond the occasional notation in a poem's title or passing mention in a piece on a different subject. Bai Juyi, for example, in his "Preface on Traveling to the Great Forest Temple" 遊大林寺序, lists the people with whom he was traveling, discusses the natural features of the landscape around the temple, and nonchalantly notes, "Thereupon I orally composed a quatrain that said..." 因口號絶句云.[48] The unfortunate result of these situations being so common, at least from a modern scholar's perspective, is that there are few detailed contemporary descriptions of oral composition of poetry in the Tang that give as much context as we might like.

Descriptions of oral composition typically use one of two terms, either *kouzhan* 口占 or *kouhao* 口號 (as in the case of Bai's comment above). The former has an earlier provenance, appearing in reference to oral com-

---

46. *Wei shu*, 7.187.

47. It is worth recalling that prior to the widespread use of word processors in modern America, physicians, attorneys, and other professionals would often dictate their notes, letters, and briefs to tape for assistants to transcribe later.

48. Zhu, 43.2756.

position in a passage in the *Han shu* biography of Zhu Bo 朱博 that reads, "The administrative clerk of the lower hall entered and Bo orally composed a dispatch" 閤下書佐入博口占檄文.[49] *Kouhao*, however, is far more frequently used and has earlier associations with poetry specifically.[50] Poems with either of these two terms in the title represent an extremely small but important subgroup of the Tang poetry that survives today.[51] In the *Quan Tang shi* 全唐詩 ("Complete Tang Poetry"), compiled in the Qing dynasty, there are eighty-one poems in all, of which seventy-nine use the term *kouhao* and two use *kouzhan*.[52] Thus the percentage of shorter Tang poems overall that make an explicit claim of orality remains minute. Nor is there anything in the content of the poems themselves that would make them stand out as orally composed (unless this fact is mentioned in the poem itself) beyond the title. However, they do typically share at least one formal trait; the majority are quatrains, with

---

49. *Han shu*, 84.3401. While "dictated" would be smoother translation for *kouzhan* in this case, I have used "orally composed" to better reflect the *Hanyu dacidian's* definition of the term in this usage: "To compose poetry or prose orally (*suikou* 隨口) without making a written draft." See Luo Zhufeng, *Hanyu da cidian*, 3.3.

50. See *Hanyu da cidian*, v. 3, 11. For Ren Bantang's discussion of this term see Ren, *Tang shengshi*, 16–17. The term used in the anecdotes about Cao Pi and Wang Ju, *koushou* 口授, is typically used in reference to orally expounding pieces meant to be simultaneously recorded by another. I hence translate it as "dictate" rather than "orally compose," though the former implies the latter in these cases.

51. Titles, as they often function to set both the topic of a poem and give a brief indication of the context in which it was composed, can be useful sources of information in this regard. They do have their considerable pitfalls: there are countless examples throughout the tradition of titles being given to poems many years after the poems were composed. In such cases the titles were typically added by someone other than the poem's original author and either replaced the title that that author gave or provided one when he had not. The relationship between titles and poems could be a fluid one: many times different poems share a single title, and a number of poems come down to us from different sources with different titles in each. These cautionary facts aside, Tang poetic titles are, more often than not, the only description of a given poem's circumstances of composition we have and as such represent an important source of information. They must be used with caution, but they must be used.

52. These numbers exclude poems attributed to immortals, ghosts, those found written on animals, etc.—i.e., any poems found in *juan* 860–81 of the *Quan Tang shi*. The numbers further indicate poems rather than titles. For example, I count Du Fu's "Cheng wen Hebei zhudao jiedu ruchao huanxi kouhao jueju shier shou" 承聞河北諸道節度入朝歡喜口號絕句十二首 as twelve poems though there is only one title.

this form accounting for sixty-seven of the poems. Those that are not quatrains still tend to be relatively short; the longest poem contains only twenty lines of seven characters each. This tendency towards brevity is not surprising in poems that are described as being orally composed on the spot, but it does not set these poems apart in any significant structural or content-based way from the majority of poetry composed in the Tang.

Both *kouzhan* and *kouhao* are used for oral composition at a specific point in time, rather than either the type of oral composition Finnegan describes Eskimo poets as employing, in which the poem is composed over a longer period and then finally declaimed to an audience upon completion, or the circumstances of oral composition studied by Parry and Lord, in which epic poems were composed orally through repeated tellings in a specifically performance-oriented context. Oral composition in Tang poetry typically results in the creation of a whole piece at one temporally defined moment. The poem is an event, not an accretion.

Tang descriptions of these oral poetic events, whether in the form of titles or longer anecdotes, often highlight two interrelated aspects of composition. The first is spontaneity: rather than struggling though a lengthy period of contemplation and crafting, the poet declaims a poem whole and off the cuff. The second is the notion of a poem as an almost involuntary emotional and moral response to a particular stimulus. Both find their inspiration in the model of poetic composition put forth by the "Daxu" and discussed above. And they are connected: spontaneity is also the hallmark of a particular type of moral response based upon one's emotional and moral reactions to a situation.

There are a few poems from the Tang simply entitled "Orally Composed";[53] the majority of titles that claim oral composition, however, are more detailed in their descriptions of locations and circumstances. Depictions of oral composition may emphasize spontaneity by locating the event in a context that would make written composition difficult. The poet is inspired to compose and must do so on the spur of the moment regardless of where he finds himself. Over a third of the poem titles indicating oral composition from the *Quan Tang shi* mention locations in either a general sense (for example "On the Road" 途中)[54] or more

53. One example is Dai Shulun 戴叔倫, "Orally Composed" 口號, *QTS*, 274.3099.

54. Sun Ti 孫逖, "Orally Composed on the Road" 途中口號, *QTS*, 118.1198.

specifically (for example "Traveling and Spending the Night at Huaiyang Pavilion" 旅宿淮陽亭).[55] Some variation of "on the road" is the most common formulation, though many titles give additional details as well. Yan Chaoyin 閻朝隱 places himself in the imperial entourage in his title "Attending on the Road, Orally Composed to Imperial Command" 侍從途中口號應制.[56] Other titles emphasize the difficulty of writing by noting the poet being in transit or in motion. A number of titles describe oral composition on horseback, ranging from the straightforward "Orally Composed on Horseback at the Xu Ru Pavilion" 徐孺亭馬上口號 by Quan Deyu 權德輿 (759–818),[57] to the circumstances even less conducive to writing described by Lu Lun 盧綸 (737–98) in "Orally Composed on Horseback Upon Encountering Rain on the Road, In Parting with the Two Very Honorable Gentlemen Zhang and Liu" 途中遇雨馬上口號留别張劉二端公.[58] Meng Haoran 孟浩然 (689–740), well-known for his love of travel, places one of his oral compositions on a boat in "Orally Composed on a Boat Having Just Set Off Down the Zhe River" 初下浙江舟中口號.[59] In all these cases poetic expression figures not as the result of laborious literary crafting, but as an immediate response to one's circumstances.

Spontaneity can also imply a lack of conscious will. In the Song period, poets and critics would come near to fetishizing spontaneity, noting frequently that they "just happened" to compose their works without any forethought. We can see the beginnings of this trend in some descriptions of poetic composition from the Tang. In his prefatory material for "On the Pond" 池上篇, Bai Juyi foregrounds this aspect of spontaneity, describing how a work flows out of him without any conscious effort on his part:

When I was drunk with ale and done with my zither, I again ordered the young musicians to ascend the Central Island Pavilion and together play "Overture to Rainbow Skirts." The sounds floated along on the wind, sometimes coalescing, sometimes spreading out. Long they rose up at the edges of the bamboo, mists,

---

55. "Orally Composed While Spending the Night at Huaiyang Pavilion" 旅宿淮陽亭口號 is attributed to both Zhang Jiuling 張九齡 and Song Zhiwen 宋之問, with the text of the poem the same in each case. See *QTS*, 48.591, and 52.644.

56. *QTS*, 69.769.

57. *QTS*, 326.3657.

58. *QTS*, 276.3129.

59. *QTS*, 160.1668.

waves and moon. Before the tune was done, I was contentedly in a drunken sleep on a stone. Rising from my slumber, I happened to intone something neither poem nor rhapsody. Agui took up a brush and thereupon wrote it up among the stones. Seeing that it roughly formed a rhymed piece I called it simply "On the Pond."

酒酣琴罷，又命樂童登中島亭，合奏霓裳散序．聲隨風飄，或凝或散，悠揚於竹煙波月之際之久之．曲未竟而樂天陶然已醉睡於石上矣．睡起偶詠，非詩非賦，阿龜握筆，因題石間，視其粗成韻章，命為池上篇云爾．[60]

Bai Juyi portrays his composition as an almost unconscious natural response to his surroundings, which are described in an earlier section of the preface that details his location, the amount of land, the proportions given over to bamboo and to water, the animals that live there, and his various entertainments. He was awake, but only recently arisen from a drunken sleep. His chantings were not premeditated; he "just happened" to intone them. Finally, the product of his composition is itself not fully formed. It is neither a proper *shi* poem nor a rhapsody. Like the music that led Bai Juyi into sleep, his spontaneous composition is dreamlike and without set form. Indeed he himself does not realize what he has created until he sees it written out. It is here that Bai Juyi's preface goes beyond the simple descriptions we have seen in poem titles; he actually does tell us something about the process by which an orally composed piece might come to be written down. Bai Juyi was not intentionally dictating, in the manner of Cao Pi or Wang Ju, but his nephew Agui was conveniently present to record his sudden inspiration. That Agui transcribed the piece also opens up the possibility that he tidied up his uncle's words as he wrote them down, bringing to mind the processes of collaborative authorship discussed in Chapter 1.

A second example from Bai Juyi is his well-known "Reciting Poems Alone in the Mountains" 山中獨吟, which begins:

Each person has one addiction,	人各有一癖，
my addiction is to composition.	我癖在章句．
The myriad attachments have all dissolved,	萬緣皆以銷，
this sickness alone hasn't yet left.	此病獨未去．
Whenever I meet a beautiful scene,	每逢美風景，

60. Zhu, 617.3706.

or beloved family or old friends, 或對好親故・
With a loud voice I intone a piece, 高聲詠一篇，
dazed as if I had encountered a god. 怳若與神遇・[61]

Again composition is an automatic response to the scenes and people Bai Juyi meets, something not entirely under his control. In "On the Pond" he "just happened" to chant out the piece; in "Reciting Poems Alone in the Mountains" composition is a compulsion, the single remaining attachment from which he cannot free himself. As in "On the Pond," Bai describes composing in a liminal state of consciousness, driven into an almost religious stupor by the urge to compose poetry. Bai Juyi builds on the notions of poetry as involuntary response explored in the "Daxu" to shape an image of himself as a spontaneous free spirit who is in touch with a poetic force that transcends himself and over which he has only limited control.[62]

If Bai Juyi ties oral composition to being in a state of liminal consciousness, then Han Yu's "Preface to the Stone Tripod Linked Verse" 石鼎聯句詩序 links it to phenomena bordering on the supernatural.[63] The preface describes a meeting of three men: a Daoist named Xuanyuan Miming 軒轅彌明, a *jinshi* graduate named Liu Shifu 劉師服, and an editor of the Imperial Diary in the Palace Library named Hou Xi 侯喜. Miming is described as being old, extremely ugly, and allegedly able to "catch ghosts and cage sea-serpents and hornless dragons" 捕逐鬼物拘囚蛟螭. As the three sit together at Liu Shifu's home, Miming challenges them to a write verses about the stone tripod set on a nearby stove. The description of the contest begins as follows:

[Liu Shifu] did not know [the Daoist] was a literary man. Upon hearing this request he was greatly pleased. He immediately took up a brush and wrote up the first two lines. He next passed this to Hou Xi. Hou Xi leapt up and quickly continued below those lines. The Daoist laughed and said, "Is this all there is to your

61. Zhu, 7.407.

62. Such an image is strikingly at odds with the meticulous approach he actually took to most matters of his literary output, a contrast of which the poet himself was surely well aware.

63. Qian, *Han Changli shiji*, 849–51. For a full translation and discussion, see Pollack, "Han Yü and the 'Stone Cauldron Linked-verse Poem.'" For a translation and brief discussion see Hightower, "Han Yü as Humorist," 17–19.

poetry?" He then put his hands in his sleeves, shrugged his shoulders, and sat down leaning against the north wall. He said to Liu: "I do not understand the writing of the common world. Write for me." Thereupon he chanted loudly....
不知其有文也·聞此說，大喜，即援筆題其首兩句·次傳於喜，喜踴躍，即綴其下云云·道士啞然笑曰：子詩如是而已乎·即袖手竦肩，倚北牆坐，謂劉曰：吾不解世俗書，子爲我書·因高吟曰···[64]

As the contest progresses, Miming continues to dictate and the other two continue to compose in writing. Miming's capping lines surpass them each time. Eventually they admit defeat and beg to become his pupils. He chants forty more characters to finish the poem and then rejects their request, saying, "None of this is worth talking to you about. Could this be literature? I merely composed at the level you were capable of. This is not what I learned from my master and am able to do" 此皆不足與語，此寧爲文耶·吾就子所能而作耳，非吾之所學於師而能者也.[65] They then ask him what script he understands (敢問解何書) and he refuses to answer.

That a mysterious character with unusual abilities is the one of the three to utilize pure oral composition both complements and expands the role of spontaneity attached to oral composition in the pieces examined above. Miming's refusal or inability to write is not directly tied to his being the better poet, but a connection is implied. As the two scholars grow increasingly frustrated, Han Yu repeatedly notes their use of brushes while Miming simply leans back and intones. Their verses are forced; his flow naturally, or even preternaturally. The piece is a satire that plays off qualities associated with oral composition, such as Bai Juyi's hints at otherworldly inspiration for his poems. The illiterate geezer turns out to be a Zhuangzian sage whose compositions are beyond the realm of mundane writing (and include amusing verbal puns). Han Yu assumes his readers are aware of the associations between spontaneity and oral composition from the "Daxu." As a satire, the work also shows that important though these associations were, they were not necessarily taken dogmatically, but rather could be manipulated for humorous intent.

---

64. Qian, *Han Changli shiji*, 850.
65. Ibid.

This humorous (and most probably quite fictional) treatment highlights the use of orality as a trope with a certain set of associations, ranging from spontaneity to moral authenticity. Even if we cannot trust that the poem titles, prefaces, and anecdotes describing oral composition are accurate portrayals of specific historical practices, we can gain something from considering how they use the idea of orality to encourage a certain type of reading of the poems they contain.

We see the more serious aspect of oral composition as a trope in its ties to emotional and moral expression. The "Daxu" emphasizes the role of emotions in poetic production, claiming that when they are "stirred," a chain of events begins that ultimately results in a poem. Tang descriptions of oral composition often follow suit in depicting poems as emotional responses. Lü Wen 呂溫 (772–811) entitled one of his quatrains, "I Was Moved When Reading My Little Brother's Poem and Thereupon Orally Composed [This] to Show Him" 讀小弟詩有感因口號以示之.[66] Similarly, Du Fu has a set of orally composed poems entitled: "Upon Receiving the News That All of the Hebei Military Commissioners Have Entered the Court, I Was Joyful and Orally Composed Twelve Quatrains" 承聞河北諸節度入朝歡喜口號絶句十二首.[67] There is nothing unusual in the Tang about conceiving of poems, whether composed orally or in writing, as emotional responses to one's circumstances. The claim of orality here does, however, serve a particular purpose. By recalling the "Daxu" with its model of a specifically oral poetic response to emotions, the title instructs the reader to interpret the poems in that light. Lü Wen and Du Fu show themselves as responding instantaneously. They do not fetch brush and paper, struggle over what words to use, and finally construct a poem though a process of laborious crafting and revision. The poems come to them in the moment and they are compelled to give them voice. The added information that the title supplies thus attempts to influence the reader to assume that that these particular examples of poetic expression have a spontaneous moral and emotional content that might not be clear from the words of the poems themselves.

Emotions can be complex, and some poets perhaps felt that a simple title was insufficient to convey the feelings behind their spontaneous crea-

66. *QTS*, 371.4169.
67. Qiu, 18.1624–29.

tions. In Quan Deyu's preface to his poem "Orally Composed on Horseback at the Xu Ru Pavilion" cited earlier, he describes in detail the circumstances that led to the poem's composition:

South of Zhongling's[68] East Lake there is a pavilion. In the pavilion are two stelae. One is the Summoned Scholar Xu[69] tablet that the late Master "Winding River" Zhang[70] composed. The other is the stele at the Pool for Setting Free Living Things that Master "North Sea" Li[71] composed. Alas! The two gentlemen have long ago accorded with the transformations [of nature] and left, yet the full-flowering of their writings are passed on throughout the world. At the beginning of the Zhenyuan reign period (785–805) I served in this region. Whenever I would greet or see people off at the city outskirts, I would often pass by this area. Because of their support for capable men and love of living things, they were both pinnacles of pure humanity. I thus sigh that I am not able to live in the same age as these two worthies and discuss the ups and downs of the changes in literature. The pavilion's foundation is ruined, with the seal script characters [on the tablets] covered in moss and the pedestals worn thin. Yet it is as if their ancient spirit remains. One feels the past still present, and there is a great road by the side and a calm lake below. The waves flow back and forth through time inexhaustible. Thereupon, while on my horse I orally composed a single quatrain to lodge my melancholy.

鍾陵東湖之南有亭，亭中有二碑，一則故曲江張公所製徐徵君碣，一則北海李公所製放生池碑．嚱夫！二君子久隨化往，而二文之盛，傳於天下．貞元初，余爲是邦從事，每將迎郊勞，多經是間，且以其尚賢好生，皆醇仁之首也．因歎不得與二賢同時，論文變損益，亭址圮壞，苔篆礴趺，古風如在，感舊依然，而通馗在側，平湖在下，波流轂擊，日月無窮，因於馬上口號絕句詩一首，以寄愀愴．[72]

Quan Deyu's preface serves more as an expanded title than as a detailed description of oral composition *per se*. It combines aspects of many of the types of titles examined earlier. He describes his location: a pavilion housing stelae or stone tablets with inscriptions by literary and political figures

---

68. In modern Jinxian County 進賢縣 in Jiangxi 江西.

69. Figure from the Later Han, courtesy name Junqiu 君求. The title "Summoned Scholar" (*zhengjun* 徵君) indicates one who did not actually serve in the bureaucracy but was summoned to court on the basis of his reputation.

70. That is, Zhang Jiuling.

71. That is, Li Yong 李邕 (678–747), important calligrapher, writer, and early mentor of Du Fu. He was killed in Li Linfu's 李林甫 (d. 752) purges in 747.

72. *QTS*, 326.3657.

from earlier in the dynasty. He then describes the emotions elicited by his location and the associations the stelae bring forth. Finally, he tells of a situation in which writing would be difficult—riding a horse—and explains that he orally composed the following poem to give expression to his feelings of melancholy.

Not surprisingly, the poem itself, while short, provides no specific evidence that Quan Deyu composed it orally. It reads:

By the lakeside the overgrown pavilion overlooks the lake,	湖上荒亭臨水開，
On the tortoise shell writing and seal script characters, lichen and moss build up.	龜文篆字積莓苔。
Winding River and Northern Sea, where are they today?—	曲江北海今何處，
They've both flowed off to the East, they have left and will not return.	盡逐東流去不迴。

Yet Quan Deyu's work gains deeper meaning when the preface explains the context more fully. The reader immediately understands the poem's references and is informed prior to reading the poem itself that it represents a spontaneous outpouring of melancholy. This claim of oral composition, then, is best seen here as part of that occasional frame. It serves to emphasize the idea of the poem as an immediate emotional response. Indeed the poem, with its clever but not terribly artful play with the earlier men's names and the motions of water, does not itself display the same type of spontaneous emotion indicated by the title and preface. It depends on the latter to give it greater depth. There is, of course, a certain irony in such a lengthy description of spontaneity. The need to make this claim with a preface far longer than the poem itself undercuts the very idea of a truly meaningful immediate moral response.

In a world in which a poem could be a measure of one's innate moral sense, the implications of different readings were not always limited to the realm of aesthetics. When the rebel general An Lushan 安祿山 (ca. 703–57) and his forces seized the capitals in 756, the poet Wang Wei was captured and forced to serve the usurping regime despite claimed attempts to poison himself and feign muteness. After the Tang armies recaptured the capitals, he was held on charges of sedition. A loyalist poem he is said to have orally composed during his imprisonment by An Lushan was cited as a mitigating factor that led to his release.[73] The title reads, "While I Was Imprisoned at the Bodhi Temple, Pei Di Came to See Me and Said that the Rebels Had Music Played at the Frozen Jade Pool, But When the Performers Lifted Up Their Tones in an Instant It Made Their Tears Fall. I Secretly Composed This Orally and Recited It to Pei Di" 菩提寺禁裴迪來相看説逆賊等凝碧池上作音樂供奉人等舉聲便一時淚下私成口號誦示裴迪. The performance of music at Frozen Jade Pool is a famous incident in which An Lushan forced the musicians from the Pear Garden Conservatory (*liyuan dizi* 梨園弟子) to perform for him and his retinue. The musicians were said to have wept and in some cases to have thrown down their instruments in protest.[74] Wang Wei's poem itself consists of only two couplets of seven-character lines with nothing in the content itself that would indicate oral composition:

In ten thousand homes broken hearts bring forth smoke in the wilds,	萬户傷心生野煙，
The hundred officials, when will they again attend court?	百僚何日更朝天。
Autumn locust tree leaves fall in the empty palace,	秋槐葉落空宮裏，
At the head of Frozen Jade Pool, pipes and strings are played.	凝碧池頭奏管弦。[75]

There is an undeniable sense of loss in this poem. Emptiness (空 *kong*), so often used by Wang Wei with Buddhist connotations, is here part of a straightforward lamentation of absence. With the Emperor gone the officials cannot attend court and the pipes and strings of the musicians are played for naught. Lamentation, however, is distinct from protest, and if the poem is to be read as an act of bravery, its title has an essential part to play. To begin with, it places Wang Wei in prison when he heard from his friend Pei Di 裴迪 (b. 716) about the incident at Frozen Jade Pond. It is this context that transforms a work of melancholy to one of defiance. The

73. As Marsha Wagner (*Wang Wei*, 53–54) points out, the intercession of his politically powerful brother was probably far more important in his rehabilitation.

74. For a well-known account of the incident and Wang Wei's poetic response, see Zheng Chuhui, *Minghuang zalu*, 41.

75. *QTS*, 128.1308.

connotation of the image of the empty palace is no longer simply that the Emperor is missing, but rather that no one fills his place. Assuming part of An Lushan's goal in having the Pear Garden musicians play was to take the trappings of rule for himself, Wang Wei's suggestion that the musicians play for an empty palace becomes more provocative. Knowing Wang Wei composed it while held captive by An Lushan, we now take the poem as an audacious mocking of Wang Wei's captor and thus as evidence that the poet had not betrayed the Tang.

These hints of protest, though present in the poem itself, are brought into sharper relief by the context the title supplies and the claim that the poem was orally composed. If oral composition traditionally implied a direct connection to the emotions and the poet's innate moral sense, then by claiming orality for the poem, the title posits that it represents Wang Wei's spontaneous moral response upon hearing Pei Di's story about the Pear Garden musicians playing at Frozen Jade Pond. That he was supposed to have recited the poem aloud further strengthens its role as evidence of loyalty. Wang Wei not only felt sadness at the plight of the empire under An Lushan's attack, he was willing to proclaim this feeling while imprisoned. If we rather imagine Wang Wei writing the poem as a reflection after the rebels were defeated, all connotations of brave defiance would be lost. The poem could then be read as a transparent attempt to appear repentant in the face of a charge of sedition. Whether Wang Wei actually orally composed a protest poem while in prison is not an issue for the points being made here. What is important is the fact that the trope of oral composition still carried certain implications of the moral and emotional authenticity described in the "Daxu" and had a key role to play in setting the context for certain poems.

The question of how much oral composition of poetry took place during the Tang is complex and difficult to answer from the surviving sources. There are, however, some intriguing patterns in these sources. When we look at the frequency of poem titles that claim oral composition in the *Quan Tang shi*, a noticeable trend emerges: there is a significant drop in the number of such titles after the High Tang, with Liu Yuxi 劉禹錫 (772–842) in the Mid-Tang being the last major poet to have more than one or two such poems attributed to him. Of the eighty-one poems overall through the Tang, fifty-six are attributed to poets prior to or roughly contemporaneous with Lu Lun (737–98). Of these, Du Fu has the greatest number by far with twenty-two, most of which are parts of poetic sets. Wang Wei, Meng Haoran, and Li Bai also have several attributions. In the Mid-Tang period, Quan Deyu, Liu Yuxi, and Lü Wen account for the most poems with five, seven, and three respectively. Interestingly, despite their sizable collections, Yuan Zhen has only one poem in response to an orally composed poem[76] but no orally composed poems of his own, and Bai Juyi has but one poem attributed to him with any indication of oral composition in the title.[77] In the Late Tang the numbers are even smaller, with only Du Mu and Li Qunyu 李群玉 (813–60) having one attribution each.[78] What makes these numbers all the more surprising is that the overall amount of poetry surviving from the Mid- and Late Tang is far greater than that for earlier periods.

We might be tempted to conclude from these numbers that there was less orally composed poetry in the later portions of the dynasty. That, I believe, would be a mistake. We must not forget that these numbers cannot be trusted to tell us anything conclusive about the actual amount of oral composition occurring in these periods. They can only tell us how much of this poetry was recorded, labeled specifically as oral in the title, and survived in written form long enough to make it into the *Quan Tang shi*. There is clear evidence that many orally composed poems did not get recorded. An entry from the *Da Tang xinyu* hints that we are only getting part of the picture from what has survived. After describing an outing where many poems were composed (some on horseback, thus implying orality), the anecdote notes that "there were many pieces, and they were not all recorded" 文多不盡載.[79]

In his "Introduction to the Collection of Liu and Bai's Matching Poems" 劉白唱和集解, Bai Juyi offers a possible reason for his lack of recorded oral compositions: "As for the other [poems], which followed a momentary whim or were the product of drink, and were generally produced orally, they are not included in this number" 其餘乘興扶醉率然

76. *QTS*, 409.4547.

77. *QTS*, 441.4928.

78. For Du Mu, see *QTS*, 524.6005. For Li Qunyu, see *QTS*, 569.6600.

79. Liu Su, *Da Tang xinyu*, 8.128.

口號者，不在此數.[80] This comment raises the question of whether these poems were not included in the collection because they were the products of whim and drink or because they were oral compositions. Eliminating poems that were in the former category would excise large parts of Bai Juyi's extant collection. Moreover, Bai Juyi was notoriously unwilling to discard his own writings.[81] It is more likely that the significance of oral composition in this case is that these poems were never written down and thus could not make it into the collection. Their exclusion was thus in part a practical matter.

There is, however, the possibility that even if the frequency of oral composition remained the same throughout the dynasty, the perceived importance of a claim of oral composition as part of the context of such works somewhat decreased. We might conclude that as writing became more common, orality lost some of its close associations with moral authenticity. Or perhaps the increased emphasis on poetry as an art rather than primarily a social skill may have caused poets to look askance at the verse they produced casually and spontaneously in social settings.[82] I suspect that these scenarios are all possible to different degrees, yet the evidence is simply too limited to say so with any confidence. With such a small number of poems that directly make a claim of orality surviving (and let us recall that about a quarter of them are attributed to Du Fu alone), the data simply do not support building a traceable narrative of change. We thus return to oral composition as an ephemeral phenomenon. It probably accounted for a great deal of poetic composition in the Tang, and before and after that period, yet we can only view it from a distance. Even then we are looking at written traces of sounds we will never hear.

Circulation

Just as the earliest works of Chinese literature were likely orally composed, so did they circulate in this mode as well. Indeed, the *Han shu* attributes

80. "Liu Bai changheji jie" 劉白唱和集解, Zhu, 69.3711.

81. See discussion in Chapter 5.

82. This dichotomy is obviously greatly simplified. All Tang poetry existed between these two poles, which were themselves not at all mutually exclusive. For an in-depth discussion of this issue and related ones, see Stephen Owen, *End of the Chinese 'Middle Ages'*, 107–29.

the very survival of the *Shi* during the Qin bibliocaust to the fact that they were memorized and transmitted orally, claiming that "they met with the Qin and remained intact because they were recited from memory and not only [written] on bamboo and silk" 遭秦而全者，以其諷誦，不獨在竹帛故也.[83] There is abundant evidence that oral transmission not only continued through the Tang period and beyond, but that it remained an important force in the survival of works that would have otherwise been lost. Descriptions of the compilation of poetry collections from all periods of the Tang, for example, make reference to a reliance on oral sources.[84] In his biography of the influential Early Tang poet Chen Zi'ang 陳子昂 (661–702), Lu Cangyong 盧藏用 writes of collecting poems from oral sources: "[Chen Zi'ang's] writings were scattered and lost. Many were obtained from people's mouths. Those that survive today are ten *juan*'s worth" 其文章散落，多得之於人口，今所存者十卷.[85] The Five Dynasties writer Xu Xuan's 徐鉉 (916–91) preface to the works of Jiang Jiangong 江簡公 similarly notes that he collected written copies of Jiang's works from a number of sources, but that he also depended on the fact that "some have been circulated orally" 或傳於人口.[86]

Oral circulation is a topic no less controversial in the scholarly literature than oral composition, and it will again be useful to begin with a definition. My focus here is not on so-called "pure" oral transmission, that is, an extended period of transmission from one person or group to another by oral means alone in which no writing is involved. Scholarly interest in this type of circulation has long been tied to the study of folk literature and the search for works that could be seen as "pure" expressions of the folk, often envisioned as illiterate. Folk songs have, in certain periods, influenced literary culture in China, yet the mainstream poetic culture of the Tang was a highly literate one. A search for chains of oral transmission unsullied by writing would likely be fruitless. For my purposes here, any instance in which a person transmits a poem to another by

83. *Han shu*, 30.1708.

84. See Chapter 5 for a more detailed discussion of poetry collections for individual writers.

85. Lu Cangyong, "Chen Zi'ang biezhuan" 陳子昂別傳, *QTW*, 238.2424.

86. Xu Xuan, "Hanlin xueshi Jiang Jiangong ji xu" 翰林學士江簡公集序, *QTW*, 881.9213.

oral means alone counts as an example of oral circulation. Following Finnegan, I do not consider a poem's having been written down at some point in its circulation to eliminate the possibility of oral circulation.[87] It is the specific moment of circulation that determines orality, not the poem's history or future. If a poet composed a poem in writing and then recited it aloud to a group of friends, he circulated his poem orally, whether his friends committed it to memory, set it down in writing themselves, or quickly forgot it altogether. This definition is a broad one, but as with my definition of oral composition, it will allow us to examine a wide array of Tang poetic practices. In what follows, I approach oral circulation from a variety of perspectives, investigating the role of audience, similarities to commercial markets, and the loss of authorial control and tenuousness of survival inherent in oral modes of poetic transmission.

Audience

The nature of a poem's audience differed depending on whether it was heard or read. Oral circulation involved a level of intimacy that could be missing in written forms of transmission. The sounds of poetry were the sounds of human voices, most often of friends, acquaintances, and family members, and the limitations of voice and hearing required close proximity between speaker and audience. Extended written transmission over time and space did not necessarily indicate the level of popularity of a given work, as a single copy of a text could survive and move from place to place without continued reproductions.[88] For a poem to circulate orally, however, required that a continuous succession of people enjoyed it enough to remember it and repeat it to others, who in turn did the same. We are not talking about an age of mass communication. A modern song becomes a hit when a great number of people listen to a much smaller number of broadcasts. In the Tang, even in performance contexts, we can assume that only a very limited number of people would hear any given

87. See Finnegan, *Oral Poetry*, 17.

88. As I will discuss in more detail in Chapter 4, the "Qinfu yin" manuscripts are an excellent example of this phenomenon. These manuscripts transmitted the poem from the tenth to the twentieth century not through continuous circulation and reproduction, but simply by surviving.

recitation of a poem. Oral circulation in the Tang meant one person chanting or singing to another or at most a small group.

The focus of much oral transmission in the Tang was from the poet himself to specific individuals, whether friends and family of the poet or figures of notable social status. Du Fu begins his poem "Expressing What Has Stirred Me" 遣興 with a proud description of his young son Zongwu 宗武:

Jizi is a fine lad,	驥子好男兒，
It was last year when he learned to speak.	前年學語時．
He asked to know the names of our guests,	問知人客姓，
And was able to recite his old man's poems.	誦得老夫詩．[89]

One of the many facets of Du Fu's poetry was the attention he devoted to his family. No Tang poet wrote more about his wife and sons; he clearly enjoyed sharing his poetry with them as well. This intimate example of the poet passing on his poems orally, sharing them with a child who has only just learned to speak, points to something larger about the way people learned the poetic language. A father teaching poetry to a young son was likely a very common occurrence in Tang elite society. Before he begins to learn how to read and write the classics, Zongwu has already been introduced, orally and aurally, to the rhythms and intonations of poetry. If Du Fu is telling us the truth (and parents do have a tendency to exaggerate their children's accomplishments), then Zongwu could recite poetry almost as soon as he could speak.

In a discussion of the connection between the oral and the written in cultures in which there was a written classical language substantially divorced from the spoken vernacular, Ong claims that by the Middle Ages in Europe, "no one who spoke [Latin] had learned it as a first language, a mother tongue, orally acquired, tied to the first growth of consciousness out of the early infant's or child's unconscious: everyone who knew Latin had learned it through the use of writing."[90] If the example of Du Fu's son is representative, Ong's notion of a clear division between a written language and a spoken vernacular has less validity for poetry specifically in

89. Qiu, 4.326.
90. Ong, "Orality, Literacy, and Medieval Textualization," 6.

Tang-period China, at least for social and cultural elites. It is true that most Tang poetry was composed in the "classical language" of literary Chinese, yet it would be wrong to assume that it was as dependent on the use of reading and writing as were the texts of the true classics that made up the Confucian canon in the Tang.[91] The structures and rules of poetry were very much alive both on the tongues and in the ears of people in the Tang, as we can see in this comment from a proud father about his son.

That Du Fu would share his poetry with his toddler son through recitation is not surprising; this mode of presentation dominated face to face poetic exchange during the Tang between highly literate adults as well. Suffusing so much of elite life, poetry was an integral part of personal interactions, and focusing on poetry solely as a literary endeavor risks neglecting its important social aspects. There are numerous examples of poetic exchange or transmission from one individual to another conducted in writing,[92] yet oral recitation was arguably the dominant mode of presenting individual poems to a friend or acquaintance when meeting face to face. Returning to Du Fu, we find a typical example portrayed in his preface to "Recalling the Unusual Occurrence When Attendant Censor Su Visited Me on the River, I Composed a Poem in Eight Rhymes" 蘇大侍御訪江浦賦八韻紀異:

Attendant Censor Su Huan loved quietude. When he traveled on the banks of the Yangzi, he did not contact the hangers-on of the regional government and had long been cut off from politics. He was in a sedan chair on the riverbank when he unexpectedly visited my boat. I had already set out tea and wine inside. I asked [Su Huan] to recite some of his recent poems and he was willing to intone several. Their skill and strength were plain and strong; the words and lines were moving.

91. I am making a distinction here between the poetic language and more grammatically complex forms of literary Chinese used in prose works, which I discussed in Chapter 2. We do not, unfortunately, know the poems that Zongwu could recite at such a young age, but the larger point of poetry being a set of patterns learned at a very young age still, I believe, holds true.

92. Some examples will be discussed in detail in Chapter 4.

蘇大侍御渙，靜者也，旅於江側·凡是不交州府之客，人事都絕久矣·肩輿江浦，忽訪老夫舟楫，已而茶酒内·余請誦近詩肯吟數首，才力素壯，詞句動人·[93]

Like Du Fu's comment that his son could recite some of his poems, this anecdote gives us a glimpse of what was probably common practice in the Tang: friends would expect each other to have a recent poem or two set to memory and ready to present as a common part of social exchange. In this context Du Fu encounters Su Huan's works not as impersonal characters on a page, but as the sounds coming from a friend's mouth in a casual setting. Su Huan is clearly not composing orally on the spot; Du Fu had asked to hear some of his "recent poems," yet the oral mode of presentation effectively reproduces the "Daxu" model and its promise of emotional truth. The literary and the social are closely intertwined here. Du Fu does consider Su Huan's poems as works of literature, praising them for specific literary qualities. At the same time the nature of poetry makes the literary personal. Du Fu lauds not only Su Huan's works but his character as well. The role of audience (here limited to only Du Fu himself) in this anecdote is different from that found in claims of broad circulation. Du Fu is not claiming that his friend's poems are popular, but rather that they are good, and it is his judgment as an individual that he relies on to buttress his claim.[94]

Claims of oral circulation are often closely tied to questions of fame and the spread of a poet's reputation. Saying that a wide array of people recited a poet's works thus implied a more intense level of popularity than did simply noting that they circulated in general or appeared in written form, and writers often employed observations that a poet's works were widely declaimed as praise for those works and the poet in question. An entry in the *Da Tang xinyu* quotes the poem "Losing My White Falcon" 失白鷹 by Shan Fan 山範 and goes on to state that the poem was "widely recited by people of the age" 甚爲時所諷詠.[95] This same work makes a similar claim about Zhang Wencheng's 張文成 "Song of Yan" 詠燕,

93. Qiu, 23.2014.

94. In his discussion of the *shihua* 詩話 ("Talks on Poetry") genre, Owen argues that they appeal "to values in which words have worth because they are elicited by chance from an interesting person." See *Readings in Chinese Literary Thought*, 362.

95. Liu Su, *Da Tang xinyu*, 8.129.

writing that "in the age there were none who did not recite it" 時人無不諷詠.[96] Su Jiang 蘇絳, in his "Funerary Inscription for Director of Granaries Jia" 賈司倉墓誌銘, writes of Jia Dao 賈島 (779–843) that "his towering lines are recalled in the mouths of men" 孤絶之句記在人口.[97] The letters and poems that Bai Juyi and Yuan Zhen sent to each other are filled with similar complimentary notes, focusing heavily on the broad popularity their poetry clearly enjoyed. A typical example is found in Yuan Zhen's preface to one of the first compilations of Bai Juyi's literary collection. He writes of Bai Juyi's poems, "They are spoken by the mouths of every noble and consort, every herdboy and groom" 王公妾婦牛童馬走之口無不道.[98]

Because oral circulation required a certain degree of intimacy and the efforts of so many individual actors, a sure sign of popularity was the ability of poems to orally circulate beyond a writer's circle of acquaintances to a broad and even anonymous audience. Some texts thus describe not only widespread recitation of a poet's works, but explicitly specify that they passed from person to person amongst a wide audience in this fashion as well.[99] In his preface to a collection of Sun Ti's writings, Yan Zhenqing 顏眞卿 (708/9–784/5) states that Sun Ti's poems "transcended this age and were spread around orally" 冠絶當時・布在人口.[100] The *Tangshi jishi* 唐詩紀事 quotes Yang Danian 楊大年 as noting of the poet Lu Yanrang's 盧延讓 works that, "Yanrang's poems survive today. There are also those who are most fond of them and spread them orally" 延讓詩至今存，人亦有絶好之者，其播人口.[101] The *Tangshi jishi* makes a similar claim about a single poem of the writer Cui Ya 崔涯, "Knight Er-

96. Ibid., 8.128–29.

97. *QTW*, 736.7937.

98. Yuan Zhen, "Preface to Mr. Bai's *Changqing* Collection" 白氏長慶集序, *Yuan Zhen ji* 元稹集, 51.555.

99. Widespread recitation is, of course, different from oral circulation *per se* and there is a subtle difference in the claims being made here. For example, in modern America, the works of Shakespeare are widely recited. They are not, however, actively transmitted through the oral medium. If one is going to memorize and recite Shakespeare's works, it would typically be done though texts rather than solely by hearing others' recitations.

100. Yan Zhenqing, "Shangshu xingbu shilang zeng shangshu youpushe Sun Ti wengong ji xu" 尚書刑部侍郎贈尚書右僕射孫逖文公集序, *QTW*, 337.3416.

101. Ji Yougong 計有功, *Tangshi jishi*, 65.973.

rant" 俠士, stating that "this poem has often been transmitted orally" 此詩往往傳於人口.[102]

Often times such comments take the form of a report to the poet himself that his works have spread beyond the scope of his awareness. In his "Sent to Reminder Du" 寄杜拾遺, Ren Hua 任華 writes:

Reminder Du, do you know
That yesterday there was someone able to recite several pieces of "yellow silk words?"[103]
I thought them strange and extraordinary and asked about them particularly.
As it turns out, he said they were the work of Du the Second...
杜拾遺，知不知，昨日有人誦得數篇黄絹詞·
吾怪異奇特借問，果然稱是杜二之所爲·[104]

There are two levels of praise operating here. Ren Hua is lauding the quality of the verses themselves, using the claim of surprise to give the praise a patina of authenticity. He did not find the works he heard recited "strange and extraordinary" simply because he knew they were by his old friend Du Fu. Rather, as he did not discover this fact until later, his judgment was based on the merit of the works themselves. Ren Hua further implies that the works were not only extraordinary, but popular as well. They had circulated orally to the extent that they had gone beyond Du Fu's close friends and had even come back to such people (including Ren himself) by another route.

If circulating poems among family and friends was an ordinary aspect of social life in the Tang, having one's works reach the imperial ears was a more rarified achievement. The emperor stood in an interesting position in the cycle of circulation. One value of circulation was that it showed the breadth of one's audience: the wider the circulation the better. In this context it is ironic that the most prestigious audience was, in fact, the smallest: it consisted of one man. At the same time, emperors were likely near the end of a long chain of transmissions. Other than works by poets they already knew personally—those who were a part of their retinue and regularly accompanied them on outings and the like—emperors only en-

102. Ibid., 52.797. For the poem itself see *QTS*, 505.5741.
103. That is, beautiful poems.
104. *QTS*, 261.2903.

countered other works after they had already circulated widely enough to penetrate the palace walls, whether through entertainers or along other paths.[105] They may have been a small audience, but they were also one that proved a base of extensive circulation preceding them.

It is thus not surprising that we find claims of poems reaching an imperial audience functioning in a similar way to claims of broad oral circulation; they serve as high praise for the poet in question and proof of expansive popularity. And again, it is oral transmission in particular that is highlighted in these comments. The goal is for a poet's poem to be performed for the emperor, not left for him to read. Li Bai, who eventually fell out of favor with the emperor Xuanzong and was expelled from court in 744, nevertheless achieved the important goal of having his poetry reach the imperial ears. As Ren Hua writes to him, "Your new poems are passed around in the mouths of palace women/fine lines never leave the Luminous Ruler's mind" 新詩傳在宮人口，佳句不離明主心.[106] Bai Juyi employs similar terms in praising Yuan Zhen: "When [Yuan Zhen] was in the Hanlin Academy, Muzong had, altogether, requested many hundreds of his poems and ordered his attendants to chant them. In the palace he was called 'Yuan the Talent'" 在翰林時，穆宗前後索詩數百篇，命左右諷詠．宮中呼為元才子.[107]

I would argue that orality as a specific mode of transmission in these latter examples is meaningful because of its seemingly contradictory aspects of intimacy and popularity. In Ren Hua's couplet "mouths" (*kou* 口) and "mind" (*xin* 心) appear in parallel positions, strengthening the connection between the sounds of Li Bai's works and the thoughts of the emperor. Even if Li Bai and Yuan Zhen were not directly reciting their poems to Xuanzong and Muzong, as Su Huan shared his recent works with his friend Du Fu and Du Fu himself taught his poems to Zongwu, their voices were being heard by the most important ears in the realm. At the same time, the emperor is the ultimate arbiter of fame. He is, in an

105. The *Pine Window Miscellany* 松窗雜錄 of Li Jun 李濬 notes Emperor Wenzong 文宗 asking a courtier, "Who first came out with this poem on the peony that is being sung in the capital these days?" 今京邑傳唱牡丹花詩，誰為首出. See Ren, *Tang shengshi*, 527.

106. "Sent to Li Bai" 寄李白, *QTS*, 261.2903.

107. Zhu, 70.3736.

important sense, the aim of all circulation and having him as an audience proves that a poet's work had spread widely. To group a father teaching his poems to his young son with a palace lady singing to the emperor might seem odd at first glance, and there is no doubt that they involved very different levels of intimacy. Yet the strong connections between author and audience that oral transmission implied resonated in both contexts. The emotional immediacy of the human voice expressing itself remained in even the most literate of circumstances.

COMMERCIAL MARKETS

The different audiences for orally circulated poetry in the Tang implied different motivations behind that circulation. A father may have recited poems to his son without commercial or economic motives,[108] but such figures as exam candidates, important officials, and the emperor existed in a nexus of capital transactions, whether that capital was social or monetary. Focusing on poems exclusively as literary works or as sources of biographical data risks obscuring the far more varied roles that poetry actually played in Tang life. Poems could be expressions of one's innermost emotions, but they also had value as commodities, advertising, and entertainment.

Although it was written poetry that was more often bought and sold as a commodity in the Tang,[109] the oral aspects of poetry mattered in a context of supply and demand as well. The *Jiu Tang shu* biography of the poet Li Yi 李益 (748–827), for example, states that "each time he would compose a piece, it would be sought out with gifts by the musicians in the palace entertainment quarters, who would sing it as a performance for the emperor" 每作一篇，爲教坊樂人，以賂求取唱爲供奉歌詞.[110] Poems function as true commodities here. There was a demand, as the emperor was apparently particularly fond of Li Yi's works. Musicians who could obtain new works by the poet could thus please the emperor and gain his favor. Li Yi in turn received tangible goods in exchange for his

108. Though as the ability to compose poetry became an increasingly important determinant of success on the civil service examinations, there would have indeed been some economic incentives for training one's sons to be skilled poets.

109. See my discussion in Chapter 4.

110. *JTS*, 137.3771.

poetic works and the more important benefit of having his works reach imperial ears. Carrying this theme further, we might say that the musicians "added value" by setting the works to music and performing them for the emperor. They took raw material and changed it to resell it at a profit to themselves. Whether Li Yi recited his works to the paying musicians or gave them a written copy, it is clear that the poems reached their pinnacle of value when they were performed for the emperor in oral form. Commercial forces both benefitted from and encouraged poetic circulation.

In more cases, poems functioned not as commodities themselves, but as catalysts in larger commercial markets. In this context, poetry's ties to commerce were perhaps nowhere closer than in the entertainment quarters of the capital cities of Chang'an and Luoyang. Amidst the mix of scholar officials, exam candidates, professional singers, and courtesans (these latter two categories largely overlapping), poems were both currency and advertising. They were sought out, acquired, and passed on for profit, imparting value not only to their authors but to others who used them properly as well. In this context of gossip, song, and exchange, oral circulation in particular found fertile ground.

The examples above show that broad oral circulation brought praise or fame to the poet himself. The rapidity of this mode of transmission meant that it could quickly spread the fame of others as well. In the *Beili zhi* 北里志 ("Record of the Northern Quarter") Sun Qi 孫棨 (fl. 880) relates a story of meeting a courtesan named Liu Tainiang 劉泰娘 who, in spite of her great beauty, was not well known as she lived in an area of the city not renowned for its fine courtesans.[111] One night, Sun, who had encountered her earlier in the day and inquired as to the whereabouts of her home, paid her a visit and posted a poem that sang of her praises there. In his text, he claims that when other travelers heard it, "the next day those who visited her came in lines of carriages" 詰朝詣之者，結駟於門矣.[112] As the woman lived in a less frequently visited area of the city, it is unlikely that the men in these lines of carriages would have encountered Sun Qi's origi-

111. Liu Tainiang appears to also be the subject of Liu Yuxi's poem "Song of Tainiang" 泰娘歌, *QTS*, 356.3997.

112. Sun Qi, *Beili zhi*, 37. See also Rouzer's (*Articulated Ladies*, 263–265) discussion of this anecdote from a different perspective.

nal text so soon after he posted it. Word of mouth, or oral circulation, on the other hand, allowed the woman's fame to spread quite quickly.

A similar anecdote in the *Yunxi youyi* 雲谿友議 ("Friendly Chats at Misty Brook") underscores the rapidity with which poems could circulate when transmitted orally. Fan Shu 范攄 says of Cui Ya, "Each time he would post a poem in a brothel, everybody would chant it in the alleys and streets. If he praised a place, then carriages and horses would come continuously. If he disparaged it, then they would be stricken with panic for their cups and plates" 每題一詩於娼肆，無不誦之於衢路，譽之則車馬繼來，毀之則盃盤失錯.[113] Here again rapid and extensive transmission is the key to the commercial value of the poem: praise is useless if people do not hear it. We might think of such poems as the equivalent of modern advertising ditties. They sometimes had value in their own right as works of literature, but they were also part of a commercial context in which they had something to sell. The better or more memorable the poem, the more effective it would be.

In both these examples poems play multiple roles and impart value to a variety of different actors. As rapidly circulating works of literature, they served to spread the fame of their authors. These were not anonymous works but poems by specific named individuals who were surely pleased that their poems spread so quickly; the entertainment quarters were filled with important people who would be a desirable audience. As advertisements, these poems increased the value of the subjects they praised, in this case brothels and courtesans.[114] Finally, they provided information, reliable or not, to customers. On the surface we are at some remove from the ideals of the "Daxu" here, but perhaps these examples afford a closer look at the reality of the different social and commercial roles poetry played in the Tang. Yet even in this less exalted context, we can find the qualities attributed to poetry in the foundational critical works of the tradition. The idea of poetry as a conveyer of truth persists. If the anecdotes are to be believed, poems by Cui Ya and Sun Qi were taken as expressions of their true feelings. That these feelings were about their experiences being entertained by courtesans does not negate the "Daxu" model so much as

---

113. Fan Shu, *Yunxi youyi*, 32–33.

114. See Rouzer's (*Articulated Ladies*, 277) discussion of poems written on a courtesan's wall as a form of advertisement.

simply re-imagine it in a very different context. Moreover, part of the value of poetry in these contexts, as opposed to other modes of expression, is exactly that it makes language last. Cui Ya's comments in mentioning to a friend that he enjoyed himself at a given brothel would have been unlikely to spread like wildfire through the quarter. When he expressed his praise in a poem, with all the structural and phonological attributes that genre involves, the words became more memorable and apt to be passed along.

I argue above that the palace musicians "added value" to Li Yi's works by setting them to music and performing them. I would thus like to close this discussion of the connections between commerce in oral circulation by considering a well-known anecdote that deals with public performance of poetry in the Tang. Finnegan sees the key distinction between oral and written poetry as ultimately residing in performance. There may be no discernable and consistent "oral style," but issues of performance can still differentiate important aspects of oral poetry from poetry in written form.[115] Such scholars as Ren Bantang and Robert Ashmore have shown that performance, whether as an actual mode of poetic presentation or as a rubric for interpretation, is indeed a constant presence in much of Tang poetry. My interest here, however, is not in performance itself, but in how questions of art are closely tied with those of popularity and value in a discourse whose aesthetic judgments had become increasingly tied to issues of economy.

Bai Juyi and Yuan Zhen, perhaps more than any other Tang poets, were keenly aware of the quasi-commercial roles their writings played. Bai Juyi in particular controlled the contents of his collection and access to it very tightly, and both writers made frequent mention of the popularity of their poems and of instances of those poems being recited, copied, and exchanged by others. Bai's oft-anthologized "Letter to Yuan the Ninth" 與元九書 includes an intriguing indication of the interplay of poetic circulation, performance, and value. In a typically self-congratulatory mode, he writes to Yuan Zhen:

When I came to Chang'an again, I also heard that there was a Military Commander, one Gao Xiayu (772–826), who wanted to marry a singing girl. The girl

115. Finnegan, *Oral Poetry*, 133.

boasted loudly: "I can recite Academician Bai's 'Song of Lasting Pain.' How could I be like any other girl?" Because of this she raised her price.
及再來長安，又聞有軍使高霞寓，欲娉倡妓·妓大誇曰：我誦得白學士長恨歌，豈同他妓哉·由是增賈·[116]

This is, we should not forget, Bai Juyi's own claim, so let us begin with him. He clearly intends this story to reflect favorably on himself, portraying his famous work as literally adding value to the singing girl through her connection to it. She is not claiming that she can recite just any lengthy poem (which would indeed make her like "any other girl," or at least any other singing girl in the entertainment quarters), but rather this one in particular. For Bai Juyi, this shows that his work has circulated widely, not simply because it is known in the capital, but because it is sufficiently famous that this singing girl can assume that Gao Xiayu will recognize the work and agree that it has something exceptional about it. The singing girl, in this case, has demonstrated a special skill, but one whose value is primarily derived from Bai Juyi's own skill and reputation.

Granting, for the sake of argument, that Bai Juyi did hear a story to this effect and that the story was true, the implications in his retelling remain misleading. The ability to simply memorize and recite "Song of Lasting Pain" would be unlikely to increase a singing girl's income or marriage price as doing so would not, in and of itself, be difficult. In the quite recent past, Chinese high school students would regularly memorize such works of similar length, such as Bai Juyi's "Song of the Pipa" 琵琶行, and professional singers in the Tang could be expected to have been much more adept at such feats. We can also assume that it was not particularly difficult to get access to a piece such as "Song of Lasting Pain," as such works were, essentially, in the "public domain" and the work appears to have been well known at the time. Bai Juyi may have restricted access to certain copies of his collection, as we will see below, but he could not control the circulation of his poetry by other means.

A more convincing explanation for the singing girl's raised price (and recall that we are never told if Gao Xiayu agreed to pay it) is suggested by Ren Bantang's discussion of this claim: it was not that she could recite "Song of Lasting Pain" but *how* she did so. Her ability as a performer, not

116. Zhu, 415.2793.

her particular repertoire, made her exceptional. Ren writes that "a skilled singer could develop the profound and subtle meanings in a poem, awaken people and attain a pleasant impression."[117] *Songde* 誦得, the same term Du Fu uses to describe Zongwu's ability to recite the poems Du Fu had taught him, is used here in a different sense. Ren argues that *song* is a description not of mere recitation or chanting, but of skilled singing accompanied by music. Such a performance, if done properly, could bring out the structures, effects, and rhetorical methods used in a piece in a way that simple recitation could not.[118] The added value was thus mutually bestowed. Our anonymous singing girl did depend on Bai Juyi's skill as poet: he had authored a piece whose subtleties and profound meanings were worth teasing out. At the same time, it took skillful performance to bring these features to an audience. The words of the poem by themselves were not enough.

In this context Finnegan's notion that performance is the key area of distinction between oral and written modes of poetic presentation becomes clear. Orality provides something that goes beyond the written text. We have seen how knowing (or believing) that a poem was composed orally can change the way we read it; actually hearing a poem performed aloud by a singer who was able to interpret the poem in the way that she presented it, with the modulations of her voice and the passions that they conveyed, could likewise radically alter one's experience of a poetic work. This is one important way in which song could "make language last" in the Tang, a feature that poets themselves understood well.[119] We already know that the rhythms and sonic patterns of some poetry made it easier to create and remember. By adding additional layers of nuance and meaning, oral performance makes the experience of a poem all the more memorable and increased the likelihood that the poem would continue to spread.

Authorial Control and Tenuous Survival

Claims of oral composition were meaningful: they implied spontaneous literary creation that promised a particular type of access to the poet's

117. Ren, *Tang shengshi*, 15.

118. Ibid.

119. Note that the poet Li Wei 李蔚 (d. 879) once ordered a singing girl to spread his works 命謳者傳之 (Ji Yougong, *Tangshi jishi*, 60.919).

moral and emotional sense. This promise, however, is potentially undercut the moment an orally composed poem in the Tang became a written text. Once a poem left its author's lips, the process of separation from him began. The above accounts by Bai Juyi and Han Yu of this process are the only descriptions of transcribing orally composed poems to survive from the Tang; each implies the possibility that what was transcribed differed from what the poets originally intoned. In his preface to "On the Pond," Bai Juyi portrays himself as composing in a state of near delirium. It is only when he looks at what Agui has written down that he sees his chantings have become a "rhymed piece." Likewise, Han Yu's mysterious monk Miming claims that he does "not understand the writing of the common world," thus implying a disconnect between the sounds he produces and the mundane written script that attempts to capture them. In each case the direct line from emotion to spontaneous poem remains intact, but there is a disjunction between that oral poem and the version that is recorded. A new actor has intervened in the person of the transcriber. The accounts do not draw specific attention to this moment, but the possibility of alteration lurks, planting the seed of doubt as to whether or not the later reader can ever have full access to the poets' true emotions.

Similar concerns can sometimes surround oral transmission. The logic of a commercial market is often observable only in the abstract, or at some remove from the individual transactions that are part of the market as a whole. When the parts are looked at separately from the totality, the result is somewhat more chaotic. Oral circulation could be intimate, but it was also a widespread and effective way of transmitting poetry from its original author to an audience that could number far more members than the author could possibly encounter himself. This larger story of success, however, can obscure the innumerable instances of instability that were also an important part of the reality of this mode of poetic circulation in the Tang. As works spread beyond a poet's circle of friends and acquaintances, they would inevitably change, and the connection between the poet and the work he had originally created would be weakened. Similarly, just as oral circulation proved a poem's popularity because it required a continuous chain of actors to remember it and recite it to others, so too were orally circulated poems in constant danger of disappearing. An existence based on the fickle tastes and flawed memories is a tenuous one, and more poems surely perished than were eventually published.

Oral circulation implies not only popularity but also speed. Freed of the constraints of brush, paper, and manual reproduction, poems could spread both widely and quickly. In his "Funerary Inscription for Sir Xue, Instructor in the Directorate of Education" 國子助教薛君墓志銘,[120] Han Yu writes, "He composed the poems 'Turkic Horse' and 'Round Hillock.' Before the people of the capital had ever seen his writings, they had all spread them to each other orally until they knew them well" 作胡馬及圓丘詩，京師人未見其書，皆口相傳以熟.[121] The race between written and oral circulation is here explicit, and orality was bound to have the upper hand. In this example we again see poems move with the logic of a market. The demands of the audience ensure that the supply will find the fastest and most efficient way to reach them.

However, the efficiency of this mode of transmission came with a price; it entailed a commensurate lack of authorial control, as poets could exert even less influence over oral circulation than they could over written circulation of these same works.[122] Underlying descriptions of rapid oral circulation, we sometimes find a sense that the poems in question have taken on a life and direction of their own. Lin Song's 林嵩 "Preface to Zhou Pu's Poetry Collection" 周朴詩集序 portrays an audience so hungry for the poet's new works that they could not wait for a whole poem to be completed. Lin writes:

> The gentleman was slow and deliberate when composing poetry. In a full month he would only get a couplet or a line, but what he came up with was sure to surprise people. Before he had managed to complete a full piece, [the couplets and lines] would have already spread orally.
> 先生爲詩思遲·盈月方得一聯一句，得必驚人·未暇全篇，已布人口.[123]

As discussed in Chapter 4, the practice (or at least the conceit) of laboring for a prolonged period of time over not only a single poem, but even a single line or word, became increasingly prominent in the Mid- and Late Tang. This more time consuming mode of composition clearly left Zhou

---

120. Xue being Xue Gongda 薛公達. See *XTS*, 新唐書, 151.4952.

121. Ma, 361–362.

122. The issue of controlling the circulation of one's work will come up again in Chapter 5 when we examine Bai Juyi's management of his various literary collections.

123. *QTW*, 839.8742.

Pu (d. 879) unable to fully meet the demand for his works. We do not know how the portions of his incomplete poems entered the public domain: perhaps he would try out a line or two on a visiting friend who would then repeat them to others. Even if this passage is more praise for Zhou Pu than historical fact about the circulation of his poems, the tension between careful craft and control on one hand, and oral transmission and the rapidity it entailed on the other, is clearly present.[124]

We catch a glimpse of how poems were both spread and altered in oral contexts in what is perhaps the most famous Tang anecdote of oral circulation and performance: the "bet on singing in the tavern" 旗亭賭唱 anecdote from the early ninth century *Jiyi ji* 集異記 ("Records of Collected Marvels") by Xue Yongruo 薛用弱. As Xue tells it, the poets Wang Changling 王昌齡 (d. ca. 756), Gao Shi, and Wang Zhihuan 王之渙 (688–742) were drinking at a tavern when a group of musicians from the imperial Pear Garden Conservatory and four beautiful singing girls appeared and began performing the "famous songs of the time" 當時之名部.[125] The poets secretly made a bet on which one of them would have the greatest number of his poems set to music and sung by the performers. In the end, Wang Changling wins with two quatrains to Gao Shi and Wang Zhihuan's one each, though Wang Zhihuan does enjoy the honor of having correctly predicted that the most beautiful of the singers (諸妓之中最佳者) would choose one of his own quatrains.

As many scholars have pointed out, there is little doubt that the specific event this anecdote portrayed never took place.[126] Since it was clearly meant to be believable, however, it can tell us something about the ways in which poetry might have circulated in more informal contexts in this period and what attitudes poets themselves might have had towards the methods and implications of such transmission. To begin with, the mode of circulation is oral. These poems are sung rather than written on the

124. It is interesting to note the surprising parallels between the situation this anecdote portrays and the rapid circulation of textual, audio, and visual materials on the Internet in recent times. Incomplete versions of eagerly anticipated songs, films, and novels are frequently "leaked" before the official versions are released. While the financial issues are certainly different from what they were in the Tang (when works were not copyrighted), questions of creative control are quite similar.

125. Xue Yongruo, *Jiyi ji*, 11.

126. See Ashmore, "Hearing Things," 15; and Owen, *Great Age of Chinese Poetry*, 93.

tavern wall. Moreover, they are sung by performers who are clearly not personal acquaintances of the poets themselves; the poets are confident that their works have circulated widely enough to return to their ears by paths unknown. The works must also have had some currency in the palace if musicians from the Pear Garden Conservatory had set them to music. We see here how poems could circulate both into and out from the palace. Poems that had been performed for the emperor did not languish there; the same performers who entertained the emperor often performed in the entertainment quarters and elsewhere in the capital as well. These were not works specifically written for an imperial audience, but rather works that had circulated to the palace musicians and been set to music by them.

The anecdote also reveals that poems circulating as song were not necessarily complete, and could become unmoored from the original occasional context that gave them much of their emotional power. Gao Shi's quatrain as performed by the singing girl is only the opening of what elsewhere appears as a twenty-four line poem.[127] The original poem, "Weeping for District Defender Liang the Ninth of Shanfu" 哭單父梁九少府 was a somber lament for the death of a friend. Ashmore points out the reader's shock at Gao's "raucous response to hearing it sung" and notes that the quatrain circulated independently from the rest of the poem at the time of the compilation of the *Jiyi ji* and later.[128] Although quatrains excerpted from longer poems could and did circulate independently in written modes of circulation, works that became parts of performance repertoires, in the palace and elsewhere, appear to have been particularly susceptible to such fates.[129]

Tang poets themselves typically did not see the loss of control that wide oral circulation entailed to be entirely problematic. Indeed, we might assume that they were in fact happy that their poems were spread-

---

127. *QTS*, 212.2215.

128. Ashmore, "Hearing Things," 22–23. Owen (*Great Age of Chinese Poetry*, 93) makes the point that this anecdote may well have been invented as a way to "set off some very famous quatrains."

129. Wu Xiangzhou (*Tangshi chuangzuo yu geshi chuanchang guanxi yanjiu*, 70–71) discusses this phenomenon in some detail, noting a Qing critic's dismay at the version of a Wang Wei piece that, in very different versions, was a popular performance piece. See also Owen, *Great Age of Chinese Poetry*, 93–94.

ing in any form. Gao Shi expresses neither surprise nor disappointment that a work that ostensibly displayed his great sorrow at a friend's passing has been cut up to entertain customers at a bar. He himself appears to have divorced the poem from its original context and can enjoy it as a piece of entertainment and the subject of a wager. Even if the individual words of this quatrain have not changed from what Gao Shi originally composed (which, of course, we can never know), the quatrain as a whole has become something other than what it was before it circulated. This is, after all, a fictional anecdote, and we should not attribute the response of the Gao Shi described here to the actual historical figure. Yet if this anecdote (which was popular and appears in a number of sources) accurately portrays its cultural context, it shows that while oral circulation brought poems quickly to a broad audience, it often changed them in the process. This phenomenon is hardly unique to the Tang; as Finnegan notes, speaking broadly of oral traditions, "exact verbal transmission through oral tradition" appears to be nonexistent, despite the previous claims of some folklorists.[130]

If poets themselves did not always mind their works taking on lives of their own, still, widespread oral circulation was not necessarily regarded positively. If a commentator did not like the works that spread so quickly, praise could be turned on its head and become a lament. In Du Mu's funerary inscription for Li Kan 李戡 we find a particularly biting example. Du Mu writes that Li Kan had complained of Bai Juyi and Yuan Zhen's poems that:

> Of those who are not proper scholars and refined men, most have been ruined by them. They have spread among the common people and are written on screens and walls. Sons and fathers, daughters and mothers pass them along to each other orally. Their lewd words and indecent talk are like winter's cold and summer's heat. They enter into men's flesh and bone and cannot be expelled.
> 非莊士雅人，多爲其所破壞．流於民間，疏于屏壁．子父女母交口教授．淫言媟語，冬寒夏熱入人肌骨，不可除去．[131]

Rather than a marketplace, the salient metaphor here is disease. Like an infection, Bai Juyi and Yuan Zhen's poems spread uncontrollably and

130. Finnegan, *Oral Poetry*, 140.
131. Du Mu, *Fanchuan wenji* 樊川文集, 8.136.

poisoned those who heard them. While both written and oral circulation are noted in this passage, orality plays the more important role in giving the complaint its power. Oral transmission was faster than its written counterpart, as we have seen, and could affect even those who were illiterate. Poems written on walls could also be more easily avoided. One need only turn away from the offending verses. The sounds of chanting, however, are more insidious. They could come from a stranger passing on the street or even a family member. It is a different sort of control that is being lost here, but one no less important. Brief though the lives of verses spoken aloud might have been, they implied an immediacy and passion that could be infectious.

The fears of Du Mu and Li Kan notwithstanding, it is likely that few orally transmitted poems enjoyed the staying power of those by Bai Juyi and Yuan Zhen. In the contexts in which oral circulation often took place, poems led a particularly tenuous existence. Through the stories of scattered survivals, we see indications of how much was surely lost. Finnegan describes a certain type of oral poetry as "topical and ephemeral poems, usually short, [that] 'catch on' in a community and pass from mouth to mouth, often in an incredibly short time, to become widely popular (or popular within a particular group of people) and then, often, to be forgotten again."[132] She goes on to highlight the informality of this mode of transmission and points out that it "perhaps ultimately depends on face-to-face and unorganized contact."[133]

The entertainment quarters in the Tang are a case in point. Most Tang poems were, after all, short, and we have seen how face-to-face contacts between friends were frequently occasions for chanting either one's own recent poems, or poems that one had recently heard from others. The situation in the entertainments quarters was different from other contexts of circulation not in kind, but rather in intensity. With a large number of literate people in a small area where fame and reputation, whether as a scholar-official or a courtesan, could influence one's career, poems that served as both gossip and advertising were bound to be passed along quickly and widely. The spontaneous and informal nature of this setting, however, strongly implies that many of these poems were indeed ephem-

---

132. Finnegan, *Oral Poetry*, 157.
133. Ibid.

eral; they existed only briefly on the lips of a singing girl or drunkenly brushed on a slip of paper by a young exam candidate. The number that survived is surely dwarfed by those that quickly faded away; they were the background noise of Tang literary culture.

An anecdote from the *Beili zhi* highlights the fragility of poetry as it existed in the entertainment quarters and reminds us that much of the poetry we have today has survived through luck and fortuitous coincidence. Sun Qi tells of a denizen of the pleasure quarters named Yan who entertained numerous exam candidates and would often request that they compose poems for her as keepsakes. She fell gravely ill but continued to host guests and drink and perform music with them late into the night. Upon her death, several exam candidates wrote eulogies to her and sent them to her family. As the family was unhappy that none of these men had helped to pay her funeral expenses, they threw the writings into the street. These were later retrieved by one of her neighbors, Camelback Liu, who some said may have been her lover in secret. He placed a number of the works before her coffin and sang them out mournfully. Some poor scholars encountered him and had him sing the songs, of which he had memorized four, again. Sun Qi writes, "From this point on they spread widely through Chang'an and were often sung by mourners" 自是盛傳於長安，挽者多唱之.[134] Had Camelback Liu not happened upon these works lying in the street, they might never have been set to music and given voice. Had the group of impoverished scholars not appeared just as Liu was singing, the poems might have enjoyed but a single performance and not become a standard part of mourners' repertoire.

Yet these poems did survive, passing through both oral and written modes of circulation. Behind this anecdote the specter of loss remains. Not only did these four poems survive through a chain of lucky coincidences, they were merely small parts of a larger set. These were the poems Camelback Liu remembered; we do not know how many he forgot or never learned in the first place. Even the best-trained memories were imperfect, and human voices quickly faded away. The remarkable amount of poetry surviving from the Tang should never lull us into forgetting the innumerable works that disappeared soon after they were composed.

---

134. Sun Qi, *Beili zhi*, 30–31. See also Rouzer's discussion (*Articulated Ladies*, 269–73).

As noted in the introduction to this chapter, scholars tend to see oral and written literature in some form of conflict, where oral literature is slowly disappearing as it is superseded by writing, with its greater ability to endure over time and space. Over centuries this may well be the case. The proportion of poetry appearing in writing rather than existing only in oral form is surely far greater in the Ming than it was in the Han. At the same time, such an argument wrongly assumes, almost like misunderstandings of Darwinian evolution, that the older forms will die out completely as the newer forms flourish. Orality did not die out in China. Because cheaper and more readily available paper made writings more accessible, more people read poetry in written form in the Tang than in earlier periods. These same people, however, almost always recited the poems they were reading aloud. Poetry came to life through the medium of the human voice, even when the person reciting was the only one to hear that voice.

The oral and the written were not, in any meaningful sense, in conflict in the Tang. Yes, there are more poems surviving from earlier in the period that claim oral composition. But there are more claims of poets' works circulating orally in the later years of the Tang. One might further assume that as poetry became increasingly tied to commercial forces in some contexts, oral modes of circulation would become less prominent.[135] Orally transmitted poems, after all, are in some sense less stable than written ones. Yet this is not what the available sources tell us. Not only was orality not a hindrance in commercial contexts, it was often a strength. Poems that functioned as advertisements for courtesans and brothels (and, of course, for the poets themselves) spread more rapidly in oral form than they ever could have as written texts in a manuscript culture requiring constant copying. They could also change form and appear in a variety of performance contexts, both private and public, that would further widen their circulation. In many of these contexts, the malleability of orally transmitted verse was key to its success. To fit different types of perform-

135. It is important to keep in mind that this indeed happened in only certain contexts. Most poetry composed and circulated in the Tang that was not closely connected to what could be meaningfully called a commercial market.

ance, it had to change, as we saw in the case of Gao Shi's vastly truncated poem that won him a bet against his friends. Tang poets may not have explicitly asked for people to change their works in the course of transmission the way certain troubadour poets did, but they clearly approved of even substantial alterations in certain contexts, if it meant greater circulation than the original poems would otherwise enjoy.[136]

An emphasis on orality was not something forced on Tang poets and their audiences by low levels of literacy or deficits in written texts; on the contrary, it represented cultural preferences that existed independent of these factors. There was no conflict between the oral and the written in the Tang. Both modes of composition and circulation were constant features of literary culture. In different contexts they would have different connotations, and one might be more prevalent than the other at any given time, but the general picture is one of complementary co-existence, not competition.

136. Wu Xiangzhou (*Tangshi chuangzuo*, 23, 31–33) argues that poets would sometimes specifically craft their poems in such a way that they would be more likely to be set to music.

FOUR

Written Composition and Circulation

As important as oral composition and transmission were, it is ultimately because a significant amount of Tang poetry was written down that it continues to exist today. Every Tang poem that has survived to the present was recorded in writing at some point, in almost all cases during the Tang itself. If the oral components of Tang poetic culture were marked by ephemerality, the written aspects fostered preservation and historical continuity. One did not preclude the other; rather the oral and written cultures of Tang poetry existed simultaneously and in general harmony, both playing off of and supporting each other.

Indeed the same can be said for much of the poetry that preceded the Tang. The status of the *Shi* as a frequently memorized text may have helped it survive the Qin bibliocaust relatively intact, but it had already begun to be written down by that point. The *Han shu* entry noted in the previous chapter stated that it was "not only [written] on silk," implying that such a mode of transmission and preservation had become widespread by the time Qin Shihuang's burning of the books took place.[1] A similar situation is found with the *Chuci* 楚辭. Most likely composed and transmitted orally for many years, it had become a set of written texts by the early Han at the latest. David Hawkes points out that Liu An 劉安 (179–122 BCE), a Han prince in the southern region of Huainan 淮南,

1. The *jinwen* 今文 versus *guwen* 古文 debates about the *Shi* in the Han further indicate that written versions of the text had become dominant in many circles. See Loewe, *Early Chinese Texts*, 415.

was "commissioned to write an introduction to Qu Yuan's famous poem 'On Encountering Sorrow.'"[2] More direct evidence for portions of the *Chuci* existing in written form comes late in the second century BCE when Sima Qian 司馬遷 (ca. 145–ca. 85) writes in the *Shiji* 史記 that he "read 'On Encountering Sorrow,' 'Heavenly Questions,' 'Calling Back the Soul,' and 'Lament for Ying' and was saddened by the aims expressed" 余讀離騷、天問、招魂、哀郢，悲其志.[3]

As a mode of composition, writing had become sufficiently commonplace by the late third century that some accounts of composition describe it as the primary way in which literary texts are created. When Lu Ji imagines the concrete action of composing in his *Wenfu*, he consistently refers not to vocalizing but to the act of writing. Of the composer he writes, "With strong feelings he puts aside the book and takes his writing brush / to make it manifest in literature" 慨投篇而援筆、聊宣之乎斯文.[4] Other descriptions in the text are in a similar vein, with a composer pictured in a contemplative mood as he "held the brush in his lips" 含毫[5] and literature like "clouds rising from the forest of writing brushes" 雲起乎翰林.[6] Orality is not absent here, and indeed there are indications that it is still an important stage before the act of writing specifically. As Lu Ji describes it, "A stream of words flows through lips and teeth" 言泉流於唇齒,[7] and writing can merely follow along, as this is "something only the writing brush and silk can imitate" 唯毫素之所擬.[8] Writing does not yet operate entirely free of orality in this vision of composition, but it does appear to be the primary mode of literary expression.

The important role of writing in poetic culture becomes most clear in the one anthology that defined the Tang poet's education in poetry from earlier periods, the *Wenxuan*. And even though, as discussed in Chapter 2, most literate men in the Tang committed portions of the *Wenxuan* to memory, it existed primarily as a set of written texts from the time of its original compilation. David Knechtges notes that the Liang, during which

---

2. Hawkes, *Songs of the South*, 29.
3. Sima Qian 司馬遷, *Shiji* 史記, 84.2503.
4. *Wenfu*, 20. Translation from Owen, *Readings in Chinese Literary Thought*, 94.
5. *Wenfu*, 60. Translation Ibid., p.117.
6. *Wenfu*, 89. Translation Ibid., p.122.
7. *Wenfu*, 241. Translation Ibid., p.175.
8. *Wenfu*, 241. Translation Ibid., p.175.

the *Wenxuan* was compiled, witnessed the early stages of literary criticism and scholarship[9]—trends that could only exist in a context that included access to large numbers of written literary texts. This access was provided by the famously substantial library of Prince Xiao Tong, the *Wenxuan*'s compiler, which was said to have held some 30,000 *juan*.[10] In fact, it appears that only works that existed in available textual form were included in the anthology, regardless of the renown of their author.[11] Oral versions, even if the only sources available, were not deemed acceptable.

If earlier periods saw a gradual rise in the importance of poetry as a specifically written culture, the Tang witnessed a dramatic increase over earlier periods of this phenomenon. A purely oral culture requires nothing more than speech, hearing, and memory to transmit its works from person to person. Written cultures, especially ones as highly developed as that of the Tang, have far greater material prerequisites for facilitating the spread of literature. Reading and writing undertaken on a large scale require available, affordable, and conveniently usable materials. The bamboo slips and silk of earlier periods in Chinese history served to preserve and transmit texts on a limited scale, but were less than ideal for widespread use. Bamboo slips were cumbersome and difficult to keep bound together, and silk was prohibitively expensive for all but the wealthiest members of society. Paper, which the Chinese had begun to make in at least a rough form as early as the reign of the Han Emperor Wudi (140–87 BCE), was being used as a writing material by the second century CE at the latest.[12] By the beginning of the Tang, there had already been numerous and important advances in the production of paper,[13] and by the Mid-Tang, massive amounts were being used by the government to run its af-

---

9. Knechtges, *Wen xuan, vol. 1*, 4.

10. Ibid., 6.

11. See Knechtges's (*Wen xuan, vol. 1*, 42 and 541*n*262) discussion of the omission of Wang Xizhi's 王羲之 "Preface to the Third Day, Third Moon, Orchid Pavilion Poems' 三月三日蘭亭詩序.

12. See Twitchett, *Printing and Publishing in Medieval China*, 13. T. H. Tsien further describes the invention of paper and its spread in *Written on Bamboo and Silk*, 131–39. A much more detailed account of the invention, use, and manufacture of paper before the Tang is found in Pan, *Zhongguo kexue*, 33–134.

13. For a brief discussion of these advances in paper technology, see Tsien, "Paper and Printing," 42–47. Again, Pan Jixing (*Zhongguo kexue*, 102–83) covers this material in considerably more detail.

fairs.[14] Reliable statistics on the number of people specifically employed as scribes are difficult to come by, but we do know that during the Kaiyuan period the Academy of Scholarly Worthies (*jixian dian shuyuan* 集賢殿書院) alone employed some ninety scribes at a time.[15] The Tang thus clearly fulfilled the material prerequisites for widespread production and reproduction of texts.

The previous chapter argued for recognition of the continued importance of orality in Tang literary culture, noting that scholars often overlook its role when examining Tang poetry. In the present chapter I do not focus on making a similar argument for the role of writing, but rather take it for granted. We know that people in the Tang composed, read, and reproduced poems in writing. The evidence is widespread, voluminous, and beyond dispute. This chapter instead focuses on the details of *how* people wrote, read, and reproduced poetry in the Tang. The first section below deals with written composition and examines what we can deduce from the available sources about the connotations of composing in writing rather than orally during the Tang. I then turn my attention to the written circulation of poetry, examining the different ways that poetry was transmitted in this form, including the inscription of poetry in (and on) public locations and the sending of written poems by means of the postal system and other methods. I also briefly consider the connection between circulation of written poems and commercial markets. The final section looks at the actual copying practices that were used in the dissemination of poetry in the Tang. Because our accounts of copying are more numerous and detailed than descriptions of oral transmission, we can approach the question of how works were altered in the course of transmission with a greater degree of thoroughness here. It is clear that changing works, even engaging in what could be called rewriting, was a common practice. From the point of view of later critical approaches to Tang poetry, this degree of textual instability is troubling in that it often indicates movement away

14. Yang Jidong notes that "in the middle of the Tang period, the Department of Public Revenue (Duzhi) alone had to use 500,000 sheets of paper every year to draw up the budget of the empire. It has also been estimated that in the Kaiyuan years (713–41) the number of books possessed by the Academy of Scholarly Worthies and other departments of the central government had already reached about 500,000 scrolls which were copied on 16,000,000 sheets of paper." See Yang Jidong, "Writing in the Tang," 11.

15. Pan, *Zhongguo kexue*, 150.

from the text as originally created by the author (though the authors themselves sometimes revised works already in circulation as well). Not unlike medieval European writers, however, Tang authors rarely expressed concern over this phenomenon.

Composition

Though poetry would maintain close ties to oral expression throughout the pre-modern period, from the time of the *Wenfu* at the latest, composition was most often closely associated with the act of writing.[16] This holds true of the entire Tang period as well. Accounts of poetry gatherings and competitions from early in the dynasty, when they specifically mention a mode of competition, invariably describe poems being written (and then often gathered together to be judged). More detailed descriptions from later in the dynasty focus on written composition as well. In the "Discussion of Literary Ideas," attributed to the High Tang poet Wang Changling and preserved in the *Bunkyō hifuron*, we find writing playing a consistent role in descriptions of and advice for poetic composition. In some cases writing is simply one part of the mechanical activity of composing, as when the text suggests, "You must always carry paper, brush, and ink on your person. When inspiration comes you can immediately record it" 紙筆墨常須隨身，興來即錄.[17] Other sections of the text are more explicit about writing as the final stage of the process of poetic composition that begins with an internal stirring and ends with a written poem:

> Now when one's writing is roused, first it moves the *qi*. The *qi* is born in the heart and the heart puts it forth in words. It is heard by the ear, seen by the eye, and recorded on paper.
> 夫文章興作，先動氣，氣生乎心，心發乎言，聞於耳，見於目，錄於紙。[18]

16. Sylvia Huot describes a similar shift in Old French poetry in the European medieval period: "Overall, it is possible to document a general shift of focus, in the later thirteenth and fourteenth centuries, from lyric performance to lyric composition, with the latter defined ever more insistently as an act of writing rather than one of song or declamation." See Huot, *From Song to Book*, 4.

17. *Wenjing mifulun*, 139.

18. Ibid., 130.

A similar passage from the same essay almost perfectly mirrors the description in the "Daxu," discussed in the previous chapter, of how poetry is produced:

> A poem is based on that which the mind is on intently. In the mind it is being intent; coming out in words it is a poem. The affections are stirred within and manifested in words, and only after this does one write them on paper.
> 詩本志也，在心爲志，發言爲詩，情動於中，而行於言・然後書之於紙也・[19]

In these passages writing is almost an afterthought. It is less a part of something we might call "written composition" (in juxtaposition to "oral composition") than it is simply recording something that one has already composed. Writing is clearly an accepted part of the compositional act, but composition remains, in an aesthetic sense at least, an oral endeavor. As the text says at another point, only after the images for the poem fully resemble their sources and one has determined the tonal regulations should one write the poem down on paper (如無有不似，仍以律調之定，然後書之於紙).[20]

A few decades later, we begin to find indications in some works that the act of writing itself had become a more integral part of the composition process. In his "Letter in Reply to Li Yi" 答李翊書, one of the most famous descriptions of literary composition from the Tang, Han Yu describes writing as fully entwined with his mode of composing. Though the almost unstoppable flood of words that he describes seems a natural fit for oral composition, when he speaks of how he transforms his emotions into words, they are written ones: "When it is grasped in the heart and pours from the hand, it comes like a flood" 當其取於心而注於手也，汩汩然來也.[21] The end product emerges not through his mouth, but from his hand. Furthermore, this is so natural to Han Yu that he does not specify the particular significance of writing itself. For Han Yu, writing had be-

---

19. Ibid., 129. The passage from the "Daxu" reads, "The poem is that to which what is intently on the mind goes. In the mind it is 'being intent'; coming out in language, it is a poem" 詩者，志之所之也・在心爲志，發言爲詩・情動於中，而行於言. See Owen, *Readings in Chinese Literary Thought*, 40–41. My translation intentionally echoes Owen's translation of the original passage from the "Daxu" for comparative purposes.

20. *Wenjing mifulun*, 130.

21. Ma, 3.170.

come an integral part of composing in a culture that was more literate and accustomed to dealing with written texts than in any previous time in Chinese history.

In spite of (or perhaps because of) its clear ubiquity, the features of written composition as a particular mode of poetic production prove difficult to pin down. Poets would occasionally specify that they had composed a poem in writing, as with Du Fu's "Traveling at Night I Write My Feelings" 旅夜書懷,[22] but there are no equivalents to *kouzhan* or *kouhao* that writers would commonly use in titles or elsewhere to denote written composition. It should also be clear by now that the content of a given poem itself, in almost all cases, can tell us little about the mode in which that poem was originally composed. Finally, we cannot meaningfully define "written composition" as merely descriptive of compositional circumstances in which no oral declamation is involved (as I similarly define "oral composition" as composition without writing); the written and oral aspects of poetic culture were closely intertwined during the Tang and it is likely that poets would almost always vocalize to some degree when they were both writing and reading. Truly silent written composition, just like silent reading, was an exception to typical practice. As a working definition, let us consider examples of composition that involve writing at the time of composition or as part of the compositional process to count as cases of written composition. The presence of an additional oral component complicates this definition in some contexts, but does not substantially undermine its usefulness in terms of the issues we will examine in this chapter.

Lacking poetic titles indicating written composition, we must turn to descriptions of the compositional process to get a sense of the roles that writing played when people composed poetry. The number of such descriptions is limited, as are the details they provide. There is no set of detailed accounts that deals with both the material and psychological or philosophical aspects of writing, though many different accounts deal with one or the other.[23] As the dynasty progressed, such descriptions became

---

22. Qiu, 14.1228.

23. Han Yu deals with the psychological and philosophical aspects of composing, though his example may well be too idiosyncratic to serve as a model of general Tang practice. The situation for medieval European writers is similar. Carruthers (*Book of Memory*,

more numerous (or at least a greater number of such descriptions survive from later in the dynasty), and by examining a range of materials we can bring into sharper focus certain features of written composition. These descriptions highlight two seemingly contradictory roles of writing as a mode of poetic composition. Some portray written composition as a highly spontaneous, even performative act of immediate creation akin to what we have seen with oral composition (though as I argue below, spontaneity functions differently in written composition). In other accounts, writing is associated with a disjunction between experience and poetic production in which the notion of artistic effort becomes an explicit part of the compositional process. Writing here slows down and even lengthens the chain of events that eventually culminates in a poem and thus moves away from the more automatic model presented in the "Daxu."

Spontaneity and Performance

As I argue in the previous chapter, claims of oral composition in the Tang often played off of the ideas in the "Daxu" to imply that an orally composed poem represented a spontaneous moral response to a specific situation. Spontaneity was not, however, the sole preserve of orality. Writers frequently describe written composition in ways that highlight immediacy as well. In the poem "Spring Begins" 立春, Du Fu writes of sudden feelings of nostalgia for the glory days of Chang'an and Luoyang brought on by a spring platter of fresh greens (春日春盤細生菜，忽憶兩京全盛時).[24] Anxious to capture the moment in writing, in the last line of the poem he writes: "I called my son to find some paper and at once wrote a poem" 呼兒覓紙一題詩. Here written composition closely follows the "Daxu" model. Du Fu's poetic response is an immediate reaction to feelings brought on by external stimuli. If the traditional model assumed orality, it still proved useful for describing writing.

Spontaneity works differently here from how it works in such examples of oral composition as Du Fu's "Upon Receiving the News That All of the Hebei Military Commissioners Have Entered the Court, I Was

---

199) notes, "We have very few specific medieval accounts of people doing what we call composing." However, the detailed instructions she quotes from Quintilian (202–206) are far more comprehensive than any accounts that I know of from the Tang.

24. Qiu, 18.1597.

Joyful and Orally Composed Twelve Quatrains," discussed in the previous chapter. In that case the title foregrounds the mention of oral composition, influencing the reader's understanding of compositional circumstances from the beginning. In "Spring Begins," Du Fu notes the mode of composition only at the very end of the piece. He portrays himself as stimulated by events to compose immediately, but does not instruct us to initially read the poem through the lens of knowledge of his mode of composition. This last line transforms the poem into a history of itself, beginning with the emotional trigger and ending with the expressed need to capture and display the emotions in structured form. At the same time, the history includes an ellipsis: we see the inspiration for the poem and know that a poem is to be written, but Du Fu tells us nothing about the process of actually composing the poem itself. The end sends us back to the beginning and remains quiet about the work of turning emotion into art.

In oral composition, spontaneity is an inherent part of the compositional process as dictated by the ideas in the "Daxu." In this instance of written composition, spontaneity is merely implied; it resides silently in the gap between intention and the completed poem. Du Fu's haste to take up paper and brush leads us to imagine the poem pouring out of him without pause as Han Yu claims his work did. And as with Han Yu, the channel for that outpouring is written, not oral: Du Fu does not call on his son to transcribe a spontaneous oral declamation, instead requesting the tools necessary to mold a poem as a piece of writing himself.

Writing also allows the possibility of revision in a way that an instantaneous oral response would not, and accounts of written composition sometimes betray an anxiety about that possibility. A poem that could be substantially revised calls into question the moral legitimacy that the "Daxu" model's focus on immediacy implies. Interestingly, accounts of written composition that emphasize spontaneity often address this possibility obliquely by describing the piece in question as perfect in its initial instantiation, with no need for later corrections and changes. Han Yu's account of Zhang Xun, whose near-perfect memory we saw in Chapter 2, also notes of the military hero that "when he composed, he would take paper and brush and immediately write. He never made use of drafts" 為文章，操紙筆立書，未嘗起草.[25] Just as Zhang Xun's memory stored

25. Ma, 2.77.

texts perfectly, so did his hand produce them. The military man's decisive actions as a soldier and strategist are mirrored by an ability to compose rapidly and without any need for second-guessing.

An anecdote about the Early Tang poet Wang Bo 王勃 (649–676) describes his compositional process in more detail and likewise portrays his written works as emerging fully formed:

Wang Bo's writing was resplendent, and those who requested it were many. His gold and silk piled up. With his mind he wove for his clothes, with his brush he tilled for his food. Yet he was not terribly meticulous. First he would grind several measures of ink. Then he would get a bit drunk, pull a blanket over his head, and lie down. When he woke up, he would pull out his brush, complete a piece and not change a single word. People called these "belly drafts."
勃屬文綺麗，請者甚多，金帛盈積，心織而衣，筆耕而食．然不甚精思，先磨墨數升，則酣飲，引被覆面臥，及寤，援筆成篇，不易一字，人謂之腹藁．[26]

Rather than the regimented mind of a military man like Zhang Xun, here we see a spontaneous (and drunken) free spirit. At the same time, there is a curious sense of constructedness to Wang Bo's spontaneity: each stage and prop is carefully prepared ahead of time, from his ink to his alcohol. These preparations undermine our notion of what a spontaneous artistic creation should be and complicate the idea that what the writer produces is truly the immediate outpourings of his heart. The account counters this suspicion by explicitly denying revision, claiming that Wang Bo would "not change a single word."

As we saw in the previous chapter, the performative aspects of poetry in an oral mode could come out both in the act of composition, and in later oral interpretations of previously composed works by singers and others. Written composition could be described in performative terms as well, with writing figured as an act of display. An anecdote from the beginning of the Jianzhong 建中 reign period (780–784) included in Duan Chengwu's 段成武 *Youyang zazu* 酉陽雜俎 describes the various martial abilities of the Hebei General Xia, such as archery and horseback riding, and goes on to note that he "was also able write a full page while on

26. Fu, *Tang caizi zhuan jiaojian* 唐才子傳校箋, 1.32.

horseback" 又能走馬書一紙.[27] Here writing is a physical skill, part of a set of "cultural" (*wen* 文) abilities noted to balance the general's talents in the military (*wu* 武) sphere. It may even be taken as an intersection of these two spheres, with a *wen* activity being performed in a *wu* context. General Xia is clearly putting on a display, and the content of what he would write is less important than the way he would write it.

Sylvia Huot, in her discussion of the shift from composing poetry orally to composing it in writing in medieval France, uses the term "lyrical writing" to "designate the act of poetic creation as represented in lyrico-narrative texts of the thirteenth and fourteenth centuries."[28] She notes that "lyric composition is conceived at once as an act of writing and as an inspired performance."[29] Performance and display were nowhere more important in Tang China than at the court of Xuanzong and no poet was as given to display as Li Bai. The following anecdote from the *Benshi shi* is a good example of a Tang version of Huot's idea of lyrical writing:

[The Emperor] thereupon summoned Li Bai. At that time Prince Ning had invited Li Bai to drink and he was already drunk. Upon arriving he bowed ceremoniously though with an air of dissolution. The Emperor knew [Li Bai] thought lightly of regulated verse and would claim that it was not his strong point. Yet he ordered him to compose ten regulated poems in five character lines for palace musical performances. Li Bai knocked his head on the ground and said, "Prince Ning has given me drink and now I'm drunk. If Your Majesty will allow me not to be in awe, only then can I exhaust my flimsy skills." The Emperor said, "It is allowed." He then had two eunuchs prop him up by the armpits and ordered ink to be ground and a brush to be moistened to give to him. He further ordered two people to spread out columned red silk before him. Li Bai picked up the brush and let out his thoughts. For a while he did not stop and the ten pieces were immediately complete. He did not add a single dot. His brush technique was vigorous and quick, climbing like a phoenix and grasping like a dragon. In [the poems'] tonal regulation and parallelism, everything was utterly perfect.

---

27. Duan Chengwu 段成式, *Youyang zazu* 酉陽雜俎, 53. Note that the binome *zouma* could also refer simply to doing something very quickly. In the context of this anecdote with its description of other feats specifically performed on horseback, the more literal reading seems appropriate.

28. Huot, *From Song to Book*, 4.

29. Ibid.

遂命召白·時寧王飲酒，已醉，既至拜舞頹然·上知薄聲律，謂非所長，命為宮中行樂五言律詩十首，白頓首曰：寧王賜臣酒，今已醉；倘陛下賜臣無畏，始可盡臣薄技·上曰：可·即遣二内臣腋扶之·命研墨濡筆以授之·又令二人張朱絲欄於其前·白取筆抒思，略不停綴，十篇立就，更無加點·筆跡遒利，鳳跂龍拏律度對屬無不精絕·[30]

This is a popular anecdote that appears in a number of different sources. While we might not be able to credit each detail with perfect historical accuracy, the account as a whole brings together a number of common tropes of written composition. Like Wang Bo, Li Bai composes after imbibing. The connections between drink and free-flowing verse are long-standing and inevitably bring to mind Tao Qian's "Biography of Master Five Willows" (*Wuliu xiansheng zhuan* 五柳先生傳). There is also a tension here between meticulous order and spontaneous expression. Xuanzong does not give Li Bai free reign to write what he pleases but rather specifically requests works that conform to the strict rules of regulated verse, rules that Li Bai is said to disdain. Like a medieval French illustration Huot describes in which a poet "holds his pen aloft and gestures expansively as though on the verge of bursting into song,"[31] Li Bai's physical movements are depicted in dramatic terms, full of motion and speed, wild like mythical beasts. Yet in the end, the works this unbridled display produces conform perfectly to the strict regulations that Xuanzong and the genre of regulated verse impose. Again we see a claim of almost instantaneous perfection with no need for revision. In this case, however, the emphasis is less on anxiety about revision than on a need to show how order and spontaneity can coexist in perfect harmony.

Throughout the anecdote there are explicit connections to performance: Xuanzong requests works that will later be set to music and performed in the palace, though the promise of a later performance is less important than the display that Li Bai puts on in the act of composition itself. Tellingly, there is little focus on the content of the actual poems Li Bai has written in the anecdote. Indeed, after quoting just one of the ten poems, the text states that "there were many pieces, and they were not all

---

30. Meng Qi, *Benshi shi*, 65.

31. Huot, *From Song to Book*, 4.

recorded" 文不盡錄.[32] It is worth noting how different this is from most descriptions of oral composition in which mention of the mode of composition was meant to set the stage and give a context for the poems, not to be the focus of attention itself. The context may have been important, as with Wang Wei's poems composed while imprisoned for treason, but it never overwhelmed the content.[33] Here Li Bai's act of lyrical writing overshadows the lyrics themselves, and the tale of his dramatic behavior has become far better known than the single poem remembered in connection to it.

Writing as Artistic Effort

Tang descriptions of written composition did not all portray inspired free spirits creating perfect verse in a state of drunken spontaneity. In many anecdotes, writing is closely associated with the very opposite phenomenon, a prolonged compositional process marked not by speed but by meticulous effort. Stephen Owen notes that in the Mid-Tang period we find a new focus on the idea of laboring over a poem and of "a temporal disjunction between the putative experience that occasioned the poem and the act of composition."[34] This disjunction is often located precisely in the act of writing. There is a hint of this in Du Fu's "Spring Begins," where the hidden period between inspiration and the finished poem implies but obscures the effort of writing. Portions of the *Bunkyō hifuron*'s "Discussion of Literary Ideas" more explicitly deal with writing as a stage separate from the moment of immediate inspiration. The passage cited earlier in which poets are instructed to always carry paper and brush so as

32. Meng Qi, *Benshi shi*, 65. Sanders (*Words Well Put*, 241) notes that the poem "has no political or moral overtones, but is simply an appreciation of the beauty of the emperor's palace ladies..."

33. It is intriguing that in an anecdote detailing both the preparations for composition, such as the grinding of ink and the provision of a moistened brush and special silk, and the physical movements of Li Bai's brush, that no indication of vocalization (or lack thereof) is made. I do not think, however, that much can be made of this. There are times when silent writing is noted and they appear to be exceptional. One might assume that in such a situation Li Bai would vocalize but that this was not considered particularly noteworthy in and of itself. If we assume the anecdote is fictitious, then we must similarly imagine the author simply saw no point in adding such a detail.

34. Owen, *End of the Chinese 'Middle Ages'*, 108.

to immediately record inspirations carries a further warning: "If you lack brush and paper, as when traveling away from home, your ideas will often be hurried and rushed" 若無筆紙，羈旅之間，意多草草.[35] Certain aspects of the "Daxu" model remain in the passage as a whole. Inspiration is beyond the poet's control to create; he should be prepared to capture it when it comes. Yet rather than emerging fully formed in voice, poetic expression must be mediated by brush and ink to reach its aesthetically proper culmination. The text proposes an interesting dichotomy: the poet should "immediately record" (*jilu* 即錄) but simultaneously avoid being "hurried and rushed" (*caocao* 草草). Simply "singing it out" would be too hasty; he must take the time to put his thoughts into written words, ensuring that inspiration cannot be lost but also that it does not flow out without direction. Writing thus serves as a point of mediation between inspiration and expression.

The extent to which poets followed the type of advice given in the "Discussion of Literary Ideas" in practice is difficult to determine, but one of the most famous descriptions of poetic composition from the ninth century does contain certain striking similarities to some of the essay's suggestions. The Late Tang writer Li Shangyin's 李商隱 (813?–858) "Short Biography of Li He" 李賀小傳 includes the following description of the short-lived but highly influential Mid-Tang poet Li He's 李賀 (791–817) compositional technique:

> He would always go off riding a donkey followed by a young Xi slave. On his back he carried an old tattered brocade bag. If he happened to get something, he would write it down at once and throw it in the bag. When he went back in the evening, his mother had a serving girl take the bag and empty out its contents, and when she saw how much he had written, his mother burst out with, "This boy won't stop until he has spit out his heart." Then she lit the lamps and gave him his dinner. Li He next had the serving girl get what he had written; then grinding ink and piling up paper, he would complete them, at which point he would throw them into another bag.

35. *Wenjing mifulun*, 139.

恆從小奚奴，騎距驉，背一古破錦囊，遇有所得，即書投囊中．及暮歸，太夫人使婢受囊出之，見所書多，輒曰，是兒要當嘔出心乃已爾．上燈與食，長吉從婢取書，研墨疊紙足成之，投他囊中．[36]

The process this passage describes potentially resolves the contradictory implications in the "Discussion of Literary Ideas" to "immediately record" in order to keep one's verse from being "hurried and rushed." By dividing the compositional process into two stages, Li He reaps the benefits of both spontaneous inspiration and meticulous craft. As Owen argues, the verb *de* (得), "to get" is the key to the first stage. What the poet "gets" is often unexpected and beyond his control, serving as a sort of raw material; it is not a finished poem itself but rough pieces that can be molded into a polished work.[37] Here we see how quickly recording momentary inspiration keeps the final composition from being rushed. Without writing, the poet might be expected to immediately expand an inspired line or couplet into a finished poem. By simply recording and storing away such fragments, he instead gives himself the time in the second stage to put the pieces together into a finished work. Whether or not Li He actually composed this way, it is clear that the model is an appealing one for Li Shangyin, who was writing in a period by which the notion of working on a poem over a substantial stretch of time was widely accepted.[38]

The "Daxu" model survives here, but in fractured form. As a completed piece, a poem is no longer fully the product of an automatic response to circumstances, but rather the result of considered craft and intentional shaping over time. Yet there does remain something beyond the poet's control. The fragments that Li He gets on his daily jaunts come of their own accord. He is prepared to capture them, but is not able to call them up at will. The

36. Wang Qi 王琦 et al., eds., *Li Changji geshi: Sanjia pingzhu* 李長吉歌詩，三家評注, 13. The translation is taken from Owen, *End of the Chinese 'Middle Ages,'* 110. Owen discusses this passage at length (110–13, 118) and although my reading of it is informed by his, my focus is on different aspects of the piece.

37. Owen, *End of the Chinese 'Middle Ages,'* 113. Even if Li Shangyin is not specific about what Li He would get, leaving open the possibility that he wrote full poems that he would simply revise later, the fact that Li Shangyin describes the poet's work in the final stage as "completing" (*zucheng* 足成) implies not revision but either finishing fragmentary pieces or putting such pieces together into a greater whole.

38. See Owen, *End of the Chinese 'Middle Ages,'* 114 for more discussion of this issue. See also his "Spending Time on Poetry," 157–78.

disjunction between inspiration and the final work of art that writing allows may not be part of the earlier model of poetic production, but it effectively captures changing ideas of the relationship between poets, their raw materials, and what they strove to create out of them.

A striking feature of this passage is its emphasis on the materiality of written poetry. Poems, or at least their constituent parts, are things to be tossed into bags and emptied out onto tables. They required the grinding of ink and piling of paper. And if the costs they entail are mainly psychic, there is an undeniably physical component as well. Li He's mother's concerns must be read in the context of Li He's untimely death at a young age: he exhausted his resources to create these bags full of poems until he had nothing left.[39]

In the mature manuscript culture of the Tang, the act of writing was ubiquitous, but the associations of written composition shifted over time and in different contexts. Writing might simply record the traces of the results of oral composition, without itself being central to the composition process, as suggested in the *Bunkyō hifuron*. It might be the natural conduit for the production of literary works that flow forth fully formed, as Han Yu, Du Fu, and the anecdote about Li Bai—who "picks up the brush and lets out his thoughts" 取筆抒思—imply. Such a model allows writing to become performative, a display of extravagant creative motion that produced perfection in an instant. Or writing might be the technology that allows the poet to piece together full poems from hard-won fragments, as Li Shangyin tells us Li He did: the unique characteristics of the written word—that it endures across time and space—allow the poet to both be spontaneous and perfect the products of that spontaneity through the hard work of turning emotions into art.

Circulation

Ming-sun Poon has written that "in the Tang the popular form of literature was restricted to poems because they could be orally disseminated."[40]

39. Owen points out that the passage portrays Li He as a kind of "poetry machine that needs constant attention" from his mother and various servants. See Owen, *End of the Chinese 'Middle Ages,'* 113.

40. Poon, "Books and Printing in Sung China," 71.

Such claims notwithstanding, the evidence for written circulation is far more abundant in both volume and detail. Tang poets wrote down their compositions, copied them out again and again, and did their best to see those copies spread widely. They inscribed poems on every imaginable surface, from monastery walls to living flesh. Taking advantage of the durability of the written word, they sent their poems to influential officials living in the capital and to friends exiled to the furthest reaches of the Tang state (and beyond). Crucially for Tang poetry's continued survival, they also copied down other people's poems in great numbers and circulated them, even buying and selling them on occasion. Indeed, were it not for written circulation of poetry in the Tang, the term "Tang poetry" would now refer to a long-dead social phenomenon rather than to a substantial set of texts that people continue to read, interpret, and enjoy. In this section I turn my attention to the details of this process and investigate the most important modes of written circulation of poetry in the Tang.

To begin once again with a definition, any examples of texts circulating in written form meet the criterion for written circulation. This includes examples as diverse as someone reading a scroll of his friend's poems or a traveler encountering an anonymous verse inscribed on the wall of a post station. As with oral circulation, there is no need for a demonstrable chain of "pure" transmission. If an anecdote tells us that Bai Juyi came home one night, recited to his nephew poems that he and Liu Yuxi composed together earlier, and had the nephew write them down and send them to Yuan Zhen, this would be an example of written circulation. Likewise, if Yuan Zhen notes in a poem that he was reading a scroll of poems by Du Fu, this would also qualify. It is not necessary to have an account of the actual transcription or copying of a poem to know that someone had indeed written it down.

As we have seen, general comments in funerary inscriptions, prefaces, and similar writings that a person's works "circulated widely in the age" are quite common, even to the point of cliché. Descriptions of written transmission in particular are less common and more specific than general mentions of circulation. These descriptions frequently take the form of simple statements that a poet's works were circulated by writing, such as Lu Guimeng's 陸龜蒙 (d. ca. 881) comment that a friend's poems were "widely circulated and copied among people" 人間盛傳寫.[41] Quan Deyu makes a similar statement in his "Biography of Master Wuzun" 吾尊師傳, writing that "each time he composed a piece, everybody copied and circulated it" 每製一篇人皆傳寫,[42] as does Li Ao 李翱, noting of Dugu Ji 獨孤及 (725–777) that "each time he wrote something, it was immediately copied and circulated by those junior to him" 每爲文輒爲後進所傳寫.[43] Such comments differ little from similar remarks about oral circulation and indeed, the modes of circulation are sometimes discussed together, as with Lu Cangyong's praise of Chen Zi'ang that "At that time his writings were copied and circulated in Luoyang, and in the markets, shops, streets, lanes, and alleys they were continually recited" 時洛中傳寫其書・市肆閭巷・吟諷相屬.[44]

Lu Cangyong emphasizes the local appeal of Chen Zi'ang's verse; other writers focus on the wide geographic reach of written circulation. Having established that "Yuan the talent's" poetry enjoyed the favor of the imperial ear, Bai Juyi goes on to claim, "From the Six Palaces, the Two Capitals and the Eight Regions to the southern barbarians and the foreign kingdoms in the east, they all copied and circulated [his poems]" 自六宮兩都八方至南蠻東夷國，皆寫傳之.[45] An anecdote in the *Da Tang xinyu*, providing more detail and perhaps less exaggeration, reports an international audience for the works of Zhang Wencheng: "Later, emissaries from Silla and Japan entered the court. They all had people go copy his writings and then left. Such was the distance to which his talent[ed] writings spread" 暹羅日本使入朝，咸使人就寫文章而去，其才遠播如此.[46] We have seen claims that poems enjoyed a wide circulation through oral means, but the written medium would have been particularly appropriate for spreading works to distant places, especially those such as Korea and Japan where Chinese poetry in textual form would be far more intelligible than oral versions of the same. These texts also functioned as valuable cultural commodities, tangible objects from the capital

41. *QTS*, 617.7113.
42. *QTW*, 508.5165. Note that this is not necessarily about poetry specifically.
43. *QTW*, 639.6449.
44. *QTW*, 238.2412.
45. Zhu, 70.3736.
46. Liu Su, *Da Tang xinyu*, 8.129.

of what was unquestionably the dominant economic and cultural force in the region.[47]

Sending Poems

Accounts of written transmission, whether based on fact or romantic fantasy, often take advantage of the ability of written texts to reach audiences far removed from each other in space and time. Unlike successive oral transmission over similar distances, written transmission relies on the very materiality of the medium to convey a direct message from poet to reader. In one well-known story from the Tang, a soldier finds stitched into his uniform a poem commiserating the bitterness of his life on the border and expressing a wish that the author and the reader meet in the next life. The uniform, as it turns out, had been stitched in the palace. Emperor Xuanzong hears of this and demands that the author reveal herself. The woman eventually comes forward and is rewarded by being freed from the palace and given in marriage to the soldier who found her poem.[48] Only through the medium of the written text could the woman's verses find an audience so distant while simultaneously keeping her message a secret.

Written transmission plays a similar though more complex role in another story of communication between a neglected palace woman and a sympathetic man on the outside:

At Ascension Gate in Luoyang, Gu Kuang was strolling with three poet friends in the park. He sat down by a stream and found a large *wutong* leaf. On it was written a poem that said:
顧況在洛乘門，與三詩友遊於苑中，坐流水上，得大梧葉，題詩上曰：

Once I entered the depths of the palace,	一入深宮裏，
Year after year I never saw spring.	年年不見春。
I recklessly write on a slip of leaf,	聊題一片葉，
Sending it off to a man with feelings.	寄與有情人。[49]

47. Poetic texts, in this case, would have served a function similar to that served by Buddhist sutras brought back from China to Korea and Japan. I discuss poetic texts as commodities in more detail below.

48. Meng Qi, *Benshi shi*, 35.

49. Ibid., 37. See discussion in Sanders, *Words Well Put*, 260–61.

The next day, Gu Kuang writes a response poem on a leaf he himself tosses into the stream at a point upstream from the palace and later receives a response on a third leaf, found by a friend of his downstream. This last couplet of the final poem expresses the woman's sadness:

I sigh to myself that I'll never be a leaf on the waves.	自嗟不及波中葉，
Rising and falling, riding spring, traveling wherever I might.	蕩漾乘春取次行。[50]

Gu Kuang and his foliaceous correspondent never do meet in the flesh; the only trace of the woman remains her words on the *wutong* leaf. The materiality of this mode of poetic transmission is key to the story on two levels. Logistically, it allows the woman to convey her words to another who is distant from her without the intercession of an intermediary who might alter her text or possibly report her implicit adulterous intentions. On a more abstract level the leaf and the words written upon it serve as a stand-in for the woman, as she suggests through her explicit envy of the leaf and its ability to leave the palace and follow its own whims. The notion of "riding spring" (*chengchun* 乘春), with its clear sexual connotations, strengthens the connection between the woman and the medium of her emotional and poetic transmission. Her words are indeed *her* words in a fundamental sense: they are the very marks that she made with her own hand. She cannot escape her lonely life in the palace, but her poem gives her a material and emotional presence beyond its walls.

Despondent palace women were hardly alone in their desire to reach others far away through their poetic texts. Poetry was an important means of personal communication throughout the Tang, and writers made constant use of both official and unofficial postal systems to send their works to friends, family members, and influential officials living in other locales. Given the legendary status of their friendship, it is easy to forget that Bai Juyi and Yuan Zhen actually spent very little time in close geographic proximity to one another. They conducted most of their relationship through written correspondence, more often than not in the form of exchanged poems, with these works at times standing in for the absent friend. In the preface to "Inscribing Poems on a Screen: a Quatrain" 題詩

50. Meng Qi, *Benshi shi*, 37.

屏風絕句 Bai Juyi writes of possessing Yuan Zhen's poems: "The best thing is to place them by my seat—it's like seeing the person I long for" 不若置之座右，如見所思.[51] Similar circumstances were shared by numerous others in the Tang. Friends were often separated by travels or official duties, and poetry sent by post was arguably the primary mode of informal communication for many. Though most poets could not take advantage of the official postal system (unlike Bai Juyi and Yuan Zhen), they would regularly make use of traveling merchants, relatives, and friends to send their poems to others.[52]

The ultimate goal of sending poems by post was circulation directed to a specific and limited audience: typically the recipient and perhaps his friends and family.[53] Yet while the number of recipients for a given poem or set of poems might be small, the number of poems transmitted this way could be substantial. Poets would often send several poems in a single mailing, sometimes as many as one hundred at a time.[54] Moreover, the use of this method of disseminating written poetry was extensive. The total number of poems in the *Quan Tang shi* whose titles alone indicate that they were sent to someone else through some form of post number in the thousands, and this figure represents a fraction of the actual number of poems disseminated this way. For instance, a great number of Bai Juyi's poems to Yuan Zhen were clearly delivered by post, though this is not noted in the title of most. The same is probably true of most poets, though on a smaller scale.[55]

---

51. Zhu, 17.1091.

52. Fan Zhilin, "Tangdai shige de liuchuan (shang)," 268.

53. Note that a poet could circulate such sent poems to a much wider audience in other contexts. In "While Copying Out Recent Poems to Send to Weizhi, I Just Happened to Write This on the End of the Scroll" 寫新詩寄微之偶題卷後, Bai Juyi writes, "The copying finished, I recite and look them over, a full roll of melancholy / Pink paper and small silver hooks. / Before I let them be sent off to Weizhi / They've already been circulated by others to Yuezhou" 寫了吟看滿卷愁，淺紅牋紙小銀鉤．未容寄與微之去，已被人傳到越州. The specific audience for this mailing is small (Yuan Zhen alone), but the poems had previous circulated in other modes to a much larger audience. See Zhu, 24.1694.

54. Fan Zhilin, "Tangdai shige de liuchuan (shang)," 267. One hundred is a number often associated with one scroll, though this would of course vary.

55. Fan Zhilin, "Tangdai shige de liuchuan (shang)," 267.

The use of the official and unofficial post was a constant throughout the dynasty, with every major poet having a number of works whose titles indicate this method of circulation. Not surprisingly given the size of his surviving corpus and his extensive correspondence, Bai Juyi has the greatest number, with 285 such poems (while Yuan Zhen has but 59, almost all of which were written to Bai Juyi). Interestingly, the second highest total in the dynasty belongs to the Buddhist monk Qiji 齊己 (fl. 881), with 208. Scholar-officials, monks (both Buddhist and Daoist), and women all seem to have made broad use of this method of transmitting their poems.

The range of recipients, compositional circumstances, subject matter, and length of sent poems was extensive. Some poets wrote while traveling to maintain contact with family back home, such as Meng Haoran's "Sent to My Younger Brother upon Entering the Gorges" 入峽寄弟.[56] Other poems merely indicate that they were sent to an unnamed friend, for example Meng Yunqing's 孟韻卿 (born ca. 725/26) "Sent to a Friend While on the Road" 途中寄友人.[57] Poems were sent off to mountain recluses, such as Chu Guangxi's 儲光羲 "Sent to Mountain Man Sun" 寄孫山人,[58] and to scholar officials, such as Jia Dao's "Sent to Attendant Censor Liu" 寄劉侍御.[59] In terms of the poems themselves, beyond the clues given in the titles there is nothing distinct about either their subject matter or length that would indicate they were written to be sent to others. This particular format did not favor shorter compositions, as orally composed poems frequently did.

Whether sent by leaf or post, the prevalence of sent poetry highlights the centrality of the social function of poetry in the Tang. Just as oral recitation of poetry was integral to social interactions when educated men gathered, written exchanges of poetry were a part of almost all casual written correspondence in the Tang. Letters to friends would, more often than not, include poems; poems might also be sent by themselves, taking the place of a letter. The conceit of poetry as a direct expression of the poet's deepest emotions and aims made poems a natural medium for

---

56. *QTS*, 159.1618.

57. *QTS*, 157.1610. It is possible that in such cases the original title specified the friend in question, with this degree of specificity disappearing with subsequent transmissions.

58. *QTS*, 139.1419.

59. *QTS*, 573.6668.

communicating at a distance. In these written missives the poem as a physical object stands in for the poet herself, used to maintain or forge ties with individuals across the empire or across the city. Poetry becomes a personal message sent from the poet to a particular and limited audience. It was a means of transmission that allowed the writer to retain some control over his work, as he designated his audience and presumably in many cases recorded the poems himself. Yet that control would always be limited, as recipients would often take the poems they received and spread them even further.

Inscribing Poems

In spite of its wide availability, paper was not the only medium for circulating written poetry in the Tang. The popular practice of inscribing poems on walls and other objects in public places had a substantial influence on the circulation of poetry as well.[60] When Yuan Zhen claims of Bai Juyi's poetry that "ever since there has been poetry, there has never been such wide dissemination" 自篇章已來，未有如是流傳之廣者 to bolster his praise,[61] he reports that his friend's poems "are written on the walls of every palace, monastery, and post station" 禁省觀寺郵候牆壁之上，無不書.[62] Hyperbole aside, Yuan's statement reflects the fact that poems had become part of both the natural and manmade landscapes during the Tang. If poetry remained an oral and aural art in many contexts, it also became increasingly prominent as a visual presence in this period.[63]

There are interesting parallels between publicly inscribed poems and oral circulation in some contexts. Like oral circulation, public inscription could quickly circulate poems to a wide audience, increasing the fame of

---

60. For an introduction to this practice and some of its particular manifestations in later periods, see Zeitlin, "Disappearing Verses," 73–125. For more detailed discussions see Wu Chengxue, "Lun tibishi" and Luo Zongtao, "Tangren tibishi chutan."

61. *YZJ*, 51.555.

62. Ibid.

63. Poems were certainly written on public objects in prior periods, but the practice became much more widespread during the Tang. Fan Zhilin notes that only in the Tang did this "become a form of conscious and commonly utilized method of 'publishing.'" See Fan Zhilin, "Tangdai shige de liuchuan (shang)," 273. Wu Chengxue ("Lun tibishi," 5) notes, "Poems written on walls flourished greatly during the Tang, the extent to which almost everyone wrote them and there were few places where they were not written."

the author in the process.[64] It could also be a part of personal exchanges between friends or patrons, as the well-known practice of leaving a poem when visiting someone and finding them away attests. Of course it was even more common to inscribe a poem when the person was in and made such a request. Yet unlike oral circulation, inscribed poems could also serve as a form of proto-printing, in which a single public exemplar could be the source for a great number of copies, whether written down or remembered. Finally, inscribed poetry reminds us of the intense materiality of poetry in the Tang. Inscribed poems quite literally became a part of the surfaces on which they appeared and could survive or perish with those surfaces.

If the primary goal of inscribing poems in public locations was circulation, it was a type of circulation very different from that achieved by sending poems through the post. Whereas the latter was a private affair with a specific intended audience, the former was a pubic act aiming at broad circulation to unknown readers. The clear advantage of this method is that it would allow a great number of people access to a poem while only requiring a single copy in the initial stage of dissemination. Poets would thus often inscribe poems in places where large numbers of people congregated and passed through, such as post stations, popular scenic sites, inns, monasteries, and temples. The extensive geographical range of the Tang empire, especially at its height, meant that members of the literary elite (essentially all of whom wrote poetry) would often travel considerable distances, inscribing poetry wherever they went and thus significantly increasing the geographic and popular spread of their poems.[65] There are

---

64. It is unclear from the sources how often the author's name would be attached to publicly posted poems. Most anecdotes do not specify whether or not this is the case. While many center on the fact that the reader recognizes the poem and the author, they often do not make it clear if this recognition comes through the poem itself, without the assistance of an attached name.

65. Fan Zhilin, "Tangdai shige de liuchuan (shang)," 272–73. In one interesting if clearly anomalous case, an object with a poem inscribed upon it would actually itself move from place to place. A passage from the *Youyang zazu* (8.77) describes a man in Jingzhou 荆州 who, "from his neck on down was tattooed all over with the poems of Secretary Bai Juyi" 自頸以下，遍刺白居易舍人詩. Conveniently, he was "also able to [recite] from memory the ones on his back" 背上亦能闇記. Note also that while the text claims the poems are Bai Juyi's, the first line cited is actually from Yuan Zhen's poem, "Chrysanthemum" 菊花. See *QTS*, 441.4560. The second line quoted is from Bai Juyi's poem "Floating

in fact many Tang poets for whom their only surviving poems are those copied from public inscriptions.[66]

Tang writers took full advantage of the opportunities for circulation that public inscription of poems provided. The number of such works that survived to be included in the *Quan Tang shi* is substantial. In that anthology there are well over a thousand poems that indicate in their primary title that they were inscribed on some surface or object other than ordinary paper or scrolls.[67] It should be noted that this number does not include alternate titles given by the *Quan Tang shi* (and there are a number of such examples).[68] Beyond these, many hundreds of poems mention inscribing a poem without noting this in the title itself.[69] It appears that

---

on Lake Tai, I Wrote About This to Send to Weizhi" 泛太湖書事寄微之. See *QTS*, 447.5025. Carrie E. Reed notes that aside from this passage, "no other example describes literary texts permanently inscribed on the body." See Reed, "Tattoo in Early China," 371.

66. Luo Zongtao, "Tangren tibishi chutan," 179.

67. Focusing on Tang poems written on walls specifically, Luo Zongtao ("Tangren tibishi chutan," 155) uses a stricter set of criteria to come up with about four hundred poems. To be included in his list a poem must 1) indicate in the title that it was written on a wall, 2) reveal in the content of the poem itself that it was written on a wall, and 3) have other related materials that prove it was written on a wall. Luo's criteria are useful ones to ensure that the poems he is looking at in more depth are definite examples of the practice of writing poems on walls. My larger number based on titles from the *Quan Tang shi* probably gives a better sense of the extent of writing on public objects overall.

68. I would conjecture that the high number of alternative titles of this sort may be a result of how collections were compiled. An untitled poem copied from the wall of a temple by a compiler might well be given a title such as "Written on a Temple Wall" by that particular compiler. Another compiler working from a different source that did give a title to the poem would use the title he found with the poem, resulting in multiple titles. This could lead to two different though compatible conclusions. It might indicate that fewer poems were originally given titles noting that they were to be posted than the number of titles in the *Quan Tang shi* would suggest. At the same time, it might indicate that the overall frequency of poems being written up in public spaces, regardless of their titles, was far larger than the *Quan Tang shi* titles imply. While this is simply a conjecture, it is worth noting that poems with titles indicating that they were sent to someone (*ji* 寄) have alternative titles far less frequently. Fan Zhilin ("Tangdai shige de liuchuan (shang)," 273) also suggests that many poems that do not indicate as much by their titles or contents were probably posted publicly at some point.

69. This phenomenon is noted by Fan Zhilin, "Tangdai shige de liuchuan (shang)," 273; Luo Zongtao, "Tangren tibishi chutan," 153; and Wu Chengxue, "Lun tibishi," 5. For some examples see Zhang Ji's "Traveling to Lingyan" 遊靈巖, *QTS*, 242.2723; Han Hong's 韓翃 "Seeing off District Defender Nan Returning to Shouchun" 送南少府歸壽春,

the practice of inscription was widespread throughout the period. The numbers of inscribed poems from the later parts in the dynasty are higher, but this is a function of the greater numbers of poems of all sorts that survive from the Mid- and Late Tang. What is clear is that essentially every major Tang poet from Wang Ji through Wei Zhuang has surviving poems that were originally inscribed somewhere. Lending some credence to Yuan Zhen's claims about Bai Juyi's omnipresent poetic traces, the *Quan Tang shi* records over one hundred poems of this sort for Bai, far outnumbering those of any other poet, though even Bai's total is dwarfed by the overall numbers through the period.

Tang poets left few surfaces untouched. For obvious reasons, walls were popular sites to post poems. Following is a partial list of the types of locations mentioned in titles, with examples in parentheses:

1. plain walls (Yang Ningshi's 楊凝式 "Inscribed on a Wall" 題壁)[70]

2. ale shops (Wang Ji's "Inscribed on an Ale Shop Wall" 題酒店壁)[71]

3. private studios (Chen Zi'ang's "Inscribed on Li the Third's Studio" 題李三書齋)[72]

4. the walls of courtesans' residences (Sun Qi's "Inscribed on the Wall of the Courtesan Wang Funiang" 題妓王福娘牆)[73]

5. hermits' lodgings (Wang Wei's "Traveling to Where Mountain Man Li Resides, I Thereupon Wrote This on the Wall of His Room" 遊李山人所居因題屋壁)[74]

6. pass fortifications (Cui Hao's 崔顥 "Inscribed on the Tower at Tong Pass" 題潼關樓)[75]

QTS, 243.2727; Zhao Jia's 趙嘏 "Seeing Off a Monk Returning to Mt. Lu" 送僧歸廬山, *QTS*, 549.6349; and Xiang Si's 項斯 "Meeting a Friend on the Road" 途中逢友人, *QTS*, 554.6421. These represent just a few of many examples.

70. *QTS*, 715.8217.

71. *QTS*, 37.484.

72. *QTS*, 84.905.

73. *QTS*, 727.8328.

74. *QTS*, 126.1274.

75. *QTS*, 130.1328.

7. religious buildings (Chang Jian's 常建 "Inscribed on the Dharma Hall" 題法院)[76]

8. private homes (Meng Haoran's "Inscribed on the Wall of My Host in Chang'an" 題長安主人壁)[77]

9. inns (Qian Qi's 錢起 "Inscribed on a Hostel on a Winter's Night" 冬夜題旅館)[78]

10. bridges (Wei Yingwu's 韋應物 "Inscribed on a Stone Bridge" 題石橋)[79]

11. post stations (Xue Feng's 薛逢 "Inscribed on White Horse Post Station" 題白馬驛)[80]

It is also clear that essentially any somewhat flat surface was fair game: paulownia leaves, such as Wei Yingwu's "Inscribed on a Paulownia Leaf" 題桐葉;[81] trees, such as Du Fu's "Inscribed on a Peach Tree" 題桃樹;[82] paintings, such as Huangfu Ran's 皇甫冉 "Inscribed on a Painted Screen" 題畫帳二首;[83] and even scrolls of other poets' works, such as Bai Juyi's

---

76. *QTS*, 144.1463. Fan Zhilin ("Tangdai shige de liuchuan (shang)," 275) notes that monks would whitewash certain walls in temples and monasteries to provide a clean surface for poets to write on.

77. *QTS*, 160.1665.

78. *QTS*, 236.2609.

79. *QTS*, 193.1995.

80. *QTS*, 548.6330.

81. *QTS*, 193.1995.

82. *QTS*, 226.2448. It is true that both this example and that of the paulownia leaf are ambiguous in that the titles could simply indicate the topic of the poem. However, there are other examples in prose pieces from the Tang in which the formulation makes it clear that the poem is physically written on the tree. For one such example see Wang Dang, *Tang yulin*, 3.259, in which Luo Jun 駱浚, a copyist for the Bureau of General Accounts, is described writing a quatrain on a cypress tree (題詩一絶於柏樹). In this case the preposition *yu* (於) indicates that the poem is written on the tree rather than about the tree. Wu Chengxue ("Lun tibishi," 6) notes that poems inscribed on trees would often be carved into the tree and thus last longer. Luo Zongtao ("Tangren tibishi chutan," 162) notes that "inscribed on a tree" (*tishu* 題樹) could also refer to inscribing a poem next to or near a tree on a wall or other surface.

83. *QTS*, 249.2799.

"Having Read a Collection of Poems by Li [Bai] and Du [Fu] I Thereupon Write This at the End of the Scroll" 讀李杜詩集因題卷後.[84]

In many cases poets would apply their brushes to these surfaces directly. As the dynasty progressed, an increasing number of locations popular for inscribing poems also made use of poetry boards (*shiban* 詩板),[85] special wooden plaques upon which poets would write their works.[86] The first mention of their use in a Tang poem is by a poet active in the first half of the ninth century, Zhang Hu 張祜, though they were undoubtedly used earlier.[87] His poem "Inscribed on the Old Room of the Abbot Lingche" 題靈徹上人舊房 reads:

It is lonely at the empty gate of Zhi Daolin,	寂寞空門支道林，
Poetry boards fill the hall, of those past who "knew the tone."	滿堂詩板舊知音。
The autumn winds blow the leaves below the old corridor,	秋風吹葉古廊下，
On half a rope bed, the lamp's shadows are deep.	一半繩床燈影深。[88]

84. Zhu, 15.956.

85. In the Song and later these were often called *shipai* 詩牌.

86. See discussions in Luo Zongtao, "Tangren tibishi chutan," 159–60 and Wu Chengxue, "Lun tibishi," 6.

87. Fan Zhilin's ("Tangdai shige de liuchuan (shang)," 276) claim that "poets would frequently bring up poetry boards in their poems" is not born out by the poems themselves, as there are fewer than a dozen pieces in the *Quan Tang shi* that mention poetry boards specifically. One possible reason for this is that poetry boards *per se* were considered incidental as a surface for writing. In other words, if a poet was inscribing a poem on a poetry board to put up at a monastery, he would indicate in the title or poem that it was inscribed on the monastery, not on the poetry board itself. For some examples of poems that do mention poetry boards, see the following: a fragment couplet by Gao Qu 高璩, *QTS*, 597.6908; Weng Tao's 翁洮 "Matching Fang Gan's 'Inscribed on Li Pin's Cottage'" 和方干題李頻莊, *QTS*, 667.7640; Zheng Gu's "Seeing off Advanced Scholar Wu Yanbao Traveling South after Passing the Exams" 送進士吳延保及第後南遊), *QTS*, 676.7744; and Qi Ji's "Thinking About My Friends in the Way at Daolin Temple" 懷道林寺道友. Poetry boards are also mentioned in the preface to Liu Shanfu's 劉山甫 "Inscribed on the Shrine at Green Grass Lake" 題青草湖神祠, *QTS*, 763.8664. Luo Zongtao gives some additional examples on pp. 159–60.

88. *QTS*, 511.5840. Lingche was a well-known monk and poet. Zhi Daolin is a Jin 晉 dynasty monk, here probably standing in for Lingche.

Monasteries were especially well known for their use of poetry boards. Wu Chengxue notes that there were two particular types: one on which monks would ask poets to inscribe a poem directly, and others upon which people would transcribe and put on display poems that had already been inscribed on walls or other surfaces.[89] There does seem to be a connection between the increased use of poetry boards after the High Tang period and a similar increase in poems inscribed at Buddhist sites. All mentions of poetry boards from surviving poetic sources postdate the High Tang, and up through that period Wang Wei is the only prominent poet with a number of works inscribed on Buddhist locations. By the Mid-Tang, most well-known writers had many and their numbers include poets who did not write frequently or positively about Buddhism in their works.[90] Temples and monasteries were public spaces whose audiences were not limited to devoted religious followers. As centers of learning and de facto lending libraries, they inevitably attracted large numbers of literate men—the primary actors in the process of written poetic transmission.[91] The use of poetry boards may well have been both cause and effect of their increasing popularity as places to inscribe poetic works.

An anecdote from the *Tang zhiyan* gives a sense of how poetry boards could aid circulation not only as templates for copying, but as physical objects that people could gather and transport to new spots (unlike walls and trees):

Li Jianzhou (a.k.a. Li Pin 李頻) had once traveled around Westlake in Mingzhou's Cixi County inscribing poems. Some time later, Li Qing was serving as Governor of Mingzhou. When Li [Pin] was made a supernumerary in the Bureau of Criminal Administration he asked him to take the poetry boards and pass them on to a military convoy that was heading to the capital.
李建州，嘗遊明州磁溪縣西湖題詩；後黎卿爲明州牧，李時爲都官員外，託與打詩板，附行綱軍將入京。[92]

89. Wu Chengxue, "Lun tibishi," 6.

90. Fan Zhilin, "Tangdai shige de liuchuan (shang)," 275.

91. For a discussion of monastic libraries in the Tang, see Drège, *Les Bibliothèques en Chine*, 194–208.

92. *TZY*, 13.149.

Poetry boards could thus capture the best aspects of both texts written on paper and poems inscribed in public places. Intended for display, they could enjoy a wide audience when put up in temples and other places where travelers and others congregated. Their portability meant that they could also be moved to new locations and find new audiences. After Li Pin's poems had been on display in Cixi County for some time, he was able to get Li Qing to help him move them to the capital, where they would enjoy even broader exposure.

If circulation, whether wide or narrow, was the preeminent goal of publicly inscribing poems, was that method effective at achieving this goal? The evidence suggests that people did indeed read inscribed poems, and that they regarded them as a legitimate way of encountering and enjoying new verse. As Luo Zongtao suggests, the evidence is fragmentary and scattered but convincing when viewed in the aggregate. One clear form of evidence is the substantial number of poems that note either in prefaces or in the body of the poems themselves that they were written after reading publicly inscribed poems.[93] Bai Juyi, Liu Yuxi, and Yuan Zhen have a number of such works, but one of the best-known examples involves Xuanzong himself. While strolling in the Eastern Palace, the emperor came upon Xue Lingzhi's 薛令之 (*jinshi* 706) poem "Self-Lament" (*zidiao* 自悼) inscribed on a wall. Inspired, "he sought a brush and wrote [a poem] next to it" 索筆題其傍.[94] Like poems exchanged in and as letters, such responses to inscribed poems parallel the oral exchange of poems in social situations. But rather than intimate exchanges, these are public reactions to public statements: the poet who inscribed the first poem might never see the response, but those who came later would see both. We are reminded again that even as poetry was conceived of as a spontaneous outpouring of emotion, it was also a fundamentally interactive practice. Response in kind was part of the audience's role, and inscribing poems allowed that practice to occur over time and space and between individuals who might never meet.

Other examples of people reading inscribed poems demonstrate the role that such works could have in spreading not only a poet's writings,

93. Luo Zongtao, "Tangren tibishi chutan," 177–78.

94. *QTS*, 215.6.

but his reputation as well. Needless to say, the more prominent one's audience, the better, and Zhang Bayuan 章八元 was fortunate in that regard:

In the past in Chang'an there was a pagoda at the Ci'en Monastery. In the front and back were a great number of poetry boards [with the works] of famous writers. Bayuan had also written works up there. There was one that said, "I still thought it strange that the birds flew above the level plain / they themselves were startled by the speech of men, half-way up in the sky." Later Yuan [Zhen] and Bai [Juyi] came to the foot of the pagoda and read them all. They then got rid of them all, leaving only Bayuan's there. They chanted it for a long time and said, "His fame is well deserved."
初長安慈恩寺浮圖，前後名流詩版甚多，八元亦題，有云：「却怪鳥飛平地上，自驚人語半天中．」後元微之、白樂天至塔下遍覽，因悉除去，惟存八元版在，吟詠久之，曰：「名下無虛士也．」[95]

Bai Juyi and Yuan Zhen seem not to have encountered Zhang Bayuan's verses in the past (though they had heard of him). By inscribing them at an oft-visited locale such as a monastery, Zhang gained exposure to an audience that might well have escaped him if he circulated his works by means of individual paper copies alone.[96] Moreover if the two famous writers were so impressed by Zhang's works, they might further pass them along to their friends or perhaps recommend they pay a visit to the pagoda to see the poems themselves.

Post stations and monasteries were effective places to put one's works on display, but less obvious locations could sometimes reap results as well, as this anecdote about Luo Jun 駱浚 attests:

Luo Jun was a copyist for the Ministry of Revenue. He always admired the various managers and wrote a quatrain up on a cypress tree [to this effect]...It so happened that a commissioner of the Ministry of Revenue was making a tour of the various offices. He saw this poem and asked his attendants about it. They said it was written by Luo Jun.
駱浚者，度支司書手也．嘗健羡一雜事典，題詩一絶於柏樹．．．會度支使巡諸司，見此題，問左右云：浚所爲也．[97]

95. Fu, *Tang caizi zhuan*, 2.113.

96. Of course the fate of the poems Bai Juyi and Yuan Zhen disposed of shows that this method also could have its problems.

97. Wang Dang, *Tang yulin*, j. 3, 259–60.

The commissioner is impressed by the poem, noting that because "the style of the words is not base and the language is ancient and strong," 詞氣不卑言語古壯, that "his character is fine" 人品亦佳.[98] He subsequently makes Luo Jun an inspector for the Ministry of Revenue. This theme of a lowly person gaining recognition through an anonymous poem inscribed in a public place was a popular one in the Tang, its most famous expression being the *Platform Sutra*'s depiction of the illiterate monk Huineng 惠能 proving his enlightenment through a *gatha* he dictates to be written on the wall of a hall in the monastery.[99] In the case of the tale of Luo Jun, we find a similar theme in a wholly secular context. The anecdote further reminds us that poetry was often read as a window into the moral qualities of the poet and hence his suitability for office. The commissioner's response to Luo's impressive verse is to give him a promotion in an area that arguably had little to do with his ability as a poet. From the commissioner's point of view, however, Luo's poetic skills revealed a larger underlying moral sense. Publicly inscribed poems thus aided the circulation of not only poetry, but of reputations.

Poets would not only inscribe their own poems on public locations, they would also occasionally write up works of other poets, be they friends or simply poets they liked. There are a number of instances of this practice,[100] though Bai Juyi and Yuan Zhen again provide the clearest and most fully described examples. In "On a Wall at the Kaiyuan Temple in Langzhou[101] I Inscribe Letian's Poems" 閬州開元寺壁題樂天詩, Yuan Zhen writes,

Thinking of you I just happen to copy out your poems,	憶君無計寫君詩，
The copying complete, a thousand lines, to whom do I speak them?	寫盡千行說向誰．

98. Wang Dang, *Tang yulin*, 259.

99. See Yampolsky, *Platform Sutra*, 132.

100. See Pi Rixiu's 皮日休 (ca. 834–ca. 883), "Presented in Response to Luwang's 'Summer: Four Poems in Four Rhymes'" 奉酬魯望夏日四聲四首, *QTS*, 616.7103, in which he mentions posting one of Lu Guimeng's poems. Bai Juyi and Yuan Zhen either engaged in this practice far more than others, or simply wrote about it with greater frequency. It is very possible that both are the case.

101. In modern Sichuan.

I inscribe them on a wall at the east
    temple in Langzhou, 題在閬州東寺壁，
When will I know a time that I will
    see you? 幾時知是見君時。[102]

As is often the case, Yuan Zhen shows a keen focus on both circulation and on reporting circulation.[103] Interestingly, his first inclination is to spread Bai Juyi's poems in an oral mode: having copied out a number of the poems, he wants to discuss them with someone. Being alone, he instead writes them on a temple wall where he can be sure others will see them and then reports his actions back to Bai Juyi.

Bai Juyi, having learned of his friend's actions, responds in kind:

Answering Weizhi (At the west[104] temple in Langzhou, Weizhi personally inscribed my poems. I am, in turn, writing one hundred of Weizhi's pieces on this screen, and we informed each other with a quatrain).
答微之（微之於閬州西寺手題予詩予又以微之百篇題此屏上各以絶句相報答之）.

You copy out my poems, overflowing temple walls, 君寫我詩盈寺壁，
I inscribe your lines, filling a screen. 我題君句滿屏風。
Meeting each other again, where will it be? 與君相遇知何處，
Two leaves of floating duckweed, amidst a great sea. 兩葉浮萍大海中。[105]

On the surface it might seem that Yuan Zhen was doing more to promote the wide dissemination of his friend's poems than Bai Juyi offered in return, since writing them on a temple wall ensured a wide audience for the poems. Yet it is clear that Bai Juyi is aiming at circulating Yuan Zhen's poems as well. In a poem written that same year (817), "Inscribing Poems on a Screen: a Quatrain," noted above, Bai Juyi writes:

Thinking of you, I pick out your
    poems to make a screen, 相憶采君詩作障，

---

102. *YZJ*, 20.226–27.

103. For other examples see both Yuan Zhen's preface to Bai Juyi's collection and "The Camel Pass Post Station: Two Poems" 駱口驛二首, *YZJ*, 17.194, in which Yuan Zhen reports seeing poems by Bai Juyi and others written on the post station walls.

104. This difference, i.e., that Yuan Zhen refers to Langzhou's east temple and Bai Juyi the west one, is unresolved in the commentaries I have read.

105. Zhu, 17.1092.

I write them out and collate them myself, not refusing the labor.	自書自勘不辭勞·
When the screen is complete, people will compete to copy them.	障成定被人爭寫，
Because of this, the price of paper in Nanzhong will be high.[106]	從此南中紙價高·[107]

The context of the previous poem implied the issue of furthering circulation; here it is made explicit. Much as Bai Juyi enjoys simply having Yuan Zhen's poems with him as a substitute for his friend's companionship, he is also compelled to share that companionship with as many others as possible by posting Yuan Zhen's poems where others could copy and spread them.

If each friend promised the other a wider audience for his poems as a result of the new act of inscription, the locations of the inscriptions point to different sorts of audiences. Inscribing a poem on a post station or temple, as Yuan Zhen does for Bai Juyi, would likely lead to broad exposure. Posting poems where any passer-by could read them was akin to publication in an age before there was a true publishing industry. Print culture is anonymous: a writer typically cannot know everyone who buys or otherwise obtains a copy of his works when they are printed on any significant scale. This is true as well of a poem inscribed in a temple or post station. The poet (or in this case, his friend) might still control his text at this stage, but by writing up the poem in a public place he loses control of his audience, as well as any future reproductions of his poem.

Bai Juyi, in contrast, writes Yuan Zhen's poems on screens. If these screens remained in Bai's home, as seems likely, Yuan's works would reach a much more limited audience. There are hundreds of examples of poems being written on the walls of private dwellings and in the chambers of monks, where they were far less likely to gain wide exposure (though they would admittedly be more accessible than as a rolled-up scroll stored in a trunk). Bai Juyi's creating a screen of Yuan Zhen's poems for the explicit

---

106. This is a reference to a comment about the rapid circulation and popularity of Zuo Si's 左思 (ca. 253–ca. 307) "Rhapsody on the Three Capitals" 三都賦, which was said to cause the price of paper in Luoyang to go up 洛陽紙貴 because of the great numbers of copies of the work being made. It had become a cliché of praise.

107. Zhu, 17.1091.

purpose of dissemination was unusual; it is a move not attested to in other writings.[108] Yet this treatment of Yuan Zhen's poems can also be seen as a precursor to print culture. Bai makes a master copy specifically to facilitate the rapid creation of other copies of a text. Displaying poems within the home of a close friend or a host or patron would ensure a known direct audience, namely the friend or host, and an additional indirect audience—others in the same social circle who would be likely to visit the person and read the poem. This is a dissemination whose goal, in terms of audience, is quality rather than quantity. In these cases it *does* matter who reads the poems, and the goal is not that "every herdboy" can be heard reciting them.

Like poetry sent by post, this more focused but limited dissemination is closely related to the prominent social role that poetry played in the Tang. While it may have been treated as a commodity at times, poetry was not typically produced for consumption by a mass audience. Part of its value lay in its role as something meaningfully exchanged between a poet and his patron or between two friends. When Meng Haoran wrote a poem on the wall of his host in Chang'an or Li Bai did the same for Mr. Ziyang of Suizhou,[109] there was something to be gained by both parties in such an exchange: the patron obtained a tangible sign of his connection with the high culture of the day and, in the case of Li Bai, a link with a poet who was quite well known in his own time. The poet in turn, beyond any financial support he might have received from the patron, gained exposure to other people of the class most likely to serve as patrons. This would be especially important for such poets as Li Bai and Meng Haoran who enjoyed little if any success in their official careers.

These exchanges were not always based on a relationship of economic patronage or even social advantage. A poet such as Wang Wei had little need of patrons for financial support, but he wrote a number of poems whose titles state that they were written on the walls of various acquain-

108. While there are examples, many of which are noted in this chapter and the previous one, of people spreading poems from public postings, especially in the entertainment quarters, I know of no other examples of a writer specifically claiming that he posted the poems of another for this purpose.

109. See Li Bai, "Written on the Wall of Mr. Ziyang of Suizhou" 題隨州紫陽先生壁, *QTS*, 184.1873.

tances of lower social status, such as Daoist and Buddhist monks. The social role of poetry here is simply part of the general practice of elite literate society during the Tang, whether one is a monk in a cell or an official at a country retreat outside of Chang'an. Just as Xuanzong demanded that Li Bai compose for him, so did social equals encourage each other to write poems for display in their homes. The significant number of titles that describe writing a poem on a friend or acquaintance's wall strongly implies that the practice was a common component of social etiquette. The social role of this type of casual poetic exchange is made explicit in such titles as the monk Huaichu's 懷楚 "Thanking a Friend for Paying Me a Visit and Leaving a Poem" 謝友人見訪留詩.[110] This type of exchange is different from a formal exchange of matching poems following particular rhymes and topics, yet it remains an important and probably even more typical example of how poetry functioned in the everyday relationships and interactions of the Tang literate class. The dynasty's most famous pair of friends, Yuan Zhen and Bai Juyi, liked to have each other's poems physically present as reminders of their friendship, and in this regard at least, there is little reason to believe that they were exceptional.[111]

The practice of inscribing poems, whether in public or private, returns us to the importance of the material aspects of written poetry in the Tang. A poem inscribed in the home of a friend or patron was a physical presence that, unlike a chanted poem, would endure long after the moment of inscription had passed. It could serve as a memento of an occasion for the friend as well as enduring proof of a connection to the poet to display to others. This ability to endure was also a crucial part of inscription as a means of transmission. It allowed a wider audience, who may well have not known the poet personally, to read his works and perhaps copy or memorize them, thus potentially circulating them even further. Inscription could move poems from the private to the public sphere without further effort by the poet and indeed without even his knowledge. When in exile in Tongzhou 通州 in 815, Yuan Zhen wrote to Bai Juyi that he had

110. *QTS*, 823.9284.

111. The importance of these material reminders in the face of separation could become even stronger when a friend had passed away, as attested to by Ouyang Zhan's 歐陽詹 (ca. 756–ca. 798) "Gazing on the Place Where My Late Friend Wrote Up a Poem" 睹亡友題詩處, *QTS*, 349.3910.

encountered one of Bai's poems on a pillar at an inn on the river. In his preface-length title to a poem he writes in response, Bai gives some of the history of the lines his friend had happened upon:

On the day that Weizhi arrived in Tongzhou, his temporary lodgings had not yet been arranged. He saw that there were a few lines of characters on a dusty wall. Reading them, it turned out that it was one of my old poems...but he did not know who had inscribed it. Weizhi could not stop sighing, then composed a piece and sent it to me together with my original poem that he had transcribed. When I examined this poem, it turned out that it was a quatrain that I had given to a Chang'an singing girl, A Ruan, fifteen years before when I had just passed the exams.
微之到通州日，授館未安，見塵壁間有數行字，讀之即僕舊詩．．．然不知題者何人也．微之吟歎不足，因綴一章兼錄僕詩本同寄．省其詩，乃十五年前初及第時贈長安妓人阿軟絶句．[112]

Bai Juyi's original poem began as a private gift to a singing girl, probably both recited and presented to her as a written text. Traveling by paths unknown, over a decade later it ended up some one hundred and fifty miles away on a pillar at an inn, written there by an unknown hand. Interestingly, Bai himself envisions the poem arriving in Tongzhou through oral circulation, writing, "Who would have known it had been passed along through recitations to Tongzhou" 可知傳誦到通州.[113] At the same time, we are reminded of the poem's status as a distinctly physical object when Yuan Zhen writes in his own poem that that he saw Bai's verses because he "all of a sudden turned towards the broken eaves, at a spot where they were damaged and leaky" 忽向破檐殘漏處.[114] We can imagine that the inscribed poem had been covered over with dust and was only revealed because of a fortuitous leak. If the poem did find its way to Tongzhou through oral circulation, its appearance there in written form is what ultimately allowed it to survive to be discovered by Yuan Zhen.

This single anecdote encapsulates a number of roles played by written poetry in the Tang and the different ways that inscription in particular participates in these roles. A poem that began as a private social exchange

112. Zhu, 15.922. Stephen Owen discusses this poem in *Mi-Lou: Poetry and the Labyrinth of Desire*, 52–55.

113. Zhu, 15.922.

114. *YZJ*, 20.224.

between a poet and a singing girl who may well have been his lover ends up inscribed on that most public of places, a riverside inn. Its audience there remains anonymous, but was presumably broad. Yuan Zhen's discovery of the poem returns it to the private social sphere, where it serves as a reminder of his good friend and the happier times they shared in the past.[115] When Yuan Zhen transcribes the poem and sends it back to its original author along with a new poem about the discovery, an additional chapter in its circulation has begun. Bai Juyi's response, in both the poem itself and its lengthy title, serves to reintroduce the poem to a new audience. Though ostensibly written as a response to his friend, it is clear that Bai intended his poem to circulate to a much wider group of people. Anna Shields points out that "the detailed account in the rest of the title seems aimed at providing context for readers other than Yuan Zhen."[116] We see here that written circulation could be just as dynamic and adaptable as its oral counterpart. Inscribing poems, whether the intended audience was a single person or thousands of passersby, kept poems in the public eye and ensured that the possibility of further circulation remained alive, often along paths their authors could not have foreseen.

Market Circulation

Publicly inscribed poems could be a form of advertising; they were "given away" in the hope that they would circulate widely and spread the reputation, literary or otherwise, of their author. They had value, but more as part of the accumulation and exchange of cultural capital than as objects that were traded in a conventional market. Yet writings were, at least in some limited contexts, also bought and sold as a true commodity in the Tang, as objects having value in and of themselves. We know that, despite some claims to the contrary,[117] bookstores had long flourished in large

115. Anna Shields, ("Remembering When," 346) notes, "For contemporary readers old enough to remember, these poems would serve as vivid reminders of the era in which the two men were celebrities."

116. Shields, "Remembering When," 346.

117. Poon ("Books and Printing in Sung China [960–1279]," 154) has commented of the Tang that "without the printed books, there was not much that a bookstore could sell, because people made manuscript copies primarily for their own use."

metropolitan areas in China, especially capital cities, and that there was a long-standing practice of selling books and writings of many sorts.[118]

Accounts of buying and selling poetic texts in particular fall into two broad categories: utility and enjoyment. Evidence for the latter, people buying poetry for their own reading pleasure, is scanty and inevitably comes back to the writings of Bai Juyi's circle about their own works. Yuan Zhen writes of his and Bai Juyi's poems:

> As for making fair copies and printings and putting them out for sale in markets or swapping them for ale and tea, it is like this everywhere. Around Yangzhou and Yuezhou they often write and print various poems of Letian and myself and sell them in the market.
>
> 至於繕寫模勒，衒賣于市井，或持之以交酒茗者，處處皆是．揚、越間多作書模勒樂天及予雜詩，賣於市肆之中也．[119]

Within the context of this preface for one of Bai Juyi's collections, it is clear that the claim here is one of popularity; people buy and sell Bai and Yuan's poems because they enjoy reading them. There is no sense that the works are used for other purposes beyond possibly resale to others who would also want to read them. Later in this same piece, when Yuan writes: "There was also a merchant from Jilin (in southern Korea) who searched the market thoroughly, himself claiming, 'My country's Chief Minister will invariably exchange a hundred in gold for a single piece...'" 又雞林買人求市頗切，自云：本國宰相每以百金換一篇,[120] the implication is the same: these poems are valuable because people like them. They are willing to pay for the pleasure of reading and possessing them as written texts. This is how we would typically envision a market for literary works: people buy things they want to read. Yet other than these comments from Yuan Zhen, there is little to suggest that there was much of a direct market for poetry in the Tang based on people's desire to read good poetry.

---

118. There are a number of Tang poems that refer to the selling of books. Some examples include Wang Jian's "Given to Commandant-Escort Cui Li" 贈崔禮駙馬, *QTS*, 300.3411; Lü Wen's "Song of the Library of High Official Zhao Rong" 上官昭容書樓歌, *QTS*, 371.4172; Xiang Si's "Spring Longings in Ningzhou" 寧州春思, *QTS*, 554.6470; and Li Zhong's 李中 "Written on *Xiucai* Wang's Wall" 書王秀才壁, *QTS*, 747.8499. See also a brief discussion in Huang Zhengwei, *Fang keben*, 7. For a brief discussion of bookselling in the Liang, see Tian, *Beacon Fire and Shooting Star*, 83–85.

119. *YZJ*, 51.555. The text in smaller type indicates Yuan Zhen's original notes.

120. *YZJ*, 51.555.

What we find instead in accounts of buying and selling poems in the Tang is a market for poetry based primarily on its utilitarian value. Recall the example of Li Yi, discussed in the previous chapter: "Each time he would compose a piece, it would be sought out with bribes by the musicians in the palace entertainment quarters, who would sing it as a performance for the emperor." An anecdote in the *Tang zhiyan* describes a similar situation, claiming that Wen Tingyun 溫庭筠 (ca. 801–910) "treated his writings as commodities" 以文爲貨 and sold them to exam candidates.[121] In both of these accounts people bought works of literature for their utility. Li Yi's writings were known to please the emperor, while candidates hoped that passing off Wen Tingyun's compositions, either in whole or in part, as their own would bring them success on the exams.[122]

It appears that this market for poetry (and other writings) to be used in the pursuit of examination success was well-developed, at least in the capital. An anecdote from the *Tang zhiyan* shows that it involved an interesting supply chain:

> Xue Baoxun, who called himself the "Diamond Vajra," was fond of circulating great numbers of his writings. In the Taihe reign period, there were at least a thousand or more nominees for office and scrolls piled up at the gates of high officials. Most of them ended up paying the expenses for the gatekeepers and old women servants' oil lamps. Those who enjoyed their ease because of this said, "If the scrolls were from Xue Baoxun, then our take would be twice as much as usual."
> 薛保遜好行巨編，自號金剛杵．太和中，貢士不下千餘人，公卿之門，卷軸塡委，率爲閽媼脂燭之費，因之平易者曰：若薛保遜卷，即所得倍於常也．[123]

The scrolls in question were commonly known as "circulated scrolls" (*xingjuan* 行卷)—small, self-compiled collections that exam candidates and others seeking positions and patronage would circulate among offi-

121. *TZY*, 11.121.

122. It is true that in the case of the Li Yi's poems, they are ultimately purchased because someone, the emperor, enjoys them, but the passage does not imply that musicians were paying for the works simply because they themselves liked them.

123. *TZY*, 12.136.

cials and others important figures.[124] Containing works of both poetry and prose, by the Mid-Tang they had become an increasingly important means of demonstrating one's literary talent to the right people.[125] As we can see from the above anecdote, the scrolls did not always make it to their intended destination.[126] That servants could make a profit from reselling the scrolls—most of which were presumably from writers who had not yet made a name for themselves—implies a healthy market for at least some sorts of literary works in the capital.

Though this anecdote does not specify why people were interested in buying the discarded poems of desperate exam candidates, it is unlikely that purchasers took them home for their own reading pleasure. Rather, a number of anecdotes suggest that they hoped to find superior works that they could pass on as their own. There were obvious risks attendant to this practice, as the following anecdote from the *Da Tang xinyu* suggests:

In the Tang, when Director Li Bo was in charge of Qizhou, there was a Mr. Li, claiming to be a recommended candidate, who came to pay him a call. It just so happened that Bo was quite ill, so his son met [Li]. When he read the poetry scroll he presented, they were all Bo's poems. He then went back and gave them to Bo, who said in surprise,
"This is the scroll that I circulated when I was an exam candidate; they've only changed the name."

124. Other terms for this practice include "presented scrolls" (*toujuan* 投卷) and "warmed scrolls" (*wenjuan* 温卷). See Fu, *Tangdai keju yu wenxue*, and Cheng, *Tangdai jinshi xingjuan yu wenxue*. See also Mair, "Scroll Presentation in the T'ang Dynasty." Mair focuses primarily on judgments passed on this practice and whether or not it resulted in good poetry. He does not address its effect on the circulation of poetry *per se*. Fan Zhilin briefly mentions *xingjuan* in "Tangdai shige de liuchuan (shang)," 271. For the general practice of appealing to high officials known as *ganye* 干謁, of which *xingjuan* are a part, see Ge, "Lun Chu Sheng Tang wenren de ganye fangshi" and Xue Tianwei, "Ganye yu Tangdai shiren de xintai." For a fascinating reconstruction of a *ganye* anthology of poetry, see Timothy Wai Keung Chan, "Restoration of a Poetry Anthology by Wang Bo."

125. Mair ("Scroll Presentation in the T'ang Dynasty," 48–55) points out that the practice was popular enough to meet with considerable opposition from critics who felt it undermined the sanctity and utility of the exam system by relying on favoritism and flattery.

126. For other examples of this see Moore, *Rituals of Recruitment*, 147–48.

The next day, he sent his son to invite Mr. Li. He calmly examined him, saying, "My father respectfully enquires, is it not the case that this scroll was composed by the Cultivated Talent?"[127]

When Mr. Li heard these words his face colored and he said, "These are the writings of my life of heart-breaking work. I'm not lying!"

The son further said, "This is a scroll from when my father took the exam. Neither the paper nor the brush has changed. I again ask the Cultivated Talent not to lie."

He hastily replied, "Up to now I really have been lying. Twenty years ago, I actually bought it in a bookstore in the capital for a hundred cash. I really didn't know it was the worthy and esteemed Director's excellent compositions. I'm overcome with fear!"

唐郎中李播典蘄州日，有李生稱舉子來謁·會播有疾病，子弟見之，覽所投詩卷，咸播之詩也·既退，呈于播，驚曰：此昔應舉時所行卷也，唯易其名矣·明日，遣其子邀李生， 從容詰之曰：奉大人咨問，此卷莫非秀才有製乎·李生聞語，色已變，曰：是吾平生苦心 所著，非謬也·子又曰：此是大人文戰時卷也，兼牋翰未更，卻請秀才不妄言·遽曰：某向來誠爲誑耳·二十年前，實於京輦書肆中以百錢贖得，殊不知是賢尊郎中佳製，下情不勝恐悚·[128]

This is a candidate who clearly wishes his scroll had been left unread at the gate. Beyond the humor here, the story reveals much about how circulation worked in a market context. To begin with, we know that Li acquired the scroll by purchasing it at a bookstore in the capital; he is even specific about the price he paid, a not insignificant amount at the time. Considering the two anecdotes together, we can imagine a cycle in which bookstores bought neglected *xingjuan* from such sources as the gatekeepers noted in the *Tang zhiyan* account, who would be unlikely to simply sell the scrolls themselves.[129] Fan Zhilin has speculated that bookstores must have employed scribes of some kind,[130] but the story of Li Bo's scroll presents an alternative possibility. As Li Bo implies and his son makes clear, the writings Mr. Li presented were not only Li Bo's own poems,

---

127. In other words, Li.

128. Liu Su, *Da Tang xinyu*, 13.205.

129. This is, of course, speculative, but it is probable that gatekeepers and servants would be illiterate and not be considered the best source for plagiarizeable literary works. In either case, we do know that this particular scroll was purchased at a bookstore.

130. See Fan Zhilin, "Tangdai shige de liuchuan (xia)" 唐代詩歌的流傳(下), 143.

they were apparently the actual scroll that he circulated when he himself had come to take the exams many years before. In other words, the scroll itself had gone through a process of circulation that took it from Li Bo to senior literati he hoped to impress many years ago, then to the bookstore, to Mr. Li, and eventually back to Li Bo. In this case there was no reproduction: where Yuan Zhen claims that people copied his and Bai Juyi's poems to sell them, Mr. Li's bookseller simply resold a scroll that had come into his hands. A single physical text was involved at each stage of circulation.

The point of this particular anecdote is the ironic coincidence of the scroll returning under another name to its original author. More interesting is the degree to which buying poems and other literary works for the express purpose of deceptively passing them off as one's own appears to have been a widespread practice. Fu Xuanzong notes that "Plagiarism was the most obvious abuse of [the practice of] *xingjuan*.[131] Oliver Moore points out that candidates knew "that circulated writings were often traded from one user to the next. Disputes concerning authorship had long been an endemic feature of writing for the examinations."[132] In such cases value derived from the interchangeability of the writings in question. Works were purchased not because they were identifiably by a famous author, but specifically because their authorship had been obscured. Mr. Li claims that he did not know that the poems were Li Bo's (and there is little reason to doubt him on this point), implying that the bookseller or his supplier had removed Li Bo's name from the scroll prior to selling it. The account of Mr. Li's error, not the only anecdote of this sort,[133] shows that many writings, in the process of circulating as commodities, had become unmoored from their creators.

Related issues of authorship arise when the market treats poems as a commodity whose value *does* derive, in part, from their purported authorship. Returning to Yuan Zhen, we find him lamenting a lack of quality control that seems to accompany the popularity of his and Bai Juyi's works:

---

131. Fu, *Tangdai keju yu wenxue*, 292.

132. Moore, *Rituals of Recruitment*, 146.

133. For a similar anecdote see Wang Dang, *Tang yulin*, 7.650. This anecdote is also noted in Mair, "Scroll Presentation in the T'ang Dynasty," 54–55.

As for more extreme examples, there are those who go as far as to steal our names, illicitly seeking to sell [poems] themselves, or confusedly mix [their poems and ours] together. There is just nothing to be done about it.
其甚者，有至於盜竊名姓，苟求自售，雜亂間廁，無可奈何。[134]

Yuan goes on to note that the Chief Minister from Jilin, who was allegedly willing to pay a hundred in gold for a single poem of theirs, can discern obvious fakes in an instant (其甚僞者，宰相輒能辨別之).[135] Bai and Yuan's poems are valuable specifically because of their famous authors. Rather than take Bai and Yuan's poems and affix their own names to them, the canny businessmen that Yuan mentions attached Bai and Yuan's names to their own implicitly inferior works to meet market demand. Hidden behind Yuan's self-aggrandizement is the tacit admission that perhaps it was not so difficult to pass off inferior poems as works of the great Bai Juyi and Yuan Zhen. A true connoisseur, such as the official from Jilin, could make the distinction, but apparently many could not.

Surviving anecdotes that describe the ways poems were bought and sold are limited and likely do not give us a full picture of the commercial market for poetry in the Tang. The dearth of casual references to buying and selling poetry intended for pleasure reading is, however, informative. The evidence suggests that people wrote, recited, and copied poems they liked; they did not buy and sell them.

The fact that so many anecdotes about buying and selling poems tend to focus on the ways in which the poetry market could go awry tell us something about Tang attitudes towards the commercial market for poetry, whatever its extent. Even though the increasingly active market for poetry and other contemporary literary works facilitated circulation of these writings, it also destabilized one of the foundations of traditional literary criticism, the connection between poets and their authors. Anxiety about the destabilization of this relationship runs through many of the accounts we have seen here. Stories of candidates caught fraudulently circulating purchased *xingjuan* to their original authors serve as revealing cautionary tales. The surprising number of stories with such a theme may not prove that many exam candidates actually met such an ironic fate, but it does tell us that writers were concerned about the practice of circulating

134. *YZJ*, 51.555.
135. Ibid.

works under false pretenses.[136] Bai Juyi and Yuan Zhen were similarly anxious that fraudulent practices were undermining their relationship with their own writings. Rather than having their names erased, they were added where they did not belong. In both cases, the increased exposure market circulation provided came, appropriately enough, at a price, as authors lost control over the works they had created.

Textual Reproduction and Change

Whether written on leaves or letters, inscribed on a temple wall or sent on a scroll to an influential official, all the poems we have considered here were written texts, and the manner in which those texts were produced and reproduced have important implications for the question of textual stability in the Tang. There were two basic modes of circulation for written works in the Tang. A single copy of a work could repeatedly change hands, going from one reader to another. The *xingjuan* sold by Tang booksellers sometimes circulated this way, as we saw in the anecdote about Li Bo's scroll returning to him. A more common and effective method of written transmission was based not on passing around a single physical copy of text, but by producing one or multiple copies of it that were then used as the basis for further copying. When Quan Deyu says that "everybody copied and circulated" 人皆傳寫 Master Wuzun's new works, he is clearly referring to circulation through this type of textual reproduction.

The same advances in the technology and availability of paper that allowed the Tang government to make such extensive use of the written medium also made it much more convenient for private individuals to engage in reproduction of texts on a wide scale. Private copying was, throughout the Tang and earlier periods, the primary means by which people acquired writings for their personal libraries. As we shall see in Chapter 5, literary collections were typically copied by authors themselves,

---

136. Another example from the *Tang zhiyan* involves an exam candidate named Yang Heng 楊衡 whose works are stolen by a cousin who passes them off as his own and succeeds in exams as a result. The cousin does, however, claim that he did not dare use Yang Heng's favorite line from one of his poems. This assuages much of Yang Heng's anger at the theft of his poems. See *TZY*, 2.18. See also Fu's (*Tangdai keju yu wenxue*, 292–93) discussion of this anecdote.

family members, close friends, or students. This level of informality proves to be the rule for the written reproduction of poetry in the Tang. In the preface to his "Sent to Dongchuan" 使東川,[137] Yuan Zhen describes a typical situation:

On the seventh day of the third month of the fourth year of the Yuanhe reign period (809), I was sent to Dongchuan as an Investigating Censor. While traveling, I composed thirty-two poems altogether. The Editor of the Imperial Diary in the Palace Library Bai Xingjian copied them out for me as the "Dongchuan Scroll." As for what I am recording today, there are only quatrains and ancient-style verse in the seven-syllable line.
元和四年三月七日，予以監察御史使東川，往來鞍馬間，賦詩凡三十二章．秘書省校書郎白行簡，爲予手寫爲東川卷，今所錄者，但七言絕句長句耳．[138]

This is textual reproduction removed only slightly from the original source of the works being copied. Whether Bai Xingjian was transcribing Yuan Zhen's poems from oral declamation, or, as is more likely, copying out a series of written poems onto a single scroll, it was probably done with the close cooperation of the original author. In this case, there is no specific indication that the goal was to further disseminate Yuan Zhen's works; Bai Xingjian (who was Bai Juyi's brother in addition to being a friend and poetic correspondent of Yuan Zhen) was simply putting a number of his friend's poems into a more formal format and presenting them as a scroll back to Yuan Zhen.

Younger relatives were also put to work as informal scribes for their elders when the need to copy poetry arose. Han Yu, in "Drunk, Presented to Zhang Shu of the Imperial Library" 醉贈張祕書, writes, "Amai does not understand writing / but has a deep knowledge of *bafen* archaic script. / When the poems are done we'll have him copy them..." 阿買不識字，頗知書八分．詩成使之寫...[139] The "Amai" referred to here is probably Han Yu's nephew. Though Qian Zhonglian suggests that it is possible that Amai could copy out characters without always understanding their meaning but was not really illiterate[140] (as was true of some printing block

137. In present-day Sichuan.
138. *YZJ*, 17.193.
139. Qian, *Han Changli shiji*, 391.
140. Ibid., 393.

carvers in later periods), the comment is more likely meant as a joke by Han Yan comparing the young child's handwriting to archaic script.[141] On a more somber note, Han Yu's good friend Meng Jiao 孟郊 (751–814) laments his own lack of a son in his poem "Regrets of Age" 老恨, writing, "With no sons to copy my writings / my elderly chantings mostly just drift away" 無子抄文字，老吟多飄零.[142]

Whether they had sons or not, most poets were themselves the primary copyists of their works throughout their lives, and their goal was dissemination, if only on a small scale. Poets were not professional scribes. With the possible exception of some examination candidates and aspiring officials who were over-zealous in spreading around their *xingjuan* (to the financial benefit of Chang'an's gatekeepers), there is no evidence that they would make large numbers of copies of their works. They focused instead on copying out poems when the need arose to give them to a specific person, as in this anecdote from the *Tang yulin* about the poet-monk Jiaoran:

> There was a monk from Wuxing named Zhouyi, styled Jiaoran,[143] who was skilled at regulated verse. When he once paid a call to Wei of Suzhou,[144] he feared that his poetic style wouldn't suit Wei. So he expressed his feelings on the boat by composing dozens of pieces of ancient-style verse to present to him. Wei did not praise any of them and Zhouyi was most disconsolate. The next day he copied out his older works. Wei recited them and admired them much more.
> 吳興僧晝一，字皎然，工律詩．嘗謁韋蘇州，恐詩體不合，乃於舟抒思，作古體十數篇爲獻，韋皆不稱賞，晝一極失望；明日寫其舊製之，韋吟諷，大加嘆賞．[145]

The immediate intended audience here is quite small, probably consisting only of Wei Yingwu himself. There is no specific implication that Jiaoran intends Wei to further disseminate his poems. He copies out his older poems, those in regulated verse, after Wei fails to praise any of the pieces in the ancient style. Jiaoran either had copies of these older works on hand

141. This has been suggested by Stephen Owen in unpublished lecture notes.

142. *QTS*, 584.6767. As we will see in Chapter 5, Bai Juyi and others frequently employed younger relatives to copy parts of their formal literary collections.

143. This is clearly the monk Jiaoran (730–99), whose secular name was Xie Zhou 謝晝 with the pen name Qing Zhou 清晝. See Wang Dang, *Tang yulin*, 3.259 for a discussion of this change in the text.

144. That is, Wei Yingwu 韋應物 (737–ca. 792).

145. Wang Dang, *Tang yulin*, 3.259.

or was copying them out from memory. In either case he would thus be making a "fair copy" to give to Wei. By doing so, Jiaoran disseminates his poetry, but on a very small scale, reminding us again of the close connection between poetic circulation and poetry's social role of communicating emotions between individuals.

Han Yu gives us a sense of how a writer might use his poetry as part of an attempt to gain employ in his series of three "Letters to the Prime Ministers" 上宰相書. After passing the *jinshi* exam in 792, Han Yu failed three times to pass the placement exam, the *boxue hongci* 博學宏詞, that would have hastened his search for an actual position in the bureaucracy.[146] Desperate for official employment, Han Yu wrote three letters to the prime ministers requesting that they appoint him. The first letter concludes:

I dare not take delight in myself. From the works I have composed in the past, I have hastily chosen a number of acceptable poems and written them on a separate scroll. I hope that you will deign to look at them for me.
小子不敢自幸，其嘗所著文，輒採其可者若干首，錄在異卷，冀辱賜觀焉.[147]

Like Jiaoran, Han Yu directs the circulation of these poems to a very limited audience and with a specific purpose: to sufficiently impress the prime ministers that they see fit to grant him employ. Although Han Yu's attempt failed (hence the need for the later two letters in the series[148]), it shows that poets took it upon themselves to copy out their poems in such circumstances and that much of the early stages of circulation of these poems should be attributed to this type of private and very small-scale copying by writers themselves.

Much copying in the Tang was not just of a writer's own poems but of the works of others. The most basic reason for copying new works one encountered was simply to acquire one's own copies. We should never forget that personal copying was how people in the Tang probably ob-

146. As Hartman (*Han Yü*, 29–30) points out, Han Yu did pass the exam the first time he sat for it in 793 but had his name removed from the list of successful candidates by a prime minister.

147. Ma, 3.158. A portion of this passage is cited in Mair, "Scroll Presentation in the T'ang Dynasty," 58.

148. Ma, 3.92–95.

tained most written works. But copying could serve other purposes as well. Writing out model texts had long been an integral part of the traditional education system based on memory and textual reproduction. As we saw in Chapter 2, students learned the Classics by reciting and copying them—a practice that they would often continue even in their later years. The *Guoshi bu* 國史補 ("Supplemental History of the Tang") notes of Zhang Shen 張參: "Zhang Shen served as Director of Studies in the Directorate of Education. When he was old, he would often copy out the *Nine Classics* by hand, as he thought that copying books was better than reading books" 張參爲國子司業，年老，常手寫九經以謂讀書不如寫書.[149] The act of copying reproduced not only the works themselves, but in some sense the original act of composition. It put the copyist in the shoes of the author as he wrote out the same text. Copying thus was, as the English word implies, imitative, and resulted in a deeper knowledge of the text than would simply reading it. For someone of advanced age such as Zhang Shen, copying served as part of a continuous practice of inculcation rather than an attempt to learn a new work, as he had surely long ago memorized many of the sections of the works he would copy out.[150]

Students had copied out the Classics as part of their education for centuries; by the Tang, the set of texts commonly copied in school included the works of contemporary writers to a much greater extent. In his preface to "A Poem Lamenting the *Jinshi* Yan Zizhong" 傷進士嚴子重詩, Pi Rixiu recalls, "When I was in the village school, I copied the collection of Secretary Du Mu in my books" 余爲在鄉校時簡上抄杜舍人牧之集.[151] Indeed, copying poetry in particular was often part of the curriculum for elite Tang youth.[152] With poetry as part of the civil service exam

149. Li Zhao 李肇, *Xinjiao Tang Guoshi bu* 新校唐國史補 in Yang Jialuo, *Tang Guoshibu deng bazhong*, 3.54.

150. Scholars have long recognized the important role Buddhism played in the educational roles of copying and later printing books. John Kieschnick discusses these topics and also the role of Buddhism in the veneration of books as physical objects in China. See Kieschnick, *The Impact of Buddhism*, 164–85.

151. *QTS*, 614.7083. This is noted as well in *Tangshi jishi*, 66.994.

152. See Li Bincheng, *Sui Tang Wudai shehui*, 363. Note also Yuan Zhen's claim that "I saw various children in the village school competing at practicing poetry. When I called to them and asked [about the poems], they all answered: 'Teacher teaches us the poems of Letian and Weizhi'" 見村校諸童兢習詩，召而問之，皆對曰：先生教我樂天微之之詩. *YZJ*, 51.555.

for much of the Tang, children began mastering its forms at an early age; copying the works of acknowledged masters was a natural part of the learning process. Adults would also employ copying contemporary writings as part of their program of study. Liu Zongyuan 柳宗元 (773–819) notes in his "Preface to Seeing Off Master Fangji" 送方及師序 of Fangji that, "Whenever he encountered the writings of an accomplished scholar, he would immediately make a fair copy with his own hand and review it tirelessly" 遇達士述作，手輒繕錄，復習而不懈.[153]

Imitation, however, is never perfect, and copies inevitably differ from originals. This is nowhere more true than in a manuscript-based literary culture like the Tang in which each reproduction had to be done by hand and depended on the unreliable tools of the eyes, ears, mouth, and memory. Textual reproduction resulted in textual change, whether intentional or otherwise, and created a very different kind of text from what we find in later print-based literary cultures. As noted previously, Gerald Bruns makes a useful distinction between open and closed texts. The latter refers primarily to finalized texts as they exist in print, which "closes off the act of writing and authorizes the results. The text, once enclosed in print, cannot be altered—except at considerable cost and under circumstances carefully watched over by virtually everyone...."[154] Texts in a manuscript culture, by contrast, are "open"; they are subject to change with each individual act of textual reproduction.[155] I note above that people circulating plagiarized *xingjuan* under a variety of names destabilized the relationship between literary works and authors. This is just one part of the larger progressive undercutting of authority by repeated textual reproduction in manuscript cultures. Bruns continues: "Originality, Imitation, Transla-

153. Liu Zongyuan, *Liu Zongyuan ji* 柳宗元集, 25.666.

154. Bruns, "Originality of Texts," 113. The last part of this statement, that changes in print would be "carefully watched over by virtually everyone," clearly would not apply to all print cultures. The limited print runs of early publication efforts in the Song, for example, certainly have more in common with manuscript production than do more formal and official printings in later times. See Chia, *Printing for Profit*.

155. Speaking of hand-copied texts in early China, written primarily on bamboo strips, Mark Edward Lewis notes that "Writings transmitted in such media have a fluidity and openness that sharply contrasts with the fixity and clear limits to which we have grown accustomed." See Lewis, *Writing and Authority*, 54.

tion, Plagiarism: one way to engage these topics is to conceive of them as events that record the gradual loss of authority...."[156]

The circulation of written works in the manuscript culture of the Tang simultaneously increased the spread of a writer's works and influence and decreased his ability to control those works, or his authority over them. Yuan Zhen complains about what is essentially the dilution of the Bai and Yuan "brand" due to other people taking the names of the famous poets and affixing them to their own works. It is telling that this complaint appears in the context of self-satisfied account of the wide circulation their "real" poems enjoyed. As the poems circulated, they were inevitably changed, and it is not beyond the realm of possibility that Yuan may not have recognized poems that had started out as his or Bai Juyi's authentic works. Consider the example of how Yuan's poems might have circulated presented in Bai's "Writing Poems on a Screen: a Quatrain," cited earlier. Bai claims that he wrote Yuan's poems on a screen so that others could come and copy them ("When the screen is complete, people will compete to copy them / because of this, the price of paper in Nanzhong will be high"). Note that the first copies that such people produced with Bai Juyi's screen as their source would be copies of the third generation at least. The poems were originally sent to Bai Juyi by Yuan Zhen (though we do not know their textual history before this point). Bai Juyi then copied them out on the screen himself. He claims that "I write them out and collate them myself, not refusing the labor" 自書自勘不辭勞. The term I translate as "collate" here, *kan* 勘, has a range of meanings that includes revising and checking and correcting a text against an authoritative original. There is a strong implication that textual change was a constant risk. Other people would then come and copy from Bai's copy, most likely not taking the same care as he did in their own copies. If Bai Juyi's hopes for the circulation of his friend's poems were fulfilled, these copies would have served as sources for further copying and even possible oral transmission as well, with additional alterations at each step. Dissemination thus implies not only movement away from the original author in a geographic or temporal sense, but in a textual sense as well.

My suggestion that Yuan Zhen and Bai Juyi's poems may have changed so much through the course of transmission that they themselves would

156. Bruns, "Originality of Texts," 114.

no longer recognize them is only speculation, but it is clear that circulation entailed change. In the preface to his "Twenty-four Poems on Dwelling in the Mountains," the monk Guanxiu 貫休 (832–912) laments the effects that circulation had on some of his works:

In the fourth or fifth year of the Xiantong reign period, I composed twenty-four "Dwelling in the Mountains Poems" while in Zhongling. When I put down my brush, they were snatched away by someone. Later on, some of them were spread around, written on the walls of dwellings and some were recited by people. Sometimes I would hear one or two of them and they all had mistakes in words and lines.
愚咸通四五年中，於鍾陵作山居詩二十四章，放筆，被人將去．厥後或有散書于屋壁，或吟詠於人口，一首兩首，時時聞之，皆多字句舛錯．[157]

Guanxiu's loss of authority is explicit: his poems were literally stolen from him. The greater loss of authority here is one that occurs with all circulation. When Guanxiu encounters the works written up on walls or overhears them recited, he finds that they have changed and are filled with what he considers errors, because they are divergences from the poems as he originally wrote them. We have no way of knowing whether these changes were introduced intentionally or by mistake in the course of the transmission, but it is reasonable to assume that they would not be seen as the latter by the people reciting the poems and writing them on walls.

Indeed there is ample evidence that people in the Tang had few compunctions about changing poems when copying them. In an anecdote in the *Tang zhiyan* concerning the poet Zhao Mu 趙牧 (fl. 860s–70s), Wang Dingbao quotes part of Zhao's poem "Facing the Ale" 對酒 but then notes that "the rest of the work is particularly relaxed and lively, but it's long and I haven't recorded it" 其餘尤工輕巧，辭多不載.[158] In this case Wang Dingbao at least lets us know that he is truncating the poem. When the singing girl in the story of the "wineshop bet" discussed in Chapter 3 excerpted a quatrain from longer poems, she gave no such notice.

157. *QTS*, 837.9428. I was alerted to this important passage by Xiaofei Tian's talk, "Possession and Loss: Tao Yuanming, Su Shi, and Acquiring a Mountain," delivered at Harvard University on October 21, 2002.

158. *TZY*, 10.110.

If some people would truncate works they copied to avoid the work of recording a lengthy piece, others would take on the extra burden of adding to pieces. In an anecdote from the *Guoshi bu*, we find Liu Fang 柳芳 (eighth century) not only copying a friend's works, but actually collaborating on them after the friend had passed on: "Liu Fang and Wei Shu (d. 757) were great friends and both served in the position of Historiographer. After Shu died, some of works remained unfinished. Fang continued many of them and made them into scrolls" 柳芳與韋述友善，俱爲史官・述卒後，所著書有未畢者，多芳與續之成軸也.[159] As this account is second-hand, we do not know if Liu Fang specifically informs the reader of these scrolls which parts of which works are solely by Wei Shu and which are the result of collaborative authorship. In either case, there is no malicious deceit here, unlike the case with plagiarized *xingjuan*. But the fact remains that whether through lengthening or truncation, reproduction and circulation clearly resulted in works undergoing significant change.

Other examples show that copyists could make even more thorough alterations in works they copied based on their judgments of the content. Gao Yanxiu's 高彥休 (b. 854) story of a Tang *jinshi* surnamed Wei 韋 provides a brief but intriguing glimpse of how collections of poetry would be copied long after their original compilations. Wei had acquired a courtesan in Luoyang who was not only beautiful, but was also apparently a skilled copyist and amender of poetic texts. Gao writes:

> Wei once had her copy out the poems of Du of the Ministry of Works.[160] The version he had acquired was full of errors. When the courtesan corrected them as she was copying, the order of the text was clear. Because of this, Wei was especially infatuated with her.
> 韋曾令寫杜工部詩・得本甚舛缺，妓隨筆鉛正文理曉然，以是韋頗惑之・[161]

159. Li Zhao, *Guoshi bu*, 1.20. It should be noted here that it is not clear what types of works Liu Fang is continuing. If they were the historical works on which they had collaborated, this anecdote would take on a different meaning. Liu does, however, specifically note that they were Wei Shu's own writings, and the implication seems to be that he is compiling his friend's literary collection.

160. That is, Du Fu.

161. Gao Yanxiu, "*Jinshi* Wei Sees the Deceased Courtesan," in Li Shiren 李時人, ed., *Quan Tang Wudai xiaoshuo* 全唐五代小說, 2085. I thank Xiaofei Tian for bringing this passage to my attention.

Copying here is not mere reproduction of a text, but alteration of the text's contents as well. Again, we can only speculate as to what would constitute an "error" and be in need of "correction," but it was apparently not a question of a few miswritten characters. The claim that the courtesan would "correct" 正, and clarify the "order of the text" implies large-scale alteration: she changed the meaning of the texts so that what had previously been confusing now made sense (at least to her and Wei).

There are two very different ways of interpreting this editorial practice. One is that while the courtesan was indeed altering the contents of the texts at hand, she assumed that she was simply restoring them to their original state of clarity from which they had departed in the long process of transmission. In such a scenario the courtesan would be acting as a good Lachmannian textual critic, saving the author's original intent from the abuses of careless scribes. The other possibility, and one that I think fits better with the reality of Tang editorial practices, is that people in the Tang simply did not think it was wrong to alter poems written by others to make them either more understandable or even "better" in some way. Thus the more extensively poems circulated, the more likely they were to undergo substantial textual change.

Revision was not only the prerogative of those who copied other writers' works. Poets themselves would frequently alter their works for reasons ranging from aesthetics to social standards of proper behavior. An oft-cited example of revision is the Late Tang poet Zheng Gu's 鄭谷 poem "Middle Age" 中年, in which he writes, "Growing old and frail, I take delight in increasing my study of poetry, / again I take some earlier pieces and revise a few couplets" 衰遲自喜添詩學，更把前題改數聯.[162] We do not know whether these were works already in circulation or whether they had not yet circulated and that any changes would be noticed only by Zheng himself. That is, he may not have been changing works that had already entered into public circulation but rather engaging in something more akin to a prolonged process of composition and revision prior to considering a poem complete and presenting it to others.

---

162. *QTS*, 676.7747. The translation is Owen's, from *End of the Chinese 'Middle Ages'*, 114. Owen argues that revision of poems had come to be accepted as a common stage of composition in the Mid- and Late Tang.

It is worth briefly noting that many of these issues would ultimately affect print culture in China as well. Manuscript and print cultures differ in important ways, but they coexisted and influenced each other from late in the Tang to the end of the imperial period. As Lucille Chia has pointed out, "written and printed texts were easily and routinely transformed into each other, a process that persisted even after the use of printing became widespread."[163] While a single print run might be expected to produce generally identical texts, woodblock printing in China was never entirely separate from its manuscript roots. Preparing woodblocks for the first printing of a text always entailed at least one stage of manuscript transmission. To carve the printing blocks, a copyist had to write out a fair copy of the text on very thin paper. The printer would then paste this copy, called the *tiexie yang* 貼寫樣, face down onto the blocks where it would serve as the guide to the actual wood carvers.[164] In other words, each new cutting of printing blocks required manual copying of texts and thus risked introducing into print the same types of variants that manuscript transmission entailed.

As revisions such as those Zheng Gu undertook were not a result of circulation, they do not represent a loss of authority over his works. The changes Guanxiu saw in his works did reveal such a loss, and when given the chance he was eager to reassert his authority. A second passage from his preface to "Twenty-four Poems on Dwelling in the Mountains" shows the monk reclaiming his poems:

> In the *xinchou* year of the Qianfu reign period,[165] while taking refuge from bandits at a mountain temple, I happened to acquire a copy of [the poems]. Their style was rustic and common, their manner low and muddled. How could I let them be heard by sophisticates? One day I took out a brush and reworked them.

---

163. Chia, *Printing for Profit*, 11.

164. This process is described in Twitchett, *Printing and Publishing in Medieval China*, 70; Tsien, *Paper and Printing*, 196–201; and Pan, *Zhongguo kexue*, 317–18. The latter notes that there are very few writings from the Tang on the procedure and that much of what we know is actually deduced from more recent practice. Chia (*Printing for Profit*, 42) notes that this process "made the bond between the manuscript and the final printed version far more intimate than was the case in Western typographic printing, in which both the text and the image could diverge drastically from the manuscript original and did so increasingly with time."

165. The year 881, which is actually the first full year of the Zhonghe reign period.

Some I kept, some I cut out. I corrected some and added to some. They actually came to twenty-four pieces and were indeed quite brilliant.
洎乾符辛丑歲，避寇於山寺，偶全獲其本，風調野俗，格力低濁，豈可聞於大雅君子．一日抽毫改之，或留之、除之、修之、補之，卻成二十四首，亦斐然也．[166]

Guanxiu does not merely restore these reacquired poems to what he recalls having originally written, but rather uses the opportunity to undertake a full-scale revision of the set. Portions and even whole poems are taken out, others are added and rewritten. His explicit goal was to improve them, feeling their style no longer appropriate for a sophisticated audience.

We do not know whether Guanxiu's displeasure with the poems as he received them years after their original composition was due to changes that had taken place in the transmission process or to the fact that his own literary standards had changed. If it is the latter, then his willingness to rewrite them so thoroughly is all the more revealing. These were not works that he had kept stored in a trunk since his youth and decided to revise in his old age; they were poems that had already circulated widely in a number of media. Thus, Guanxiu's rewording is an unabashed altering of works that had long been publicly circulated, albeit without his blessing, and not part of the more prolonged compositional process that became accepted in the Mid- and Late Tang. Moreover, while Guanxiu does explain the revisions, he maintains the conceit that these are the same poems. The title remains unchanged, as does the number in the set, indicating that he did not see these new versions as completely new works.

It is only fitting that our discussion of open texts returns us in the end to *xingjuan*. This mode of circulating literary works not only destabilized the relationship between author and text, it required constant recopying and revision. An entry from the *Tang zhiyan* shows the perils of being careless when presenting one's *xingjuan*:

When the *jinshi* candidate, Chu Dai, sealed up two rolls and called to submit them he inadvertently took the scroll for [Liu] Zizhang and presented it personally to [Lu] Wei. Wei read it. Numerous characters violated Wei's family taboos one after the other, so that Wei, looking utterly shocked, saluted and retired. Dai

166. *QTS*, 837.9428.

was in a panic to confess what had been a huge error, and subsequently delivered a long note of apology...[167]

進士褚戴緘二軸投謁，誤以子長之卷面贄於威；威覽之，連有數字犯威家諱，威因拱而矍然・戴錯愕白以大誤，尋以長牋致・・・[168]

There was great importance given to avoiding taboos based on the family name's of the recipients of such writings and, as Oliver Moore notes, "Every submission necessitated re-copying all the documents and employing the taboo avoidances that new addressee's name and ancestral names demanded."[169] Such changes to texts might at first glance seem trivial, especially in a culture so accustomed to avoiding taboo characters. But we must take into account the cumulative effect of practices such as these. Not only were texts repeatedly recopied, but each new copy was intentionally changed to fit a different set of new taboos. It is likely that a given candidate would keep a master set and that each new copy would represent a discrete set of alterations. However, as *xingjuan* were apparently plagiarized with abandon, recopyings could result in an accumulation of changes such that texts might begin to look quite different. This would be especially true for poetic texts, in which the demands of rhyme, and depending on the poetic form, tonal alternation and parallelism, could require large-scale revisions.

In his discussion of manuscript culture in medieval Europe, Bruns asks, "What sort of finality does a manuscript possess, particularly in relation to the rights, privileges, and conventional arrogations of a 'latter hand'?"[170] The finality possessed by many poetic texts in the Tang was clearly limited. Revision and alteration by the "latter hands" of copyists and readers were unavoidable parts of the circulation process. The more a work circulated, the less authority its author retained.

Tang writers had a fluid view of textual integrity. We do see glimpses of resistance on the part of authors and readers to this tendency towards

---

167. Translation from Moore, *Rituals of Recruitment*, 151.

168. *TZY*, 11.124.

169. Moore, *Rituals of Recruitment*, 150. This topic is also discussed by Fu (*Tangdai keju yu wenxue*, 281–82, 284). Interestingly, Fu notes that candidates would sometimes have other people, including in one case the candidate's daughter, copy out the final version to be sent. See also Cheng, *Tangdai jinshi xingjuan yu wenxue*, 21.

170. Bruns, "Originality of Texts," 115.

textual alteration, whether through transmission or otherwise. Guanxiu may have been willing to revise his own poems, but he still considered changes introduced by others in the course of circulation to be "mistakes." Indeed, as Cherniack has pointed out, Chinese scholars had long recognized and condemned certain textual changes that occurred in the course of transmission.[171] This condemnation, however, was typically focused on unauthorized changes in the Confucian Classics or in historical documents. Contemporary poetry in the Tang was of a different category. Authors may have resisted some forms of textual change, but they surely recognized its inevitability.

The culture of written poetry in the Tang was a complex one that contained numerous contradictory impulses and trends. Anecdotes portray written composition as both spontaneous and labored. It could take place in a single inspired performance, as with Li Bai's composition for Xuanzong, or over the course of many distinct stages, as we saw in Li Shangyin's portrayal of Li He's compositional technique. Poetry in written form also brings into play new questions of materiality. Written poems could endure over time and space in a way that a single oral recitation could not; poems sent to a friend or written on a wall could serve as keepsakes and mementos. Thus just as orality played a part in the social functions of poetry, so did writing. The latter, moreover, extended the reach of social poetry as it could be sent over great distances and preserved over time. Materiality also introduced a different set of issues of value and commerce. To the extent that poems were turned into a commodity, it was primarily for utilitarian reasons and on a very limited scale. Commercial markets in-

---

171. Cherniack ("Book Culture," 9) cites instances of "unsanctioned change" being noted as early as the *Lü shi chunqiu* 呂氏春秋 ("*Spring and Autumn Chronicles of Mr. Lü*"). Note also the concerns of the Tang writer Lin Han 林罕, who writes in his "Preface to Mr. Lin's 'Origins of Characters: A Compilation of Brief Discussions'" 林氏字源編小說序, "I will thus write it with my own hand and engrave the stones. I hope by this that it will never perish. First of all this avoids the mistakes of transmission by copying. Second of all it avoids the labors of brush and ink" 乃手書刻石期以不朽一免傳寫之誤二免翰墨之勞. See *QTW*, 889.9293. Stone engravings from which one would take rubbings were important precursors to block printing and the fact that Lin Han recognizes the advantages of this mode of textual reproduction is intriguing.

creased the possibilities for circulation, but simultaneously undermined both the control an author had over his works and the relationship between a poet and his poetry. Finally, though writing could fix texts, at least temporarily, in a way that the more ephemeral act of oral declamation could not, the existence of a written text that a poet could revisit, revise, and improve undermined this very notion of permanence and the idea of capturing in verse a single spontaneous emotional response to a specific circumstance. More importantly, accounts make it clear that texts were often altered in the course of circulation by many actors other than the original author himself, again calling into question some of the basic assumptions of traditional literary criticism. The Tang conception of a poetic text was more fluid, and thus the notion of maintaining a single version of a given poem was less important than it would be in later dynasties. This reality of written poetry in the Tang, which we confronted in concrete form in Chapter 1 with the multiple manuscript copies of "Qinfu yin," presents a complexity that can be daunting, but it underscores the importance of basing our critical approaches on a thorough understanding of the true context of the production and circulation of poetry in the Tang.

FIVE

Individual Literary Collections

Literary collections consisting of the works of a single author, generically known as *bieji* 別集, *wenji* 文集, or in the case of collections containing only poetry, *shiji* 詩集, have played a number of crucial roles in the circulation and transmission of poetry during the Tang and were arguably one of the most important routes by which Tang poetry was transmitted to later dynasties. Poets themselves were acutely aware of the importance of compiling a collection to ensure the preservation of their works and reputation beyond their death, and such collections became near ubiquitous in the Tang.[1] As a basis for many anthologies compiled in the Tang itself (and thus for the original print editions of Tang poetry that appeared in the late Tang and Song dynasties), individual literary collections compiled in the Tang have exerted substantial influence on how poetry was re-

---

1. Fan Zhilin, "Tangdai shige de liuchuan (shang)," 278. It has been estimated elsewhere that there were probably no fewer than a thousand such collections compiled during the Tang. See Shang, *Zhongguo gudian wenxue*, 245. Note also that most literary collections referred to as *wenji* contain a substantial number of pieces from prose genres as well. In some case the prefaces to these collections will specify the various genres included. For most Tang versions of collections (as opposed to collections constructed or reconstructed in the Song or later, of which there are far more surviving) prefaces will either not note genre at all or will use a general term such as "poetry and prose writings" (*shibi* 詩筆). My discussion focuses specifically on poetry, as this is the topic of the larger study and also the focus of most collectors and the main content of most collections in numerical terms. At the same time, many of the issues I will address here apply to the circulation and preservation of prose writings contained in literary collections as well.

ceived and read throughout the imperial period and indeed on how it continues to be received and read today.

The first chapter of this study presented examples of the material reality of poetry during the Tang in as authentic and direct a form as we have access to today—surviving Tang manuscripts. This final chapter looks at the experience of confronting that reality through the eyes of some of the few people in the Tang to actually write about it in detail: the compilers of literary collections.[2] I first examine the full process of compiling a literary collection during the Tang, from collecting the poems to editing and copying them into a formal collection. I focus on the Tang prefaces to these collections, not as literary works in their own right (though they are also that), but as sources of evidence for the particulars of how unpolished

2. There were clearly other contexts in which people collected poems in a formal mode (that is, not simply for personal reading pleasure), the most obvious being when compiling anthologies of verse by multiple poets. These anthologies are indeed crucial to our understanding of poetic tastes during different periods of the Tang era, tastes which are often quite different from what later anthologies and critical opinion would imply. Unfortunately, unlike the compilers of collections of individual literary collections, anthologists whose prefaces and other writings survive very rarely talk about the quotidian aspects of the process of collecting poems (I will discuss one major exception, Gu Tao's 顧陶 *Tangshi leixuan* 唐詩類選, later in this chapter). Their concerns tend to focus on aesthetic rather than material issues. As a result, they have very little to tell us about how poems actually circulated. We can deduce that the poems they include in their anthologies circulated widely enough for the compilers to acquire copies, but that process could vary greatly depending on the relationship between the compiler to the poets in questions, the compiler's administrative position, and even his social standing. Again, these are issues the prefaces and other contemporary writings about multi-author collections simply do not address. One possible explanation for this may be that multi-author anthologies were probably made up of works the compiler already knew (and, of course, liked). In other words, he would have already possessed the constituent parts of the anthology he was compiling (Gu Tao, who was interested in a generally representative anthology, is again an exception). In the case of individual collections, the compiler began not with the works themselves, but with a category—works by a given author—that he then had to fill by gathering together poems that fit. For a broad and insightful examination of Tang and pre-Tang collections of poetry, see Yu, "Poems in Their Place." For a comprehensive account of the aesthetic and cultural issues surrounding the compilation of a collection of song lyrics just after the end of the Tang (with important discussions of other anthologies as well), see Shields, *Crafting a Collection.* Wu Qiming examines Tang anthologies in two articles, "'Tangren xuan Tangshi' liuchuan, sanyi kao" and "Tangdai shixuanxue luelun," collected in his *Tangyin zhiyi lu.* Chen Shangjun expands on Wu's work in his "Tangren bianxuan shige zongji xulu" from his *Tangdai wenxue congkao.*

materials were transformed into those collections. These accounts, brief though they often are, bring together the major themes of this study. They tell of collecting poems from oral sources, written sources, and even by seeking out people who had set to memory works that were otherwise lost. They reveal a world in which the materiality of poetry still mattered deeply and the survival of literary works was recognized to be distinctly tenuous. The costs and effort required for textual reproduction in an age before print meant that any given person was unlikely to have multiple copies of a given work; poems were thus seen as being in constant danger of falling out of circulation and disappearing for good.

Examining collections also allows us to revisit issues of textual stability and the link between an author and his ostensive works. While collections preserved poems, they also changed them. One important goal of collections was to tie poems to particular authors. At the same time, the actual process of compilation could destabilize the basic connection between an author and his poems. Some works might be omitted so as to craft a particular image of the poet. Spurious pieces might be included and authentic ones altered with the same end in mind. Writings about collections also clarify the limits of the commercialization of poetry in the Tang. We have seen that poetry was tied to commerce in certain contexts, but the ways compilers put together and describe collections demonstrate that literary works were not yet a commodity in the manner they would be in the later age of commercial printing. Finally, collections and their prefaces reveal meaningful differences between the attitudes of Tang collectors and compilers towards their work and the approaches of those who would undertake similar endeavors in the Song. The Tang sources show us a literary world in which the fluidity of poems and of their textual manifestations was accepted as the norm. The relative scarcity of texts meant that collectors likely did not often find themselves confronted with a large number of variant texts of the same work and thus did not see constant variation as a particular problem. This is a very different world from that which the expansion of print technology, the proliferation of texts, and the advent of a more scholastic and commercial attitude towards poetry created beginning in the Song and continuing to the present.[3]

---

3. For an extensive discussion of the history of the Tang literary collections that exist today (in printed, not original manuscript, form), see Wan, *Tangji xulu*.

Gathering the Texts

Accounts of the first stages of compiling a literary collection—gathering together the materials that would ultimately form the basis for that collection—often emphasize the difficulties faced by the compiler. Through their depictions of loss, the prefaces portray the tenuousness of poems as physical objects always subject to the hazards of social upheaval, intentional destruction, and simple neglect. This concern is especially prominent in writings from the Early and High Tang. Poets of the seventh and eighth centuries showed far less interest in maintaining their own collections than did their successors in later periods, and the compilers of their works are thus particularly focused on this issue of loss. As Lü Cai notes in his preface to the collected works of Wang Ji, "Many of the poems and rhapsodies he composed are scattered and lost. With the collecting and searching as yet unfinished, I have for the time being compiled [his works] into five *juan*" 所著詩賦，並多散逸，鳩訪未畢，且緝成五卷.[4] According to Lü's account, Wang Ji often wrote in a state of spontaneous drunkenness, his poems being recorded and circulated only through the efforts of "those who enjoyed them" (*haoshizhe* 好事者).[5] The implication is that without the efforts of these "fans," even more of Wang Ji's works would have disappeared.

Wang Jin 王縉 (d. 781) expresses a similar anxiety about the works of his elder brother Wang Wei. In his "Memorial on Presenting Wang Wei's Collection" 進王維集表, of 764, Wang Jin laments, "Some [of his works] were dispersed among his friends, some were left in bamboo cases. I recently searched for them and still worry about those that are scattered and lost" 或散朋友之上，或留篋笥之中・臣近搜求，尚慮零落.[6]

4. Lü Cai, "Donggaozi houxu" 東皋子後序, *QTW*, 160.1640.

5. *QTW*, 160.1639.

6. *QTW*, 370.3756–57. For a slightly different wording of the cited passage, see Zhao Diancheng, *Wang Youcheng ji*, 494. Note that Wang Wei and his brother were members of two elite clans, their father's being the Taiyuan Wangs 太原王 and their mother's the Boling Cuis 博陵崔. Fan Zhuanzheng 范傳正, who compiled a collection of works by Wang Wei's contemporary Li Bai about fifty years after the latter's death, describes Li Bai's poems as being in a state similar to that of Wang Wei's. In his "New Funeral Tablet for the Tang Reminder of the Left, Hanlin Academician, Master Li" 唐左拾遺翰林學士李公新墓碑, Fan Zhuanzheng writes of the poems in the collection that, "Sometimes I obtained them from literati of the time, sometimes I got them from his ancestral clan

Wang Wei's status as a poet quite famous in his own day and, moreover, a member of two of the Tang's most important aristocratic families, must have ensured that there were a good number of his poems both in circulation and in the possession of members of his social circle. At the same time, the upheaval of the An Lushan Rebellion, during which Wang Wei was accused of treason, clearly made locating copies of his various works a more difficult endeavor than it might otherwise have been.

Some poets were so critical of their own literary output that they themselves endangered its survival, leading compilers to desperate measures likely to result in questionable attributions. Wang Shiyuan 王士源, the compiler of the first known collection of Meng Haoran's poems, encountered circumstances substantially more difficult than those faced by Lü Cai and Wang Jin in their efforts. He writes:

> Whatever Haoran composed he would soon destroy or discard without editing or copying it down, often sighing to himself that the written text did not capture his intent. Since his wanderings and wayfarings were many, his pieces and drafts were scattered and lost. I have offered rewards for them, gathering them from parish and hamlet, but don't have even half of them.
> 浩然凡所屬綴，就輒毀棄，無編錄，常自嘆爲文不逮意也・流落既多，篇草散逸，鄉里搆採，不有其半・[7]

Unlike Wang Ji, who was merely neglectful of the material of his literary legacy, Meng Haoran took to heart the notion from the *Yijing* that "writing does not fully capture speech, and speech does not fully capture meaning" 書不盡言，言不盡意, and destroyed much of what he created before it could be ordered or even recorded. Moreover, as Meng only held an official position for a very short time, had numerous friends, and spent much of his life traveling, his works were necessarily difficult to find in any

---

members. I compiled the incomplete fragments in order to circulate the collection in the age" 或得之于時之文士，或得之于公之宗族，編緝斷簡，以行于代. See Fan Zhuanzheng, "Tang zuoshiyi Hanlin xueshi Li gong xin mubei," in Qu Tuiyuan and Zhu Jincheng, *Li Bai ji jianjiao*, "fulu" 2.1781–82.

7. Wang Shiyuan, "Meng Haoran ji xu" 孟浩然集序, in Meng Haoran (Tong Peiji, ed.), *Meng Haoran shiji jianzhu*, 433. This translation is based on Paul W. Kroll's in "Wang Shih-yüan's Preface," 350.

one location.[8] Extreme actions on the part of the poet inspired extreme actions by the compiler. Using a method that is unique in the descriptions of Tang poetry collection (though quite possibly not unique as an actual practice), Wang Shiyuan "offered rewards" for poems ostensibly by Meng Haoran. It goes without saying that such a practice would provide great incentive to come up with poems in Meng's style, thus throwing the legitimacy of many attributions into doubt. Yet even this methodologically flexible collection process and the imitations it likely inspired left Wang Shiyuan bemoaning how limited his discoveries ultimately remained.

If Meng Haoran's poems suffered at the hands of their self-critical creator, the writings of other poets fell victim to larger forces. Liu Yuxi's preface to Lu Xiang's 盧象 collection simply states, "Seventy-three years after he died, his grandson Yuanfu presented [Lu Xiang's] remaining drafts to me and begged for words to show with it. Having gone through chaos and turmoil, many pieces had been scattered and lost. Those that survive today come to twelve *juan*..." 公下世後七十三年，其孫元符捧遺草來乞詞以表之·嘗經亂離，多所散落，今之存者，十有二卷.[9] Liu Yuxi thus makes explicit what Wang Jin only implied: rebellion and social upheaval could take a toll not only on people but on literary works as well. Li Yangbing's 李陽冰 preface of 762 to a collection of Li Bai's works, the *Tang Li hanlin caotang ji* 唐李翰林草堂集 ("Grass Hut Collection of Hanlin Academician of the Tang, Li"), describes encountering the poet on his death bed, surrounded by tens of thousands of rolls of writings in draft form, unordered and uncorrected. Li Yangbing writes, "Since the troubles in the Central Plains, [Li Bai] had fled [that] land for eight years. Of [the works] he had composed at that time, nine out of ten are lost. Of those that survive today, all of them were obtained from other people" 自中原有事，公避地八年，當時著述，十喪其九·今所存者，皆得之他人焉.[10] The "troubles" to which he refers are, of course, the An Lushan Rebellion, during which Li Bai, like Wang Wei,

---

8. Kroll notes that Meng's "official rank was quite humble, only one step from the bottom of the thirty-rung bureaucratic ladder" and that he held it for less than a year. See Kroll, *Meng Hao-jan*, 79–80.

9. Liu Yuxi, "Tang gu shangshu zhuke yuanwailang Lu gong wenji xu" 唐故尚書主客員外郎盧公文集序, in *Liu Yuxi ji* 劉禹錫集, 19.234.

10. Qu Tuiyuan 瞿蛻園 and Zhu Jincheng 朱金城, eds., *Li Bai ji jianjiao*, "fulu" 2.1790.

was accused of treason, in this case for his association with a prince who attempted to set up his own state.[11] In his years of imprisonment and wandering between 755 and his death in 762, Li Bai's works were scattered and eventually reassembled in part by the poet himself. Yet even his diligent efforts to reclaim his writings and pass them on to be ordered and prefaced resulted in a collection that represented but a fraction of his earlier oeuvre.

The related case of Luo Binwang 駱賓王 (ca. 640–84), one of the famed "Four Elites of the Early Tang" (*Chu Tang sijie* 初唐四傑),[12] is interesting in that his works were both lost and recovered thanks to intrigue and decisions made at the highest levels of court. Xi Yunqing 郗雲卿, the compiler of Luo's collection, writes:

> In the Wenming reign period (684) [Binwang] schemed together with Jingye[13] in Guangling to raise a righteous rebellion. The rebellion failed, leading him to flee. This then caused his literary collection to be completely scattered and lost. Later, the court of Emperor Zhongzong[14] sent down an order to seek out Binwang's poems and writings, commanding me, Yunqing, to collect them. The recorded ones that were missing at that time came to ten *juan*. This collection is made up of pieces stored in private homes and it is indeed worth circulating among those who enjoy [such things].
>
> 文明中，與敬業於廣陵共謀起義兵．事既不捷，因致逃遁，遂致文集悉皆散失．後中宗朝降敕搜訪賓王詩筆，令雲卿集焉．所載者，即當時之遺漏，凡十卷．此集並是家藏者，亦足傳諸好事．[15]

Xu Yunqing's account implies that these works had apparently ceased to circulate. They were no longer in the public domain but rather stored

11. For a brief account of this incident and Li's travels in the years that followed, see Owen, *Great Age of Chinese Poetry*, 117–18.

12. For a full discussion of the *Chu Tang sijie*, see Owen, *Poetry of the Early T'ang*, 79–150.

13. Xu Jingye was also known by the surname Li 李. His grandfather, originally named Xu Shiji 徐世勣 (594–669), was a rebel from Shandong who eventually became a military leader for the Tang and was granted the imperial surname Li. In 684 Xu Jingye raised a rebellion against Empress Wu that ultimately failed. The rebellion and Luo Binwang's role in it are covered in Twitchett, *Cambridge History of China*, vol. 3, 294–300.

14. Zhongzong ruled for most of January and February of 684 and for the period from 705–10 after the restoration of the Tang. See Kroll, "True Dates of the Reigns," 25–26.

15. Xi Yunqing, "Luo Binwang wenji xu" 駱賓王文集序, from *Luo Cheng ji* 駱丞集, 1.

away in private homes. This situation is not surprising given the political upheavals at the time. And just as Wang Shiyuan's rewards provided incentive to "discover" that one had a number of Meng Haoran's poems in one's procession, so did Luo Binwang's association with a failed rebellion surely make people more likely to either destroy their copies of his poems or at least keep quiet about them until the political winds changed, as they eventually did.

In all these cases poems are portrayed as fragile things, and whether through neglect, the author's own hand, or the impact of historical events, they were easily lost or destroyed. Underlying this anxiety over their fragility is a keen awareness of the materiality of literature in this period. Poems could be destroyed, scattered, and lost—as we have seen throughout this study—because they were essentially rare objects. That is, even in the case of the best-known and socially best-connected writers, the arduous process of textual reproduction in an age before print meant that there would always be limits on how many copies of any given work could exist. There were no print runs, and very few contexts in which such works of literature as poems were sold and purchased. It was thus a real possibility that all copies of a given work might disappear.

Writers in the Mid- and Late Tang period typically took a more active role in maintaining a set of their literary works that could eventually be ordered into a formal collection; this may have been due, at least in part, to an awareness of the possibility of loss, but the reality of frequent exiles and relocation connected to official employment was surely an important factor as well.[16] There are a number of examples of writers who passed on their collected writings to trusted friends when they feared that their writings might be at risk. In his preface to Liu Zongyuan's collection, Liu Yuxi recounts how Liu Zongyuan left him a letter, saying, "I'm ill-fated to die demoted, and so trouble an old friend with my remaining drafts" 我不幸卒以謫死，以遺草累故人.[17] The term "remaining drafts" (*yicao* 遺草) is similar to the *caogao* 草稿 that Li Yangbing relates having

16. I will return to the issue of changing attitudes towards literary collections in the Mid- and Late Tang below.

17. Liu Yuxi, "Tang gu shangshu libu yuanwailang Liujun wenji ji" 唐故尚書禮部員外郎柳君文集紀, *Liu Yuxi ji*, 19.236–67.

received from Li Bai. Both indicate works that are in need of revision and are being passed on in such a state out of a sense of urgency. Yuan Zhen's "Xushi ji Letain shu" 敘詩寄樂天書 ("Letter Discussing Poetry, Sent to Letian") from 812 similarly describes how Yuan, when he was demoted and exiled to Jiangling 江陵 for his political involvements, left a set of texts with Bai Juyi.[18] Unlike Liu Zongyuan, however, Yuan Zhen sets out the content of these materials in considerable detail, discusses his ideas on poetry, and distinguishes ten specific forms (*ti* 體) among his poems, ranging from "poems of social criticism in the ancient style" (*gufeng* 古諷) to "poems of seductive allure in ancient and modern style" (*jingu yanti* 今古艷體).[19] He writes, "From when I was sixteen to this seventh year of the Yuanhe reign period, I've already accumulated over eight hundred poems… When I recently came to the capital, they happened to be in my boxes and trunks. I'll deposit all of them with you when I leave for Tongzhou" 自十六時，至是元和七年，已有詩八百餘首・・・昨來京師，偶在筐篋，及通行，盡置足下.[20] Though Yuan Zhen may have left his works with Bai Juyi out of fear that they would perish with him in exile, he had apparently prepared them well in advance, as evidenced by their being carefully ordered and categorized by type. It was probably this categorical schema that inspired Bai Juyi, the Tang's most dedicated custodian of his own works, to come up with a similar system to classify them.[21]

Even in the Late Tang, when maintaining copies of one's own works had become common practice, the task facing a compiler could be difficult. In his postface to Du Mu's literary collection, the *Fanchuan wenji* 樊川文集, the poet's nephew Pei Yanhan 裴延翰 relates that Du Mu had requested that he compile his works and write a preface for the resulting

18. Jiangling is in modern Hubei. For a detailed discussion of Yuan Zhen's political career and opinions see Hwa, "Yuan Chen." Hwa (105) speculates that Yuan Zhen left his works with Bai Juyi partly out of fear that he would not be allowed to return to the capital.

19. See Shields, "Defining Experience."

20. Yuan Zhen, "Xushi ji Letian shu," *YZJ*, 30.352.

21. This is based on claims made by both Angela C. Y. Jung Palandri and Hwa. See Hwa, "Yuan Chen," 121; and Palandri, *Yüan Chen*, 64. Owen (*Late Tang*, 77–78) notes that Yuan was probably the first poet "to actively compile his own collected works, with explanatory materials (in the form of prefaces or letters…."

collection. Unfortunately, while feeling ill one day, Du Mu gathered thousands of pages of his writings and burned all but a small number of them.[22] Not one to be daunted, some years later Pei Yanhan went about putting together the collection from other sources. "Even though I went to hidden and difficult-to-find places," he wrote, "I did not think of many thousand *li* as being far. I insisted on having the works copied out and shown to me" 雖適僻阻，不遠數千里，必獲寫示.[23]

Du Mu's actions, though apparently the result of fever-induced illusion, were similar in effect to Meng Haoran's more methodical attempts to destroy works that he found wanting. Both examples show that the dangers faced by poems were not limited to chaos and rebellion; simple authorial discontent and even temporary delusion were threats as well. Yet beyond its amusing twist, Pei Yanhan's postface does give us some insights as to the state of a poet's draft manuscripts. In describing the documents that Du Mu set aflame, Pei Yanhan hyperbolically states that there were "a hundred thousand pages (*zhi* 紙)," whereas collections were more frequently described in terms of either scrolls, *juan* 卷, or pieces, *pian* 篇. Even if Du Mu had not burned his works, the image of Pei Yanhan—or any other compilers—having to edit, order, and copy thousands of pages of text gives us an idea of just how difficult an undertaking putting together a collection could potentially be.

A final example from the late Tang demonstrates the broad range of sources of which compilers would avail themselves in their pursuits. In his preface to the monk Guanxiu's second collection, the *Chanyue ji* 禪月集 ("Chan Moon Collection"),[24] Tan Yu 曇域 gives a detailed description of the process he went through to compile his teacher's works:

The burial procedures were complete and the mourning finished. On their free days sometimes special worthies would come asking, sometimes guests from court would come seeking. Sometimes they would read one or two of our late teacher's works and sometimes jot down a couple of lines.... Everyone begged me, Tan Yu,

22. Pei Yanhan, "Fanchuan wenji houxu" 樊川文集後序, in Feng, *Fanchuan shiji zhu*, 5.

23. Feng, *Fanchuan shiji zhu*, 5.

24. Guanxiu's first collection, the *Xiyue ji* 西岳集 ("Western Peak Collection"), was put together by the monk himself in 896 and prefaced by Wu Rong 吳融.

to collect and edit the earlier and later poems, prose pieces, and encomiums that he had composed. Every day someone came to inquire [about the work] and I had no time to resist them. I thereupon sought out and examined draft manuscripts and people who had set [his works] to memory. There were around a thousand pieces. Then I had printing blocks carved of the whole set and entitled it the *Chan Moon Collection*.

葬事既周，哀制斯畢．暇日或勛賢見訪，或朝客見尋，或有念先師一篇兩篇，或記參句五句．．．眾請曇域編集前後所製歌詩文贊．日有見問，不暇枝梧．遂尋檢稿草，及暗記憶者，約一千首．乃雕刻成部，題號禪月集．[25]

Most accounts depict collection efforts as focusing on the location of written texts, with source materials described in distinctly physical terms: they might be "scattered and lost," or "stored" (*cang* 藏) in "cases" (*qie* 篋);[26] authors also speak of "disordered drafts" that are "piled up." Pei Yanhan requested that texts be copied out or shown to him. Tan Yu's account describes similar materials, noting that he sought out "draft manuscripts" (*gaocao* 稿草), like those passed on to their compilers by Li Bai and Liu Zongyuan. However, his mention of "those who had set his works to memory" or, more literally, "who silently remembered them" (*anjiyizhe* 暗記憶者), clearly speaks of a different type of source, indicating that Tan Yu sought out people who had memorized works by Guanxiu and could reproduce them. Whether he would have these people recite the pieces so that he could write them down, or have them write them out from memory themselves, is not clear. In either case, his preface offers strong evidence that at least some collection compilers made use of both written and oral sources when putting together collections. It is also the first mention in the Tang of printing blocks being carved for a literary

---

25. Tan Yu, "Chanyue ji xu" 禪月集序, *QTW*, 922.9604.

26. Such cases are the most common storage place cited in prefaces. See Shen Ziming's 沈子明 account of storing Li He's collection, described by Du Mu in "Li Changji geshi xu" 李長吉歌詩敘, Wang Qi 王琦 et al., eds, *Li Changji geshi*, 1.11. Other examples include Wang Wei's poems, about which Wang Jin writes, "...a few were left in bamboo cases" 或留篋笥之中, and the works of Cen Shen 岑參 (715–70), discussed below, whose heir is said to have "possessed [Cen Shen]'s remaining writings and stored them in a case" 有公遺文貯之筐篋. See Du Que 杜確, "Cen Jiazhou ji xu" 岑嘉州集序, *QTW*, 459.4692.

collection, and thus gives us a glimpse of the diverse literary world of the Late Tang—a world in which oral culture, manuscript culture, and the beginnings of print culture coexisted and overlapped.

Tan Yu's extensive efforts to gather as many of his master's works as possible returns us to the reality of how much he and other compilers must have missed. Monasteries were important sites of textual preservation in the Tang—and yet the works of such a prominent monk as Guanxiu, who was also a well-known writer, artist, and calligrapher, were scattered and difficult to locate. One can only assume that those of ordinary scholar officials or of the more peripatetic poets, such as Meng Haoran, Li Bai, and Du Fu, would have suffered even greater losses. By detailing what has survived, prefaces inevitably remind the reader of what has not. The clearest examples of this are a number of prefaces noting that the compiler was able to find only fragments of certain works, or ephemeral traces that remained to give a hint of what was missing. Thus, Dugu Ji's preface to the works of Li Hua lists a long series of titles of works ranging from stele inscriptions to *shi* poems, and then notes, "All of them were lost because of the [An Lushan] Rebellion. The names survived but the pieces themselves have disappeared" 並因亂失之，名存而篇亡.[27] Li Hua himself expresses a strikingly similar note when, in his preface to the works of Xiao Yingshi 蕭穎士, he says of Xiao's writings that have been lost, "While the titles of the pieces survive, sections and lines are missing. This is what in antiquity was called 'to have the meaning but lack the words'" 其篇目雖存，章句遺落・古所謂有其義無其詞者也.[28] The act of collection itself thus creates, ironically, the figure of loss: only when someone attempted to compile the entirety of an author's works were the gaps discovered and given concrete expression in prefaces. The loss of some or even many of an author's works did not become a fact until an attempt definitively to "set" a collection had been made. Setting the collection also set the lacunae in the collection.

27. Dugu Ji, "Jianjiao shangshu libu yuanwailang Zhaojun Li gong zhongji xu" 檢校尚書吏部員外郎趙郡李公中集序, *QTW*, 388.3947.

28. Li Hua, "Yangzhou gongcao Xiao Yingshi wenji xu" 揚州功曹蕭穎士文集序, *QTW*, 315.3198.

Editing and Copying

The materials gathered or received by compilers[29] were never considered to be finished products; rather, they were the raw materials out of which a collection could be made. Both the compilers and the writers themselves consistently refer to these sources as "uncorrected" (*weixiu* 未修), "neither ordered nor copied" (*wu bianlu* 無編錄), or as "drafts" (*caogao*, *yicao*). The implication of such terms was that the pieces would undergo intentional alteration in the process of being turned into finished collections—they would be fixed and improved. In her study of textual transmission in the Song, Cherniack points out that "the sanction for textual change was from the beginning implicit in the role of the editor as one who transmits."[30] She demonstrates that even with the Confucian classics, "where the desire for textual perfection and the prohibition against change posed by traditional authority are at their strongest,"[31] change and emendation were constant features of transmission and reproduction. If this was so with the classics, one can imagine it would be even truer of works that lacked any sort of canonical authority and tradition. A Qing-dynasty editor might have been disinclined to alter a line in one of Li Bai's by then well-known and oft-anthologized works, but it is doubtful that Li Yangbing or even Fan Zhuanzheng would have felt similar compunction in compiling the earliest collections of his poems.

The first step in the editorial process—choosing which poems to include (and thus which to exclude)—followed the example set by Confucius himself in his legendary editing of the poems of the *Shi*. The "Hereditary House of Confucius" (*Kongzi shijia* 孔子世家) from Sima Qian's *Shiji*, a prominent source for the legend, reads as follows: "In ancient times there were over three thousand of the *Shi*. Then Confucius got rid of redundant ones and chose those that would propagate ritual and right-

29. Compilers, who played an active role in ordering and editing the contents of a collection, often in addition to composing a preface, must be distinguished from simple preface writers who were only responsible for a preface to head the collection. Although the two roles frequently overlapped, this was not always the case.

30. Cherniack, "Book Culture," 18–19.

31. Ibid., 19.

eousness" 古者詩三千餘篇，及至孔子去其重，取可施於禮義.[32] Sima Qian's account makes it clear that one element of Confucius's motive in "culling the poems" (*shanshi* 刪詩) was to give a moral import to the work by cutting out the licentious pieces and keeping only those that could be interpreted as setting appropriate ethical examples.

Tang preface writers are not often explicit about the need to cut out certain poems (and certainly never imply that their subjects wrote licentious poems). However, the following passage suggests that such selectivity was considered a normal part of the compilation process and did not bear mentioning unless unusual circumstances applied. Sun Guangxian's preface to the Buddhist monk Qiji's poetry collection, the *Bailian ji* 白蓮集 ("White Lotus Collection"), states:

> As for all the draft copies of poems from the master's life, he never had the spare time to cull them. All of a sudden he unexpectedly died and his disciple Xi Wenbing was given [the writings] that had been collected. He was then able to edit them into 810 pieces that he bound as ten *juan* and entitled *The White Lotus Collection*.
>
> 師平生詩稿，未遑刪汰，俄驚遷化．門人西文併以所集見授，因得編就八百一十篇，勒成一十卷，題曰白蓮集．[33]

Here we see "culling" (*shantai* 刪汰) noted because Qiji died before he could perform this essential task himself. The responsibility then fell upon his disciple Xi Wenbing.

Let us return for comparison to Guanxiu's *Chanyue ji*, which must have been compiled by Tan Yu under similar circumstances. Guanxiu's works at the time of his death can be put into three general groups. The first consisted of the works included in his self-compiled collection of 896, the *Xiyue ji* 西岳集 ("Western Peak Collection"), which would have already gone through the culling process. The second group comprised the works that he had written in the sixteen years since then and that were in his possession. There is no indication as to whether or not he had begun preparing these to be put into collection form. The third group contained those works that Tan Yu describes hunting down from both written and

---

32. *Shiji*, 47.1936–37. Note that this legend, though it had already come under attack by the Tang, was still an important cultural template. For a more detailed treatment of Confucius's purported editorial roles, see Cherniack, "Book Culture," 15–17.

33. Sun Guangxian, "Bailian ji xu" 白蓮集序, *QTW*, 900.9390–91.

oral sources after Guanxiu's death. Given Sun Guangxian's description of how Qiji's collection—also the work of a prominent poet-monk edited by one of his disciples—was put together, it is very likely that Tan Yu culled poems from at least the second group of Guanxiu's works, and definitely from the third. In other words, works originally gathered for a collection would not necessarily be included in that collection. They were merely raw source material that still needed to be picked through and culled.

According to Sima Qian, Confucius's criteria for exclusion were both practical and moral: he eliminated poems that either were redundant or did not propagate "ritual and righteousness" (*liyi* 禮義). The standards underlying Tang editorial practices were more varied. In the self-preface to his own collection, Sun Qiao 孫樵 (fl. 860–88) implies an aesthetic basis, stating that, of the two hundred pieces he looked over, "I gathered those worth looking at—thirty-five sections—and compiled them into ten *juan*. I stored them in a bamboo chest in order to pass them down to my sons and grandsons" 叢其可觀者，三十五篇，編成十卷，藏諸篋笥，以貽子孫.[34] For his part, Bai Juyi excludes some works from his collection of matching poems composed with Liu Yuxi because of their lack of formality: "As for the other [poems], which followed a momentary whim or were the product of drink, and were generally produced orally, they are not counted here."[35] In other contexts, however, Bai Juyi cannot bear to exclude certain pieces despite the informal circumstances of their composition and the knowledge that a later editor will likely remove them. His "Letter to Yuan the Ninth" of 815, which also served as the *de facto* preface for an early version of his primary collection, states:

> As for these remaining miscellaneous poems, some were coaxed out by a certain time or thing; they came forth as a laugh or a chant and were put together hastily and are not what I would typically esteem. They were only taken up on occasions when relatives and friends were gathered or parting, to release sorrow or add to joy. In my arranging and ordering today, I haven't been able to cut them out. At

---

34. Sun Qiao, "Zixu" 自序, *QTW*, 794.8326. It should be noted that no poetic genres are included in Sun's list of his own writings. There is also a problem with the use of the term *pian* 篇 here: it is typically a measure word for a piece of writing, yet thirty-five pieces seems a small number to fill ten *juan*. At the same time, as the pieces in this case were probably prose rather than poetry, some may have been quite long.

35. Zhu, 69.3711. I noted this passage in Chapter 3 as well.

another time when someone collects and disseminates my writings for my sake, it will be fine to omit them.

其餘雜律詩，或誘於一時一物，發於一笑一吟，率然成章，非平生所尚者，但以親朋合散之際，取其釋恨佐懽．今銓次之間，未能删去，他時有爲我編集散文者，略之可也．[36]

Bai Juyi here may be the exception that proves the rule. He feels that his reluctance to cut out certain poems goes against the norm and thus begs explanation. Moreover, he states that he would not object to someone else omitting the poems in a later version of the collection—of which there were many, though most were also compiled and edited by Bai himself.

Other editorial standards employed in the Tang are more troubling from the standpoint of our construction of literary history, in that compilers intentionally shaped the image of the writer to conform to their own views. The above-mentioned collection of Wang Ji's poems in five *juan*, compiled and prefaced by Lü Cai prior to the poet's death, was not the only collection of Wang's poems put together in the Tang. In fact, as Ding Xiang Warner has pointed out in her recent study of Wang Ji, "[u]ntil the 1980's, no reader since the end of the Song dynasty had recorded seeing the original five-*juan* collection of Wang Ji's works."[37] By the end of the Song, Lü Cai's collection had been eclipsed by another collection, compiled by one Lu Chun. Lu Chun's collection was actually a redaction of Lü Cai's original compilation, and its postface is appropriately titled "Postface to the *Culled* Collection of Master Donggao" (*Shan Donggaozi ji houxu* 删東皐集後序). Lu removed from Lü's original collection any works that did not conform to his ideal of Wang Ji as a free spirit in the mold of Tao Qian or Ruan Ji.[38] As I note in the Introduction, he "expunged those words of purposive intent and [so] made complete [Wang's] ambition to be unbound."[39] In doing so he reduced the contents of the collection by more than half and provided readers with a far less

36. Bai Juyi, "Yu Yuanjiu shu," Zhu, 45.2795.

37. Warner, *A Wild Deer*, 4. See also Tian, "Misplaced."

38. Lu Chun, "Shan Donggaozi ji houxu," in *Wang Ji shiwenji jiaozhu*, 388. See also Warner, *A Wild Deer*, 4–5.

39. Jin Ronghua, ed., *Wang Ji shiwenji jiaozhu*, 388. Note that "purposive intent," translated *youwei* 有爲, is the antithesis of the Daoistic ideal of "non-action" (*wuwei* 無爲) and corresponds with Lu Chun's association of Wang Ji with Zhuangzi earlier in the postface.

nuanced portrayal of Wang Ji's works than they would have received from Lü Cai's original collection.

Most Tang editors appear to have been less extreme than Lu Chun in their standards (or at least less forthright in explaining them), but it may well be that a similar process took place in innumerable other instances. It is doubtful that Wang Shiyuan accepted and paid for every poem presented to him as a work of Meng Haoran—and what better measure upon which to base his acceptance or rejection than whether or not a work "sounded like" Meng Haoran to him? The result would be a more uniform style that would build on itself and attract the attribution of more poems in that style to Meng Haoran. For other poets, political consideration surely came into play. When Li Bai and Wang Wei died, it had not been long since they had been charged with treason; Li Yangbing and Wang Jin would have been wise to consider any potentially controversial works to be among those mourned as "scattered and lost."[40]

Selectivity in the compilation process could also involve selecting only a certain type of poems from those available to balance a pre-existing image of a given poet. The first mention of Du Fu's poems in collection form is found in an example of a compiler who gathered a selection of poems together specifically because the more commonly circulated works in a certain area did not give what he saw as the correct portrait of the poet. In his "Du gongbu xiaoji xu" 杜工部小集序 ("Preface to a Small Collection of Du of the Ministry of Works"), Fan Huang 樊晃 notes that there is a sixty-*juan* collection of Du Fu's works that circulates in the south, though he has not seen it personally.[41] His concern is that "those [poems] that poets in the eastern areas circulate orally are all just his works with playful topics and amusing discussions. They have never known that he has lofty and upright compositions" 江左詞人所傳誦者，皆公之戲題劇論耳，曾不知君有大雅之作.[42] To remedy this Fan puts together a

40. Recall as well that Wei Zhuang made sure his brother omitted from his poetry collection what was surely his best-known work, "Qinfu yin."

41. This preface is a standard starting point for any discussion of the early circulation of Du Fu's works. See, for example, Chen Shangjun's "Dushi zaoqi liuchuan kao," 308. Owen ("A Tang Version of Du Fu," 58) however, notes that the provenance of this preface is questionable and it thus must be used with caution.

42. Qiu, "fubian," 2237. See Owen, "A Tang Version of Du Fu," 59 for a discussion of this translation of 劇論.

small collection of 290 works divided into six *juan* to be circulated in the east. He still, however, holds out hopes of finding the "formal collection" 正集 as well.[43] It is not that Fan feels Du Fu's full collection is somehow misleading, but rather that he (and others in his area) do not have access to it. It is also important to be clear that Fan does not believe that the poems well-known through oral transmission are spurious, just that they are only a part of a more complex whole. The smaller set of works he puts together, with the specific intent to circulate them, is meant to provide a counterbalance to the image of Du Fu one would get from the works he heard circulating in his locale. Of course readers who only encountered Fan Huang's small collection (possibly including Yuan Zhen in the last decade of the eighth century),[44] would have also had an erroneous view of the nature of Du Fu's full poetic personality, albeit one that Fan probably preferred. Whether for reasons of aesthetics, image, or politics, it is clear that many individual literary collections in the Tang represented not the totality of an author's available works, but a selection from among them.

The process of reshaping a writer's oeuvre did not come to an end once the culling of unwanted works was complete. A formal collection was finished only when a final fair copy had been made of the selected works, and

---

43. Qiu, "fubian," 2237. The distinction Fan Huang is making between types of poems here is an interesting one. This study has largely avoided connecting different types of circulation with the specific contents of various poems. We simply do not know enough about how specific poems circulated to say that, for example, parting poems that mention singing girls circulated orally while poems about the fall of the Han were transmitted in written form. Moreover, some poems with quite somber topics could circulate, albeit in truncated form, in more jovial contexts, as we saw in the case of Gao Shi's winning quatrain in the "bet on singing in the tavern" in Chapter 3. However, Fan Huang here does tie certain types of poems with certain types of circulation. He explicitly claims that the playful and amusing poems are ones that are circulated orally 傳誦. We do not know if he intended his new collection to circulate primarily in writing, but as noted below, it may well be connected with the collection that Yuan Zhen was reading years later. When Yuan Zhen writes about the Du Fu poems he admires, they are ones dealing with such topics as the An Lushan Rebellion and are anything but playful (see Owen, "A Tang Version of Du Fu," 59 and Yuan Zhen, "Yuefu guti xu" 樂府古體序, *YZJ*, 23.255). Unfortunately, as we know neither the actual poems that Fan Huang heard nor those he included in his new collection, we can do no more than speculate.

44. In his "Xushi ji Letian shu," (*YZJ*, 30.352), Yuan Zhen mentions reading a collection of Du Fu poems with "several hundred pieces" 杜甫詩數百首.

this stage offered a last important opportunity for editorial changes.[45] Du Que's preface to Cen Shen's collection is one of the earliest accounts we have of the process, and it is typical in its lack of detail. Du writes, "I accepted the command to edit and arrange [the works] and thereupon ordered that a fair copy be made. I divided them into different categories and bound them into eight *juan*" 受命編次，因令繕錄，區分類聚，勒成八卷.[46] Elsewhere in the preface he notes that he received the works from Cen Shen's heir, who had been storing them in trunks. In other words, we see here a very brief summary of the entire editorial process, from obtaining the pieces to editing them and having a copy made. We know that Du Que did not make a final fair copy himself, and he leaves unanswered the important question of whom he ordered to do so.

This information is, however, provided in many other prefaces, and it is clear that such copying was not done by professional scribes under anything resembling the strict conditions one might find in such official contexts as the Directorate of Education.[47] We saw earlier that when a reader wanted a copy of a poem, most often he copied it by hand himself; the same level of informality is found in preparing final copies of collections. In his "Wusilan shi zixu" 烏絲闌詩自序 ("Self-Preface to the Black Silk Door Poems"), Xu Hun 許渾 (ca. 787–854) describes finding himself with a surfeit of free time of which he took advantage to put together his own collection. He writes:

> I edited and compiled my new and old [works] into five hundred pieces and set them on my table. I worked at leisure and took my time, as the aim was not fame... I wrote out this copy in my own hand.
> 編集新舊五百篇，置於几案間．聊用自適，非知之志也．．．手寫此本.[48]

The impression here is one of informality. Putting together a finished copy of one's literary collection was an activity of leisure, done late in

45. Editorial change here being considered distinct from other changes, whether intentional or otherwise, that would occur in the process of transmission after the collection was compiled.

46. Du Que, "Cen Jiazhou ji xu," *QTW*, 459.4692.

47. The exacting standards of which are described in Cherniack, "Book Culture," 58–61. Note that these standards still resulted in innumerable textual emendations.

48. Xu Hun, "Wusilanshi zixu," *QTW*, 760.7903.

life.[49] Even Bai Juyi, known for his scrupulous attention to his various collections, left the job of copying at least sections of them to his young nephew. In the 829 preface to the collection of his matching poems with Liu Yuxi, he writes:

I thereupon ordered my young nephew Gui to edit, copy, and bind them into two *juan*. He then wrote out two copies. One I gave to Gui and one I presented to Mengde's (i.e., Liu Yuxi) young son Lun. Each was ordered to store them away, and attach them to the collections in each household.
因命小姪龜兒編錄，勒成兩卷・仍寫二本，一付龜兒，一授夢得小兒崙朗，各令收藏，附兩家集.[50]

The significance of the editing and copying practice employed by Bai Juyi becomes clear when the full extent of his collection project is set forth. So far as we know, Xu Hun wrote out a single copy of what was a relatively short collection. Bai Juyi's collection, on the other hand, was a conglomeration of numerous sub-collections. Multiple copies of the full collection were all carefully accounted for and distributed. In an 845 postface written about a year before his death, Bai Juyi gives a useful summary of the various copies of his collection and a sense of the meticulousness with which he managed them:

I, Mr. Bai, previously composed the *Changqing Collection* in fifty *juan*. Yuan Weizhi [Zhen] wrote the preface. The *Later Collection*, in twenty *juan*, I prefaced myself. Today I again continue the *Later Collection* with five *juan* and write an account of it myself. Altogether they come to seventy-five *juan*, with poems and writings great and small, in all three thousand eight hundred and forty pieces. There are five copies of the collection: one is in the Sutra Cache Hall of the Donglin Temple on Mt. Lu; one is in the sutra cache at the Nanchan Temple in Suzhou; one is in the *Vinaya* Storehouse Building in the Pota Hall at the Shengshan Temple in the Eastern Capital; one I've given to my nephew Gui; and one I have given to my grandson Tan Getong. Each of the [latter two] is stored in their homes to be passed down to posterity. As for the ones copied out by people from Japan, Silla, various other countries, and the two capitals, they are not accounted for here. There is also the *Collection of Continued Matching Poems of Yuan and Bai*, seventeen *juan* in all; the *Matching Poems of Liu and Bai* in five *juan*; and the *Sightseeing and Banqueting Downstream from Luoyang Collection* in ten *juan*.

49. Xu Hun's preface was written in 850 when he was about sixty-three.
50. "Liu Bai changheji jie" 劉白唱和集解, Zhu, 69.3711.

These writings are all copied out from the larger collection and circulate separately today. Those not in the primary collection and circulating falsely under my name are all spurious.

白氏前著長慶集五十卷，元微之爲序．後集二十卷，自爲序．今又續後集五卷，自爲記．前後七十五卷，詩筆大小凡三千八百四十首．集有五本：一本在廬山東林寺經藏院，一本在蘇州南禪寺經藏内，一本在東都聖善寺鉢塔院律庫樓，一本付姪龜郎，一本付外孫談閣童，各藏於家，傳於後．其日本、新羅諸國及兩京人家傳寫者，不在此記．又有元白唱和因繼集共十七卷，劉白唱和集五卷，洛下遊賞宴集十卷，其文盡在大集内錄出，別行於時．若集内無而假名流傳者，皆謬爲耳．[51]

The comments on the various sub-collections are of particular interest, with Bai Juyi's statement that they were "copied out" from the larger collection standing as a unique piece of information about Tang copying practices. First, smaller occasional collections must have been put together and re-copied to form one larger collection. But subsequent circulating versions of those occasional collections would be copied out of the larger and more general grouping. This indicates that Bai Juyi saw his primary literary collection as functioning as a sort of standard, a formal version of the various writings from his life. Moreover, as we know that his nephew had only made two copies of at least one of the constituent parts of this collection, the three or more copies of the complete collection each represented new productions. Not even taking into account the different versions copied and circulating in Japan and Korea or considered spurious, it is clear that a great number of texts were copied and recopied many times. And if Bai Juyi's nephew continued to serve as the primary copyist, he was a busy man. According to the very rough estimate proposed by Stephen Owen, producing a single copy of Bai's collection in its later stages would have required over thirty-two days of steady labor based on the relatively fast rate of twelve characters per minute, eight hours a day.[52] The picture that emerges from Bai Juyi's account is one of multiple reproductions, and thus opportunities for emendations and errors, before the completed collection was made available to the public.

---

51. "Baishi Changqing ji houxu," Zhu, "waiji," 3.3916–17.

52. Owen, "Butterflies Dangling in a Spider's Web: The Literary World of the 830s," unpublished paper delivered at Princeton University, April 20, 2002, 6–7.

Bai Juyi's writings suggest the maximum possible size of a collection and the extent of the editing and copying process. They do not, however, provide much detail on how copying might take place, especially if more than one person was involved. Wei Ai's 903 preface to the collection of his brother Wei Zhuang fills in some of these gaps. After noting that written versions of many of Wei Zhuang's earlier poems had been destroyed and that the poems were preserved only in oral form—the *kousongzhe* (口誦者) that had been set to memory and could be recited—Wei Ai goes on to describe the creation of his brother's *Washing Flowers Collection*: "Taking advantage of free days, I would record things from among my brother's drafts. From time to time I would also silently record from his chantings. I arranged [everything] into [three characters missing] and titled it the 'Washing Flowers Collection,' sharing the intent of the one who lived in Duling (i.e., Du Fu)" 藹便因閒日，錄兄之稿草中，或默記於吟詠者，次爲□□□，目之曰浣花集，亦杜陵所居之義也.[53] Wei Ai was thus working with both written and oral sources. As it was assumedly Wei Zhuang himself who remembered his own poems, and not other people (as had been the case in the compilation of Guanxiu's collection), Wei Ai could at least show his transcriptions to his brother and check whether corrections were needed. Still, the editing and copying process is again shown to be an informal one performed not by a professional scribe but by a family member.

The picture that ultimately emerges from these accounts of the editing and copying process is one of substantial flexibility. Tang individual literary collections typically represented not all of an author's works but a selection based on any number of criteria. Moreover, rather than being a record of a writer's works as they were originally composed and even circulated, collections consisted of edited and corrected versions of those works. Earlier I noted the distance between modern readers and Tang poetry as Tang poets produced it; an important stage in the development of this distance was the significant changes that poems often underwent between their original composition and their enshrinement in collections, sometimes even while the author was still alive. As presentations of a literary history, Tang literary collections were both selective and mediated

53. Wei Ai 韋藹, "Wanhua ji xu" 浣花集序, in *Wei Zhuang ji jianzhu*, "fulu" 4.483–84.

by the changing tastes of authors and the judgments of their compilers, editors, and copyists.

Returning to the larger question of the connection between and author and his works, we find that collections play an ambiguous role. They do indeed strengthen the connection by declaring that a given poem is by a given author and putting it in the context of his other works. At the same time, because poems were altered, omitted, and added based on standards that we would not recognize as preserving the authenticity of literary products from a modern critical perspective, the connection between an author and the works *attributed* to him continued to be undermined. As we shall see below, this was not at all troubling to a Tang audience, but it does call into question the way critics typically approach these works.

Roles of Collections in Tang Literary Culture

Whether compiled in response to imperial command or simply as an attempt to gather together the works of an author one admired, literary collections played two essential and interrelated roles in the literary culture of the Tang: preservation and circulation. Poems led precarious lives in this period; they existed not in multiple copies of printed books but rather as individually hand-copied scrolls and sheets of paper. They might be written on walls at temples and post stations or passed from mouth to mouth by singing girls in the entertainment quarters. All of these media were susceptible to the unruly forces of entropy. The promise of the *Book of Documents* that song would make language last offered little solace in the face of the reality of constant loss so often lamented by compilers. The effort required for textual reproduction further made the circulation and dissemination of literary texts a slower and more laborious process than it would be in later periods. Prefaces to literary collections accordingly show an acute concern with preservation and circulation and a conviction that literary collections themselves are crucial to ensuring that both occur.

Central to the issue of loss is the physicality of poems in the Tang. When authors and compilers discuss literary works they often speak of them in a very material sense, not as disembodied works that would always exist somewhere (as we might think of much literature today),[54] but as actual documents that could be permanently lost or destroyed. This notion of literary works as vulnerable physical objects is clear in Bai Juyi's poem of 835, "Written on My Collection Cabinet" 題文集櫃:

I cut cypress to make a cabinet for writings,	破柏作書櫃，
The cabinet was sturdy and the cypress was strong.	櫃牢柏復堅．
And whose collection is stored there?	收貯誰家集，
The inscription says "Bai Letian."	題云白樂天．
My life's endeavor has been writing,	我生業文字，
Since I was young until my elder years.	自幼及老年．
Altogether there are seventy juan,	前後七十卷，
More or less three thousand pieces.	小大三千篇．
I truly understand that in the end they'll be scattered and lost,	誠知終散失，
But cannot bear for them to be hastily tossed aside.	未忍遽棄捐．
I open [the cabinet] and lock it shut myself,	自開自鎖閉，
Placing it in front of my study curtain.	置在書帷前．[55]

Following the convention of prefaces, Bai Juyi quantifies his life's literary output in terms of pieces and scrolls. He focuses not on worries that his works will be forgotten, but that they will be scattered and lost. His concern is very much with their physical existence as written documents. While conceding that the process of entropy cannot be forestalled forever, Bai is yet determined to resist it by keeping this copy of his works close by under lock and key. His aim is preservation.

The poet here shows little concern with other people actually reading his poems. Bai Juyi knew that his works circulated widely in the world; we have seen Yuan Zhen's claim that, "ever since there has been poetry, there has never been such wide dissemination." Contemporaneous writings, such as Du Mu's comments bemoaning the spread of Bai and Yuan's poems seen in Chapter 2, suggest that this may indeed not have been an

54. For example, while I might worry about my copy of *Hamlet* being lost or destroyed for financial or sentimental reasons, I can be confident that there is little risk of *all* copies of *Hamlet* being destroyed. *Hamlet* exists in my consciousness as a work independent of its individual physical incarnations.

55. Bai Juyi, "Ti wenji gui" 題文集櫃, Zhu, 30.2072.

empty boast. It is perhaps because of this that Bai's concern with his collection throws into such sharp relief the contrast between a writer's works as an abstract oeuvre and his collection as a material manifestation of that abstraction. Confident that he was being read, Bai Juyi's energies centered on keeping specific copies of his works physically secure. Nowhere is this concern more obvious than in the descriptions he wrote of copies of his collection deposited at various monasteries. His "Account of the Donglin Temple Literary Collection of Mr. Bai" 東林寺白氏文集記, written in the same year as the poem on his collection cabinet, ends with this unusual request:

From time to time the elders would ask for my literary collection so that it could also be placed in the sutra cache. But I would merely agree tacitly that I would do this some other day. Up to now, it has been over twenty years [since then]. Today, altogether my writings come, great and small, to 2,964 pieces, arranged into sixty *juan*. With the ordering complete, I am depositing it in the cache....I further request that the elders of this temple and the monk in charge of the cache follow the example of the literary collection of Master Yuan[56] and not lend it out to outsiders or let it pass the temple gates. That would be fortunate indeed!
時諸長老請余文集，亦置經藏·唯然心許他日置之，迨茲餘二十年矣·今余前後所著文大小合二千九百六十四首，勒成六十卷·編次既畢，納于藏中···仍請本寺長老及主藏僧依遠公文集例，不借外客，不出寺門，幸甚·[57]

Bai Juyi wanted his collection protected, not passed around. He expected that interested parties would themselves take the initiative to come and see the collection if they wished to read or copy it. This same request was made the following year when he deposited an additional copy of the manuscript at the Shengshan Temple. In his "Account of the Shengshan Temple Literary Collection of Mr. Bai" 聖善寺白氏文集記, he requests that his collection "... not leave the hall and not be lent out to official guests. If there is someone who is interested they can just go look at it [there]" 仍請不出院門，不借官客，有好事者，任就觀之.[58] We may take Bai Juyi at his word that he was, to some extent, simply responding to repeated requests from the temple elders to donate a copy of his

56. The monastery's founder, Huiyuan 慧遠.
57. Bai Juyi, "Donglinsi Baishi wenji ji," Zhu, 70.3768–69.
58. Bai Juyi, "Shengshansi Baishi wenji ji," Zhu, 70.3770.

collection to them. He was the most famous poet of the day, and such a gift would surely have been much prized. Moreover, Bai Juyi associated depositing copies of his collection at temples with the accumulation of Buddhist merit.[59] At the same time, there is no doubt that he was well aware of the potential benefits, in terms of preservation of the collection, of keeping it stored in the sutra cache of a prominent temple. Such a method of storage certainly did not preclude circulation, since temples were popular destinations in the Tang and people were apparently welcome to read and copy as much of Bai's collection as they saw fit when visiting temples that held copies. Yet Bai Juyi's primary concern remained with keeping the deposited copies safe.

If Bai Juyi's obsessive focus on preserving his collection as the ultimate representation of his life's work was unusual, for the Mid- and Late Tang periods this was often as a matter of degree, not of kind. Numerous other writers express a hope that compiling works into a formal collection with a preface will by itself serve to preserve them. In his preface to the works of Li Guan 李觀 (766–94), Lu Xisheng 陸希聲 writes:

> Ever since the devastation of the Guangming rebellion,[60] the world's literary collections have mostly disappeared. I obtained Yuanbin's[61] writings by the River Han. Fearing that they would still be wiped out, I arranged them into three sections and discussed their meaning at the beginning.
> 自廣明喪亂，天下文集略盡．予得元賓文於漢上，惜其恐復磨滅，因條次爲三編，論其意以冠於首.[62]

Lu Xisheng explicitly claims a connection between arranging and prefacing this set of Li Guan's works and keeping them from harm: the act of collecting was by itself an act of preservation. Scattered poems were gath-

---

59. In two prefaces to copies of his collection that he deposited in temples, Bai Juyi explicitly claims that he is doing so to make up for his past misdeeds and establish the basis for his future salvation. This motivation, however, appears to apply only to depositing the copies at the respective temples, not to the actual compilation of the collection. See "Shengshansi Baishi wenji ji," discussed immediately above, and "Suzhou Nanchanyuan Baishi wenji ji" 蘇州南禪院白氏文集記, Zhu, 71.3788.

60. In other words, the Huang Chao rebellion.

61. Li Guan's style name (*zi* 字).

62. Lu Xisheng, "Tang taizi jiaoshu Li Guan wenji xu" 唐太子校書李觀文集序, *QTW*, 813.8550.

ered together and recopied; and if some were eliminated in the process, those that remained were given a new life.

Collections also preserved works by contextualizing them. As part of a collection they gained the company of other works that might implicitly help to situate them both as points in the biography of the author and as examples of his literary style. An isolated poem tells the reader only about itself; as part of a collection it is a piece in a larger construction. Prefaces contribute to this contextualization by giving biographical information about the writer; putting his literary output in historical, contemporary, and aesthetic contexts; and making arguments about what is valuable and interesting about the author's works. Pauline Yu has written that prefaces trace "forms to their sources, works to their prototypes, and authors to their predecessors" and that they "verify the venerable genealogy of the genres included as well as the concrete historicity of the works themselves."[63] These two types of context, in turn, would preserve the poems when the dissemination process began anew. In essence, a collection tells the reader that these are no longer isolated poems discovered at random or uttered in a transitory moment, but that they are rather part of a body of work with specific and knowable historical and social connections. We see this context at work when Lu Xisheng makes a connection between "discussing their meaning" and keeping the poems from perishing. His preface gives the works additional weight. It implies that they were worthy of collection and critical attention. In a second preface to the collection of Meng Haoran's poems compiled by Wang Shiyuan that I will discuss in more detail below, a certain Wei Tao 韋縚 writes, "If these poems had not met Master Wang, then they would have been nothing but a few dozen sheets of old paper" 此詩若不遇王君，乃十數張故紙耳.[64] Here and in many other cases we have seen, the preface is also a record of the tenuous past of the works that went into the collection. As an account intended thereafter to accompany the collection, it serves as a warning to future readers, informing them that what they are reading came perilously close to disappearing and that they should thus treat it with care. This

63. Yu, "Poems in Their Place," 170. While Yu is speaking primarily about anthologies, her point is valid here as well.

64. Wei Tao, "Meng Haoran ji xu" 孟浩然集序, *QTW*, 307.3124.

context both explains the survival of the collection and implicitly entreats the reader to continue the ongoing process of preservation.

Lu Xisheng's portrayal of himself as saving Li Guan's works from the brink of the oblivion into which many other works had fallen implies that Li Guan's writings were not in wide circulation. Yet even works that had enjoyed substantial dissemination were seen as needing to be compiled into a collection and prefaced to preserve them. In his preface to the collected poems of the monk Fanggan 方干, written near the end of the dynasty, Wang Zan 王贊 writes:

When I was young I obtained many dozen pieces of the master's poems and was especially fond of them. At that time the master was still alive, but he lived far away and we were never able to meet. Later his reputation was increasingly given tribute and among those who composed poems there were many able to chant [his works]. But then the master died. This year I ran into Sun Yan of Yue'an in Jing. He had been close to the master from early on. He took out and showed me the "Biography of Master Xuanying [i.e., Fanggan]" that he had composed. He then said, "I went with [Fanggan's] nephew, Yang He, to see the [master's] disciple, the monk Juyuan, and gathered up his remaining poems. We obtained over 370 pieces and separated them into ten *juan*." He wanted me to write a preface for [the collection], hoping that together they would not perish.
予爲兒時，得生詩數十篇．心獨好之，生時尚存，地遠莫可相見，其後生名愈藉，爲詩者多能諷之，而生歿矣．今年遇樂安孫郃於荆，早與生善，出示所作玄英先生傳，且曰：「與其甥楊弇洎門僧居遠收掇其遺詩，得三百七十餘篇，析爲十卷．」欲予爲之序，冀偕之不朽．[65]

Unlike Lu Xisheng or Xi Yunqing, Wang Zan does not claim that the works in question were in any proximate danger and does not imply that it was he alone who saved them. At the same time, he directly ties his preface to the continued survival of the works in Fanggan's collection, relating Sun Yan's hope that by being together the collection and the preface would both "not perish" (*buxiu* 不朽). The collection might not have come into being were it not for the compilation efforts of Sun Yan and Yang He, but it would not live on and serve its intended purpose without the addition of his preface. Again we see a distinction between Fanggan's literary legacy as an abstraction and as a concrete set of texts. The former

65. Wang Zan, "Xuanying xiansheng shiji xu" 玄英先生詩集序, *QTW*, 865.9069–70.

appeared to be safe, as both his fame and his poems had spread widely, to the extent that Wang Zan claims that many people could recite his works from memory. Yet Sun Yan, Yang He, Juyuan, and Wang Zan all understood that with the poet's death, fame could quickly fade and poems remembered could be forgotten. By collecting the poems together and giving them a literary, biographical, and historical context, they could both preserve a physical set of texts and the larger literary oeuvre that it represented.

Important as preservation was, it was typically not an end in and of itself. Works were preserved so that they could ultimately be disseminated both in the present (often described in prefaces as to "circulate in this time" 行於代) and into the future. In some contexts these two goals could come into conflict. As we have seen, many of the precarious conditions in which poems could be found in the Tang were actually conducive to circulation. Poems written on post-station walls might not survive long in such a state, but they had a far greater chance of catching the attention of travelers who might remember or copy them than did poems stored away securely in a cabinet of strong cedar. Likewise, singing girls would surely move on to new songs as old ones went out of style, yet they also served as an important means of spreading those works that were in fashion for a time, no matter how briefly. In contrast, though the copy of Wang Wei's collection locked up in the Imperial Library may have been physically secure, it was unlikely to gain a broad audience in such conditions.[66]

Most collections in the Tang were not, of course, compiled for storage in the Imperial Library, and prefaces clearly state that one of the primary goals of compilation was to provide a broad audience with access to the works. Xi Yanqing notes that the works of Luo Binwang that he found stored in private homes were "worth circulating among those who enjoy [such things]." That is, they were worth bringing back into the public realm. Fan Huang compiled a new set of Du Fu's poetry with the specific

66. As Fan Zhilin ("Tangdai shige de liuchuan (shang)," 283) points out, "The primary responsibility of the Imperial Library was storing books; it was certainly not open to the outside. Only the emperor, high court officials, and related functionaries would have opportunities to read there." It is unclear whether these people would be allowed to make copies for personal use or for dissemination.

intent of "circulating it in the east" 行於江左 in order to counteract the oral circulation of Du Fu's less morally serious verse.[67] Tan Yu states that he put together a new collection of Guanxiu's works specifically in response to popular demand. People wanted access to his master's poetry, and a collection would bring a large number of such works together for people to enjoy and copy. The fact that Tan Yu then had printing blocks of the collection carved further supports the idea that the ultimate purpose of his labors was to circulate the works more widely. In a similar vein, Yan Zhenqing makes the connection between compiling a collection and circulating works explicit in his preface to the collected works of the High Tang writer and official Sun Ti, writing, "I thereupon compiled and edited his literary collection into twenty *juan*, setting it out below. I hope that people who enjoy [his works] will copy them out and chant them in order to pass them down to eternity. Indeed, what need is there for storing them on famous mountains and placing them in chambers of stone?" 乃編次公文集爲二十卷，列之於左・庶乎好事者傳寫諷誦，以垂乎無窮，亦何必藏名山而納石室.[68] Dissemination, in this case, *is* preservation. Protective storage is deemed unnecessary when one's works reach the level of popularity Yan Zhenqing foresees for those of Sun Ti.[69] The compilation of collections remains a key part of the overall circulation process, as it gives people access to a substantial number of works at one time and location.

Circulation in the contemporary era seems to be the prime concern for Xi Yunqing, Fan Huang and Tan Yu. Like Yan Zhenqing, many other compilers are more interested in passing works on to later generations and audiences. Wang Shiyuan laments that Meng Haoran's deeds will go unrecorded by official historians as Meng never held a position in the bureaucracy, and cannot bear the thought that his "excellent rhymes will be severed from this point on" 妙韻從此而絶. He writes:

> Having no other important affairs, I am passing [Meng Haoran's works] down for posterity so that hereafter all those within the seas wearing the robe and cap

67. Qiu, "fubian," 2236.

68. Yan Zhenqing, "Shangshu xingbu shilang zengshangshu youpushe Sun Ti wengong ji xu," 尚書刑部侍郎贈尚書右僕射孫逖文公集序, *QTW* 337.3416.

69. Yan Zhenqing was proved correct to some degree. Sun Ti's collection does not survive though many of his individual works do.

of officialdom and with the official's tablet stuck in their belts will remember him when passing through Xiangyang, and look over his writings.
既無他事，爲之傳次，遂使海內衣冠縉紳，經襄陽思睹其文.[70]

His earlier description of Meng Haoran's carelessness towards his own literary legacy, and the lengths to which he had to go to save what was left of the poet's output, give the reader a distinct sense of the tenuousness of poems left on their own. Yet clearly these poems rescued from falling into, at best, obscurity, and at worst, oblivion, were not meant to be hidden away for safe keeping. The larger intent of dissemination and circulation into the future underlies the act of preservation. It was not enough to know that the poems continued to exist. To remember Meng Haoran and read his poems, later generations had actually to have access to them as well. Dissemination of the poems in the form of a collection increased the chances that this would happen.

Writers compiling their own works were also cognizant of the important role collections would play in securing them an audience beyond their own lifetimes. Thanks to his poetry's widely attested contemporary popularity, Bai Juyi may have been unconcerned about increasing the circulation of his poems in his day. He was, however, well aware of the importance of future readers for his works, especially those pieces that did not enjoy much acclaim at present. In his letter to Yuan Zhen accompanying his very first collection, he writes:

Coming to [my poems] of allegorical remonstrance, their ideas are stimulating and their speech unadorned. As for the [poems of] leisure and pleasure, their thoughts are calm and their words meandering. Because they are unadorned and meandering, it is only fitting that people do not cherish them. The only one living in the world with me today who cherishes them is you. However, a hundred thousand years hence, how could we know that there won't appear someone like you who will cherish my poems?
至於諷諭者，意激而言質，閑適者，思澹而詞迂．以質合迂，宜人之不愛也．今所愛者，並世而生，獨足下耳．然千百年後，安知復無如足下者出而愛我詩哉．[71]

---

70. Wang Shiyuan, "Meng Haoran ji xu," *Meng Haoran shiji zhu*, "fulu," 433; cf. Kroll, "Wang Shih-yuan's Preface," 356.

71. "Yu Yuanjiu shu," Zhu, 45.2795. Amusingly, Bai Juyi includes himself as a possible future audience for his own writings. In his "Account of Mr. Bai's Fragrant Mountain

Note that preservation remains an important aspect of Bai Juyi's goal. He was including these poems in the first phase of the collection on which he would continue to lavish great care. Yet access to the works is his main concern, rather than an afterthought. He wants his poems to get to others: it is for that reason that they must be preserved. Bai Juyi is also not explicitly focused on the material nature of his literary products in this passage. These poems are characterized by their content, not by where they are to be kept or the rules governing access to them.

The notion of works of literature as material objects did, however, play a part in issues of circulation to a more specific future audience, namely one's descendants. In some cases writers thought of the works they would be passing down in an abstract sense. Sikong Tu 司空圖 (837–908), for example, states that an important purpose of his collection is "no more than perhaps to startle awake my sons and grandsons" 庶警子孫耳.[72] However, there are many cases in which the works to be passed down to posterity are described as a very material inheritance. As noted previously, Sun Qiao compiled his collection of pieces "worth looking at" with the express intent of passing it on to his sons and grandsons. He did not merely want them to know of his literary works, but to possess physical copies of them, stating that he "stored them in a bamboo case" for this purpose. Actual copies of works in collections thus represented a bond between a writer and his descendants or other family members, a bond that could be valuable not only emotionally but socially as well. In his "Explanation of Mr. Liu's Summary Collection," Liu Yuxi describes a request from his son-in-law:

> The other day my son-in-law Master Cui of Boling reported to me: "When I was heading to the capital, eminent men often asked how many new writings of my father-in-law I had and wanted me to go get some. But I answered that I had none and shame instantly rose up in my face. Today I am again going west and

---

Temple Collection of [Works from] Luoyang," he imagines himself coming back in a later life to read his own collection: "How can I know that in another life I won't again travel to this temple, and gaze once more on these writings?" 安知我他生不復游是寺，復睹斯文. See "Xiangshansi Baishi Luozhong ji ji" 香山寺白氏洛中集記, Zhu, 71.3806.

72. Sikong Tu, "Zhongtiao wangguangu xu" 中條王官谷序, *QTW*, 807.8488–89. Note that this text is elsewhere referred to as the "zixu" 自序 to the *Yimingji* 一鳴集. See Wan, *Tangji xulu*, 335. There are also some small textual differences in the version cited by Wan.

hope to have something to end this shame." Thus I picked out one of every four pieces to make my "collection summary" and gave it to this lad. I don't dare circulate it very far.

他日，子婿博陵崔生關言曰：「某也鄙游京師，偉人多問丈人新書幾何，且欲取去．而某應曰無有，輒媿起於顏間．今當復西，期有以弭媿者．」由是删取四之一，爲集略，以貽此郎，非敢行乎遠也．[73]

Liu Yuxi displays a reticence about wider circulation (though perhaps only as a move of self-deprecation) matched with a desire to pass on his works to close relations. The physicality of pieces is what is important here. Liu Yuxi's son-in-law is expected to have actual texts of his writings, as opposed to merely knowledge about them or the ability to recite them. Liu Yuxi, in turn, compiles this sub-collection to grant him that possession. The works are not passed on as abstract vehicles of moral suasion or literary models so much as physical proof of a connection with the author. Being Liu Yuxi's son-in-law might have given the young man a right to claim a familial connection, but he apparently required actual copies of the writer's recent works to be able to claim a literary inheritance as well.[74]

Some of the strongest evidence that authors envisioned collections as an important means by which to pass on copies of their works to descendants is found in examples of writers who worried that they would be unable to do so in the manner they had hoped. Yuan Zhen's poem, "Sighing to Myself, I Send This to Letian" 自歎因寄樂天, laments that since "Heaven has left our families without male heirs, to whom can we give our literary collections?" 天遺兩家無嗣子，欲將文集與它誰.[75] For Bai Juyi the answer to this question was his nephew and grandson. In "Written on My Collection Cabinet," he expresses his worries about his collection eventually being scattered and lost, and concludes his poem with the words, "My only response is to give them to my daughter, leave them to be passed on to my grandsons" 只應分付女，留與外孫傳.[76] And as we have seen, it was with his grandson and nephew that he ulti-

---

73. Liu Yuxi, "Liu shijilüe shuo" 劉詩集略說, *Liu Yuxi ji*, 20.250–51.

74. It is also possible that the "eminent men" wanted to copy Liu Yuxi's poems themselves. In this case, physical possession would be even more important.

75. Yuan Zhen, "Zitan yin ji Letian," *YZJ*, 22.247.

76. Bai Juyi, "Ti wenjigui," Zhu, 30.2072.

mately deposited two of the five copies of the final version of his collection, "to be passed down to posterity."

Indeed, this notion of a literary collection as inheritance is strong enough that there are examples of third parties going to great lengths to ensure that collections get passed on to rightful heirs. During the Taihe reign period (827–35) Li Yisun 李貽孫 was serving as an official in Fujian when the son of the late Ouyang Zhan 歐陽詹 (ca. 756–ca. 798) brought a set of the latter's works from Nan'an 南安 and "tearfully requested a preface" 泣拜請序. Li Yisun agreed but had not yet completed the piece when the son died. About two decades later, in the sixth year of the Dazhong Reign (852), Li writes that he "was again made Surveillance Commissioner and ordered a search for [Ouyang's] descendants. I thereupon found a grandson called Xie. I could not allow the transmission of Mr. Ouyang's writings to be thus severed. In composing this preface, I've also completed the wishes of [Ouyang's] descendants" 又爲觀察使・令訪其裔，因獲其孫曰澥・不可使歐陽氏之文遂絶其所傳也・爲題其序亦以卒後嗣之願云.[77] The transmission, *chuan* 傳, to which Li Yisun refers is clearly neither to the world at large nor simply to later times; it is a transmission of this specific set of works to Ouyang Zhan's descendants. We again see a distinction between literary works in the abstract and a given collection of those works. Even if Li had spread Ouyang Zhan's poems far and wide, it would not have resolved the issue of returning the set of works that he had been given to its rightful owners.

Li Yisun himself does not, of course, use the word "owners," yet the term is appropriate when discussing literary collections of the Mid-Tang and later. Bai Juyi and others thought of collections as property; they were tangible objects that could be passed down to selected recipients, just like land or other possessions. Stephen Owen has noted that questions of ownership in earlier periods are unusual and has discussed their increased prominence in the Mid-Tang.[78] It is important to be clear about what sort of ownership is implied here. It is not, I think, akin to modern ideas of intellectual property, and the reasons why it is not so get to the heart of the conception of works of literature as material objects that I have been dis-

77. Li Yisun 李貽孫, "Gu simen zhujiao Ouyang Zhan wenji xu" 故四門助教歐陽詹文集序, *QTW*, 544.5514.

78. Owen, *End of the Chinese 'Middle Ages'*, 24.

cussing. Bai Juyi, for example, exerted more control over his literary legacy than any other Tang figure, going as far as to declare versions of his works that were not copied out from his "official" collections to be spurious. Thus he claimed complete authority over his literary oeuvre. Authority, however, is different from ownership. Bai did not assert that he should control the circulation of his works or profit from them in any way. Those works, as linguistic patterns, were not his possessions. As their creator he could determine what they were, but once he let them out into the world, people could circulate them as they saw fit. His collections as physical objects were a different story. They were his to keep or distribute as he pleased. Moreover, he felt it within his rights to determine how they would be treated even after leaving his possession. Bai Juyi did not own his poems the way that a modern writer does, though he did own particular copies of them and exerted substantial effort to keep these safe.

Collections were thus seen by their compilers as physical repositories of literary works that could keep them safe and thereby serve as a means of circulating those works in both abstract and material senses. But did they successfully play these roles in Tang literary culture? The available evidence strongly suggests that they did. There is no question that people in the Tang, at least by the Mid-Tang, did indeed read poetry in the form of collections. Starting some decades after the An Lushan Rebellion, we begin to find a number of poem titles that refer to reading collections. The most basic are similar to the title of Meng Jiao's poem about reading the collection of his friend Zhang Bi 張碧: "Reading Zhang Bi's Collection" 讀張碧集.[79] Near the end of the dynasty, Meng Jiao's own collection is similarly mentioned in the title of Guanxiu's poem "Reading Meng Jiao's Collection" 讀孟郊集.[80] While Meng Jiao and Zhang Bi were contemporaries and friends, Guanxiu would have been reading Meng Jiao's collection well after the latter's death. An even greater temporal gap between author and reader is indicated by such works as Lu Guimeng's "Reading the Collection of Reminder Chen" 讀陳拾遺集, referring to the Early Tang poet Chen Zi'ang.[81] As noted in Chapter 4, Bai Juyi entitles one of

79. *QTS*, 380.4261.
80. *QTS*, 829.9343.
81. *QTS*, 629.7219.

his poems "I Read a Collection of Li Bai and Du Fu's Poetry and Thereupon Wrote This at the End of the Scroll" 讀李杜詩集因題卷後.[82]

Judging by references in poems and poem titles, writers in the last century of the dynasty read collections with greater frequency than their predecessors. In addition to his poem on reading Meng Jiao's collection, Guanxiu has several poems on reading other earlier poets' collections as well, ranging from Du Fu ("Two Poems on Reading the Collection of Du of the Ministry of Works" 讀杜工部集二首)[83] to Liu Deren 劉得人 and Jia Dao ("Two Poems on Reading the Collections of Liu Deren and Jia Dao" 讀劉得人賈島集二首).[84] Guanxiu's fellow monk Qiji also writes of reading Jia Dao's collection ("Reading Jia Dao's Collection" 讀賈島集),[85] as well as those of Li Bai ("Reading Li Bai's Collection" 讀李白集)[86] and Li He ("Reading a Collection of Li He's Songs" 讀李賀歌集).[87] Literary collections of contemporary writers were even used in educational contexts and were considered suitable models for young students. Recall that Pi Rixiu writes that, "When I was in the village school, I copied the collection of Secretary Du Mu in my books."[88] This marked increase in mentions of reading collections in the Mid- and especially Late Tang does strongly suggest that, as the dynasty progressed, collections were more and more often one of the formats through which readers encountered poetry.

Moreover, there are indications that literary collections were an important source for the anthologies that would become an important route for the transmission of Tang poetry into later periods.[89] In the postface to his

---

82. *QTS*, 438.4875. A more complete list of such titles, including many references to reading single scrolls not explicitly identified as collections, can be found in Xu Jun, *Dunhuang shiji*, 13–14.

83. *QTS*, 829.9339.

84. *QTS*, 829.9340.

85. *QTS*, 843.9525.

86. *QTS*, 847.9585.

87. *QTS*, 847.9585.

88. *QTS*, 614.7083. This is noted as well in *Tangshi jishi*, 66.994, and discussed in Chapter 4.

89. The question of the fate of collections in later dynasties, while important, is beyond the scope of my discussion here. For a useful examination of the Tang literary collections that survive today (many of which were compiled well after the Tang), see Wan, *Tangji xulu*. Xu Jun also notes that the Ming scholar Hu Zhenheng 胡震亨 made a list of indi-

anthology composed in the 850's, the *Tangshi leixuan* 唐詩類選 ("Categorical Selection of Tang Poetry"), the Tang anthologist Gu Tao 顧陶 discusses poets whose works he chose *not* to include and gives his reasons for doing so. Following a list of over ten poets, from Linghu Chu 令狐楚 (766–837) to Liu Yuxi, Gu Tao justifies their exclusion by saying, "Their poems are still in the world, while they have just departed it, but their literary collections have yet to circulate. Even if there were a piece or some chantings that one could obtain from people, they could still not be called things that had been recorded" 詩猶在世，及稍淪謝，即文集未行，縱有一篇一詠得於人者，亦未稱所錄.[90] This passage highlights the fact that collections gave the works they contained a formal context that they might otherwise have lacked. It is not that Gu Tao had no access to poems by these authors, many of whom were quite prominent: he admits that obtaining their poems would not be difficult. The issue, rather, is the source; he trusts collections in a way that he does not trust other sources. Unlike poems circulating less formally, poems in a collection had, by definition, been "recorded" (*lu* 錄), and this gave them a historical, biographical, and literary context that Gu Tao felt was necessary.

Gu's postface also implies that the term "*ji*" covered a broad and diverse range of textual sets in the Tang that included not only the single individual literary collections most often composed near the end of a writer's life, or after his death, but significantly smaller sets of texts as well. Discussing Du Mu, Xu Hun, and others, he explains:

> All have poems and lines that spread orally. As they died only two or three years ago, I have yet to obtain their formal collections. If I get some of the writings from the end of their lives, I'll make a separate scroll and attach it after the twenty *juan* [of the collection as it stands now]. I hope this is not looked upon with animosity. If I waited until I saw the completed versions, I would definitely fail to succeed in my compiling.

---

vidual literary collections listed in such works as the official Tang and Song histories and the *Zizhi tongjian* 資治通鑒. But as he points out, "The primary situation reflected by the bibliographies in [these works] was that of the writings stored by the government. Based only on these bibliographies and judgments about a number of books, it would be very difficult to gain a true understanding of the state of circulation of poetry collections among typical members of the scholar-official class of the time." See Xu Jun, *Dunhuang shiji*, 10–11 for further discussion.

90. Gu Tao, "Tangshi leixuan houxu" 唐詩類選後序, *QTW*, 765.7960.

並有詩句播在人口，身沒才二三年，亦正集未得．絶筆之文，若有所得，別爲卷軸，附於二十卷之外，冀無見恨．若須待見全本，則撰集必無成功．[91]

There is a distinction here between collections in general and "formal collections" (*zhengji* 正集). The formal collections appear to be those compiled after the author's death that would be intended as a more inclusive—or at least broadly representative—presentation of the writer's works. As we have seen in the examples of Du Fu, Bai Juyi, Liu Yuxi, and others, smaller collections were frequently compiled and circulated while the authors were still alive. Such collections would be expected to have lacunae. Often times, this was intentional. Fan Huang was not attempting to gather all the poems by Du Fu he could, as these would include the less serious verses whose popularity he desired to counter with his carefully chosen set of works. There is also the assumption that the living authors continued to write after the smaller collections had been compiled. It is those "last works" composed later in the authors' lives, their *juebi zhi wen* 絶筆之文, that Gu Tao would only be able to acquire when their *zhengji* circulated. He is not excluding certain poems by Du Mu on aesthetic grounds, but is simply waiting until he can acquire them as part of a formal collection. This postface thus sheds light on what constituted a "collection." We can see that the term "*ji*" covered a broad range of materials including, but not limited to, formal collections.[92]

The diversity of materials labeled as *ji* in the Tang should not be taken to imply that larger formal collections did not circulate, as there is ample evidence that they did. Beyond Gu Tao's stated desire to acquire *zhengji*, there are other examples of people in the Tang reading full collections. Fan Huang knew that a much larger collection of Du Fu's works (that he specifically refers to as a *zhengji*) was circulating in the south. Recall that in 836 Bai Juyi wrote of depositing a copy of his collection as it then stood at Shengshan Temple in Luoyang with the following limitation: "I still

91. Ibid.

92. The finds at Dunhuang provide even more direct evidence in the form of documents entitled "collection" that are far shorter than what we might expect from the content descriptions found in Tang prefaces. As Xu Jun (*Dunhuang shiji*, 9) puts it, "Obviously, there is a significant difference between the Dunhuang manuscript poetry collections and the traditional notion of a 'poetry collection.' "

request it not be lent out to official guests. If there is someone who is interested he can just look at it [here]." In the postface to the final version of his collection, written in 845, he also lists this as one of his designated collections, the implication being that he has updated it in the nine years since first depositing it at the temple. In fact, one of his friends *was* interested enough to "just look at it [there]." Bai Juyi's contemporary, the writer Li Shen 李紳 (772–846), entitled a poem "On Bai Letian's Literary Collection" 題白樂天文集 and included a prefatory note stating: "Letian stored his writings at the Eastern Capital Shengshan Temple, calling them 'Mr. Bai's Literary Collection.' I have composed this poem to praise them" 樂天藏書東都聖善寺，號白氏文集，紳作詩以美之.[93]

Bai Juyi's collection was protected by his admonitions that it not leave the temple. Other collections traveled more widely, and their fate reveals that collections were further altered after their compilation. While not a compiler of the collection proper, Wei Tao wrote a second preface for a collection of Meng Haoran's poems that he had acquired and that included the preface by Wang Shiyuan discussed above. Wei Tao writes:

> In the Tianbao period, I unexpectedly obtained a collection of Haoran's writings, and Shiyuan had, in fact, written the preface for it. The structure of the phrasing was so outstanding that, chanting them, I forgot my weariness. The writing was not in a single hand, and the paper and ink were thin and weak... If these poems had not met Master Wang, then they would have been nothing but a few dozen sheets of old paper... I have made a fair copy and added a table of contents. Moreover, to honor the pure talent of Shiyuan, I have dared to add my own description at the beginning of the scroll. I will respectfully present this volume to the Imperial Library, in hopes that it will not perish for many ages and its fragrance will be transmitted without end.
> 天寶中，忽獲浩然文集，乃士源撰爲之序傳．詞理卓絶，吟諷忘疲．書寫不一，紙墨薄弱．．．此詩若不遇王君，乃十數張故紙耳．．．余今繕寫，增其條目，復貴士源之清才，敢自述於卷首．謹將此本，送上秘府，庶久而不泯，傳芳無窮．[94]

Wei Tao's preface is dated to the third day of the first month of the ninth year of Tianbao (February 13, 750), which puts it some ten years after

93. *QTS*, 483.5495.

94. *QTW*, 307.3124. For Daniel Bryant's translation, which is different from mine in some important ways, see Bryant, "The High T'ang Poet Meng Hao-jan," 368–69.

Meng Haoran's death and five years or less after Wang Shiyuan's compilation of his collection of Meng's works. Assuming that Wang had made a fair copy of the collection when he originally compiled it, it is clear that the writings Wei Tao obtained were later-generation copies. Perhaps the most interesting comment he makes is that the writing was not in a single hand. Wei's comment raises the possibility that this collection was not an exact copy of the original collection compiled by Wang Shiyuan, but rather portions of it and other poems by Meng Haoran cobbled together with Wang Shiyuan's preface. Without the original collection itself, Wei Tao would have had no way of knowing how faithful his newly discovered copy was to Wang's compilation; by making a fair copy of the collection and presenting it to the Imperial Library, he gave this new version a legitimacy it might have lacked had it stayed in the condition in which he found it.

The tale of the different stages Meng Haoran's poems went through bears revisiting. The poems that managed to survive his own destructive impulses were scattered among his friends and old haunts. By bringing them together, Wang Shiyuan intended to give them a new context that would help to preserve and circulate them. In this he was clearly successful. Yet the collection obtained by Wei Tao, fading and written in different hands, was almost unquestionably not a perfect copy of the one originally created by Wang Shiyuan. Following the latter's footsteps, Wei in turn took further steps to save the poems and ensure that they would live on. In each case the preface writer took works he saw in danger of vanishing and preserved them. And each act of preservation obscured the questionable legitimacy of its sources; Wang surely traded his rewards for some spurious poems, and Wei says nothing about verifying the provenance of the collection he obtained. We have thus moved from scattered works, some of dubious origin, to a twice prefaced collection residing in the Imperial Library. Finally, neither Wang nor Wei seems troubled by the possibility that some of these works may not have been by Meng Haoran. Their compiling and copying may have obscured the origins of their sources, but neither attempts to hide this fact, instead giving accounts of these sources in their prefaces, and allowing us a rare glimpse of this aspect of the compilation process.

Collections and Critical Attitudes towards Poetry

The collection of Meng Haoran and the many collections of Bai Juyi have figured prominently in our discussion. The contrast between the two sets of works speaks to the different methods of compilation of literary collections in the Tang and of the roles these collections played. We can be confident that Bai Juyi's collection, secure in the Shengshan Temple sutra storehouse, was in roughly the same state Bai Juyi left it when it was later read by Li Shen. The version of Meng Haoran's collection given to the Imperial Library by Wei Tao, in contrast, may have differed significantly from Wang Shiyuan's original compilation. Meng Haoran showed little interest in the material preservation of his literary legacy, frequently destroying written copies of his poems. It was left to one of his admirers, a man who had never even met him, to wander the countryside gathering the scattered remnants of that legacy. Bai Juyi, on the other hand, demonstrated a concern with his works that bordered on obsession. He kept multiple copies in different locations, updated them regularly, and even gave strict instructions on the conditions under which others would be allowed to read them. These two cases do not represent opposing poles *per se*—Bai Juyi may indeed be an extreme case, but the fact that Meng Haoran even had a literary collection compiled during the Tang differentiates him from innumerable writers who, along with their works, were more quickly forgotten—yet they demonstrate the great diversity of the process that produced and preserved Tang literary collections.

Those who compiled literary collections in the Tang undertook this task with the intent to preserve and circulate the works they were compiling. If they were members of the writer's family, they probably had the future reputation of their relative in mind. For self-compiled collections, authors had a similar set of goals, from preserving their property to passing their writings down to face the judgments of later generations. Yet we cannot allow these more practical goals to obscure the fact that, in many cases, people compiled collections of a given author's works simply because they enjoyed them and thought that others would as well. The compilation of literary collections in the Tang was not meant as an academic exercise in literary history the way it would often be in the Song. Something about how people approached even the recent literary past changed in the Song, when the collection of literary works simply for pleasure increasingly involved academic endeavors to quantify, judge, and compare editions in a way that was not at all prominent in the Tang. A full comparison of Song attitudes towards collection compilation with those in the Tang is beyond the purview of this study. But it is important to at least briefly discuss some of the roles literary collections seem *not* to have played to a significant degree in the Tang—roles that would become more pronounced later.

In her informative discussion of canons and collections, Pauline Yu has written, "In the case of the collected works of an individual author... the primary aim will be comprehensiveness, the inclusion of every work that falls under the rubric that has been established."[95] As far as the post-Tang period is concerned, Yu may indeed be correct. However, the evidence I have presented suggests that compilers of collections in the Tang often did not aim at comprehensiveness, and if they did, they saw it as only one goal among many. Tang collections were typically not all-inclusive. In many cases numerous works were deemed unworthy of inclusion in collections either by the authors themselves or by other compilers. This was an accepted part of the process of turning a set of gathered poems into a formal collection. Writers and compilers hoped that, as Pi Rixiu said of his set of self-compiled works intended to serve as an introduction to his literary abilities, "those who peruse them will find nothing to ridicule" 覽者無誚矣.[96] Scholars of literary history, as many of those who put together collections of Tang literature in later eras could be considered to be, might have seen collections as sets of data whose value was dependant largely on their comprehensiveness. Tang compilers took a more selective

---

95. Yu, "Poems in Their Place," 168.

96. Pi Rixiu, "Wensou xu" 文藪序, *QTW*, 796.8352–53. The full passage reads, "In the *bingrong* year of the Xiantong reign period (866), I 'heaved the spear' [i.e. took the civil service exam] but failed. I retreated to my prefecture and came to my villa, where I compiled and edited my writings, intending to present them to the appropriate officials. When I opened up my chest they were all bunched up, tangled as an overgrown marsh. Thus I named the book the 'Tangled Marsh of Writings'... The 'Genealogical Record of Master Pi' is written at the end and shares the intent of the Grand Historian's self-preface. Altogether there are two hundred pieces, making ten *juan*. Those who peruse them will find nothing to ridicule" 咸通丙戎中，日休射策不上第．退歸州來別墅，編次其文，復將貢於有司．登篋叢萃繁如藪澤，因名其書曰文藪焉．．．皮子世錄，著之於後，亦太史公自序之意也．凡二百篇，爲十卷，覽者無誚矣. Note that Pi Rixiu's collection cited here is a *xingjuan*.

view. Even the dedicated Wang Shiyuan admits to having placed substantial limits on the time and effort he expended searching for Meng Haoran's scattered works.

What is perhaps most telling is that there do not appear to be any Tang prefaces that entreat other people or later generations to add to collections should they encounter works legitimately ascribed to the author but not included in the collection in question. There are no requests that others "carry on the work that I have started." This fact is particularly interesting given that "lost" works are more typically described as "scattered and lost," rather than lost for good or destroyed. While there was always the potential that additional works would be found (as they often were), the notion that they ought then to be added to a pre-existing collection is not addressed by these prefaces. If there were, in fact, new poems in the version of Meng Haoran's collection discovered by Wei Tao, they were not inserted at Wang Shiyuan's request. Collections were seen as "fixed," as self-contained and complete documents, rather than as repositories that could be expanded or amended later.

Tang collectors and compilers were not literary historians who undertook these activities as part of a search for scholarly truth. They were not devoted to gathering all available versions of a poem so that they could be compared and the "true" original could be discovered. In the Song, Ouyang Xiu and his friends would debate over the proper character to fill a lacuna in a Du Fu poem until the correct original could be found.[97] Li Qingzhao 李清照 (1084–ca. 1151) and her husband would collate any new book they purchased and make corrections to it on the basis of their research.[98] Yet I have not found a single preface to a Tang collection that mentions the comparison of different versions of a poem to determine which one is more "authentic" or true to the author's original intent. Nor have I found any extant preface to an anthology compiled in the Tang that discusses such issues. Gu Tao chose not to accept certain sources, but there is no indication that he compared different versions of a given work in the compilation of his anthology. Guanxiu expresses displeasure in changes in his poems through the course of unintended circulation, but

97. See discussion in Introduction.

98. See Li Qingzhao, "Jinshi lu" 金石錄 in Wang Zhongwen, *Li Qingzhao ji jiaozhu*, 3.176–92.

he has no master copy with which to compare them. He is happy simply to change them as he sees fit.

In general, we find little concern with authenticity expressed in the prefaces. Wang Shiyuan apparently felt no need to justify his collection method. Though the offering of money in exchange for poems would seem likely to result in a great number of false attributions, he does not display any concern over the matter. Lu Chun expunged numerous poems in his attempt to present an image of Wang Ji that he found more appropriate. Yet he never claims that, based on his textual research, the excluded poems appeared to be spurious. Rather than using all the available sources to determine the truth about Wang Ji's literary temperament, Lu Chun approached the sources with his opinion already established and openly altered them to conform with that opinion. It is worth noting that both Wang and Lu are quite forthright about these activities. This fact alone tells us that they found no fault with them.

Finally, there is a notable lack of competitiveness in evidence in these prefaces. While most collectors may have made an effort to gather together as many of a given author's works as they could, there are no boasts about any collection being the most comprehensive or the "definitive" collection. This is true even when there were multiple early collections for the same poet, as was the case with Guanxiu, Li Bai, Du Fu, and others.

I would speculate that these differences between the Tang and Song may well be connected to the particular context and methods in and by which these works were reproduced and circulated. Tang collections existed not in a true commercial context, but rather in a proto version of the commercial markets that would develop after the advance of print technology. As we have seen, with the exception of *xingjuan* used for utilitarian purposes, individual poetry collections do not appear to have been commonly sold or printed, and claims that people purchased poetry for their own enjoyment are extremely rare. Just as Tang collectors were not literary historians, neither were they businessmen attempting to market a product. Absent a true competitive commercial market, such as the one which came to exist for materials related to examinations preparation, novels, short fiction, poetry, etc., in the Song and later periods, we may conclude that Tang compilers felt no particular need to elevate their versions of the collections they put together above others. While dissemination may have been an important goal, the evidence strongly suggests that it was the dissemination of a given author's works in general that was important, not that of a specific version of those works contained in one particular collection.

Printing dominated the dissemination of written works in the Song and after. It was a commercial enterprise that both responded to and created its own economic logic. The example of Guanxiu's collection, the first for which we know printing blocks were cut, is illustrative. Tan Yu portrays himself as having compiled Guanxiu's collection in response to demand. People were coming to the monastery to read Guanxiu's works and to copy them out themselves. One implication of this is that some collections by this time existed in a nexus of, if not consumerism—there is no evidence that people paid to copy out Guanxiu's poems—at least supply and demand. Printing thus appears to be a further step in satisfying the demand for texts. It would allow much more rapid and efficient circulation of Guanxiu's works than the copying of individual poems. It might also ensure that the collection circulated as a collection. The time involved in personally copying texts for one's own use meant that people were unlikely to copy out an entire collection. Why take the time to copy the poems one does not like? The preface itself, with its mention of copying out a few lines (叁句五句), implies as much. Printing would thus mean a difference in kind, not just degree, of circulation. People would still be likely to copy down individual poems that they enjoyed, but the presence of full printed collections meant that poems would be circulating in that significantly different context as well.

Because of the lack of a true commercial market for full literary collections in the Tang and the lack of readily available multiple copies of the works in question, the idea of a best or most "accurate" version of a given work in the context of contemporary poetry was not important to most Tang literati. The lack of commercial printing meant that there were fewer versions of a given work available in the Tang; a reader would rarely have multiple editions available for comparative purposes, either of individual poems or of a poet's full collection. The time and effort required to produce such copies would have been prohibitive. In a literary environment in which poems took a number of different forms and existed in a number of different media, including oral song, the idea of an "original" version was not a particularly important one. This is not to say that people did not understand that there could be different versions of a given work; quite the contrary. They did not, however, find this troubling.[99] And by being collected, the collected versions were, at least for a time, set. There were unquestionably variations, yet one can imagine that the full extent of the variations would not become as clear a problem until the proliferation of printed materials in the Song. It was only then, when the notion of a "literary marketplace" became the literal truth and when collecting became a specifically scholarly pursuit (and even obsession), that issues of comprehensiveness and authenticity would come to the fore.

Bai Juyi and Yuan Zhen once again offer intriguing counterexamples that, in this case, foreshadow the changes to come in the Song and later periods. In many ways, Bai Juyi's attitude towards his collection *was* more akin to the scholarly approaches taken towards Tang literature by Song literati than the comparatively casual, if diligent, attitudes exemplified by such Tang collection compilers as Wang Shiyuan. What was particularly unusual about Bai Juyi was that his object of study was his own literary output; he was a literary historian of himself. The careful counting of the numbers of pieces and the elaborate classificatory systems he used are simply not found in other Tang writings, with the possible exception of Yuan Zhen. Both poets also demonstrated an interest in the question of the authenticity of literary works that was unusual for their time. Yuan Zhen, in a note to one of his poems, claims that many poems circulating as his own were, in fact, fakes:

> The younger generation enjoys composing fake poems attributed to me; these circulate all over. Since I have arrived in Kuaiji someone has already written one hundred "Palace Verses" and "Miscellaneous Poems" in two *juan*. All of these are said to have been written by me. When I examined them myself, there was not a single one that was.
> 後輩好僞作予詩，傳流諸處·自到會稽，已有人寫宮詞百篇及雜詩兩卷，皆云是予所撰·及手勘驗無一篇是者·[100]

Bai Juyi also ends the postface to his final collection by claiming that any omissions or false attributions within the collection are honest mistakes

99. As the old saying has it, a man with two watches never knows what time it is. Tang compilers usually had only one watch.

100. Yuan Zhen, "Chou Letian yusi bujin jiawei liuyun zhi" 酬樂天餘思不盡加爲六韻之, *YZJ*, 22.247.

and not attempts at trickery on his part.[101] An intriguing implication of this is that perhaps Bai Juyi is admitting that he himself might not recognize a forgery!

We can never definitively determine why these two poets, more than any other Tang author, showed such a concern with authenticity and control over specific versions of their works; but the idea of commercial culture may come into play here in a reverse of my discussion above. While there is no evidence that either Bai Juyi or Yuan Zhen directly made money from their poetry by selling it as a commodity, both describe their works being used by others to make a profit. As we have seen, Yuan Zhen tells of finding his and Bai Juyi's poems for sale in a market and encountering a Korean merchant who would take them home and sell them to his country's Chief Minister. Bai Juyi claims that knowledge of his poetry would increase a singing girl's price. Thus, even if they did not personally participate in the commercial culture surrounding their literary works, both Bai Juyi and Yuan Zhen were aware that such a context existed, or at least imagined it did. Perhaps this knowledge, combined with a certain degree of natural meticulousness and self-regard, can begin to explain the exceptional motivations behind Bai Juyi's and, to a lesser extent, Yuan Zhen's compilations of their own literary collections.

Because of their voluminous writings about their collections, Bai Juyi and Yuan Zhen play what is perhaps an oversized role in any discussion of literary collections in the Tang. At the same time, they represent an important point in what we can legitimately consider a historical trend. There is little evidence of writers in the Early and High Tang giving much attention to their own collections. Li Bai and many others kept copies of their writings, but a disorganized pile of writings did not constitute a collection. It is only in Bai Juyi and Yuan Zhen's generation that we begin to see writers regularly compiling, organizing, and maintaining their collections themselves—a trend that would continue for the rest of the dynasty. We must be careful to acknowledge that this was a trend, not a wholesale change in practice. Many writers from these later periods did not engage in these activities or if they did, failed to match the enthusiasm of the period's most famous literary friends. As there are far more surviving writings on these topics from the second half of the dynasty than from the

101. "Baishi Changqing ji houxu," Zhu, "waiji" 3.3917.

first, we must also be cautious about drawing larger conclusions about historical change. Yet a change in attitude is unmistakable and calls out for some explanation.

One important factor to consider is the new Mid-Tang interest in ownership. As I discussed above, poets in the second half of the dynasty had begun to think of their works as material possessions in a way that earlier writers typically did not. They were objects that could be ordered, protected, and passed on to the next generation. This attitude was not entirely absent in earlier periods (at least with regards to literary works), but it was less pronounced.

Perhaps more importantly, there was general shift in the post-An Lushan period away from the court as the real or imagined center of literary activity. As McMullen has meticulously demonstrated, literary men in the second half of the dynasty turned from the official to the unofficial, from the public to the private, in a wide range of literary pursuits. Writings "circulated privately, to be commented on and appreciated by colleagues and friends," resulting ultimately in a "decentralized literary milieu."[102] In this context a poet's works were not just materials for a surviving relative to gather together after the poet's death, but rather a constantly evolving aspect of one's status in private literary circles.

Yet even if literature was a more private sphere of activity in the second half of the dynasty, its public role, especially as part of the exam system, remained prominent. In this vein, we might see the increasing importance of *xingjuan* in the lives of exam candidates as an important factor in the growing interest in maintaining personal literary collections. Circulating *xingjuan* as part of the cultural practices surrounding the exam began during the High Tang. As Fu Xuanzong has argued, however, it did not come into its own until the end of that period.[103] Few prominent High Tang poets appear to have circulated what we would recognize as a *xingjuan*; by the early ninth century the practice was common (albeit confined to very specific times, situations, and people in connection with the exams). It is reasonable to assume that writers who had become accustomed to creating small but formal collections of a range of their works when they were

---

102. McMullen, *State and Scholars*, 235.

103. Fu (*Tangdai keju yu wenxue*, 262) sees the practice of *xingjuan* as taking shape between 742 and 754.

young would be more likely to continue this practice on a larger scale later in their lives. Moreover, even if they did not depend on such collections for employment in the years after they had passed (or given up on) the exams, the general notion that it was important to have a representative set of one's own writings would still have been an element of how they thought about their literary production and legacy.

Finally, I think we might consider that Bai Juyi and Yuan Zhen, as prominent writers and political figures, might well have been especially influential in this specific context. Bai Juyi's literary career in particular was a long and successful one. His and Yuan's example, combined with these other social and cultural changes taking place, may well have helped create the early stages of a trend that would continue and grow not just in the Tang, but for the rest of the imperial period.

Conclusion

Tang poetry has survived. Over a thousand years after these poems first came into existence, whether as voices in the air or as ink on paper, millions of people continue to read them, recite them, imitate them, and ponder their meanings. Because Tang poetry has survived and continues to impact the cultural and literary values of so many people, it can be easy to forget where it came from. Before there was something called "Tang poetry," there were people in the Tang composing, reproducing, and enjoying these works, many of which have come down to us today in some form but far greater numbers of which have been lost. Their origins are important, and coming to a better understanding of them has been one of the primary goals of this study. Here I revisit some of the larger issues that have run through this book and consider how they might affect the way we think about Tang poetry in the future. I also briefly point to how the findings of this study connect to work in other fields such as religion and history.

We began with an examination of the material nature of poetry in the Tang by looking at some of the few examples of it that still exist—manuscript copies of Tang poems from the Tang itself and the period immediately following the Tang. Materiality mattered in the Tang in a way that it does not in our modern media-saturated culture, with its promiscuous reproduction of texts and images in a wide range of formats. The most striking aspect of the materiality of the Dunhuang manuscript copies of "Qinfu yin" is the stability it has provided. These pieces of paper—our only substantial record of a poem that was extremely popular in its day—have survived for over a thousand years. We can look at these pages and see the poem just as it existed for its original audience. We can see the traces of a distracted scribe whose eyes wandered ahead on the text he was copying before he caught himself, re-inked his brush, and continued his work. We can see the difference between a scroll with small characters written with a quick brush and a booklet with larger characters written in multiple unsteady hands. From the material clues found on these pieces of paper, be they marginalia or crossed-out mistakes, we can begin to trace a tentative story about why and how these texts were created a millennium ago.

From another perspective these manuscripts reveal radical instability. They survived, but this reminds us that they are *all* that survived of a poem so well known that it became a nickname for its author, a man who was prominent for many other literary accomplishments beyond the poem he eventually disavowed. We know more than two lines of "Qinfu yin" only because of a lengthy chain of fortuitous circumstances, ranging from dry desert air to imperialistic amateur archeologists. These texts reveal other instabilities as well. "Qinfu yin" was not a static, disembodied work that reached its wide audience in the form its author created it. It was fluid, with hundreds of alterations that changed not only the form of the work but also its meaning. Whether intentionally or by accident, the readers and copyists who kept "Qinfu yin" alive changed it in the process, making it something other than what Wei Zhuang himself had produced. The same holds true for the poetic manuscripts of the set of Gao Shi poems we examined, many of which, lacking any indication of an author, could only be connected to the poet by readers who were already familiar with the poems. In both cases circulation and survival entailed textual change. The contents of "Qinfu yin" and the poems by Gao Shi were stable enough to maintain their identities, yet unstable enough to lead us to question what those identities really mean.

The issues I have explored via these manuscripts are relevant to the study of other aspects of Tang culture as well. Materiality is arguably of even greater importance for certain types of religious texts than for the literary ones I have examined.[1] Written talismans, for example, were seen to have power not only as disembodied words but as words inscribed. The words had to take on material form to manifest certain types of religious

1. Teiser deals extensively with issues related to the materiality of religious texts in *Scripture on the Ten Kings*.

efficacy. And as Dunhuang texts from Buddhist and Daoist traditions have shown, religious texts from the medieval period were often as unstable as poetic ones. Christine Mollier has demonstrated that many Daoist works were copied directly from Buddhist sutras and that "the Buddhists showed no hesitation about trolling through Daoist collections and falsifying the writings they found there."[2] These works and parts of works would thus not only lose their connection to an original author, but would also be transposed into entirely different systems of religious and philosophical thought and practice. Indeed the "messiness" of medieval manuscript culture was a reality of all aspects of textual culture in the Tang, from Daoist talismans to the Confucian classics.

Memories were a key factor in poetic circulation and survival in the Tang as well. As we saw in the second chapter, literate men and women in medieval China were accustomed to memorization as a common way of engaging with literary texts. From an early age, men in particular learned texts by setting them to memory, most often through a method that required massive amounts of time, but allowed its practitioners to internalize texts to an extent that they became part of one's linguistic and literary identity. Though poetry was not memorized with the systematic rigor employed in learning the classics, its structures and particular aesthetic norms made it especially easy to recall. Unlike the primers learned by young schoolchildren, these poems were not structured the way they were with the explicit goal of easy memorization, but the fact that they could be quickly set to memory contributed to their great popularity.

Medieval memories preserved and transmitted innumerable texts, but they changed them as well. The often uncritically accepted myth of near-perfect memory in traditional China does not capture the more complicated reality of actual medieval practices and abilities. After adolescence, writers and readers typically did not continue to train their memories the way their medieval European counterparts did. Such formal arenas for testing memory as the exams had minimal requirements for precise memorization. Other spheres of literary activity, such as composition, required not precise memory but internalization of styles and ideas. This surely meant that many texts were indeed memorized whole or, more commonly, in part, but not with the regularity or rigor that has often

2. See Mollier, *Buddhism and Taoism*, 20.

been assumed. Poetry was easy to set to memory and was thus often passed along through memorial transmission. This helped it spread and survive, but imperfect memories reproduced texts imperfectly. Survival entailed change.

Closely tied to memory is its expression in oral poetic production and circulation. The nature of orality in Tang China presents a challenge to common Western models of the connections between orality and writing. Poetry in the Tang was an intensely oral phenomenon, as we can see not only from the many descriptions of oral practices that survive but from the mode of formal presentation on the page that written texts took. These features of poetic practice were not, as some models would have us believe, the result of an immature written culture just beginning to leave its oral roots. Rather, they were the result of aesthetic norms that valued orality in spite of a flourishing written culture that had existed for thousands of years.

Orality was also a key aspect of the survival and circulation of poems in the Tang. It allowed works to spread rapidly and widely, often bringing fame to their authors and renown to others associated with them. It was fast and cheap, but also arduous in its way. Sounds are ephemeral and can never travel far from their source. Where a written copy of a poem might circulate by itself for years, the work of oral circulation required the participation of innumerable voices and memories. Oral circulation thus bespoke popularity in a different way from written circulation. There was something special about works enjoying wide oral circulation, as attested to by comments praising poets' popularity.

In oral circulation, every instance of transmission is a new production of a poetic text. These reproductions were rarely perfect; poems changed as they spread. Indeed, many prominent contexts for oral circulation encouraged change. This is especially clear in the case of performance. Performers, whether they were entertaining the emperor or patrons in a bar, took poems apart and reconfigured them in new ways to fit the occasion or even the music that accompanied them. Textual fluidity was not anathema to these sometimes commercial contexts; on the contrary, they required it. We see something very similar at work in Tang narratives. In the course of both written and oral circulation, these works could change far more radically than poems. They could be summarized, expanded, spliced together, and even re-worded entirely.[3]

Oral circulation, effective though it was in many spheres, had its limits. And as much as poetry in the Tang was a very oral art form, it was simultaneously an intensely literate one. Poetic composition in the Tang, even in the context of rapid-fire composition in the poetry salons and competitions of the Early Tang, was most often described as involving an act of writing. Composition could be spontaneous and nearly instantaneous, or it could be a process of prolonged revision and refinement. Poems created in written form most commonly circulated that way as well. Whether on leaves or in letters to friends sent by official post, poems made their way through the empire as written texts. As we have seen, written circulation of poetry in the Tang was not limited to pages and scrolls. Poets inscribed their words on landscapes natural and man-made throughout the Tang.

The stabilizing features of written texts are clear: they persevered through time and space in a way that oral declamations could not. A poem chanted once could reach only a small number of people. That same poem written once on a poetry board in a popular Chang'an monastery could reach thousands. Poetic texts written down in a dusty Tang frontier town near the steppes survive in museums in Paris, London, and elsewhere today (and images of them are available to anyone in the world with a computer connected to the Internet).

Yet even a poem inscribed at an oft-visited locale depended on additional textual reproduction to spread. Woodblock printing did begin in the Tang, but the basic mode of producing new copies of poetic texts remained hand-copying. The use of paper and brush meant that these texts were easier to produce and thus more plentiful than medieval Europe manuscripts. The fact remains, however, that the process was so time-consuming that poetic texts circulated in limited numbers and were easily lost. Time and again, accounts tell us of textual loss on a massive scale due to everything from the fires of rebellion to the dissatisfaction of exacting authors. Those texts that did survive, as with oral circulation, changed in the process. Numerous accounts of revising and editing make it clear that Tang copyists felt little responsibility to perfectly reproduce the poetic texts they copied. These were not Buddhist sutras or the "Confucian"

3. See Sarah M. Allen, "Tang Stories" and "Tales Retold."

classics and were not treated as such. They were fundamentally fluid, whether copyists rewrote them to avoid taboo characters in the names of recipients or simply to make them into better poems.

In all these cases, texts moved away from their authors. What readers encountered differed in ways both trivial and significant from what authors had created. Throughout this study I use terms such as "loss of control" and "instability" because I believe they give an accurate account of the way texts changed in the Tang. Unfortunately these terms often have negative connotations that, though they fit certain critical attitudes towards textual fluidity, do not capture the perspectives of most writers and readers during the Tang itself. As we have seen in almost every part of this study and in the final chapter on literary collections in particular, Tang poets and even compilers of collections rarely expressed concern about these facts of circulation. Poetry infused many aspects of Tang life, but it had not yet become an object of scholarly and analytic examination the way it would in later periods.

We, however, are not Tang poets; the reality of their attitudes towards textual fidelity has implications for our scholarly approaches to the literature they produced. As Stephen Owen has pointed out, "There is much in our traditional interpretation of Du Fu's poetry and its development that would be shaken if we imagine the old man in Chengdu or Kuizhou recopying the poems of his younger days, adding and subtracting lines, changing words."[4] We do not know whether or not Du Fu did indeed substantially revise his poems in his last years, but there is clear evidence that such a practice was far from unheard of at the time.

We do know that *other* people revised Du Fu's poems after they left his hand, and this is a far more problematic reality for both traditional and most modern critical modes to face. Given the close scrutiny of individual words and phrases in traditional criticism on Tang poetry (a glimpse of which we see in the anecdote from Ouyang Xiu's *Shihua* cited in the Introduction), the substantial differences between some of the recovered versions of "Qinfu yin" might well have resulted in very different perceptions of the poem. This would be even more the case for the far shorter poems that made up much of Tang verse. Specific words matter in poetry in a way that they do not in, for example, Tang prose narratives. Short

4. Owen, "Poetry and Its Historical Ground," 109.

regulated poems are not read for the plot. A different poem about the same event with different words is just that, a different poem, and it is thus assumed to portray a different set of experiences. The notion that some of the words in a received version of one of Du Fu's poems were chosen not by him, but by a Late Tang courtesan who revised the work to make it a better read for one of her clients, throws much of the later critical apparatus into question. And such revisions represent only a partial disjunction between poem and poet. We have also seen examples in which this separation is complete. From pilfered *xingjuan* bought and sold in the alleys of Chang'an to people attributing their own verses to Yuan Zhen and Bai Juyi, the connection between a work and its purported author could be a tenuous one.[5]

While many of these issues are brought into particularly sharp relief in the case of poetry, they are also relevant for a number of fields other than medieval literature. Indeed, in any case where an interpretive apparatus ties words specifically to given individuals, the revelation of a reality that undermines that connection can prove challenging. Albert Welter has noted that Chan masters were viewed as "living buddhas" and that anecdotes about them "thus became regarded as the words and deeds of living buddhas."[6] Yet it is clear that any connection between historical personages and the words they are portrayed as saying is questionable at very best. John McRae has outlined the process by which the recorded sayings of Chan masters circulated, a process that is strikingly similar to that which I describe above for poetry. In the case of Chan encounter dialogues, the original form is presented as oral. There is then an "initial transcription," followed by "circulation, evaluation, and selection," and finally, "editorial modification."[7] The first two stages of this process involved "a complex environment of both oral and written transmission" and a close connection between the reputation of a given master and the popularity of dialogues involving him.[8] In the final stage, not unlike the final stage of com-

5. The problem of misattributions is not, of course, a new revelation. However, such problems have typically been "solved" by recourse to a poet's biography which was, in turn, often constructed on the basis of his poems.

6. Welter, *Monks, Rulers, and Literati*, 43.

7. McRae, *Seeing through Zen*, 99-100.

8. Ibid., 100.

piling poetry collections, McRae notes "a clear tendency for editors and compilers to modify their texts in order to increase the perceived religious utility of the dialogues."[9] Interestingly, the more these dialogues were circulated and modified in their written forms, the more they were reworked and re-written to have the appearance of direct transcriptions of oral events, with the attendant implications of spontaneity and immediacy.[10] A similar phenomenon is observable in the later Song period with the recording and circulating of the recorded sayings of Neo-Confucian figures. Robert Hymes has argued that the relationship between the actual words uttered by teachers and the written records of those words is a highly fluid one, with what must have been a colloquially phrased oral original ultimately transformed into a written version that may well retain a colloquial flavor, but would often be much more akin to the literary Chinese of the period.[11] In both these cases, as with that of poetry, the paths from an "original" version to those that circulated, to say nothing of those that survived to the present, are long and circuitous ones.

The problems that the material reality of literary production and circulation in the Tang pose to traditional critical approaches should not be taken lightly, yet I am not advocating a critical stance in which a biographical reading of a poem can have no role. It would be a mistake to abandon completely our understanding of, for example, Du Fu's "Qiuxing bashou" 秋興八首 ("Autumn Stirrings: eight poems") on the possibility that an unknown copyist rather than "China's greatest poet" might have been the true author of some of the finer phrases. As we have seen, the forces working against textual change were strong ones as well. We can and should still speak of the genius of particular poems and lines and even the use of a single word, but perhaps we might hesitate before tying these too closely with the author as a sole creative force and his life experiences as prime determining factors.

In dealing with the material realities of Tang poetic production and circulation, we should take advantage of what opportunities surviving texts afford. The number of poems that survive in Dunhuang manuscripts is limited, but those that do survive have much to tell us and should not

9. Ibid.

10. Ibid.

11. See Hymes, "Getting the Words Right."

be ignored. "Qinfu yin" is again a useful example. Unlike with the great majority of Tang poems, our knowledge of the poem is based entirely on found manuscripts, without the intermediate stage of the Song and later imperial print cultures. It is thus unfortunate that what may well be the new standard version of the poem, the version found in the recent Shanghai guji edition of Wei Zhuang's works, takes a 1947 critical text as the basis for *its* critical text. On this base the editor creates a new text by consulting other critical texts and the surviving manuscripts to "choose the best and follow them" 擇善而從.[12] While he does give variants in the notes, the fact remains that he has proposed a standard text that, as far as we know, had never actually existed. It is a creation of modern textual criticism, with all the substantial flaws from which the discipline suffers. When we have texts that we know existed in the Tang, and we do not even have Song printed versions as alternatives, why create a text that we are certain no one closer to Wei Zhuang's time ever read? Xu Jun, following a practice Bédier would have approved, chooses the exact text of one of the Dunhuang copies, as well as it can be reproduced in typeset form, as his base. He then gives the variants from all the other manuscripts for essentially every character position in the poem. Any typesetting naturally separates us from the materiality of the original manuscripts, but by choosing a text that we know did exist in the Tang or just after as his base (and by his very insightful writings about the manuscript culture in Dunhuang in general), Xu Jun demonstrates a willingness to convey at least some of the messy reality of the literature he examines.[13]

Other scholars working on medieval China recently have similarly provided examples of how we might meaningfully engage with manuscript culture. Variation and textual fluidity were fundamental realities of poetry in the medieval period. In her writings on Tao Yuanming and other poets, Xiaofei Tian's work has shown how we might take textual

---

12. Nie, *Wei Zhuang ji jianzhu*, 323.

13. This is not to say that we should always or even often choose Dunhuang versions of poems when available over, for example, those found in Song printed editions of the same works. If one is not focusing on material aspects of the poems, a strong argument could be made that Song printed versions might well be closer to some originals. With "Qinfu yin," however, we know that the new critical texts are inventions.

variants seriously rather than simply acknowledge them in footnotes.[14] Variants, even when we cannot definitively date them to the general period in which the author was active, can tell us much about how poems were received, interpreted, and changed in the course of transmission. Moreover, they remind us that variants were a regular part of this literature as it was produced and circulated in earlier periods. As Cerquiglini concisely put it in the quote cited at the beginning of the first chapter, "medieval writing does not produce variants; it *is* variance."

Scholars working on medieval European literature have been grappling with similar issues for some time. If their experience is any guide, we have much to be optimistic about. A more holistic approach to Tang literature that directly confronts the material realities of literary works during the Tang itself will indeed undermine certain critical approaches to that body of literature, but I believe it will open more doors than it shuts.

Tang poetry is tough; it has survived rebellions and revolutions, passing from long-departed lips to manuscripts, printed pages, and even electronic ones and zeros. Despite the vast gaps between us—its modern readers—and the period of its creation, there *is* still something familiar about Tang poetry. Confronting the reality of those gaps can be alienating, but seeking to better grasp what poetry in the Tang looked and sounded like before it became "Tang poetry" will ultimately replace that sense of alienation with a deeper and more accurate understanding of this enduring literature.

14. See both *Tao Yuanming and Manuscript Culture* and "Misplaced: Three Qing Manuscripts of a Medieval Poet." Sarah M. Allen deals with similar issues for Tang narrative in "Tang Stories" and "Tales Retold."

Appendix

Appendix: Types of Variants Found in the "Qinfu yin" Manuscripts

1. Variant Forms

Variant forms are variants that a contemporary reader would not perceive as altering the meaning found in a given character position. A common example of variants in this category is one in which a character that would now be considered to be a "simplified" character, such as 门, is used in one text while another text uses the "complex" form, in this case 門.[1] There is no difference in meaning here, just as a British writer's use of the British spelling "colour" rather than the American "color" would not indicate a different meaning of the word. In another example, some scribes used two dots known as a *chongwen hao* 重文號, or duplicating mark, to replace the second of a set of repeated characters. Other scribes (such as Servant Yin) typically wrote out the full character a second time. If in a given character position one text has a duplication mark while its pair has a full character, the variation would fall into this category. The meanings are exactly the same (but, of course, different from synonyms), yet the actual written characters are different.

Examples of this category of variants often include more than two possible forms of a character. In line 70, manuscripts S692 and P3910 use the character 娉, while P2700 and P3780 use the variant form 騁. These

1. For an example of this variant see line 21, character position 3, in which S5476 uses the character 门 while the other five versions that include this portion of the text use the character 門 instead.

forms are interchangeable and the reading of the line is unchanged. But to further complicate matters, manuscripts S5476 and P3381 use what is probably a variant of the second character, 斛. As all of these three variations appear in more than one manuscript, it is unlikely that they constitute singular mistakes by a copyist, but are rather alternative choices that would have been considered acceptable in the historical orthographic context in which the manuscripts were copied.

Even within a single manuscript a scribe may use multiple forms of a single character. The character 壹, a variant form of the character 一, meaning "one," is used frequently in the manuscripts but without any discernable patterns.[2] For example, in line 128, manuscripts S5477, P2700, P3953, P3910, and P3381 use the character 一 in the first and fifth character positions as a counter for amounts of gold and grain respectively. P3780, on the other hand, uses 壹 in both positions. And demonstrating that this is not simply a transcription choice for a given copyist, S5476 uses the character 一 in the first position and 壹 in the fifth, while S692 does just the opposite. In other words, this is not a choice dictated either by a copyist's overall preference for one form over another, or even for one over another depending on context when the use is numerical. In a related example, the copyist of P2700 frequently switches between using simplified and complex versions of the character for gate (門/门) both as stand-alone characters and as radicals.

Perhaps because this form of variation has little effect on meaning, it is the type found most frequently in these texts, accounting for just over a fifth (21.8 percent) of the variants overall across all pairs. But it is important to note that this figure is only an average and does not at all indicate that variant forms are the most frequent type of variation found in any given pair of manuscripts. In some pairs it is, accounting for 38.6 percent of the variants in the pair P3381 and P2700 and for about 31 percent of the variants when P2700 is paired with S5476 and P3381.[3] At the same time, in about one third of the comparisons, this type of variant either is not the

2. In general usage (that is, not in the context of these manuscripts) the more complicated character was often used in official or legal documents, as the character 一 would be much easier to alter into characters indicating other numbers.

3. Note that as these pairs also have some of the lowest overall variant rates to begin with, the dominance of this variant further emphasizes the pairs' similarity.

most frequently encountered or is essentially tied for that position with another category.

An objection might be raised that such variants are insignificant, in the same way that we would give little meaning to the variant spellings of the word "color."[4] However, in a manuscript culture the potential for new variation is considerable, and variant characters that might be considered interchangeable in one set of forms can grow farther apart through subsequent transmissions. In a phenomenon I call "variant drift,"[5] variant forms with the same meaning can easily give rise to later variations that end up with very different meanings. The character 壹 is much more likely to be mistakenly read and written as 荳, meaning "beans" or "peas," than would the form 一.[6] This would be a significant possibility in a context like line 128, which addresses agricultural products. Another example can be found in the variant forms of the character 關, meaning "gate" or "to close," which appears in many forms in the "Qinfu yin" manuscripts. In the fourth character position of line 26 alone we find the following forms: 関, 闲, 閑, and 開. The last of these forms is especially problematic due to its close graphic similarity to the character 開, meaning "open." With the meanings related and the forms so similar, a reader could easily mistake one for the other. The final stage of this particular example of variant drift does not appear in the "Qinfu yin" manuscripts themselves, though it is well attested to elsewhere.[7] Variants, even those that indicate the same meanings, still constitute differences between texts. Moreover, they can and do lead to further variation that gradually increases these differences as a work is repeatedly copied.

2. Graphically and Phonologically Similar

These are variants in which both the appearance and sound of the characters are quite similar. In many cases, these small differences in phonology and orthography result in much larger differences in meaning. Common

4. It is worth noting that such differences are typically counted as meaningful variation by scholars analyzing medieval European manuscripts.

5. See the more detailed discussion under category 11 below.

6. Note, however, that there are no instances of this specific variant in these manuscripts.

7. See Cherniack ("Book Culture," 110), number 1.1.7.1, for examples from other texts.

forms of this variation involve the use of different radicals or the omission of a radical. An example of the latter is found in the fourth character position of line 153, in which manuscripts S5476 and P3780 both have the character 城 (*ʂɦiajŋ*), while the rest of the texts use 成 (*ʂɦiajŋ*). In most texts this line reads 大道俱(成/城)棘子林 ("The main roads had become groves of thorn bushes") and thus 成, meaning "to become," makes more sense in context.[8] Examples with different radicals abound as well. Because the characters 河 and 何 are both pronounced "xɦa" and their respective radicals can be almost identical in many calligraphic styles, they are frequent candidates for confusion. In the first character position of line 224, P3381, P3780, and S5477 use 河 while P2700 and S692 use 何. As the character is part of the compound with 津, meaning "ford," context makes it clear that 河 ("river") is probably correct.

In both these cases one variant is clearly preferable to another and we can attribute the variation to scribal errors at some point in the transmission process. There are many other instances in which the choice is much less obvious or even impossible to make. In the sixth character position of line 26, four manuscripts use the character 警 (*kiajŋ´*) and two use 驚 (*kiajŋ*). Both appear with the character 急 in compounds that have attested Tang uses. In this case the likely meanings, "a dire situation" or "imminent danger," are quite close, though 驚急 has additional psychological implications not contained in 警急. In the line in question, 擬向潼關爲(警/驚)急 ("They readied to head to Tong Pass to deal with the crisis"),[9] both compounds make sense and there is no clear basis for favoring one over the other.

Characters with similar sounds and appearances are obviously strong candidates for scribal confusion (or choice), and it should come as no surprise that this type of variant appears frequently in the "Qinfu yin" texts. Overall they make up 17.4 percent of the variants in the pairs comparisons and are thus the second most frequently encountered category. But again we see a wide range within the various pairings. In the pairs P3953 with P2700 and P3780, this category makes up as much as 31 percent of the variants. With most other pairs the numbers are closer to 15 percent to 20

8. Note that S5477 has 且 rather than 俱 in this line.

9. There are variants in a number of these positions, but this seems to be the most likely reading of the line.

percent. Even though these numbers are lower than those for the variant forms category, unlike the variants in that category, these often substantially change the meaning of the character in question and can thus have a greater effect on possible interpretations of the poem.

3. Graphically Similar, Phonologically Distinct

Characters that are orthographically similar but phonetically quite distinct rank third in frequency and account for 13.1 percent of the variation in these texts.[10] Unlike the first two categories, this one appears with a fair degree of consistency across the different pairs. Save for pairs with P3953, whose statistics can sometimes be skewed by the small size of the sample, this category typically makes up between 11 percent and 15 percent of the variants in each pair.

These variants almost always result in significant differences in meaning. In some cases one can easily identify a particular variant as a copying error. The seventh character position of line 24, in which manuscript P3910 has the character 設 (*ʂiat*) while all the other versions use 誤 (ŋuǝ̆`), is a good example. The compound 疑誤 has attested Tang usages meaning either "to be confused" or "to misunderstand," both of which make sense in this context of an alarm indicating that the rebels are about to attack. The character 設, on the other hand, does not appear in compounds with 疑, and with a primary meaning of "to establish," it would make little sense here.[11]

Other examples of this category bring into question whether one particular variant should be privileged over another. In the fourth character position of line 93, P2700 has the character 里 (*li*) as part of the compound 千里, while the other manuscripts all have the character 重 (*trɦywŋ*`). With the latter variant the full line reads: 夜卧千重劍戟圍 ("At night I slept surrounded by a thousand layers of swords").[12] This reading makes perfect sense in context, and the fact that it appears in all the other manuscripts that contain this line is a strong argument for tak-

10. These are found in Cherniack's ("Book Culture," 109) type 1.1, "Confusions of similar graphic forms."

11. The full line reads: 朝士歸来(上/半/尚)疑(誤/設). I discuss it further below.

12. There are variant characters in the sixth position but they are of the first category, variant forms, and do not affect the meaning of the line.

ing it as the standard version. At the same time, the compound 千里, meaning "a thousand *li*," is far more common in general and would also read smoothly here.[13]

We find more complicated scenarios in other instances from this category. In the seventh character position of line 53, manuscripts P3780, P3910, S692, and S5477 use the character 盡 (*tsɦin`*), meaning "to complete." P3381, P2700, and S5476 instead use the character 畫 (*xɦwa:jk*), meaning "to paint." The full line reads: 東隣有女眉新(畫/盡) ("My neighbors to the east had a daughter, her eyebrows newly painted/complete"). In this case there is little reason to privilege one variant over the other. Both make sense in the context of the poem (though 盡 would require a more forced reading) and both are attested to in multiple manuscripts.

4. Phonologically Similar, Graphically Distinct

These variants are the reverse of the previous category; they sound the same but look very different.[14] Like the third category, these variants typically display widely divergent meanings. In the sixth character position of line 4, for example, two manuscripts have the character 塵 (*trɦin*), while another uses the homophone 陳 (*trɦin*). In the context in which they appear, 塵 is a better fit as part of a common compound, 香塵. With a basic meaning of "fragrant dust," this is both a metaphor for the walk of a beautiful woman and a Buddhist term for one of the "six dusts" of worldly entanglement. 陳, with a meaning of "to array," would make little sense here. Another example in which it is relatively easy to determine the best reading is P2700's use of the character 同 (*tɦəwŋ*) rather than 潼 (*tɦəwŋ*) in the third character position of line 26. As the line is making a clear reference to the famed Tong Pass 潼關, we can confidently consider this an error.[15]

---

13. A similar situation is found in the seventh character position of line 190, in which P3780 has the character 公 (*kəwŋ*) whereas the other manuscripts use 翁 (*ʔəwŋ´*). Both make sense in context, though a stronger argument might be made for 翁 as the standard.

14. See Cherniack's ("Book Culture," 110) type 1.3, "confusions due to similarities in sound."

15. For the sake of contrast, we might consider variants with characters that are graphically similar but phonetically quite distinct. These are often cited as evidence of written transmission, and in some cases the context makes it clear that a given variant is indeed probably a copying error.

For many variants in this category, one alternative appears to fit much better with the sense of the line than another. Yet there do remain a number of cases in which it is much more difficult to make such a determination. In the fourth character position of line 45, manuscripts P3381, P3780, and S5476 have the character 氣 (k^hi\`), here meaning "vapor" or "mist," while P3910, P2700, and S5477 use the homophone 起 ($k^hi$´), meaning "to rise up." In this context, 氣 would serve as part of a compound noun with the character 暈 (*yn*\`) indicating the ring of mist around the moon. As 暈 itself has this meaning of "mist," the character 氣 as part of a compound with it does not affect the sense of the line. The character 起, however, operates as a verb for which 暈 would be the subject. Alternate readings would be something to the effect of, "Dark clouds, the moon's ring of vapor, like surrounding layers" 陰雲暈氣若重圍;[16] or, using the variant 起, "The moon's ring of dark clouds rises up like surrounding layers" 陰雲暈起若重圍.[17] Neither 暈氣 nor 暈起 are common Tang compounds and neither is used more frequently in the extant manuscripts. Thus while these two near-homophonic characters have fundamentally different meanings and graphs, there is little if any ground to privilege one over the other.

Such variants, making up 10.1 percent of the total variants, are less prominent overall than the category of orthographically similar characters with different sounds. However, they are much more frequent in some pairings than others, accounting for 18 perccent of the variants between P3780 and P2700, but only about 2 percent of those between the pair S692 and S5476 and the pair P3910 and S5477. Both this wide range and the differences between this category and the previous one have implications for determining how these texts may have been transmitted, as discussed in Chapter 1.

---

16. *Wei* (圍) need not have military implications, though the context makes it clear that they are intended here. This is especially true of the reading with the variant 起.

17. For the sake of simplicity, I am ignoring other variants in some of these lines (e.g., 園 for 圍, in S5476).

5. Semantic Similarity

These are characters with similar meanings but completely different graphs and pronunciations.[18] These variants are relatively rare, accounting for only 4.5 percent of the variants overall, but are arguably the best examples of change in the course of transmission due to scribal choice rather than simple error.[19] In the third character position of line 163, manuscript P2700 uses the character 賊 (*tsɦəăk*), meaning "bandit" or, often, "rebel," while the rest of the manuscripts use 寇 (k^h*əw*ˋ), which has approximately the same meaning, though is also used to specifically refer to "raiders" from another land. In the sixth character position of line 4, P3780 uses the character 烟 (*ʔjian*), meaning "smoke" or "mist." Manuscripts P3381 and P2700, as noted previously, use the character 塵, meaning "dust."[20] The meanings of these two characters are not identical, but they are unquestionably close. When we examined this character position for the previous category, the compound "fragrant dust" 香塵 helped to identify the variant 陳 as a probable mistake. In this case, however, such a determination is much more difficult to make. To begin with, because of physical damage to manuscript P3780, the character immediately preceding 烟 is missing. Assuming for the sake of argument that it was the character 香, as in the other manuscripts, we are still left with no definitive answer. The compound 香烟, like 香塵, has many well-attested Tang uses and would fit quite well in this line. In both of these cases context is no help in determining the better reading and there is thus nothing to favor one reading over the other.

Interestingly, this type of variant is also found in one of the only two lines of "Qinfu yin" that had been known for hundreds of years prior to the discoveries at Dunhuang due to its preservation in the *Beimeng suoyan*. In the fourth character position of line 145, manuscripts P3381, P3780, P3953, S692, P2700, and S5476 (in addition to the received version of the *Beimeng suoyan*) all have the character 爲 (*yj*), here meaning "to become" or "to be." Manuscripts P3910 and S5477 use the character 成 (*ʂɦiajŋ*),

18. This category is not included in Cherniack's list.

19. The only pair in which they are substantially more common is P3780 and P3381, where they make up 8.4 percent of the total variants between the two texts.

20. As discussed previously, this character position has a third variant, 陳, as well.

which here would mean "to change into" or "to become." Again, the characters bear no graphic or phonological similarity, but are rather near synonyms. With either character the line could be translated as, "The Inner Treasury was burned into the ashes of brocade and embroidery."

A subset of this type is the category of graphically and phonologically distinct characters that belong to the same general category but yet have different meanings. Variants of this sort do change the meanings of the lines in which they appear. Yet they do not typically force grammatical changes in the lines and rarely provide clear evidence that one variant or another is more likely to be correct. In the third character position of line 52, manuscripts P3910 and S5477 both have the character 子 (*tsz̩´*), here meaning "son," while the rest of the manuscripts use 女 (*nriə̆´*), "daughter."[21] The meanings, appearance, and sound of the characters are all different, yet the shared general category of the meanings probably explains the variation. We find a similar situation in the fifth character position of line 214, in which S5477 uses 數 (*ʂwa:wk*), "many," with the other manuscripts all reading 千 (*tsʰian*), "a thousand," as a modifier for 万, meaning "ten thousand." Again, the resulting meaning of the line is slightly changed, but the sense and grammar remain the same.

6. Reversed Characters

Category 6, reversed characters, is straightforward: in a pair of texts, two adjacent characters appear in inverted positions. These variants account for 9.3 percent of the variants overall but are significantly more frequent in pairs involving P3953 or S692.[22] Cherniack argues that in many cases of textual transmission, characters are reversed intentionally to "improve the sense."[23] This does not often prove to be the case in the "Qinfu yin" manuscripts. In fact, these variants provide a rare opportunity to be con-

---

21. Note that this is one of the many instances in which S5477 and P3910 share a variant that does not appear in the other manuscripts. As noted above, at least a portion of S5477 appears to have been copied by the same copyist responsible for P3910. However, the strong probability that S5477 was written by multiple hands complicates matters. My conjecture is that even though S5477 is the work of a number of copyists, they were probably working from the same source. This may well be true of P3910 as well.

22. These two texts do not share the same set of reversals in most cases.

23. Cherniack ("Book Culture," 119) has classified this as type 4.2.

fident in assessing whether a variant is simply another version of the text or difference that would be considered an error by the copyist himself or a later reader. In over a third of these instances, caret-like marks appear next to characters that have been reversed from the order found in the other manuscripts.[24] In the second and third character positions of line 36, for example, manuscript S5477 has the characters 向走, while the other four manuscripts in which this line survives all read 走向. Next to these characters in S5477 a caret mark is written. It is unclear, however, whether the mark was put in by the copyist himself or by someone else. In either case, as noted previously, this is strong evidence that these texts were read over after being copied.

In almost every case, even when not corrected, these reversals do not seriously alter the meaning of the lines in which they appear. In the second of the lines of the poem found in the *Beimeng suoyan*, line 146, the reversal of the characters 盡踏 in the third and fourth character positions in S5477 and P3910 makes little difference in the meaning of the line, "On the Streets of Heaven everywhere we stepped were the bones of officials." And although these reversals sometimes change the meanings of lines if one holds to strictly grammatical readings, in many cases the result is a change in emphasis rather than larger meaning. Line 61 of manuscript S692 reads 西隣女有眞仙子, while the same line in all the other manuscripts reads 西隣有女眞仙子. The difference between "The neighbors to the west have a daughter, a true goddess" and "Among the daughters of the neighbor to the west, there is a true goddess," is not great.

7. Extra Characters

These variants, in which one line in one manuscript contains extra characters (beyond the seven that should be contained in each line of the poem), account for 8.6 percent of the variants overall. In some instances, extra characters are simply rewritten versions of a mistaken character that the copyist did not bother to cross out. In line 59 of manuscript S5477, the character 郎 (*laŋ*) appears as an extra character directly before the graphically and phonetically similar character 良 (*liaŋ*). The copyist probably realized his error and simply wrote the correct character in without crossing

24. Note that I still include these "corrected" examples in the 9.3 percent figure above.

out the incorrect one.[25] Other additions appear to be due to line skips by the scribe. At the beginning of line 66 in S5477 the copyist has begun the line with the characters 出朱門 (the last of which is an aborted attempt at the full character 門), which appear out of place here. These same three characters are found at the end of the next line, line 67, indicating that the copyist skipped ahead but realized his error in mid-character.

Some additions, however, are not clearly errors and can have a significant impact on the meaning of a line. In both line 143 of S5477 and line 172 of P2700, extra negative particles (不) clearly give the lines new readings. An interesting example of additional characters that appear to have been inserted intentionally is found in line 196. Here all the manuscripts but one end the line with the phrase 仰天哭 ("he looked up to the Heavens and wept"). Manuscript P3780, on the other hand, lengthens this phrase to the more detailed and emotive 仰天掩面哭一聲 ("he looked up to the Heavens, hid his face in his hands, and gave a single cry"). Though this violates the seven-character line in which the rest of the poem is written, it would be wrong to characterize it as a mistake rather than an embellishment. By the Tang there was already a long-standing poetic tradition of expanding and contracting lines to fit into different meters, often by adding or subtracting particles or other words less crucial for the meaning of the line. In this case, however, the added words are not filler but are likely intended to give further emotional weight to the scene the line describes.[26]

8. Missing Characters

Missing characters, in which a line in one of the texts has fewer than seven characters when others do not, make up 11.3 percent of the variants overall.[27] Many missing characters are also easily attributable to simple copy-

25. See line 78 of manuscript S5476 for two examples of this type of extra character variant in a single line.

26. The power of this emotion was not lost on at least one translator of the poem. Though P3780 is the only manuscript with these extra characters, Dore Levy's translation apparently uses this version in her rendering of the phrase as "...hiding his face in his hands and wept aloud to Heaven." See Levy, *Chinese Narrative Poetry*, 147.

27. Note that the category of missing characters does not include characters missing due to textual damage and also does not include the last third of the poem that seems to have been intentionally omitted from P3910.

ing errors such as line skips at some point in the transmission process. Line 132 of manuscript P3910 is a good example. In the other seven manuscripts this line reads 溝壑漸平人漸少 ("Ditches and gullies gradually filled [with bodies] while the people grew few"); in P3910 it reads, 溝壑漸少 ("Ditches and gullies grew few"). By consulting multiple texts we can clearly see that the copyist must have skipped from one 漸 to the other in the same line. To a reader who had only this one text (and it make sense to assume that most readers *would* only have one text), the line would be confusing indeed.

9. Commentarial Characters

With this type of variant what appear to have originally been commentarial characters have become part of the text proper—a relatively frequent occurrence in printed editions of philosophical and historical texts.[28] In these texts, however, it appears only once. In manuscripts P3780 and P2700, the characters 眇音 (*mjiaw´ ʔim*) are written horizontally in small script after the character 殍 (*pĥiaw´*), apparently as an explanation of the latter's correct pronunciation. In P3910, however, the character 殍 itself is omitted while the characters 眇音 appear as vertically written, regularly sized parts of the text proper. They make no sense in context and can rightly be deemed an error. The nature of this particular work of literature and the context of its reproduction—a popular poem being copied on a distant frontier no longer part of the Tang empire—make it unsurprising that there was little commentary or annotation, beyond this one instance, that might be accidentally incorporated into the main text.

10. Split Characters

Commentarial characters working their way into the text proper is surely a result of written, rather than oral, transmission, as are split characters, in which a scribe has at some point mistakenly written the radical and the phonetic components of a single character as two separate characters.[29] This type of variant is also quite rare, making up less than 1 percent of the total variants. Not surprisingly given the overall quality of its copying,

28. See Cherniack's ("Book Culture," 120) type 5.2.
29. See Cherniack's ("Book Culture," 112) type 1.7.

most instances of this type of variation are in the manuscript S5477, though it appears in P3780 as well. In line 187, what appears as the character 擕 in other texts is clearly written as 推乃 in S5477. Likewise, in line 193, S5477 has two characters 公羽 where P3381, S692, and P2700 have the single character 翁.[30] In both these cases the characters resulting from the split make little sense in context.

11. Variant Drift

This final category of variants, making up 2.9 percent of the variants overall, is perhaps the most difficult to explain. These are characters that seem to have little or no clear connection with each other in terms of graphic form, phonology, or meaning. They are not easily explainable by line skips, character reversals, or any of the other categories explored above. For example, in the fourth character position of line 107, manuscript S5477 and P3910 have the character 事 (*ʂɦṛ*`) while the other manuscripts all use 對 (*tuaj*`). Both variants make sense in context but there is little to connect them. Another example is found in the third character position of line 114. This section of the poem describes a rumor that the imperial forces have retaken the city of Chishui 赤水, about thirty miles from the capital. In most manuscripts the line reads: 朝若来兮暮應至 ("If they set out for here at dawn, they will arrive here by dusk!"). P2700, on the other hand, has the phonetically and orthographically unrelated character 見 (*kjian*`) in the place of 来 (*laj*). Other than both being verbs, there is little to connect them. Moreover, 来 would have as its subject the troops themselves, which would have to be taken as the object of 見. Again, both work in context but there is no clear reason for the variation. For further explanation of this category see my discussion in Chapter 1.

30. Manuscript P3780 uses the character 公 in the second character position. As it does not follow this with 羽, I have not put this variant in the present category. Determining that 翁 has been broken up at this point in S5477 is, of course, a judgment call. Based on the spacing between characters and comparisons with other instances of 翁 in this same text, I am confident that a reader (and later copyist) would likely read this 公 and 羽 as separate characters in this case.

Reference Matter

Works Cited

Akehurst, F. R. P., and Judith M. Davis, eds. *A Handbook of the Troubadours*. Berkeley: University of California Press, 1995.

Allen, Joseph R. *In the Voice of Others: Chinese Music Bureau Poetry*. Ann Arbor: Center for Chinese Studies, University of Michigan, 1992.

Allen, Sarah M. "Tales Retold: Narrative Variation in a Tang Story." *Harvard Journal of Asiatic Studies* 66.1 (June 2006): 105–43.

———. "Tang Stories: Tales and Texts." PhD dissertation, Harvard University, 2003.

Ashmore, Robert. "Hearing Things: Performance and Lyric Imagination in Chinese Literature of the Early Ninth Century." PhD dissertation, Harvard University, 1997.

Baddeley, Alan D. *Essentials of Human Memory*. Hove, UK: The Psychology Press Ltd, 1998.

———. *Human Memory: Theory and Practice*. Boston: Allyn and Bacon, 1990.

———. "Short-Term and Working Memory." In Endel Tulving and Fergus I. M. Craik, *The Oxford Handbook of Memory*. Oxford: Oxford University Press, 2000.

Bahrick, Harry P. "Long-Term Maintenance of Knowledge." In Endel Tulving and Fergus I. M. Craik, *The Oxford Handbook of Memory*. Oxford: Oxford University Press, 2000.

Bei Qi shu 北齊書. Comp. Li Delin 李德林. Beijing: Zhonghua shuju, 1972.

Bibliothèque nationale de France. *Manuscrits de Dunhuang et d'Asie Centrale Conservés à la Bibliothèque Nationale de France.* Shanghai: Shanghai guji chubanshe, 2001–.

Bloom, Jonathan M. *Paper Before Print: The History and Impact of Paper in the Islamic World.* New Haven: Yale University Press, 2001.

Bodman, Richard. "Poetics and Prosody in Early Mediaeval China: A Study and Translation of Kūkai's *Bunkyō hifuron.*" Ph.D dissertation, Cornell University, 1978.

Bol, Peter K. *"This Culture of Ours": Intellectual Transitions in T'ang and Sung China.* Stanford: Stanford University Press, 1992.

Boltz, William G. "Language and Writing." In Michael Loewe and Edward L. Shaughnessy, eds., *The Cambridge History of Ancient China: From the Origins of Civilization to 221 B.C.,* 74–123. Cambridge: Cambridge University Press, 1999.

———. "The Study of Early Chinese Manuscripts: Methodological Preliminaries." In Sarah Allan and Crispin Williams, eds., *The Guodian* Laozi, *Proceedings of the International Conference, Dartmouth College, May 1998,* 39–51. Berkeley: Society for the Study of Early China and the Institute of East Asian Studies, University of California Berkeley, 2000.

Brashier, K. E. "Text and Ritual in Early Chinese Stelae." In Martin Kern, ed., *Text and Ritual in Early China,* 249–84. Seattle: University of Washington Press, 2005.

Brown, Scott C., and Fergus I. M. Craik. "Encoding and Retrieval of Information." In Endel Tulving and Fergus I. M. Craik, *The Oxford Handbook of Memory,* 93–107. Oxford: Oxford University Press, 2000.

Brownlee, Marina S., et al. *The New Medievalism.* Baltimore: The Johns Hopkins University Press, 1991.

Bruns, Gerald L. "The Originality of Texts in a Manuscript Culture." *Comparative Literature* 32.2 (1980): 113–29.

Bryan, Elizabeth J. *Collaborative Meaning in Medieval Scribal Culture: The Otho Laȝamon.* Ann Arbor: University of Michigan Press, 1999.

Bryant, Daniel Joseph. "The High T'ang Poet Meng Hao-jan: Studies in Biography and Textual History." PhD dissertation, University of British Columbia, 1977.

Carruthers, Mary. *The Book of Memory: A Study of Memory in Medieval Culture*. Cambridge: Cambridge University Press, 1990.

Carruthers, Mary, and Jan M. Ziolkowski, eds. *The Medieval Craft of Memory: An Anthology of Texts and Pictures*. Philadelphia: University of Pennsylvania Press, 2002.

Cerquiglini, Bernard. *In Praise of the Variant*. Trans. Betsy Wing. Baltimore: The Johns Hopkins University Press, 1999.

Chafee, John W. *The Thorny Gates of Learning in Sung China*. Albany: State University of New York Press, 1995.

Chan, Chiu Ming. "Between the World and the Self—Orientations of Pai Chü-i's (772–846) Life and Writings." PhD dissertation, Madison: University of Wisconsin, 1991.

Chan, Marie. *Cen Shen*. Boston: Twayne Publishers, 1983.

Chan, Marie. *Kao Shih*. Boston: Twayne Publishers, 1978.

Chan, Timothy Wai Keung. "Restoration of a Poetry Anthology by Wang Bo." *Journal of the American Oriental Society* 124 (2004): 493–515.

Chen Shangjun 陳尚君. *Tangdai wenxue congkao* 唐代文學叢考. Beijing: Zhongguo shehui kexue chubanshe, 1997.

Chen Yinke 陳寅恪. *Chen Yinke xiansheng wenshi lunji* 陳寅恪先生文史論集. Hong Kong: Wenwen chubanshe, 1972.

———. "Du 'Qinfu yin'" 讀秦婦吟. *Qinghua xuebao* 清華學報 11.4: 951–68.

Cheng Qianfan 程千帆. *Tangdai jinshi xingjuan yu wenxue* 唐代進士行卷與文學. Shanghai: Shanghai guji chubanshe, 1980.

Cheng Qianfan 程千帆 and Xu Youfu 徐有富. *Jiaochu guangyi* 校儲廣義. Nanjing: Qi Lu shushe, 1991.

Cherniack, Susan. "Book Culture and Textual Transmission in Sung China." *Harvard Journal of Asiatic Studies* 54.1 (June 1994): 5–125.

Chia, Lucille. *Printing for Profit: The Commercial Publishers of Jianyang, Fujian (11th–17th Centuries)*. Cambridge: Harvard University Asia Center, 2002.

Chou, Shan. "Literary Reputations in Context." *T'ang Studies* 10–11 (1992–93): 41–66.

Coleman, Janet. *Ancient and Medieval Memories: Studies in the Reconstruction of the Past.* Cambridge: Cambridge University Press, 1992.

Craik, Fergus I. M., and Endel Tulving. "Depth of Processing and the Retention of Words in Episodic Memory." *Journal of Experimental Psychology: General* 104 (1975): 268–94.

Cui Lingqin 崔令欽. *Jiaofang ji* 教坊記. In Ding Ruming 丁如明, et al., *Tang Wudai biji xiaoshuo daguan* 唐五代筆記小説大觀. Shanghai: Shanghai guji, 2000.

Dagenais, John. *The Ethics of Reading in Manuscript Culture.* Princeton: Princeton University Press, 1994.

DeWoskin, Kenneth. "Lei-shu." In Nienhauser, William H. Jr., ed. and comp., *The Indiana Companion to Traditional Literature*, vol. 1. Taibei: SMC Publishing, Inc., 1986.

Diringer, David. *The Book Before Printing, Ancient Medieval, and Oriental.* New York: Dover Publications, 1982.

Downer, G. B., and A. C. Graham. "Tone Patterns in Chinese Poetry." *Bulletin of the School of Oriental and African Studies, University of London* 26.1 (1963): 145–48.

Drège, Jean-Pierre. *Les Bibliothèques en Chine au Temps des Manuscrits.* Paris: École Française d'Extrême-Orient, 1991.

Dreyfus, George B. J. *The Sound of Two Hands Clapping: The Education of a Tibetan Buddhist Monk.* Berkeley: University of California Press, 2003.

Du Mu 杜牧. *Fanchuan wenji* 樊川文集. Shanghai: Shanghai guji, 1978.

Duan Chengwu 段成武. *Youyang zazu* 酉陽雜俎. Beijing: Zhonghua shuju, 1981.

Ebrey, Patricia Buckley. *The Aristocratic Families of Early Imperial China: A Case Study of the Po-ling Ts'ui Family.* Cambridge: Cambridge University Press, 1978.

Egan, Charles H. "Were *Yüeh-fu* Ever Folk Songs? Reconsidering the Relevance of Oral Theory and Balladry Analogies." *Chinese Literature: Essays, Articles, and Reviews* 22 (2000): 31–66.

Fan Shu 范攄. *Yunxi youyi* 雲谿友議. In Yang Jialuo 楊家駱, ed., *Tang guoshibu deng bazhong* 唐國史補等八種. Taibei: Shijie shuju yinhang, 1978.

Fan Zhilin 范之麟. "Tangdai shige de liuchuan (shang)" 唐代詩歌的流傳（上）. *Tangdai wenxue* 唐代文學 5 (April 1984) (part I).

———. "Tangdai shige de liuchuan (xia)" 唐代詩歌的流傳（下）. *Tangdai wenxue* 唐代文學 6 (August 1985) (part II).

Feifel, Eugene, ed. and trans. *Po Chü-i as a Censor: His Memorials Presented to the Emperor Hsien-tsung During the Years 808–810.* The Hague: Mouton & Co., 1961.

Feng Jiwu 馮集梧, ed., *Fanchuan shiji zhu* 樊川詩集注. Shanghai: Shanghai guji, 1980.

Finke, Laurie A., and Martin B. Shichtman, eds. *Medieval Texts and Contemporary Readers*. Ithaca: Cornell University Press, 1987.

Finnegan, Ruth. *Oral Poetry: Its Nature, Significance, and Social Context*. Bloomington: Indiana University Press, 1992.

Fish, Michael B. "The Tu Mu and Li Shang-yin Prefaces to the Collected Poems of Li Ho." In Ronald C. Miao, ed., *Studies in Chinese Poetry and Poetics, Volume I*. San Francisco: Chinese Materials Center, 1978: 231–86.

Frankel, Hans H. "Cai Yan and the Poems Attributed to Her." *Chinese Literature: Essays, Articles, and Reviews* 5.1/2 (July 1983): 133–56.

Fu Xuanzong 傅璇琮. *Tangdai keju yu wenxue* 唐代科舉與文學. Shaanxi: Shaanxi renmin chubanshe, 1986.

———, ed. *Tang caizi zhuan jiaojian* 唐才子傳校箋. Beijing: Zhonghua shuju, 1987.

Fujieda Akira 藤枝晃. "The Tunhuang Manuscripts: A General Description," parts 1 and 2. *Zinbun, Memoirs of the Research Institute for Humanistic Studies* 9 (1966): 1–32, and 10 (1969): 17–39.

Gao Guofan 高國藩. *Dunhuang suwenhua xue* 敦煌俗文化學. Shanghai: Shanghai sanlian shudian, 1999.

Gao Song 高嵩. *Dunhuang Tangren shiji canjuan kaoshi* 敦煌唐人詩集殘卷考釋. Yinchuan: Ningxia renmin chubanshe, 1982.

Ge Xiaoyin 葛曉音. "Lun Chu Sheng Tang wenren de ganye fangshi" 論初盛唐文人的干謁方式. *Tang yanjiu* 唐研究 1 (1995): 119–38.

Gellrich, Jesse M. *Discourse and Dominion in the Fourteenth Century: Oral Contexts of Writing in Philosophy, Politics, and Poetry*. Princeton: Princeton University Press, 1995.

Giles, Lionel. "The Lament of the Lady of Ch'in." *T'oung Pao* 24.4 (1926): 305–80.

Goh, Meow Hui. "Wang Rong's (467–493) Poetics in the Light of the Invention of Tonal Prosody." PhD dissertation, University of Wisconsin-Madison, 2004.

Goody, Jack. *The Interface Between the Written and the Oral*. Cambridge: Cambridge University Press, 1987.

Guan Xihua 管錫華. *Hanyu guji jiaokan xue* 漢語古籍校勘學. Chengdu: Bashu shushe, 2003.

Han shu 漢書. Comp. Chen Zhi 陳直. Beijing: Zhonghua shuju, 1962.

Hanabusa Hideki 花房英樹. *Hakushi monjū no hihan deki kenkyū* 白氏文集の批判的研究. Kyoto: Ibundō, 1961.

Hartman, Charles. *Han Yü and the T'ang Search for Unity*. Princeton: Princeton University Press, 1986.

———. "Literary Chinese." In William H. Nienhauser, Jr., ed. and comp., *The Indiana Companion to Traditional Literature*, vol. 1. Taibei: SMC Publishing, Inc., 1986.

Hawkes, David, trans. *The Songs of the South*. Middlesex, Eng.: Penguin, 1985.

Herbert, P. A. "Curriculum and Content of Doctoral Examinations in Tang China." *Studies in Language and Culture* 13 (1987): 149–63.

———. "Decree Examinations in T'ang China." *T'ang Studies* 10–11 (1992–93): 1–40.

———. *Examine the Honest, Appraise the Able: Contemporary Assessments of Civil Service Selection in Early Tang China*. Canberra: Faculty of Asian Studies, Australian National University, 1988.

Higbee, Kenneth L. *Your Memory: How It Works and How to Improve It*. New York: Marlow and Company, 1996.

Hightower, James Robert. "Han Yü as Humorist." *Harvard Journal of Asiatic Studies* 44.1 (1984): 5–27.

———. "Some Characteristics of Parallel Prose." In John L. Bishop, ed., *Studies in Chinese Literature*. Cambridge: Harvard University Press, 1966.

Hou Han shu 後漢書. Comp. Fan Ye 范曄. Beijing: Zhonghua shuju, 1965.

Housman, A. E. *Selected Prose*. Cambridge: Cambridge University Press, 1961.

Hsieh, Daniel. *The Evolution of Jueju Verse*. New York: Peter Lang, 1996.

Hsiung Ping-chen. "Erh-t'ung wen-hsüeh." In William H. Nienhauser, Jr., ed. and comp., *The Indiana Companion to Traditional Literature*, vol. 2, 31–37. Taibei: SMC Publishing, Inc., 1998.

Hu Daojing 胡道靜. *Zhongguo gudai de leishu* 中國古代的類書. Beijing: Zhonghua shuju, 1982.

Huang Yongwu. *Dunhuang de Tangshi* 敦煌的唐詩. Taibei: Gongfan shudian youxian gongsi, 1987.

———. *Dunhuang de Tangshi xubian* 敦煌的唐詩續編. Taibei: Wenshizhe chubanshe, 1989.

Huang Zhengwei 黄鎮偉, ed. *Fang keben* 坊刻本. Part of series: Zhongguo banben wenhua congshu 中國版本文化叢書. Nanjing: Jiangsu guji chubanshe, 2002.

Hucker, Charles O. *A Dictionary of Official Titles in Imperial China*. Stanford: Stanford University Press, 1985.

Hult, David F. "Reading it Right: The Ideology of Text Editing." In Marina S. Brownlee et al., *The New Medievalism*, 113–130. Baltimore: The Johns Hopkins University Press, 1991.

Hung, William. *Tu Fu: China's Greatest Poet*. Cambridge: Harvard University Press, 1952.

———. *A supplementary volume of notes for* Tu Fu: China's Greatest Poet. Cambridge: Harvard University Press, 1952.

Huot, Sylvia. *From Song to Book: The Poetics of Writing in Old French Lyric and Lyrical Narrative Poetry*. Ithaca, NY: Cornell University Press, 1987.

Hwa, Lily. "Yuan Chen (A.D. 779–831): The Poet-Statesman, His Political and Literary Career." PhD dissertation, University of Illinois at Urbana-Champaign, 1984.

Hymes, Robert. "Getting the Words Right: Speech, Vernacular Language, and Classical Language in Song Neo-Confucian 'Records of Words.'" *Journal of Song-Yuan Studies* 36 (2006): 25–55.

Ikeda On 池田溫. *Tonkô kanbun bunken* 敦煌漢文文獻. *Kôzo Tonkô*, 5 Daitô, 1992.

Ji Xianlin 季羨林, ed. *Dunhuangxue da cidian* 敦煌學大辭典. Shanghai: Shanghai cishu, 1998.

Ji Yougong 計有功. *Tangshi jishi* 唐詩紀事. Beijing: Zhonghua shuju, 1965.

Jiang Tianshu 蔣天樞. *Chuci jiaoshi* 楚辭校釋. Shanghai: Shanghai guji, 1989.

Jin Ronghua 金榮華, ed. *Wang Ji shiwenji jiaozhu* 王績詩文集校注. Taibei: Xinwenfeng chubangongsi yinhang, 1998.

Jin shu 晉書. Comp. Fang Xuanling 房玄齡. Beijing: Zhonghua shuju, 1974.

Kao, Yu-kung. "The Aesthetics of Regulated Verse." In Shuen-fu Lin and Stephen Owen, *The Vitality of the Lyric Voice:* Shih *Poetry from the Late Han to the T'ang*, 332–85. Princeton: Princeton University Press, 1986.

Kern, Martin. "Methodological Reflections on the Analysis of Textual Variants and the Modes of Manuscript Production in Early China." *Journal of East Asian Archaeology* 4 (2002): 143–81.

———. *Text and Ritual in Early China*. Seattle: University of Washington Press, 2005.

Kern, Martin, and Robert E. Hegel. "A History of Chinese Literature?" Review of *The Columbia History of Chinese Literature,* by Victor H. Mair. *Chinese Literature: Essays, Articles, and Reviews*, 26 (2004).

Kieschnick, John. *The Eminent Monk: Buddhist Ideals in Medieval Chinese Hagiography*. Honolulu: University of Hawai'i Press, 1997.

———. *The Impact of Buddhism on Chinese Material Culture*. Princeton: Princeton University Press, 2003.

Kinney, Anne Behnke. *Representations of Childhood and Youth in Early China*. Stanford: Stanford University Press, 2004.

Klöpsch Volker. "Lo Pin-wang's Survival: Traces of a Legend." *T'ang Studies* 6 (1988): 77–97.

Knechtges, David. "Questions About the Languages of *Sheng Min*." In Pauline Yu, et al., *Ways with Words: Writing about Reading Texts from Early China*, 14–24. Berkeley: University of California Press, 2000.

———, trans., and Xiao Tong 蕭統, comp. Wen xuan, *or Selections of Refined Literature, vol. 1: Rhapsodies on Metropolises and Capitals*. Princeton: Princeton University Press, 1982.

Kroll, Paul W. *Meng Hao-jan*. Boston: Twayne Publishers, 1981.

———. "The True Dates of the Reigns and Reign-Periods of T'ang." *T'ang Studies* 2 (1984): 25–30.

———. "Wang Shih-yüan's Preface to the Poems of Meng Hao-jan" *Monumenta Serica Journal of Oriental Studies* 34 (1979–80): 349–69.

Landauer, T. K, and R. A. Bjork. "Optimal Rehearsal Patterns and Name Learning." In M. M. Gruneberg, P. E. Morris, and R. N. Sykes, eds., *Practical Aspects of Memory*. London: Academic Press, 1978.

Levy, Dore J. *Chinese Narrative Poetry: The Late Han through T'ang Dynasties*. Durham: Duke University Press, 1988.

Levy, Howard S., trans. "The Original Incidents of Poems." *Sinologica* 10 (1968): 1–54.

Lewis, Mark Edward. *Writing and Authority in Early China*. Albany: University of New York Press, 2007.

Li Bincheng 李斌城, et al. *Sui Tang Wudai shehui shenghuo shi* 隋唐五代社會生活史. Beijing: Zhongguo shehui kexue chubanshe, 1998.

———. *Tangdai wenhua* 唐代文化. Beijing: Zhongguo shehui kexue chubanshe, 2002.

Li Fuyan 李復言. *Xu Xuanguai lu* 續玄怪錄. Taibei: Wenshizhe chubanshe, 1989.

Li Han 李翰. *Mengqiu zhushi* 蒙求注釋. Ed. Yan Weicai 顏維材. Taiyuan: Shanxi renmin chubanshe, 1987.

Li Jianguo 李劍國. *Tang Wudai zhiguai chuanqi xulu* 唐五代志怪傳奇敘錄. Tianjin: Nankai Daxue chubanshe, 1998.

Li Ruiliang 李瑞良. *Zhongguo gudai tushu liutong shi* 中國古代圖書流通史. Shanghai: Shanghai renmin chubanshe, 2000.

Li Shiren 李時人, ed. *Quan Tang Wudai xiaoshuo* 全唐五代小說. Xi'an: Shaanxi renmin chubanshe, 1998.

Li Zhao 李肇. *Xinjiao Tang guoshi bu* 新校唐國史補. In Yang Jialuo 楊家駱, ed., *Tang guoshibu deng bazhong* 唐國史補等八種. Taibei: Shijie shuju yinhang, 1978.

Liang shu 梁書. Comp. Yao Cha 姚察 and Yao Silian 姚思廉. Beijing: Zhonghua shuju, 1973.

Lin, Shuen-fu. "The Nature of the Quatrain from the Late Han to the High T'ang." In Shuen-fu Lin and Stephen Owen, eds., *The Vitality of the Lyric Voice:* Shih *Poetry from the Late Han to the T'ang*, 296–331. Princeton: Princeton University Press, 1986.

Liu Kaiyang 劉開揚, ed. *Gao Shi shiji biannian jianzhu* 高適詩集編年箋註. Beijing: Zhonghua shuju, 1981.

Liu Su 劉肅. *Da Tang xinyu* 大唐新語. Beijing: Zhonghua shuju, 1984.

Liu Su 劉餗. *Sui Tang jiahua* 隋唐嘉話. In *Sui Tang jiahua, Chaoye qianzai* 隋唐嘉話、朝野僉載. Beijing: Zhonghua shuju, 1997.

Liu Xie 劉勰. *Wenxin diaolong zhu* 文心雕龍註. Hong Kong: Shangwu yinshuguan, 1960.

Liu Xu 劉昫. *Jiu Tang shu* 舊唐書. Beijing: Zhonghua shuju, 1975.

Liu Yeqiu 劉葉秋. *Leishu jianshuo* 類書簡說. Shanghai: Shanghai guji, 1980.

Liu Yuxi 劉禹錫. *Liu Yuxi ji* 劉禹錫集. Beijing: Zhonghua shuju, 2000.

Liu Zongyuan 柳宗元. *Liu Zongyuan ji* 柳宗元集. Beijing: Zhonghua shuju, 2000.

Loewe, Michael, ed. *Early Chinese Texts: A Bibliographic Guide*. Berkeley: The Society of the Study of Early China and the Institute of East Asian Studies, 1993.

Lord, Albert B. *The Singer of Tales*. Cambridge: Harvard University Press, 2000.

Lu Ji 陸機. *Wenfu ji shi* 文賦集釋. Ed. Zhang Shaokang 張少康. Beijing: Renmin wenxue chubanshe, 2002.

Luo Binwang 駱賓王. *Luo Cheng ji* 駱丞集. Shanghai: Shangwu yinshu guan, 1937.

Luo Zhufeng 羅竹風, et al. *Hanyu da cidian* 漢語大詞典. Shanghai: Hanyu da cidian chubanshe, 1995.

Luo Zongtao 羅宗濤. "Tangren tibishi chutan" 唐人題壁詩初探. *Zhonghua wenshi luncong* 中華文史論叢 17 (1991): 153–85.

Luria, Aleksandr R. *The Mind of a Mnemonist: A Little Book about a Vast Memory*. Trans. Lynn Solotaroff. Cambridge: Harvard University Press, 2006.

Ma Qichang 馬其昶, ed. *Han Changli wenji jiaozhu* 韓昌黎文集校注. Shanghai: Shanghai guji, 1987.

Maas, Paul. *Textual Criticism*. Trans. Barbara Flower. Oxford: Clarendon Press, 1958.

Mair, Victor H. "Anthologizing and Anthropologizing: The Place of Non-elite and Nonstandard Culture in the Chinese Literary Tradition." In Eugene Eoyang and Lin Yao-fu, *Translating Chinese Literature*, 231–61. Bloomington: Indiana University Press, 1995.

———. "Scroll Presentation in the T'ang Dynasty." *Harvard Journal of Asiatic Studies* 38.1 (June 1978): 35–60.

———. *T'ang Transformation Texts: A Study of the Buddhist Contributions to the Rise of Vernacular Fiction and Drama in China*. Cambridge: Council on East Asian Studies, Harvard University, 1988.

Mair, Victor H., and Mei Tsu-lin. "The Sanskrit Origins of Recent Style Prosody." *Harvard Journal of Asiatic Studies* 51 (1991): 375–470.

Mather, Richard B. *The Poet Shen Yüeh (441–513): The Reticent Marquis*. Princeton: Princeton University Press, 1988.

McGillivray, Murray. *Memorization in the Transmission of the Middle English Romances*. New York: Garland Publishing, Inc., 1990.

McMullen, David. *State and Scholars in T'ang China*. Cambridge: Cambridge University Press, 1988.

McRae, John R. *Seeing through Zen: Encounter, Transformation, and Genealogy in Chinese Chan Buddhism*. Berkeley: University of California Press, 2003.

Meng Haoran 孟浩然. *Meng Haoran shiji jianzhu* 孟浩然詩集箋注. Shanghai: Shanghai guji chubanshe, 2000.

Meng Qi 孟棨. *Benshi shi* 本事詩. In Wang Meng'ou 王夢鷗, ed., *Tangren xiaoshuo yanjiu sanji* 唐人小說研究三集. Taibei: Yiwen yinshuguan, 1974.

Miller, George A. "The Magic Number Seven, Plus or Minus Two: Some Limits on Our Capacity for Processing Information." *Psychological Review* 63 (1956): 81–97.

Mollier, Christine. *Buddhism and Taoism Face to Face*. Honolulu: University of Hawai'i Press, 2008.

Moore, Oliver. *Rituals of Recruitment in Tang China: Reading an Annual Programme in the Collected Statements by Wang Dingbao (870–940)*. Leiden: Brill, 2004.

Morino Shigeo 森野繁夫. Rikuchō shi no kenkyū: *"shūdan no bungaku" to "kojin no bungaku."* 六朝詩の研究：「集団の文学」と「個人の文学」. Tokyo: Daiichi gakushūsha, 1976.

Mote, Frederick W., Hung-lan Chu, and Howard L. Goodman, eds. *Calligraphy and the East Asian Book*. Boston: Shambhala, 1989.

Nan Qi shu 南齊書. Comp. Xiao Zixian 蕭子顯. Beijing: Zhonghua shuju, 1972.

Nichols, Stephen G., and Siegfried Wenzel, eds. *The Whole Book: Cultural Perspectives on the Medieval Miscellany*. Ann Arbor: The University of Michigan Press, 1996.

Nie Anfu 聶安福, ed. *Wei Zhuang ji jianzhu* 韋莊集箋注. Shanghai: Shanghai guji, 2002.

Nienhauser, William H. Jr., ed. and comp. *The Indiana Companion to Traditional Literature*, Vols. 1 and 2. Taibei: SMC Publishing, Inc., 1986 (1), 1998 (2).

———. *P'i Jih-hsiu*. Boston: Twayne Publishers, 1979.

O'Keeffe, Katherine O'Brien. *Visible Song: Transitional Literacy in Old English Verse*. Cambridge: Cambridge University Press, 1990.

Ong, Walter J. "Oral Residue in Tudor Prose Style," *Publications of the Modern Language Association of America* 80 (1965): 145–54.

———. *Orality and Literacy: The Technologizing of the Word*. New York: Routledge, 2002.

———. "Orality, Literacy, and Medieval Textualization." *New Literary History* 16 (1984): 1–12.

Ouyang Xiu 歐陽修. *Ouyang Xiu quanji* 歐陽修全集. Beijing: Zhonghua shuju, 1986.

Owen, Stephen. "Butterflies Dangling in a Spider's Web: the Literary World of the 830s." Paper delivered at "New Perspectives on the Tang: An International Conference," Princeton University, April 18–20, 2002.

———. *The End of the Chinese 'Middle Ages': Essays in Mid-Tang Literary Culture.* Stanford: Stanford University Press, 1996.

———. *The Great Age of Chinese Poetry: The High T'ang.* New Haven: Yale University Press, 1981.

———. *The Late Tang: Chinese Poetry of the Mid-Ninth Century (827–860).* Cambridge: Harvard University Asia Center, 2006.

———. "The Manuscript Legacy of the Tang: The Case of Literature," *Harvard Journal of Asiatic Studies* 67.2 (2007): 295–326.

———. *Mi-Lou: Poetry and the Labyrinth of Desire.* Cambridge: Harvard University Press, 1989.

———. "Poetry and Its Historical Ground." *Chinese Literature: Essays, Articles, and Reviews* 12 (1990): 107–18.

———. *The Poetry of the Early T'ang.* New Haven: Yale University Press, 1977. Cambridge: Cambridge University Press, 1986.

———. *Readings in Chinese Literary Thought.* Cambridge: Harvard University Press, 1992.

———. "Spending Time on Poetry: The Poetics of Taking Pains." In Olga Lomová, ed., *Recarving the Dragon: Understanding Chinese Poetics,* 157–78. Prague: The Karolinum Press, 2003.

———. "A Tang Version of Du Fu: The *Tangshi leixuan* 唐詩類選." *T'ang Studies* 25 (2007): 57–90.

———. *Traditional Chinese Poetry and Poetics: Omen of the World.* Madison: University of Wisconsin Press, 1985.

———. "What Did Liuzhi Hear? The 'Yan Terrace Poems' and the Culture of Romance." *T'ang Studies* 13 (1995): 81–118.

Paden, William D. "Manuscripts." In F. R. P. Akehurst and Judith M. Davis, eds., *A Handbook of the Troubadours,* 307–33. Berkeley: University of California Press, 1995.

Palandri, Angela C. Y. Jung. *Yüan Chen.* Boston: Twayne Publishers, 1977.

Pan Jixing 潘吉星, ed. *Zhongguo kexue jishu shi: zaozhi yu yinshua juan* 中國科學技術史：造紙與印刷卷. Beijing: Kexue chubanshe, 1998.

Pearsall, Derek. "Editing Medieval Texts: Some Developments and Some Problems." In Jerome J. McGann, ed., *Textual Criticism and Literary Interpretation*, 92–106. Chicago: University of Chicago Press, 1985.

Pollack, David. "Han Yü and the 'Stone Cauldron Linked-verse Poem'." *Journal of Chinese Studies* 1.2 (1984): 171–202.

Poon, Ming-sun. "Books and Printing in Sung China (960–1279)." PhD dissertation, University of Chicago, 1979.

Preminger, Alex, and T. V. F. Brogan, eds. *The New Princeton Encyclopedia of Poetry and Poetics*. Princeton: Princeton University Press, 1993.

Pulleyblank, E. G. *Lexicon of Reconstructed Pronunciation in Early Middle Chinese, Late Middle Chinese, and Early Mandarin*. Vancouver: University of British Columbia Press, 1991.

———. *Middle Chinese: A Study in Historical Phonology*. Vancouver: University of British Columbia Press, 1984.

Qian Zhonglian 錢仲聯. *Han Changli shiji nianji shi* 韓昌黎詩繫年集釋. Shanghai: Shanghai guji, 1984.

Qiu Zhao'ao 仇兆鰲, ed. *Dushi xiangzhu* 杜詩詳註. Taibei: Liren shuju, 1980.

Qu Tuiyuan 瞿蜕園, ed. *Liu Yuxi ji jianjiao* 劉禹錫集箋校. Shanghai: Shanghai guji, 1989.

Qu Tuiyuan 瞿蜕園 and Zhu Jincheng 朱金城, eds. *Li Bai ji jianjiao* 李白集箋校. Shanghai: Shanghai guji chubanshe, 1998.

Quan Tang shi 全唐詩. Beijing: Zhonghua shuju, 1985.

Quan Tang wen 全唐文. Beijing: Zhonghua shuju, 1983.

Reed, Carrie E. "Tattoo in Early China." *Journal of the American Oriental Society* 120.3 (2000): 360–76.

Ren Bantang 任半塘. *Tang shengshi* 唐聲詩. Shanghai: Shanghai guji, 1982.

Renoir, Alain. "Oral-Formulaic Rhetoric: An Approach to Image and Message in Medieval Poetry." In Laurie A. Finke and Martin B. Shichtman, eds., *Medieval Texts and Contemporary Readers*, 234–53. Ithaca: Cornell University Press, 1987.

Rouzer, Paul. *Articulated Ladies: Gender and the Male Community in Early Chinese Texts*. Cambridge: Harvard University Asia Center, 2001.

Ruan Yuan 阮元, ed. *Shisanjing zhushu* 十三經注疏. Beijing: Zhonghua shuju, 1957.

Rubin, David C. *Memory in Oral Traditions: The Cognitive Psychology of Epic, Ballads, and Counting-out Rhymes*. Oxford: Oxford University Press, 1995.

Saenger, Paul. *Space Between Words: The Origins of Silent Reading*. Stanford: Stanford University Press, 1997.

Sanders, Graham. *Words Well Put: Visions of Poetic Competence in the Chinese Tradition*. Cambridge: Harvard University Asia Center, 2006.

Schaberg, David. *A Patterned Past: Form and Thought in Early Chinese Historiography*. Cambridge: Harvard University Asia Center, 2002.

———. "Song and the Historical Imagination in Early China." *Harvard Journal of Asiatic Studies* 59.2 (1999): 305–61.

Schafer, Edward H. *The Golden Peaches of Samarkand: A Study of T'ang Exotics*. Berkeley: University of California Press, 1985.

Shang Xuefeng 尚學鋒, et al. *Zhongguo gudian wenxue jieshou shi* 中國古典文學接受史. Jinan: Shandong jiaoyu chubanshe, 2000.

Shaughnessy, Edward, *Rewriting Early Chinese Texts*. Albany: State University of New York Press, 2006.

Shields, Anna M. *Crafting a Collection: The Cultural Contexts and Poetic Practice of the* Hua Jianji. Cambridge: Harvard University Asia Center, 2006.

———. "Defining Experience: The 'Poems of Seductive Allure' (*yanshi*) of the Mid-Tang Poet Yuan Zhen (779–831)." *Journal of the American Oriental Society* 122 (2002): 61–78.

———. "Remembering When: The Uses of Nostalgia in the Poetry of Bai Juyi and Yuan Zhen." *Harvard Journal of Asiatic Studies* 66.2 (2006): 321–61.

Shih, Vincent Yu-chung, trans. *The Literary Mind and the Carving of Dragons: A Study of Thought and Pattern in Chinese Literature*. Hong Kong: The Chinese University Press, 1983.

Sima Qian 司馬遷. *Shiji* 史記. Beijing: Zhonghua shuju, 1989.

Slingerland, Edward. *Confucius Analects*. Indianapolis, IN: Hackett Publishing Co., 2003.

Song Qi 宋祁 and Ouyang Xiu. *Xin Tang shu* 新唐書. Beijing: Zhonghua shuju, 1975.

Spence, Jonathan D. *The Memory Palace of Matteo Ricci*. New York: Viking Penguin, 1983.

Su Ying-hui. "On the Tunhuang Studies." *Chinese Culture* 17.1 (March 1976): 64–88.

Sun Guangxian 孫光憲. *Beimeng suoyan* 北夢瑣言. Beijing: Zhonghua shuju, 1981.

Sun Qi 孫棨. *Beili zhi* 北里志. In Wang Rutao 王汝濤 ed., *Quan Tang xiaoshuo* 全唐小說. Ji'nan: Shandong wenyi chubanshu, 1993.

Taiping guangji 太平廣記. Taibei: Wenshizhe chubanshe, 1987.

Tang, Raymond Nai-wen. "The Poetry of Wei Chuang (836–910)." PhD dissertation, Stanford University, 1982.

Tansell, Thomas G. *Textual Criticism and Scholarly Editing*. Charlottesville, VA: Bibliographical Society of the University of Virginia, University Press of Virginia, 1990.

Tao Min 陶敏 and Li Yifei 李一飛. *Sui Tang Wudai wenxueshi kexue* 隋唐五代文學史科學. Beijing: Zhonghua shuju, 2001.

Teiser, Stephen F. *The Scripture on the Ten Kings and the Making of Purgatory in Medieval Chinese Buddhism*. Honolulu: University of Hawaii Press, 1994.

Thomas, Rosalind. *Literacy and Orality in Ancient Greece*. Cambridge: Cambridge University Press, 1992.

Thorpe, James. *Principles of Textual Criticism*. San Marino, CA: The Huntington Library, 1972.

Tian, Xiaofei. *Beacon Fire and Shooting Star: The Literary Culture of the Liang (502–557)*. Cambridge: Harvard University Asia Center, 2007.

———. "Misplaced: Three Qing Manuscripts of a Medieval Poet," *Asia Major* 20 (2007): 1–23.

———. *Tao Yuanming and Manuscript Culture: The Record of a Dusty Table*. Seattle: University of Washington Press, 2005.

Tsien, T. H. *Written on Bamboo and Silk: The Beginnings of Chinese Books and Inscriptions*. Chicago: University of Chicago Press, 1962.

———. *Paper and Printing*. In Joseph Needham, *Science and Civilization in China*, vol. 5: *Chemistry and Chemical Technology*, part 1. Cambridge: Cambridge University Press, 1985.

Tulving, Endel, and Fergus I. M Craik. *The Oxford Handbook of Memory*. Oxford: Oxford University Press, 2000.

Twitchett, Denis. *The Cambridge History of China, vol. 3: Sui and T'ang China 589–906, part 1*. Cambridge: Cambridge University Press, 1979.

———. "Chinese Social History from the Seventh to the Tenth Centuries." *Past and Present* 35 (December 1966): 28–53.

———. *Printing and Publishing in Medieval China*. New York: Frederic C. Beil, 1983.

Van Vleck, Amelia E. *Memory and Re-Creation in Troubadour Lyric*. Berkeley: University of California Press, 1991.

Van Zoeren, Steven. *Poetry and Personality: Reading, Exegesis, and Hermeneutics in Traditional China*. Stanford: Stanford University Press, 1991.

Veidlinger, David M. *Spreading the Dharma: Writing, Orality, and Textual Transmission in Buddhist Northern Thailand*. Honolulu: University of Hawai'i Press, 2006.

Wagner, Marsha L. *Wang Wei*. Boston: Twayne Publishers, 1981.

Waley, Arthur. *The Life and Times of Po Chü-i 772–846 A.D.* New York: The MacMillan Company, 1949.

Walther, Ingo F., and Norbert Wolf. *Codices Illustres: The World's Most Famous Illuminated Manuscripts 400 to 1600*. Köln: Taschen, 2001.

Wan Man 萬曼. *Tangji xulu* 唐集敘錄. Taibei: Mingwen shuju yinhang, 1982.

Wang, C. H. *The Bell and the Drum:* Shih Ching *as Formulaic Poetry in an Oral Tradition*. Berkeley: University of California Press, 1974.

Wang Dang 王讜. *Tang yulin* 唐語林. Beijing: Zhonghua shuju, 1997.

Wang Dingbao 王定保. *Tang zhiyan* 唐摭言. Beijing: Zhonghua shuju, 1959.

Wang Guowei 王國維. "Wei Zhuang de Qinfu yin" 韋莊的秦婦吟. *Beida guoxue ji kan* 北大國學季刊 1.4 (1923): 693–99.

Wang Li 王力. *Hanyu shilüxue* 漢語詩律學. Shanghai: Jiaoyu chubanshe, 1965.

Wang Liqi 王利器, ed. *Wenjing mifulun jiaozhu* 文鏡秘府論校注. Beijing: Zhongguo shehuike chubanshe, 1983.

Wang Qi 王琦 et al., eds. *Li Changji geshi: Sanjia pingzhu* 李長吉歌詩，三家評注. Shanghai: Shanghai guji, 1998.

Wang Xiaodun 王小盾, and Li Changji 李昌集. "Ren Zhongming xiansheng he ta suo jianli de sanquxue, Tangdai wenyixue" 任中敏先生和他所建立的散曲學、唐代文藝學. *Wenxue yichan* 文學遺產 (1996): 104–14.

Wang Zhongwen 王仲聞, ed. *Li Qingzhao ji jiaozhu* 李清照集校注. Taibei: Hanjing wenhua shiwu youxian gongsi, 1983.

Warner, Ding Xiang. *A Wild Deer amid Soaring Phoenixes: The Opposition Poetics of Wang Ji*. Honolulu: University of Hawai'i Press, 2003.

Watson, Burton, trans. Meng Ch'iu*: Famous Episodes from Chinese History and Legend*. Tokyo: Kodansha International, 1979.

Wei Shou 魏收 *Wei shu* 魏書. Beijing: Zhonghua shuju, 1974.

Welter, Albert. *Monks, Rulers, and Literati: The Political Ascendancy of Chan Buddhism*. Oxford: Oxford University Press, 2006.

Wilhelm, Richard. *The I Ching or Book of Changes*. Trans. Cary F. Baynes. Princeton: Princeton University Press, 1977.

Wilkinson, Endymion. *Chinese History: A Manual*. Cambridge: Harvard University Asia Center, 2000.

Wu Chengxue 吳承學. "Lun tibishi jianji xiangguande shige zhizuo yu chuanbo xingshi" 論題壁詩兼及相關的詩歌制作與傳播形式." In *Wenxue yichan* 文學遺產 4 (1994): 4–13.

Wu Hung. *The Double Screen: Medium and Representation in Chinese Painting*. Chicago: University of Chicago Press, 1996.

Wu Qiming 吳企明, *Tangyin zhi yilu* 唐音質疑祿. Shanghai: Shanghai guji chubanshe, 1985.

Wu Xiangzhou 吳相洲. *Tangshi chuangzuo yu geshi chuanchang guanxi yanjiu* 唐詩創作與歌詩傳唱關係研究. Beijing: Beijing daxue chubanshe, 2004.

Xiong, Victor Cunrui. *Sui-Tang Chang'an: A Study in the Urban History of Medieval China.* Ann Arbor: Center for Chinese Studies, University of Michigan, 2000.

Xu Jun 徐俊, ed. and comp. *Dunhuang shiji canjuan jikao* 敦煌詩集殘卷輯考. Beijing: Zhonghua shuju, 2000.

Xue Tianwei 薛天緯. "Ganye yu Tangdai shiren de xintai" 干謁與唐代詩人的心態. *Tangdai yanjiu* 唐代研究 5 (1994): 1–16.

Xue Yongruo 薛用弱. *Jiyi ji* 集異記. Beijing: Zhonghua shuju, 1980.

Yampolsky, Philip B., trans. *The Platform Sutra of the Sixth Patriarch.* New York: Columbia University Press, 1967.

Yan Tingliang 顏廷亮 and Zhao Yiwu 趙以武, eds. "Qinfu yin" 《秦婦吟》 *yanjiu huilu* 研究彙錄. Shanghai: Shanghai guji, 1990.

Yang Bojun 楊伯峻. *Liezi jishi* 列子集釋. Beijing: Zhonghua shuju, 1979.

Yang Jidong. "Writing in the Tang: Literature and Society in 7–10th Century China," PhD dissertation, University of Pennsylvania, 2000.

Yao Boyue 姚伯岳. *Banbenxue* 版本學. Beijing: Beijing Daxue chubanshe, 1993.

Yates, Frances A. *The Art of Memory.* Chicago: University of Chicago Press, 1966.

Yates, Robin D. S. *Washing Silk: The Life and Selected Poetry of Wei Chuang (834?–910).* Cambridge: Council on East Asian Studies, Harvard University, 1988.

Yingcang Dunhuang wenxian 英藏敦煌文獻. Chengdu: Sichuan renmin chubanshe, 1990.

Yoshikawa, Kōjirō. "Tu Fu's Poetics and Poetry." *Acta Asiatica* 16 (1969): 1–26.

Yu, Pauline. "Poems in Their Place: Collections and Canons in Early Chinese Literature." *Harvard Journal of Asiatic Studies* 50.1 (June 1990): 163–96.

———. *The Poetry of Wang Wei: New Translations and Commentary.* Bloomington: Indiana University Press, 1980.

Yuan Jie 元結. *Tangren xuan Tangshi* 唐人選唐詩. Beijing: Zhonghua shuju, 1958.

Yuan Zhen 元稹. *Yuan Zhen ji* 元稹集. Beijing: Zhonghua shuju, 1982.

Zeitlin, Judith T. "Disappearing Verses." In Zeitlin and Lydia H. Liu, eds., *Writing and Materiality in China: Essays in Honor of Patrick Hanan*, 73–125. Cambridge: Harvard University Asia Center, 2003.

Zhao Diancheng 趙殿成. *Wang Youcheng ji jianjiao* 王右丞集箋校. Shanghai: Shanghai guji chubanshe, 1998.

Zheng Acai 鄭阿財 and Zhu Fengyu 朱鳳玉, eds. *Dunhuang mengshu yanjiu* 敦煌蒙書研究. Lanzhou: Gansu jiaoyu chubanshe, 2002.

Zheng Chuhui 鄭處誨. *Minghuang zalu* 明皇雜錄. Beijing: Zhonghua shuju, 1994.

Zhou Weide 周維德, ed. *Wenjing mifulun* 文鏡秘府論. Beijing: Renmin wenxue chubanshe, 1975.

Zhu Jincheng 朱今城, ed. *Bai Juyi ji jianjiao* 白居易集箋校. Shanghai: Shanghai guji, 1988.

Zürcher, Erik. "Buddhism and Education in T'ang Times." In Wm. Theodore de Bary and John W. Chaffee, eds., *Neo-Confucian Education: The Formative Stage*, 19–56. Berkeley: University of California Press, 1989.

Index

Harvard-Yenching Institute Monograph Series

(titles now in print)

11. *Han Shi Wai Chuan: Han Ying's Illustrations of the Didactic Application of the Classic of Songs*, translated and annotated by James Robert Hightower
21. *The Chinese Short Story: Studies in Dating, Authorship, and Composition*, by Patrick Hanan
22. *Songs of Flying Dragons: A Critical Reading*, by Peter H. Lee
24. *Population, Disease, and Land in Early Japan, 645–900*, by William Wayne Farris
25. *Shikitei Sanba and the Comic Tradition in Edo Fiction*, by Robert W. Leutner
26. *Washing Silk: The Life and Selected Poetry of Wei Chuang (834?–910)*, by Robin D. S. Yates
27. *National Polity and Local Power: The Transformation of Late Imperial China*, by Min Tu-ki
28. *Tang Transformation Texts: A Study of the Buddhist Contribution to the Rise of Vernacular Fiction and Drama in China*, by Victor H. Mair
29. *Mongolian Rule in China: Local Administration in the Yuan Dynasty*, by Elizabeth Endicott-West
30. *Readings in Chinese Literary Thought*, by Stephen Owen
31. *Remembering Paradise: Nativism and Nostalgia in Eighteenth-Century Japan*, by Peter Nosco
32. *Taxing Heaven's Storehouse: Horses, Bureaucrats, and the Destruction of the Sichuan Tea Industry, 1074–1224*, by Paul J. Smith
33. *Escape from the Wasteland: Romanticism and Realism in the Fiction of Mishima Yukio and Oe Kenzaburo*, by Susan Jolliffe Napier
34. *Inside a Service Trade: Studies in Contemporary Chinese Prose*, by Rudolf G. Wagner
35. *The Willow in Autumn: Ryutei Tanehiko, 1783–1842*, by Andrew Lawrence Markus
36. *The Confucian Transformation of Korea: A Study of Society and Ideology*, by Martina Deuchler
37. *The Korean Singer of Tales*, by Marshall R. Pihl

38. *Praying for Power: Buddhism and the Formation of Gentry Society in Late-Ming China*, by Timothy Brook
39. *Word, Image, and Deed in the Life of Su Shi*, by Ronald C. Egan
40. *The Chinese Virago: A Literary Theme*, by Yenna Wu
41. *Studies in the Comic Spirit in Modern Japanese Fiction*, by Joel R. Cohn
42. *Wind Against the Mountain: The Crisis of Politics and Culture in Thirteenth-Century China*, by Richard L. Davis
43. *Powerful Relations: Kinship, Status, and the State in Sung China (960–1279)*, by Beverly Bossler
44. *Limited Views: Essays on Ideas and Letters*, by Qian Zhongshu; selected and translated by Ronald Egan
45. *Sugar and Society in China: Peasants, Technology, and the World Market*, by Sucheta Mazumdar
46. *Chinese History: A Manual*, by Endymion Wilkinson
47. *Studies in Chinese Poetry*, by James R. Hightower and Florence Chia-Ying Yeh
48. *Crazy Ji: Chinese Religion and Popular Literature*, by Meir Shahar
49. *Precious Volumes: An Introduction to Chinese Sectarian Scriptures from the Sixteenth and Seventeenth Centuries*, by Daniel L. Overmyer
50. *Poetry and Painting in Song China: The Subtle Art of Dissent*, by Alfreda Murck
51. *Evil and/or/as the Good: Omnicentrism, Intersubjectivity, and Value Paradox in Tiantai Buddhist Thought*, by Brook Ziporyn
52. *Chinese History: A Manual, Revised and Enlarged Edition*, by Endymion Wilkinson
53. *Articulated Ladies: Gender and the Male Community in Early Chinese Texts*, by Paul Rouzer
54. *Politics and Prayer: Shrines to Local Former Worthies in Sung China*, by Ellen Neskar
55. *Allegories of Desire: Esoteric Literary Commentaries of Medieval Japan*, by Susan Blakeley Klein
56. *Printing for Profit: The Commercial Publishers of Jianyang, Fujian (11th-17th Centuries)*, by Lucille Chia
57. *To Become a God: Cosmology, Sacrifice, and Self-Divinization in Early China*, by Michael J. Puett
58. *Writing and Materiality in China: Essays in Honor of Patrick Hanan*, edited by Judith T. Zeitlin and Lydia H. Liu
59. *Rulin waishi and Cultural Transformation in Late Imperial China*, by Shang Wei
60. *Words Well Put: Visions of Poetic Competence in the Chinese Tradition*, by Graham Sanders
61. *Householders: The Reizei Family in Japanese History*, by Steven D. Carter
62. *The Divine Nature of Power: Chinese Ritual Architecture at the Sacred Site of Jinci*, by Tracy Miller
63. *Beacon Fire and Shooting Star: The Literary Culture of the Liang (502–557)*, by Xiaofei Tian
64. *Lost Soul: "Confucianism" in Contemporary Chinese Academic Discourse*, by John Makeham

65. *The Sage Learning of Liu Zhi: Islamic Thought in Confucian Terms*, by Sachiko Murata, William C. Chittick, and Tu Weiming
66. *Through a Forest of Chancellors: Fugitive Histories in Liu Yuan's* Lingyan ge*, an Illustrated Book from Seventeenth-Century Suzhou*, by Anne Burkus-Chasson
67. *Empire of Texts in Motion: Chinese, Korean, and Taiwanese Transculturations of Japanese Literature*, by Karen Laura Thornber
68. *Empire's Twilight: Northeast Asia Under the Mongols*, by David M. Robinson
69. *Ancestors, Virgins, and Friars: Christianity as a Local Religion in Late Imperial China*, by Eugenio Menegon
70. *Manifest in Words, Written on Paper: Producing and Circulating Poetry in Tang Dynasty China*, by Christopher M. B. Nugent